Building and Managing a Career in Nursing

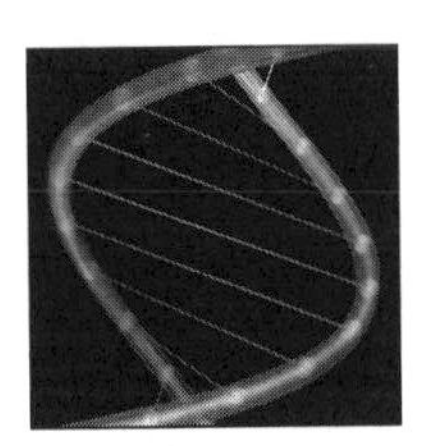

Other Books Available from Sigma Theta Tau International

- *The Adventurous Years: Leaders in Action 1973-1999,* Henderson, 1998.
- *As We See Ourselves: Jewish Women in Nursing,* Benson, 2001.
- *Cadet Nurse Stories: The Call for and Response of Women During World War II,* Perry and Robinson, 2001.
- *Collaboration for the Promotion of Nursing,* Briggs, Merk and Mitchell, 2003.
- *The Communication of Caring in Nursing,* Knowlden, 1998.
- *Creating Responsive Solutions to Healthcare Change,* McCullough, 2001.
- *Gerontological Nursing Issues for the 21st Century,* Gueldner and Poon, 1999.
- *The HeART of Nursing: Expressions of Creative Art in Nursing,* Wendler, 2002.
- *Immigrant Women and Their Health: An Olive Paper,* Ibrahim Meleis, Lipson, Muecke and Smith, 1998.
- *The Language of Nursing Theory and Metatheory,* King and Fawcett, 1997.
- *Making a Difference: Stories from the Point of Care,* Hudacek, 2000.
- *The Neuman Systems Model and Nursing Education: Teaching Strategies and Outcomes,* Lowry, 1998.
- *Nurses' Moral Practice: Investing and Discounting Self,* Kelly, 2000.
- *Nursing and Philanthropy: An Energizing Metaphor for the 21st Century,* McBride, 2000.
- *The Roy Adaptation Model-Based Research: 25 Years of Contributions to Nursing Science,* Boston Based Adaptation Research in Nursing Society, 1999.
- *Stories of Family Caregiving: Reconsideration of Theory, Literature, and Life*, Poirier and Ayres, 2002.
- *Virginia Avenel Henderson: Signature for Nursing,* Hermann, 1997.

Call toll-free 1.888.634.7575 (U.S and Canada) or +800.634.7575.1 (International), or visit our Web site at www.nursing.society.org/publications for more information.

Building and Managing a Career in Nursing

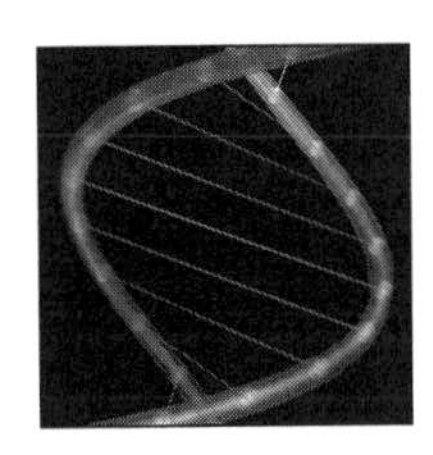

Strategies for Advancing Your Career

Terry W. Miller, RN, PhD
With 13 contributors

A Joint Publication of
The Honor Society of Nursing, Sigma Theta Tau International
And
NurseWeek Publishing, Inc.

Sigma Theta Tau International
Publishing Director: Jeff Burnham
Book Acquisitions Editor: Fay L. Bower, DNSc, FAAN
Graphic Designer: Jason Reuss
Proofreader: Linda Canter

NurseWeek Publishing, Inc.

Printed in the United States of America
Composition by Graphic World
Printing and Binding by Edwards Brothers
Cover art by Getty Images, Inc.

Sigma Theta Tau International
550 West North Street
Indianapolis, IN 46202

Visit the Honor Society of Nursing, Sigma Theta Tau International Web site at www.nursingsociety.org for more information on our books and other publications.

ISBN: 1-930538-08-1

Library of Congress Cataloging-in-Publication Data

Building and managing a career in nursing : strategies for advancing your career / Terry W. Miller.
p. ; cm.
Includes bibliographical references.
ISBN 1-930538-08-1
1. Nursing—Vocational guidance—United States. 2. Career development.
[DNLM: 1. Nursing. 2. Career Mobility. WY 16 B932 2003] I. Miller, Terry W. II. Sigma Theta Tau International.
RT82.B796 2003
610.73'06'9—dc21 2003007008

03 04 05 / 9 8 7 6 5 4 3 2 1

About the Author

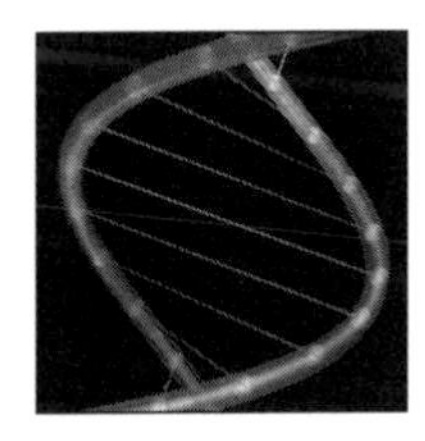

Terry W. Miller, RN, PhD

Terry W. Miller earned two bachelor's degrees, one in nursing and another in zoology and chemistry, from the University of Oklahoma and a master of science degree in nursing and PhD from the University of Texas, Austin. He currently is the dean and professor of nursing at Pacific Lutheran University and prior to that held the position of associate dean of the College of Applied Sciences and Arts and professor of nursing at San Jose State University. Dr. Miller was awarded Professor Emeritus status by President Robert L. Caret in 1999, only one year after assuming the position of dean at Pacific Lutheran University School of Nursing.

About the Contributors

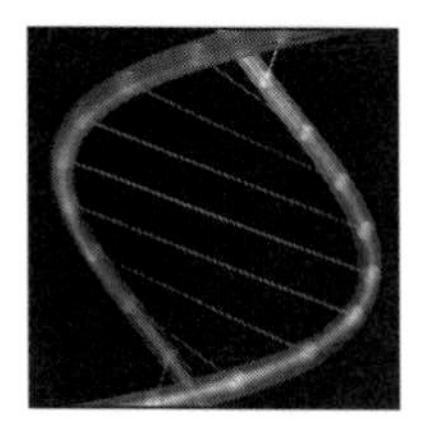

Fay L. Bower, RN, DNSc, FAAN

Fay L. Bower has over 50 years of experience in nursing, with 35 years in nursing education. She earned a bachelor of science degree from San Jose State College and a master of science in nursing and a doctor of nursing science from the University of California, San Francisco. Dr. Bower's career has included a variety of positions. She has been a faculty member, chair, coordinator of graduate programs, dean, vice president of academic affairs, and director of institutional research and planning before becoming the president of Clarkson College in Omaha, Nebraska. After retirement, she returned to academia in 2000 as chair of the Department of Nursing at Holy Names College in Oakland, California. She has written several books and many articles and is currently the book acquisitions editor for Sigma Theta Tau International.

Marcia E. Canton, RN, PhD

Marcia E. Canton received a bachelor of science degree from Long Island University; a master's degree from the University of California, San Francisco; and a master's and a PhD from Stanford University. She is currently the president of Canton Associates, a consulting firm that assists managers in improving their management skills in the areas of cultural diversity and program evaluation. Dr. Canton was associated with San Jose State University as a full professor and associate dean for the College of Applied Arts and Sciences. She now is an adjunct faculty member at Holy Names College.

Edith Jenkins-Weinrub

Edith Jenkins-Weinrub began her nursing career as an LVN. She then received her bachelor of science degree from the University of Texas at Arlington, her master of science degree from California State University Dominguez Hills, and her EdD from Nova Southeastern University. She has taught at the University of Phoenix in the nursing program and in the human service program. She also was director of nursing for ambulatory care for the San Mateo County Medical Center. Currently she is program administrator at the Bay Area Consortium for Quality Healthcare, Inc. overseeing the HIV/AIDS program and is an assistant professor of nursing in the Department of Nursing at Holy Names College in Oakland, California.

Patsy Maloney, MA, MSN, PhD

Patsy Maloney is the director of continuing nursing education and associate professor of nursing at Pacific Lutheran University, Tacoma, Washington. She received a bachelor of science degree in nursing from the University of Maryland; master of arts and master of nursing degrees from Catholic University of America; and an EdD degree from the University of Southern California in higher, adult and professional education. Dr. Maloney is certified in nursing staff development and continuing education, as well as in advanced nursing administration.

Cynthia S. McCullough, RN, MSN

Cyndi McCullough earned a bachelor of science degree from Slippery Rock University and a master's degree in nursing from Clarkson College. She has over 20 years of experience in healthcare as a staff nurse and manager. She also has experience in patient-focused care, clinical and operations reengineering, and self-directed work teams. Currently, Cyndi is employed as a senior nurse consultant with HDR, Inc. in Omaha, Nebraska, which is an architectural/engineering firm specializing in the design of healthcare facilities. Cyndi has also written several articles and is the editor of a book.

Wendell Oderkirk, RN, PhD

Wendell Oderkirk is associate professor of nursing at New Mexico State University in Las Cruces, New Mexico. He has earned a bachelor of science degree in nursing, a bachelor's degree in Spanish, a master of science degree in urban education and another in nursing and a PhD in psychological and cultural studies. Dr. Oderkirk has written articles and a book and is currently working with a National Institute of Cancer grant focusing on colon-rectal cancer screening of persons on the U.S./Mexican border.

Barbara L. Pille, RN, MBA

Barbara Pille received a diploma in nursing from Creighton St. Joseph School of Nursing, a bachelor of science and a master's degree in business administration from the University of Nebraska at Omaha. Currently, Barb is the vice president of nursing and clinical services for Quality Living, Inc. in Omaha, a head injury rehabilitation center. Barb's career has included a variety of positions including chief nursing officer at Clarkson Hospital, cardiology product line manager and risk manager for an insurance company.

Pamela Reiter, RN

Pamela A. Reiter earned a bachelor of arts in nursing from Augustana College in Sioux Falls, South Dakota, and a bachelor of science in anesthesia from the University of South Dakota in Vermillion, South Dakota. Currently, Pam is a nurse anesthetist at the University of Nebraska Medical Center in Omaha, Nebraska. She has also held staff nurse positions in medical/surgical and intensive care settings and access services.

Michelle T. Renaud, RN, PhD

Michelle T. Renaud is the division chief for the accelerated BSN program at Duke University School of Nursing in North Carolina. She earned a bachelor of science degree in nursing from the University of Connecticut, a master of science degree in nursing from the University of Colorado and a doctoral degree from the University of Washington. Dr. Renaud has had a long and varied nursing career including 24 years of military nursing experience in the Army Nurse Corps.

Mae E. Timmons, RN, EdD

Mae Timmons received a bachelor of science degree in nursing from St. Louis University School of Nursing, a master's degree in nursing from the University of California in Los Angeles and an EdD from the University of San Francisco. Currently, Dr. Timmons is an associate professor in the graduate nursing program at Clarkson College in Omaha, Nebraska. Dr. Timmons' experience includes working in one of the first intensive care units in Dallas, Texas; teaching in various educational institutions; and serving as director of a graduate program for several years. Dr. Timmons was instrumental in designing and developing the majority of online courses in the education option of the graduate program at Clarkson College in Omaha, Nebraska.

Michaela N. Tolo, RN

Michaela Tolo received a diploma in nursing from Clarkson Hospital School of Nursing. Currently, she is the clinical services coordinator for access services for Nebraska Health System. Michaela has been employed by the same health system for the past 26 years. She has held a variety of positions as a nurse in gastrointestinal, renal and gynecologic areas and in outpatient and admitting services. Michaela was instrumental in developing and implementing the pre-admission screening program for the health system and is currently developing a centralized scheduling program.

Arthur Wallace, RN, MSN, CEN

Arthur Wallace was awarded a bachelor of science degree in nursing from the University of Maryland and a master of science degree in nursing from the University of Texas Health Science Center in San Antonio. He is currently the deputy executive director/director, clinical operations, TRICARE Pacific, Honolulu, Hawaii. Art was selected as the first male White House nurse supporting Presidents Bush and Clinton. His experience includes burn and trauma nursing, chief nursing officer and chief executive officer in various hospitals in the U.S. and abroad.

Robinetta Wheeler, RN, PhD

Robinetta Wheeler received a bachelor of science in nursing from New York University; a master of science in nursing degree from San Jose State College; and a PhD in sociology from the University of California, San Francisco. Dr. Wheeler's experiences include clinical, management, education, research and entrepreneurial assignments. In addition to being associate professor of nursing and director of NEXUS, a distance education teleconferencing program, at Holy Names College, she is employed at Stanford Medical Center and the Veterans Affairs Palo Alto Health Care System.

Foreword

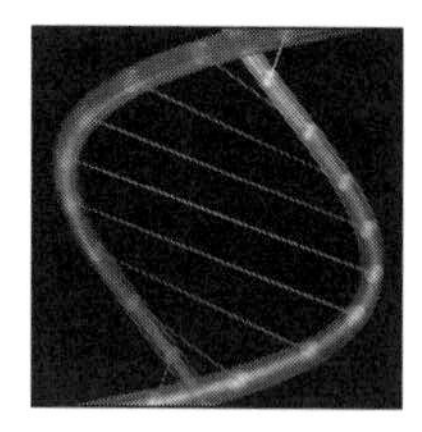

Dr. Terry Miller has presented a distinctive approach to building and managing a career. The content of the book is based on research in nursing and areas supportive to nursing. Miller's objective was to incorporate what good research exists outside nursing, while recognizing how the profession is distinguishable from as well as analogous to other professions. Using a research-based approach to career development, Miller worked with 13 expert contributors who could offer information from different perspectives. It impressed me that he successfully carried research from his dissertation to this publication. As the former dean of nursing in the university where his doctorate was awarded, it is my wish that all dissertations could be so relevant.

For the individual looking for a more satisfying career path in nursing or for the individual seeking a first career, *Building and Managing a Career in Nursing* will provide valuable information. The variables significant to career management and development are explored by the book's contributors. A broad range of topics is included, from information about development of a career to planning for retirement and the stages in-between.

To exemplify their message and support their theoretical discussions, the contributors use stories. In addition to information on how to search and interview for a position, the reader is given details on how to choose a position. I found the anecdotes and stories compelling.

One typically considers a career choice to be a lifetime decision. We know from studies that many individuals change careers as many as 10 times. Choosing a career is an overwhelming responsibility. This is true for the nurse who has not yet selected a specific professional track as well as the nurse who wishes to redirect his or her career. More literature is needed to help individuals search for a career. Very little addresses the career concept from beginning to end, including career changes and career reclamation. *Building and Managing a Career in Nursing,* written by experienced professionals, provides that information.

Billye J. Brown, RN, EdD, FAAN
Past President of Sigma Theta Tau International, 1989-1991
Retired Dean and Professor Emeritus
The University of Texas, Austin

Introduction

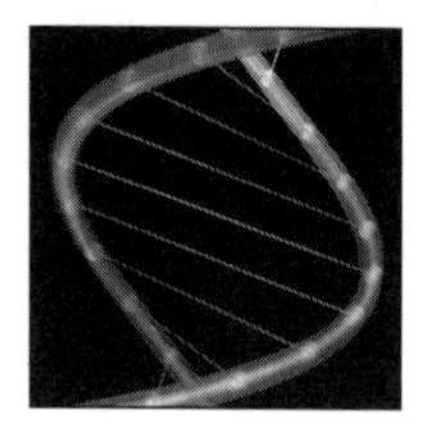

This book presents a unique approach to creating and managing careers in nursing. The authors discuss careers from five perspectives: discovering a career, developing a career, changing a career, reclaiming a career and using tools for career decision-making. Each area is explored from a theoretical perspective, with some chapters providing real examples of how nurses have managed their careers. The final part of the book presents strategies used by successful nurses as they search, match, choose and build support for their careers. Mentoring, as well as taking personal responsibility, is addressed as an important aspect of career development. The models and discussions are based on grounded research and real-life examples. This book can help anyone considering nursing as a career, as the authors provide a comprehensive exploration of career management every nurse should know about.

Contents

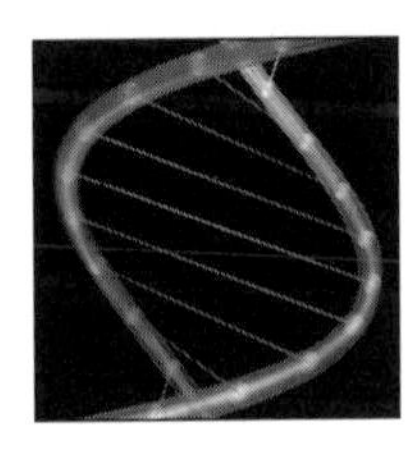

Unit I
Discovering a Career

Chapter 1

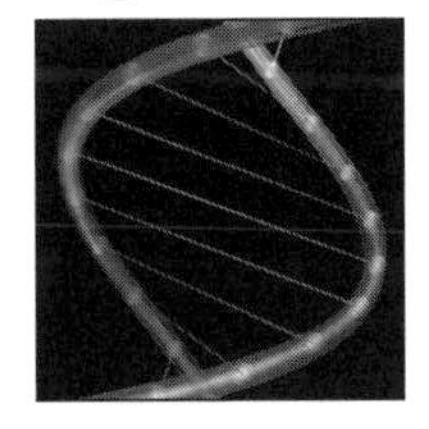

Work Versus Career

by Terry W. Miller

Specialized training alone is not enough. It may get you that first job; but if it is all you have to offer an employer, it may also bury you in that first job (Henry Ford II).

INTRODUCTION

Career choice and development affect all aspects of adult life. Work is directly linked to individual and family status, as well as to survival in society (Perlmutter-Bloch & Richmond, 1997). In Western society, work is a major source of status, identity and gratification (Yost & Corbishley, 1987). Finding meaning in work is critical if a person is to avoid stagnation and boredom (Berquist, Greenberg, & Klaum, 1993). Yet many people do not enjoy their work and do not understand how others find real enjoyment and personal fulfillment in what they do for an income. Many factors, such as not having a career-orientation to one's work, contribute to this failure.

Outdated myths and erroneous assumptions limit possibilities and restrict the potential of some people entering the workforce. If people approach work as a series of tasks merely to be done to the satisfaction of others in a supervisory capacity over them, work can be grueling, monotonous and unfulfilling. It is important to choose work that fits personal values and to understand how a real career is something far more than a particular job or series of jobs. If nothing else, a career offers more psychological control over the work environment. This chapter provides a career orientation for the person considering the profession of nursing as life's work.

WHAT IS A CAREER?

Career is often defined in terms of advancement, professional status and occupational stability. For example, career can be defined as a course of professional life or employment, which affords the individual opportunities for personal advancement, progress or achievement (Oxford University Press, 1996; Webster's, 1995). Career can also be defined in less restrictive terms as an evolving sequence of work experience over time (Arthur, Hall, & Lawrence, 1989) or a pattern of work-related experiences that spans the course of a person's life (Greenhaus, Callahan, & Godshalk, 2000).

There are many types of careers, with some being far more demanding of the individual in terms of educational preparation, level of responsibility, challenge and expected level of commitment. Some careers are highly structured and place-bound, while others may require periodic relocations and progressive levels of independence and accountability. Professional careers often involve job transitions, returning to school and some relocation.

Having a career is more analogous to a journey than a person's state of employment. Yet having a career is more than a series of jobs with an increase in pay and benefits over time. Understanding the values most commonly reflected in American culture helps explain the social significance of having or not having a career in the United States. Kohl (2000) and Althen (1998) identify values held by most Americans. These values include individualism and privacy, equality, informality, future orientation, change and progress, and time. These values also include achievement, action, work and materialism. The last four, if not all of the values listed, can be correlated with how a career is defined.

Having a career and being career-oriented imply changes in the work situation and status over time are to be natural and positive. Having a work orientation that demands personal action and being oriented to the future, as well as the present, also fit with having a career perspective of one's work. Kohl (2000) claims Americans do not believe in the power of fate or luck and have a responsibility to pursue a better life. Change in one's work status, leading to development, improvement and progress is perceived as more important than stability, continuity and tradition. Finally, many Americans pride themselves in having climbed the "ladder of success" and believe the future should and will be better than the present. Regardless of whether there is acceptance of what Kohl and others identify as core American values, these values inherently support having a career orientation over not having one.

Americans frequently ask each other, "What do you do for a living?" or ask children what they want to be when they grow up. Such personal questions indicate how much Western society values others because of what they do for income. Although having a career is usually viewed as a positive attribute in American culture, some people become physically and emotionally entangled in a lifelong pursuit of achievement. Some of the literature suggests work is occupying a larger part of most people's time, and that the average workweek has increased significantly for people in managerial and professional fields.

The term work/life balance has appeared in recent career development literature (Hansen, 1996). In the 1990s, Silicon Valley newspapers such as the *San Jose Mercury News* documented how successful people were leaving the area at young ages and relocating to more remote areas. Pursuit of a less-hectic lifestyle was often cited as the reason. Yet lifestyle, more than workload, may be the real culprit that exhausts people, dissolves families and creates career discontent. Pacing oneself through work, and ultimately a career path, is important in order to achieve a desirable balance between career goals and personal life goals.

Another potential downside of being career-oriented occurs when a person pursues a career with little regard for others or in ways that place personal success and advancement over what is attributable to the work of others. Ironically, this form of careerism limits the person's potential for professional growth and advancement in several ways. Successful people who have careers understand the need to support others in their careers, as well as receive support for their own career aspirations. It is unhealthy to make work the only goal, and it is destructive to make a career so important it discounts or devalues others and their contributions.

Career Myths

Harris-Tuck, Price and Robertson (2000) address several myths of the "American dream" that have important implications for understanding what a career offers a person in today's society. These myths include:

1. Good workers don't get fired. However, periodic restructuring of organizations and downsizing now cause many good workers to lose their jobs. This trend, which began in the 1980s, is not likely to end soon. In an article in Fortune (October 25, 2000), it was reported that "American businesses have cut back on everything, which means they've slashed perks and fired lots of workers."
2. Good-paying jobs are available without a college education. However, a college education is not only essential for most careers, it is becoming increasingly important. Few individuals are able to gain entry to a more desirable career field without a college education, and several professional fields require graduate degrees for entry. Even if a person is able to start a career path without a college education, the potential for career advancement becomes minimal without the expected degree. Fourteen million seven hundred ninety-one thousand students attended college in the United States in 2002, with 564,933 earning an associate degree, 1,237,875 earning a baccalaureate degree, 457,056 earning a master's degree, 44,808 earning a doctorate and 80,057 earning a professional degree (*The Chronicle of Higher Education,* 2002).
3. A college degree guarantees a good job. However, a college degree is only a piece of a much larger picture – timing, references, presentation, research and other factors are critical as well. The percentage of U.S. citizens earning college degrees at every level continues to increase at a faster rate than job openings. A college degree is only one criterion of several that prospective employers expect of applicants.
4. The best jobs are in large corporations. However, it is often more difficult for a large corporation to offer the best jobs or to ensure the best work environment because an expansive bureaucracy makes it difficult to address issues in a more timely manner, and the distance between top-level administration and lower-level workers can be quite a leap. Each year *Fortune* has a list of the

"100 Best Companies to Work For." Companies are recognized for coming up with creative ways to keep employees satisfied, and for offering generous severance and compassion when they had to make cuts. Seven of the top 100 companies for 2002 have less than 1,000 employees and 24 percent of them less than 2,000 employees (http://www.fortune.com/fortune/bestcompanies).

5. Go to work for a good company and move up the career ladder. However, moving up a career ladder assumes people get promoted because of their time in the organization. In reality, very few do, and they are at risk in an increasingly competitive, global economy. Increasingly, responsibility for career advancement and employability has shifted from the employer to the employee.
6. Find the hot industry and you'll always be in demand. However, a "hot industry" can cool just as quickly as it heated up. By the time this cooling begins, the media may just be starting to identify the industry as "hot." One only has to compare the "hot" job market for computer engineers, software specialists and systems analysts in the 1980s and 1990s to the present job market. It takes more than job market to assure employment, because no employee is often better than a poor performing one. Nursing is projected to be one of the "hottest industries" throughout this decade and into the next one, but a poor performing nurse will not be successful and will find it difficult to remain employed.

The previous decade marks several shifts in how people define their work and plan their careers. "Economic and cultural changes in society, technological and organizational changes in the workplace, and changes in business operations—management processes and customer orientations—are creating frustration for many workers" (Lankard, 1993). Despite any gloomy economic picture, many people are still successful while obtaining, losing and changing jobs (Schlossberg, 1997).

Critical thinking about the future and work supports the process of careful, formal planning of a career. Thinking about adult career development as a transition process of moving in, through and out of the workforce is also helpful (Schlossberg, 1997). Much of the literature regarding careers in professional fields includes information about how a person should make a conscious effort to develop a career and to plan for it before committing to some course of action (Fouad, 1994). Discussions during the preparation of a major report by the Committee on Science, Engineering, and Public Policy (COSEPUP) of the National Academy of Sciences (NAS); National Academy of Engineering (NAE); and Institute of Medicine (IOM) indicated the need for a guide designed specifically to help students plan their educational and professional careers.

CAREER PLANNING

The literature and research indicate career planning and professional development are essential for people entering their chosen vocations, staying in their vocations and defining themselves as successful in their work (Brown & Brooks, 1996). Career planning, development and decision-making have been correlated with job satisfaction, productivity and occupational retention for over four decades (Bowen & Hall, 1977; Moore, 1979; Keaveney & Jackson, 1979). Yet many people choose a job with little consideration for its career implications. Instead, they choose what is easiest or most expedient or because of the existing job market. Although these convenience factors certainly count, a more long-term perspective coupled with a heightened awareness of one's values regarding work would be more beneficial. For the purpose of this book career planning is defined as an individual process in which a person plans, manages and influences the direction of work life in order to attain long-range personal and professional goals.

Career planning includes an educational plan that will prepare, sustain and hopefully help the individual prosper along a chosen career path. It is a deliberate process that takes time and research, as well as direction and commitment. Unfortunately, much of the literature on career planning and related topics is anecdotal or commercially oriented, with little empirical evidence to back the claims or approaches. Yet, expecting work to be fulfilling over a lifetime when educational and work choices are left to chance is irresponsible and needlessly risky. Labor experts claim most individuals will work over 70,000 hours in a lifetime in work outside the home (40 hours per week times 48 weeks in a year times 35 years). This is an incredible amount of time to be devoted to something that is not fulfilling.

Benefits of Career Planning

Career planning is beneficial in several ways. Bolles (2003) describes the advantages of career planning as: (1) being in charge of the career rather than someone else controlling those decisions, (2) improved job satisfaction and effectiveness, and (3) not being underemployed and frustrated because of being in the wrong job. When the potential for being laid off is considered, the value of career planning becomes evident.

Major well-established employers may change their locations or take production or services out of the country, file bankruptcy, or even redefine their missions. For example, Boeing, the largest producer of commercial aircraft in the world, moved its headquarters to Illinois in 2002 and laid off over 32,000 workers in the state of Washington in less than six months.

During the past decade, many workers have been laid-off, creating a market for books and articles to assist "dislocated workers" (Harper, 1994; Kirkwood, 1994). Today, workforce councils in many states offer retraining grants to qualified individuals who have been laid off, to enable them to be more employable in a competitive labor market.

Case (1997) has written that "Self-confidence is key in the job search and the career development process" (p. 23). It would be difficult to have self-confidence or a realistic perception of one's career potential without a plan to guide one's career decision-making. It is not uncommon to ask job applicants where they would like to be in one to five years. Stumbling over this question is not going to create the best impression and could mean the loss of a great opportunity. Employers often view the ability to articulate a career vision during a job interview as a positive attribute. A clearly expressed vision indicates the job seeker has thought about the future and understands the value of goal-setting and long-term thinking.

The benefits of career planning become even more evident when a job applicant is asked other important questions during an interview. Without adequate preparation, it would be very difficult to articulate career goals, describe strengths, identify limitations or weaknesses in a positive manner, list major accomplishments and job-related skills, or adequately address contributions in other work settings. How to interview for a position is discussed in Chapter 22.

CAREER DISCONTENT AND FAILURE

Career discontent is characterized as dissatisfaction with work and the career it represents. It is a rejection of the present career path and is due to a refusal or an inability to internalize the value of the career as fulfilling. The expectations for the career being pursued do not match the person's expectations. Whether or not an individual's personal values fit the values promulgated by a particular career or job is the major determinant of career discontent.

Whereas people may define their work in terms of the future, planning and investing carefully, entering the right career, and sustaining any career over a lifetime are major challenges. These challenges are some of the reasons a successful career is so valuable and desired by so many.

In the early stages of career development, it is difficult to realistically determine the degree of congruence between personal values and a career course for several reasons. Naiveté, immaturity, being misled, being reactive and/or being directed by others may make it impossible to determine congruence. And when values are not self-defined, it is likely the values will be defined by the work setting. As the person gains experience and matures, the lack of self-defined values becomes apparent, so actions must be taken to get in touch with personal values.

When an individual does not identify personal values before embarking upon a career, conflicts arise through a socialization process. Socialization into a career role or job can be described as a sequential set of phases or "chain of events," like the ones listed below:

1. Transition from anticipatory to specific expectations of the role, as defined by the societal group of work peers;
2. Attachment to significant others in the social system milieu or work setting;
3. Recognition of congruency and incongruence in role expectations; and
4. Adaptation, internalization or integration of role values and standards (adapted from Hinshaw, 1977; Miller, 1991).

When people are unable or refuse to complete these four steps, they fail to fulfill the career role in the sociological sense and often experience career discontent. The following quote illustrates career discontent:

While learning the ropes, I was wild-eyed. I'd think, we'll get to clean up the environment. Then occasionally I would happen to ask the question, at our work group meetings, "Is the environment getting any cleaner?" and they would kinda go, "Ha!" So while we're supposed to be cleaning up the environment, we were taking papers from box A, processing them and putting them in box B. It was getting to me, and I began to realize that it was more political than I could handle. I consider myself pretty streetwise, but if you're really going in there and want to make a difference, the people who are appointed at the top for all the regions, the people with the final say, the bottom line, are politically appointed....There was one particular gentleman who was in the cubicle next to me whose great quote was, "Well, I used to be a radical and I used to have youthful idealism, but you get old and your values change." And he was the person who coalesced everything. I decided that I'm not going to become like that gentleman (Excerpt from field notes 6/26/90).

People perceive career discontent in several ways. These perceptions can be summarized in three ways:

- A dislike of significant others in the social system milieu or work settings associated with the career
- A dislike of work expectations associated with the career
- A recognition of the incongruence between work expectations and personal values

Career discontent is likely to be a major source of stress for the individual and the family. Because of the educational and/or experiential requirements of having a career, it is believed that changing careers is difficult and thus should be avoided. On the other hand, the alternative of remaining in a career that is stressful is equally unsuitable. If changing the circumstances does not alleviate the career discontent, a move to the next stage, quitting the job or career path, is inevitable.

Lack of information is a major factor contributing to career discontent. Unfortunately, many people base their decisions on very limited information or exposure to what is available to them. They make choices without doing any "homework." The career possibilities are greater today than ever before in human history. However, if people do not pursue sources that can accurately inform them and help them make intelligent career decisions, they are less likely to find a good job, much less the right career, and often end up discontented.

Some people approach work without being prepared for the job or the career they really want. They expect the employer to hire them because they claim they can do the work, yet they do not have the required educational preparation, ability or successful track record to support their claim. Their approach to securing desirable work is analogous to poor-performing students who apply to a highly selective educational program. Applicants who are most likely to be admitted demonstrate that they have the ability to perform at the required level. They show the people who make the admission selections how well they have met the admission criteria.

People involved in hiring wisely employ only those who can demonstrate they are the most prepared, most motivated and best qualified. They carefully consider an applicant's documented history, references and personal presentation to determine if the applicant has the potential for making a worthwhile contribution. Proper education and skill on the part of the job seeker is critical for career success, but finding work that the job seeker values is just as critical.

Some people mistakenly believe that they have to do little to keep a desirable job or position once they have a job. To complicate the situation, they often have several jobs. Peters (1994) predicted the career of tomorrow would consist of a dozen jobs, and that workers would move on and off payrolls of large and small companies in two or three industries over the course of their lifetimes. Recently, the U.S. Department of Labor has claimed that the average employee will change jobs seven times in a lifetime (Conway-Welch, 2001). A longitudinal study of almost 10,000 young men and women who have been periodically surveyed from 1979 through 2000 indicates that late baby boomers average over 9 jobs from ages 18 to 36 (U.S. Bureau of Labor Statistics, 2003). Sometimes, this moving around from job to job and bouncing back and forth between jobs creates stress and ends in job discontent.

Today's workplace is different from that of the recent past. Global competition, cultural diversity demanding cultural competency, new technologies and new management processes require a higher level of critical thinking, problem-solving and communication skills. Work is increasingly being parceled into specific projects with designated timelines. Work may be done by regular employees, outsourced to independent contractors or completed by temporary employees (Harris-Tuck, Price, & Robertson,

2000). Career-oriented people who plan for career transitions understand that as jobs change to match changes in the workplace, so must their career goals. Those people who do not understand the changing workplace and its effect on jobs and careers are candidates for discontent and sometimes failure.

It is difficult to have a career orientation if decisions related to employment are unplanned or based solely on pay. It is important to understand how a new job is going to shape career development and the potential for future employment. People who are career oriented treat their need to make money more as a long-term investment strategy than an immediate solution to one's budget needs. Jobs that offer good benefits, such as educational and advancement opportunities, are more likely to provide much higher earnings in the long run than jobs that have a higher salary at entry. A career-oriented person may actually take a salary cut on purpose to gain knowledge or experience that will better support a long-range career goal.

Attitude and Motivation

Leeds (1991) points out that if people go into situations expecting to fail, they probably will. How people approach situations reveals their attitudes toward work. Blaming others or taking on the role of victim, in most work situations, is highly destructive for a career. Most people are hired or employed to help solve problems, create or make products, and provide services. In addition, the person with a negative attitude or victim mentality poses a problem for others in the workplace. The person who becomes known as a problem is not likely to advance. Certainly, many people are victims of some form of discrimination, violent behavior, crime or tragic event. Yet, people with positive attitudes do not let the experience of being victimized define their life and work. A positive, solution-oriented attitude is important for the career-oriented individual.

NURSING AS A CAREER OR AS A JOB

Nursing offers a wide variety of career opportunities at both the generalist and specialist levels. However, some nurses view their positions as merely a job. These nurses are often referred to as "refrigerator nurses," because the motivation to be a nurse is little more than earning a living to pay for things. The characterization is not intended to be derogatory; instead it is to call attention to one of the major contributors to career failure in a wonderful profession. Nurses who have real careers tend to highly value their work and certainly enjoy what they do more than those who are merely working for a paycheck.

Throughout the Western world and increasingly in Eastern countries, work is a major source of status, identity and gratification. In American culture, life work is linked to the individual and family status, as well as to their socioeconomic survival. Although nursing's contribution to any society is crucial, the work of nurses can be under-valued. Hudacek (2000) has asked nurses to "say what you do" in a way that demonstrates how nursing makes a significant difference. She has concluded that nurses' work is important, rewarding and arduous. She also has described how nursing requires emotional strength, is diverse and is constantly changing, with caring at the core.

Nursing is truly special. Nurses' career choices affect all aspects of their lives. Most people enter nursing to make a difference in the lives of others. But nursing is also demanding and exacting—some of the reasons it is not boring or monotonous. Nursing requires skill and accountability—some of the reasons for a considerable investment in performance-based education. Not everyone can be a nurse, and it has nothing to do with "fainting at the sight of blood." Nursing is a remarkable profession fraught with challenges and permutations. It is a profession that truly makes a difference in the lives of others, as well as in the lives of those who enter and pursue a nursing career.

Unfortunately, much of the public does not understand what the modern nurse does. Many people attempt to define nursing and its status in society based on misinformation, anecdotal evidence, personal stereotypes or even misidentification. Because there are so many nurses and because they occupy so many diverse positions in today's healthcare industry, everyone knows or is related to a nurse. This plethora of nurses makes it important for the career seeker to determine whether the nurse is a real professional role model. Successful nurses are far more than kind, caring people with good intentions.

Most people define nurses by the license they hold, with registered nurses being the most common. However, the 2.5 million registered nurses in the United States vary greatly in terms of educational preparation, credentials, practice setting, level of accountability and responsibility, degree of autonomy, and income. Nurses can also be categorized according to their primary roles as practitioners, educators, administrators and/or researchers. In other words, nurses comprise a large, diversified group with well-defined professional roles both inside and outside hospital settings.

Advantages of a Nursing Career

The professional opportunities in nursing are varied and numerous, because the job opportunities are worldwide, ongoing and increasing. There are the standard positions of staff nurse, nurse educator and nurse administrator that most people associate with hospitals, nursing homes, nursing schools and other healthcare agencies. Although the majority of nurses in the United States and Canada work in hospitals, clinics, home health and extended care settings, thousands of nurses work in other diverse settings. These include K-12 schools, colleges, universities, the public health services, nonprofit agencies such as Red Cross, and unique jobs that offer major career opportunities for nurses throughout the United States and many other countries. The International Council of Nurses' (ICN) Web site offers an excellent way to learn about the international scope and career opportunities of nursing (www.icn.ch/).

The United States Army Nurse Corps is over a century old and has over 3,380 active duty nurses, as well as another 10,000 nurses in the army reserves (Caruana, 2002).

Baccalaureate and higher degree nurses are commissioned as officers and are afforded multiple opportunities for advanced training, higher education and overseas assignments. Nurses are also commissioned as officers in the United States Navy and the United States Air Force and afforded similar career opportunities.

Other nursing opportunities include occupational health nursing; camp nursing; private-duty nursing; flight nurses; and advanced practice nursing, such as family nurse practitioners (FNPs), clinical nurse specialists (CNSs), certified nurse midwives (CNMs) and certified nurse anesthetists (CNAs). Some nurses choose to see different regions of the country as contract or traveling nurses. They accept an assignment for a designated time period, usually six months to one year, and often may choose to stay or leave the position at the end of the contract period. Some nurses work for publishing firms, law firms and architectural firms. Nurse entrepreneurs have established their own consulting firms, businesses or product lines (Norwood, 2003). In some form or another they all "nurse."

CONCLUSION

People who have a socially recognized career and who value the career themselves are more likely to experience satisfaction in both their work and personal lives. Understanding the importance of career development and successfully managing a career promote the development of self, including self-esteem and the sense of self-efficacy (Heise, 1990).

REFERENCES

AHA Commission for Hospitals and Health Systems (April 2002). In our hands: How hospital leaders can build a thriving workforce. Chicago, IL: American Hospital Association (Product #2101101).

Althen, G. (1998). American values and assumptions. In P.S. Gardner (Ed.). *New directions: An integrated approach to reading, writing, and critical thinking.* Boston, MA: University of Cambridge Press.

Arthur, M.B., Hall, D.T., & Lawrence, B.S. (1989). *Handbook of career theory.* Cambridge, UK: Cambridge University Press.

Berquist, W.H., Greenberg, E.M., & Klaum, G.A. (1993). *In our fifties: Voices of men and women reinventing their lives.* San Francisco, CA: Jossey-Bass.

Bolles, R.N. (2003). *What color is your parachute? A practical manual for job-hunters and career-changers.* Berkely, CA: Ten Speed Press.

Bowen, D.D., & Hall, D.T. (1977). *Career planning for employee development: A primer for managers.* California Management Review, 20(2), 23-35.

Brown, D., & Brooks, L. (1996). *Career choice and development.* San Francisco, CA: Jossey-Bass.

Caruana, C.M. (2002, Winter). The best you can be. *Medhunters Magazine.*

Case, B. (1997). *Career planning for nurses.* Albany, NY: Delmar.

Chronicle of Higher Education (2002). *Almanac 2002-3.* Washington, DC: Author.

Conway-Welch, C. (2001). *Getting started: Career planning and your resume. Opportunities to care: The Pfizer guide to careers in nursing* (pp. 7-9). New York, NY: Pfizer Pharmaceuticals Group.

Fouad, N. (1994). Annual review 1991-1993. Vocational choice, decision making, assessment and intervention. *Journal of Vocational Behavior, 45*, 125-176.

Greenhaus, J.H., Callahan, G.A., & Godshalk, V.M. (2000). Career management (3rd ed.). Fort Worth, TX: Dryden Press.

Hansen, S.L. (1996). *Integrative life planning: Critical tasks for career development and changing life patterns.* San Francisco, CA: Jossey-Bass.

Harper, L. (1994, April 5). Work week. Job-hunt costs. *Wall Street Journal,* p. 12.

Harris-Tuck, L., Price, A., & Robertson, M. (2000). *Career patterns: A kaleidoscope of possibilities.* Upper Saddle River, NJ: Prentice-Hall.

Heise, D.R. (1990). Chapter 3: Careers, career trajectories, and the self. In J. Rodin, C. Schooler, & K. Warner Schale (Eds.), *Self-directedness: Cause and effects throughout the life course*. Hillsdale, NJ: Lawrence Erlbaum Associates.

Hinshaw, A.S. (1977). *Socialization and resocialization of nurses for professional nursing practice*. New York, NY: National League for Nursing.

Hudacek, S. (2000). *Making a difference: Stories from the point of care.* Indianapolis, IN: Center Nursing Publishing, Sigma Theta Tau International.

Keaveney, T., & Jackson, J.H. (1979). Propensity for career change among supervisors. *Human Resource Management*, 16(3), 13-16.

Kirkwood, C. (1994). *Your services are no longer required: The complete job-loss recovery book.* New York, NY: Plume.

Kohl, L.R. (2000). Why do Americans act like that? A guide to understand the U.S. culture and its values. Retrieved on November 27, 2000, from http://www.uku.fi/-paganuzz/xcult/values/Amer_values.htm.

Lankard, B.A. (1993). *Career development through self-renewal.* Washington, DC: Office of Educational Research and Improvement. U.S. Department of Education, ERIC Clearinghouse on Adult Career and Vocational education.

Leeds, D. (1991). *Marketing yourself: The ultimate job seeker's guide.* New York, NY: Harper/ Collins.

Miller, T.W. (1991). *The career creation process of persons with previous college degrees pursuing nursing as a career change.* Dissertation, University of Texas, Austin.

Moore, L.L. (1979). From manpower planning to human resources planning through career development. *Personnel, 56*(3), 9-17.

Norwood, S.L. (2003). *Nursing consultation: A framework for working with communities* (2nd ed.). Upper Saddle River, NJ: Prentice Hall.

Oxford University Press. (1996). *The Oxford English Dictionary.* New York, NY. Author.

Perlmutter-Bloch, D.P., & Richmond, L.J. (Eds.) (1997). *Connections between spirit and work in career development.* Palo Alto, CA: Consulting Psychologists Press.

Peters, T. (1994, August 22). No job description, but great business cards. *Chicago Tribune*, p. 4.

Schlossberg, N.K. (1997). *A model for worklife transitions.* Greensboro, NC: ERIC Clearinghouse on Counseling and Student Services.

U.S. Bureau of Labor Statistics (April, 2003). National Longitudinal Survey Program Employment Research and Program Development; Washington, DC 20212-0001 On-line at http://www.bls.gov/NLS (NLS data questions: nls_info@bls.gov).

Webster's. (1995). *Webster's new world dictionary and thesaurus.* Indianapolis, IN: Wiley.

Yost, E.B., & Corbishley, M.A. (1987). *Career counseling.* San Francisco, CA: Jossey-Bass.

Chapter 2

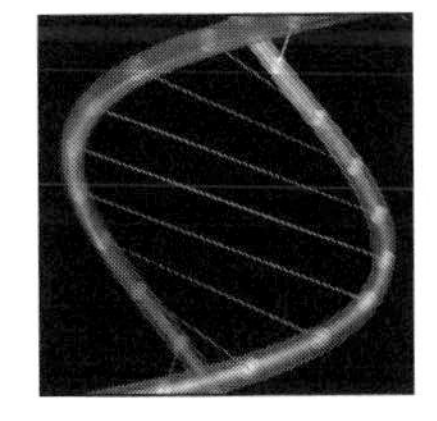

Overview of the Career Creation Process

by Terry W. Miller

> *It has to do with really looking at what you want. I think there are people in this world just going along . . . just doing what they are doing. They don't really think about it. If they're earning a comfortable living, I guess it's okay with them, and they just do it. They don't think about growth or challenge. There are people in this world who aren't interested in growing in their lifetime. That's not for me* (Excerpt from field notes 6/27/90).

INTRODUCTION

Career planning is a personal, lifelong process that gives shape and direction to work. It can greatly enhance a person's life, earnings and overall status in society. Yet, its greatest benefit comes in the form of personal fulfillment and knowing that informed decisions about the future have been made. The purpose of this chapter is to present a framework for the process of identifying and pursuing a career. Identifying a career and committing to it can be a scary proposition when it is considered as lifework. However, while needs and expectations change over time, all of us need some degree of stability and consistency.

The beginnings of career development theory, at least in the United States, can be traced back to Frank Parsons (1909). Early career theorists and counselors were linear positivists who treated career changers or people who did not know what they wanted to do for their life's work until well into adulthood as career failures. Basically, these career theorists believed people had a structural orientation and possessed relatively unchanging characteristics. These characteristics were usually described as the person's interests, talents and/or intelligence. They defined career as a vertical, lifelong commitment to a particular job. They also predominantly studied male populations and generalized their findings to female populations (Schulenberg, Vondracek, & Crouter, 1984). Fortunately, this approach to career counseling has been abandoned by all but a few.

Considerable work has been accomplished in human development that strongly indicates people can and do change significantly over time. It is no surprise that many later career theorists have discredited the static nature of Parsons' trait theory, as well as personality-based models. Some discredit because they believe the sociocultural context is constantly changing, which causes the vocational/career development context to also change (sociological or anthropological perspectives). Others discredit because they believe individuals do change as they grow older, regardless of their sociocultural context (psychological perspective).

Several common themes do emerge from a current overview of career theories. The impact of sociocultural change on career development alone has been recognized and studied since the 1980s. Many theorists since the 1980s assume that people make career decisions from a whole lifetime of experiences, as opposed to an isolated moment or single experience (Super, 1990; Osiprow & Fitzgerald, 1996; Vondracek & Lerner, 1982; Vondracek, Lerner, & Schulenberg, 1983; Hall, 1990). Also, it is assumed that many people have strong expectations of the work that occupies at least half of their waking lives. Many theorists espouse to the need for skills specific to job selection, acquisition and retention (Arthur, Claman, & DeFillipi, 1995; Greenhaus, Callahan, & Godshalk, 2000). They also recognize that many people may not be in a position to make informed career choices. Several causes of this lack of readiness have been proposed to include immaturity, environmental constraints and personality flaws (Miller, 1991).

Creating a career is a process of discovering and developing a work life that produces growth and becomes a recognizable part of an individual's identity. Some careers tend to be very regimented and require years of preparation before the individual can function as a professional in practice. Some careers tend to follow a "vertical" model where advancement is based on years in the career rather than on the ability to meet a particular set of outcomes or accomplishments. Other careers offer many choices and the ability to make lateral, as well as vertical, career moves without much difficulty.

Careers like nursing allow for location practically anywhere, while others can be very place-bound because there are only certain places where a person can do the work or find employment. A few careers, such as military careers, require periodic relocation. And there are careers that involve considerable short-term travel, while others limit the ability to travel at all. The number and variation of career opportunities can be overwhelming to anyone, so it really helps to have a strategy for identifying career goals and taking action to meet them.

Creating a career requires decision-making that builds on the advice of others, but ultimately rests with the career seeker. A helpful tool for making career decisions consists of five concepts—fun, future, focus, flexibility and feasibility. Fun in this context refers to the ability to enjoy what is being accomplished during work and not what can be acquired because of work (e.g., salary). Job discontent, if not career discontent, will be inevitable if the majority of the time at work cannot be enjoyed or any fun enjoyed occurs outside the work setting. However, beginning a new career or beginning a new job can be stressful because the "fun" may not be evident for an extended period of time.

Most people enjoy playing games but may struggle while they learn the rules. It is important to recognize that, at first, there may be little fun with career planning, but once one is oriented to the process, it becomes fun. After all, the career creation process is a plan for a major part of one's life, so what is selected is a way of "making a living" and hopefully provides personal fulfillment. The time invested in the development of a career strategy will prove valuable throughout life. It may even help avoid considerable grief, because it is important to be informed when making decisions about the future.

It helps to have a vision of tomorrow's opportunities when creating a career. Some career choices become obsolete because of advances in technology, loss of market for the skills associated with the career, redefinition or relocation to places having less expensive workforces. Other career choices are saturated with people who want the benefits associated with them without a clear understanding of what success in the career choice requires. Work and how work is done changes with time.

> *The new employee contract guarantees you nothing but the opportunity to remain employed—provided your skills are current and in demand. This stark reality translates into the need for constant self-renewal; continuous learning; and deliberate, lifelong networking* (Sukiennik, Bendat, & Raufman, 2001, p.269).

Understanding the implications of a career decision in terms of the future demands a consideration of both the actual and potential developments in the career field. This understanding also supports the need for getting a higher level, more transferable education and skill set.

Although having an awareness of trends and future possibilities is important, career creation also requires focus on the present. Focus provides a sense of purpose and direction for establishing meaningful goals. Focus takes discipline and a commitment to a direction but does not imply career inflexibility. Focus means actions for creating a career are deliberate and purposeful, as opposed to haphazard and randomly determined by environmental circumstances.

Some career seekers waste considerable time and energy predicting an unlikely career future because they do not take the necessary steps to make that future feasible. During times of personal transition and uncertainty, focus provides the structure to cope by keeping the individual "on task." Successful people in careers such as nursing demonstrate the ability to stay focused, while retaining a high degree of flexibility in a work setting.

Harris-Tuck, Price and Robertson (2000) claim a flexible career plan is time-limited, framed by a person's core focus, continually shifting and evolving. Instead of searching for a perfect, lifelong job, search for the best job, matching interests for the next four to five years. Flexible career planners think of themselves as businesses with business plans. Flexible career planning includes alternative work options and may include contract employment for a time-limited period, as opposed to an ongoing job in one organization.

Feasibility is a difficult concept to realize when making career decisions, because it requires a realistic self-assessment, as well as validation by others. Feasibility is often defined in terms of time, money and support from others, but personal ability is more critical. Some people are very unrealistic about their abilities and limitations, especially when they have little exposure to successful role models who can objectively and appropriately validate their potential for success in a given area. Every informed career decision demands a personal assessment at the time of the decision. Thus, an ongoing personal assessment is a major part of career decision-making.

DOING A REALISTIC SELF-ASSESSMENT

Self-awareness is a critical first step for any feasible career strategy. Knowing strengths and limitations, as well as likes and dislikes, creates better decision-making and helps avoid needless mistakes. To develop self-awareness, it is important to realistically assess competencies and values. Competencies are the knowledge, skills or abilities that enable good performance in a given role. Certainly, there are competencies that may be missing, but most can be learned with the right education and experiences. However, some competencies require special aptitudes or require a level of mastery that exceeds the average person's ability. Fortunately, there are many ways to assess aptitude for developing a skill set, if openness to evaluation from others in an educational context is provided.

Part of an honest self-assessment includes identifying the factors that really motivate and the factors that discourage. Often, people are unduly influenced by media representations of an occupation, failing to recognize the absurdity of the media portrayal. For example, television programs and popular literature often present nursing as nothing more than a subservient occupation for the benefit of medicine. This portrayal disregards the power and influence that nurses hold throughout the healthcare system, in schools and universities, as well as in communities and organizations, including private businesses. For example, several nurses have served in the United States House of Representatives, and many others are chief executive officers of hospitals and even large healthcare systems. Nurses are commissioned as officers in the United States Armed Services, and a few have held the rank of general.

It is important to listen closely to those with firsthand experience who have been successful in an occupation rather than those who have not succeeded or not advanced in an occupation. These are the people who can describe what a particular occupation has to offer and what will be required to succeed in it. Every person's career is different, and some occupations, such as nursing, have so many dimensions and possibilities that it is impossible to obtain a complete picture by interviewing a few individuals. Nurses who hold many different types of positions should be interviewed.

Most people are intrigued by some occupations and disinterested in others, regardless of their real experience with, or knowledge of, these occupations. Interests often reveal passions and are key for personal motivation. Personal hobbies, extracurricular activities and how free time is spent are strong indicators of what really interests a person. It is important to discover in a self-assessment what creates real interest and what it will take to be open to new ways of thinking about self. Possibly the most popular book for this endeavor is *What Color is Your Parachute?* by Richard Bolles (2003).

There also are several tools that can help people learn more about themselves. Two of the most common instruments that are fun to complete and quite informative are the Strong Interest Inventory (SII) and the Myers-Briggs Type Indicator (MBTI). Other frequently used measures to aid in career exploration are the Self Directed Search (SDS) and the Kuder Occupational Interest Survey (KOIS). All of these instruments have been developed or revised to be gender neutral or "sex fair" (Farmer, 1995).

The Strong Interest Inventory compares the test taker's interests with the interests of those who are successful in a large number of occupational fields. This inventory provides a profile on four scales: (1) work style, (2) learning environment, (3) leadership style and (4) risk-taking/adventure. This profile can help the test taker learn more about how s/he likes to work, learn, play or live. These scales can also show the test taker how to organize the current job so it is a better match with interests and desires or how life might be better structured. The test taker might also discover the preferred style is at odds with the current work environment, which might mean staying in the same career field but moving into a different role or area that is a better fit.

The Myers-Briggs Type Indicator (MBTI) offers another approach to understanding likes and dislikes. It is one of the most-used indicators of adult personality patterns. The results of the test can be used to guide decisions regarding careers, as well as to provide an understanding and appreciation of individual differences in interpersonal relationships. More specifically, it is a self-report personality inventory designed to give people information about their psychological type preferences. MBTI results indicate the respondent's likely preferences on four dimensions:

- Extraversion (E) OR Introversion (I)
- Sensing (S) OR Intuition (N)
- Thinking (T) OR Feeling (F)
- Judging (J) OR Perceiving (P)

Results of the MBTI are generally reported with letters representing each of the preferences as indicated above. Though many factors combine to influence an individual's behaviors, values and attitudes, the four-letter-type descriptions summarize underlying patterns and behaviors common to most people of that type. The MBTI is a widely used instrument for career exploration, development and counseling, as well as self-understanding. Both the Myers-Briggs Type Indicator and the Strong Interest Inventory should be administered and interpreted by a qualified practitioner. The best way to locate a qualified practitioner is to contact the human resources department at the site of employment, a career counselor, or college and university counseling centers.

A comprehensive self-assessment also includes an evaluation of education and experience. It is an attempt to examine a person's skills, personal attributes and abilities in the context of personal interests, and potential career values. Often, a comprehensive self-assessment reveals an overall attitude about work and the career potential for the person doing it, as well as what motivates the person to take action. Once the factors that motivate are identified, it is easier to develop a career strategy that will reach the desired future.

DISCOVERING CAREER INTERESTS AND NEW CAREER OPTIONS

Once career seekers complete a self-assessment, it is time to start focusing on career interests and exploring career options. Again, there are numerous books and professional counselors, as well as several computer-based tools available for accomplishing the task. Career exploration entails gathering information about career fields and occupations to determine what matches personal interests, builds on abilities and fits values. To have an effective career strategy, it is important to find information about different careers in more than one way. Some sources of valuable information are listed below:

- Want ads and career sections of newspapers
- Job titles and descriptions posted at employment agencies
- Position listings in human resource departments of organizations, agencies and businesses
- Position announcements in professional journals
- Career fairs and career centers at schools, colleges and universities
- People who will take a few minutes to answer questions about what they do

Periodically searching these sources, as identified, is valuable even if the career focus is already known or a career is well underway. Specifically, four methods are useful for career exploration. They are:

- The library reference search
- Computer search
- Personal interview and discussion
- Experiential learning

Many people do not realize the wealth of information about careers available at the local library. Some useful publications are the *Dictionary of Occupational Titles, Occupational Outlook Handbook* and *National Association of Colleges and Employers (NACE) Salary Survey.* There is more than anyone can access, much less read, in several days. Reference librarians are excellent starting points and can save a person considerable time and frustration.

Access to any online Internet service provider (ISP) enables anyone to explore multiple career options and job opportunities, as well as to become exposed to literally thousands of career-related topics and resources. The home page for America Online (AOL) has a careers and work section featuring Monster.com. This Web site has career-related subsections identified as: salary and benefits, career finder, improve yourself, research a company, start up a business, professional training, chats and boards, and explore your profession. Using a search engine, such as Google.com, and typing in career exploration provides over one-half million Web sites, including career centers at highly respected universities and organizations. Nursing can be located under the listing of healthcare.

To complement any library and computer research on a career, such as nursing, it is useful to gather information from professionals in the chosen field of interest. The insight gained through the perspectives of others provides a much better understanding of the work and if it will be a good fit. The contacts made during the process may help in the future when advancing through the personal career creation process. Again, it is important to focus on people who have been successful in their careers to learn what has helped them succeed and accomplish their career goals. Most people enjoy discussing their work when someone is genuinely interested in listening.

Experiential learning offers people a working exposure to some aspect of a career. For example, participating in cooperative education, working as a volunteer for an organization, and performing internships or some form of related employment in which the person associates with others working in an area of interest are valuable ways to gather information and gain insight into an occupation and potential career choice. Yet, this method takes the most time and should not be the only method used to map out a career pathway. Organizations and agencies, as well as the people who work in them, vary greatly. Unfortunately, a negative experience in one organization or setting with a few unhappy people could create a premature conclusion about an occupation or career line.

The result of the self-assessment and career exploration should lead to decisions about the future. Career decision-making that is strategic comes from an integration of a self-assessment and career exploration—it culminates in a career focus. This is the time to identify career goals and objectives. Career goals are broad statements of intent and provide direction for the career. Career objectives are specific and determine what actions must be taken to stay focused and heading in the right direction. In other words, career goals are for the long-term and more global; whereas career objectives are measurable and achievable in a given time frame. Meeting realistic, achievable objectives on the way to achieving career goals creates a sense of accomplishment along a lifelong career path.

LEARNING ABOUT A CAREER

Learning how to do something that is complex and challenging requires commitment and focus. For example, most nursing careers begin with several years of higher education and the successful completion of the registered nurse licensure examination before entry into professional practice is achieved. Yet, the challenge for meeting the entry to practice requirements is what makes nursing such a valuable career option. Occupations that have few or minimal requirements are open to anyone at anytime. This is why these jobs tend to be low paying and offer few opportunities for advancement and professional growth. Occupations that require a distinctive skill set, demand real expertise and meet high standards before entry protect their members by making them far more valuable to society and potential employers. These requirements also greatly enhance an individual's ability to create a sustainable position.

Too often people determine whether or not something is feasible for the wrong reasons. It is important to understand that a real career is an investment. For instance, the more invested, the greater is the potential for significantly greater rewards, higher lifelong earnings, more professional recognition and greater personal fulfillment. Investment in terms of a career is more about education, time commitment and focus than money. Although practically everyone must plan his or her finances carefully, there are many ways to finance an education if there is commitment when gratification is not immediate.

Often, excessive amounts of money are spent in an effort to minimize the educational requirements of a profession. This can be a grievous mistake, because the quality of the education may be diminished. Another mistake that often occurs is when a position is accepted based solely on the salary. Short-cutting education and professional development and accepting salary over other considerations can result in short-lived rewards and long-term dissatisfaction.

CREATING A CAREER IN NURSING

Career is something you go after. You go into it anticipating that you are going to do this for your working life, and you seek it out. I've changed, and I have gotten deeper into a career and found something lacking and saw something adjacent and more promising. That is nursing (Excerpt from field notes 6/26/90).

Creating a nursing career is the process of discovering and developing a career pathway that produces growth and becomes a recognizable part of the nurse's identity. Career creation in nursing requires more than earning a degree, being licensed and working in a nursing role. Editorials and essays in nursing literature have identified career planning and development as essential at entry to the profession, as well as throughout the time in the profession (Haylock, 2003; Katz, Carter, Bishop, & Kravits, 2001; Case, 1996; Heydman & Madsen, 1989; Morrison & Zebelman, 1982; Robinson-Smith, 1984; Hefferin & Kleinknecht, 1986).

Some nursing programs provide a career course for undergraduates, and clinical ladders are available in some healthcare agencies. Yet, too often people enter nursing without realizing their potential to create a successful career that extends well beyond any employment setting or particular job. A review of the growing number of successful nurse entrepreneurs highlights some of the possibilities.

Although it is important to assess one's progress in nursing, or any field of interest in relationship to others, one or two delays or some variation from the "norm" is not unusual. In other words, the career paths of others should not be intimidating but should be a way to learn from others. Being strategic and focused pays off because so many people treat career planning more as a luxury than a necessity for professional advancement.

The process of career creation has properties, and understanding these properties can help when considering a nursing career. These career properties include:

- Shape and direction
- A course with several stages

- Change in identity
- Variation in approach

SHAPE AND DIRECTION

The first property of the career creation process is that it has shape and direction. The shape and direction of the career process is driven by the way the individual responds to certain conditions. At least 10 conditions influence the way people pursue a nursing career. These conditions include education, practice, support, finances, time, role models, exposure, availability, convenience and motivation. For nursing, these conditions are described as follows:

1. *Education* that leads to the registered nurse (RN) licensing examination and to safe entry into the practice of nursing varies because there is more than one educational pathway to qualify for the National Certification Licensing Examination (NCLEX). These educational pathways include the following:
   a. *Associate degree in nursing (ADN) program.* This is a three-year program when the required prerequisite coursework is included.
   b. *Baccalaureate degree in nursing (BSN) program.* This is a four-year program when the required prerequisite coursework is included.
   c. *Diploma program.* This is a three-year, hospital-based program, including summers. There are few of these programs remaining in the U.S.
   d. *Entry-level graduate degree in nursing (MSN) program.* There has been an increasing number of these programs in the U.S. over the past few years. They usually require, at entry, a baccalaureate or higher degree in a field outside of nursing and some prerequisite coursework. The student acquires eligibility to complete the NCLEX at some designated time during the program.
2. *Practice* is the actual experience of providing nursing services to clients/patients. Clients/patients may be individuals, families or even a whole community.

3. *Support* is the extent to which others promote the nurse's career goals and understand what is necessary for the pursuit and maintenance of a career.
4. *Finances* are the monetary resources that must be available.
5. *Time* is the measurement of how long it takes to progress through the career creation process.
6. *Role models* are exemplars of nursing that are either emulated or rejected.
7. *Exposure* is the way a nursing career and what it entails is discovered.
8. *Availability* is having access to a program if the candidate meets the criteria for admission and applies.
9. *Convenience* is the amount of effort required to pursue a course of action.
10. *Motivation* is the personal driving force behind an action.

Conditions related to the pursuit of a nursing career either facilitate or hinder the intentional shaping of the personal career creation process. For example, having a well-paying job can be a condition for a particular career course and can be rewarding yet hindering at the same time. If earning a high salary in one field prevents the pursuit of a career in another field, the high-paying job creates conflict.

Conditions can also be cumulative, complementary or offsetting. That is, the degree and direction of a condition's impact upon an individual's career course often depends on whether or not certain other conditions exist. Conditions change with time, and the actions taken by an individual in the past and present will affect the conditions experienced in the future.

There are at least three types of actions used by people to manage the conditions they encounter while pursuing a career goal. These actions are searching, matching and choosing. Searching can occur in several different ways. For example, seeking informants who represent particular aspects of nursing is one way. Reading ads is another. There are many other strategies for searching for a career opportunity.

Matching occurs when a career goal or alternative fits the desires and interests of the job seeker. Choosing occurs when one career goal or option is selected over another. Regardless of the type of action taken in seeking a career, it has consequences. Consequences are the reasons that it is critical to make informed choices and to understand the "bigger picture" before committing to an educational program or accepting a job.

PATHWAYS FOR CAREER PURSUIT

The second property of the career creation process is that it has a course or pathway. The pathway for a nursing career has both sociological and psychological dimensions that are significant. The psychological dimensions are essentially intrinsic to the individual and partially determine the sociological forces acting on the individual. Similarly, the sociological dimension is primarily extrinsic and partially determines the psychological status of the individual.

The pursuit of a nursing career has eight stages that are not necessarily age-related in terms of cause and effect. Career changers pursuing a nursing career also pass through these stages after experiencing career discontent related to their previous career pathway. The eight stages are:

- Identifying a strong career interest
- Exploring how to pursue the career interest
- Fulfilling the requirements for entry into the career
- Identifying personal values in the context of the values inherent to the career
- Recognizing career-life linkage
- Making nursing self-linkage
- Becoming nursing career hopeful
- Having a nursing career

It is important to understand that a person can move back and forth between stages or become fixed in a stage. Movement through the career creation process depends on the actions of the career seeker. Variations among individuals are dependent on the conditions being faced and the actions taken in relation to those conditions. However, lack of action or career inertia means no movement regardless of the conditions faced.

The outcome of an individual's actions and interactions through the stages of the career creation process is dependent on the person's sense of achieving or not achieving a desirable work life. It is doubtful that an individual ever experiences a total sense of achievement. Prevailing career discontent often includes a feeling of being unfulfilled and results in personal conflict. When people experience career discontent or become disenchanted with their career goals, they have three basic options: live with it, change it or leave it.

Commitment is crucial for making a career-life linkage. Thousands of nurses today have successful, personally rewarding careers because they have taken the right actions to ensure their future. They have fun, remain focused and can determine what is feasible for them at every stage of their professional growth. Once a nurse has made a career-life linkage, the career is re-staged as early career, middle career and late career as discussed in Chapter 4.

CHANGE AT A PERSONAL LEVEL

The third property of the career creation process is identity change. A change in identity occurs when passage through the stages of the career creation process is completed. This change is influenced by others but occurs at a personal level. The degree of the identity change ranges from a shift in commitment to career goals to an identity transformation. It is sometimes hard to accept this identity transformation in others because of the high level of commitment to the career that it often entails. However, it can be a joyous situation to see someone choose a career, fulfill the requirements for entering the career and develop into a real professional committed to the selected work life.

Identity transformation is reflected in how the career pathway is perceived, experienced and evaluated. Because of a reconstruction or confirmation of personal values in relation to career work, the individual becomes someone different. This change does not usually happen suddenly, but may become evident because of a significant event. For example, many nurses early in their careers share their roles in certain experiences, such as the delivery of a baby or the death of a patient, as they begin to identify themselves as nurses.

VARIATION IN APPROACH

The fourth property of the career creation process is variation. Two basic patterns of the career creation process are common among Americans. One pattern is the "opportunistic" career course and the other is the "humanistic" career course. The patterns are basically the same until the individual reaches the values identification phase of the career creation process. The "humanistic" pathway diverges from the "opportunistic" pathway because value identification leads to a reconstruction of personal values. Individuals motivated by humanistic values seek a career that is more personal and less extrinsic. From then on, personal values become the predominant motivation for choosing a particular career. For instance, nursing represents a valuable, personally rewarding service and something to believe in. In contrast, the opportunistic perspective focuses on "there are jobs," "the pay is good," and "I can obtain what I want with less work."

However, actions have consequences, and taking a purely opportunistic approach to a career such as nursing could lead to career discontent. Life's work is long, and there are few shortcuts to success in any field. A close examination of people who are highly successful and happy in their careers reveals a sense of pride, accountability and professional identity that is internalized and irrespective of monetary gain. Yet, it does not hurt that nursing pays well, provides outstanding employment opportunities and should show significant wage gains throughout this decade.

Some authors express considerable concern over the apparent disconnection between what has been identified as the spiritual self and work. Perlmutter-Bloch and Richmond (1997), as well as Sundal-Hansen and Hansen (1996), offer approaches to more integrative life planning by attempting to model the connection between spirit and work in career development. Nursing certainly has a long history of supporting a more spiritually defined approach to career development as indicated by the number of religiously affiliated nursing programs. Miller (1991) discovered that some career changers entering nursing reaffirmed their faith, not necessarily Judeo-Christian, in something more than humanity itself.

CHANGING THE CAREER COURSE

I once chose a career that I didn't consider particularly professional, but it had great monetary gain. As I got into it, I didn't care for it at all. So I changed. It had some growth potential, but it lacked something that I cared about for me. So I guess it wasn't the correct career, because it didn't fit what I advocated.... It didn't fit my soul. (Excerpts from field notes 6/26/90).

Some sources state today's Americans will have five or more careers during their lifetimes (Austin, 2002; Statland, 2000). In reality, it is more likely they will change jobs several times over their lifetimes because there is a tendency for job promoters and people without established careers to equate job with career. In U.S. society, having a career is commonly perceived as more favorable than having a job. Certainly, being employed is a positive; however, a "career" indicates something far more than having a particular job or title. For example, most graduates who enter the nursing profession work as staff nurses. At that time in their career life, a career orientation or the level of commitment that would distinguish work from a real career in nursing may not be important; however, after three or four successful years of nursing practice, the pursuit of a master's degree may seem appropriate. While many nurses may not have entered nursing with a career orientation, it is not uncommon for that orientation to change, particularly if more education has been pursued or a wise and progressive mentor has had an influence on the nurse.

Changing a career course, like establishing a career direction, is determined by both external and internal conditions. Since the internal conditions are reflective of the person's value system and if the individual does not change this values-orientation during the career creation process, the same pattern in terms of searching, matching and choosing a new career course is likely to be repeated. If these values match the goals and inherent values of the new career path, the career creation process becomes values oriented. Therefore, anytime a career or career change is contemplated, a reassessment of the career goals, aspirations and activities in light of personal values must be assessed.

Changing to a humanistic career course links career with life in personal terms. Nursing becomes a career choice because the person perceives a match between personal values and the intrinsic nature of the profession. The following description, by a person who attempted several career options after high school, illustrates this personal values transformation.

> *In high school, I just knew I wanted to be rich. I didn't really know how I was going to attain my goal. And I didn't give it a lot of thought. That was why I didn't have a lot of direction when I first started college. . . . I figured that the chips would fall where they would, and it would become self-evident to me, in the course of my studies, what I should do. . . . Well I changed goals, I decided in college that I wanted to enter business, and that would be how I would become successful. When I did have my own business and became financially successful, I discovered that it was not fulfilling. . . . I wanted a career that would be more fulfilling, something that I could feel good about accomplishing . . . just becoming a better person. Financial wealth was not my top priority anymore. I wanted more. I wanted a career that would make me feel good about myself when I went to bed at night. I wanted something that I could look forward to everyday, in spite of its challenges and frustrations, because all careers must be frustrating at some level. I started searching for something that would fill that void, and I think I have discovered it is nursing.*
>
> *Now that I've been through school and I've been out in the real world, I've thought about things more. I learned by example and by doing what my goals and aspirations demanded. . . . Because I'm 27 now, I'm just really embarking upon what I consider to be my ultimate career. I think I'm more positive, but I don't know if I am more positive than others. . . . I think that I've proven to myself that nursing is right for me. I think nursing gives me a really strong motivation, maybe stronger than for some other people. . . . I think a lot of external influences changed me internally, and it's kind of a chain reaction.*
>
> *Seeing other people and learning from others has helped me. My mom is a nurse, and my wife is a med student. Their sharing of their experiences has helped mold me and change how I feel internally. Also, my internal thoughts and ideas have changed, so I think that is what helped me make the ultimate decision . . . my decision that is internally motivated* (Excerpt from field notes 1/28/91).

ACHIEVING BALANCE

Career choice and its development influence all aspects of life. Finding the right balance between personal life and professional work is important in order to sustain a productive career while enjoying life. Underlying this desire for balance is the need to fit career aspirations with lifestyle. As nurses advance in their careers and mature in their relationships, they find themselves living increasingly multifaceted lives. Career success often means increasing career demands and a greater sense or need for personal time. Obtaining this balance requires attention be paid to both.

Nursing is a profession with rich career opportunities (McCloskey Dochterman & Grace, 2001, p. 2). These career opportunities are projected to expand significantly throughout this decade. The nurse of the future will most likely work with a new health system yet to be determined, a system that may demand even more than the one of today. Being able to balance work with personal time demands priority setting and the ability to say "no" and how to determine when to say "yes." It may even require a career change if the job infringes on personal time.

Balance between work and one's personal life means the individual must have support systems, so when the job demands more time, the other aspects of life are taken care of. Further, an understanding and flexible employer must be available when one's personal life demands more attention. This issue of balance is an important factor when seeking a job or progressing through a career, or the individual may become the victim of "overload" and ultimately poor performance.

CONCLUSION

The process of creating a career trajectory has been described in this chapter. Specifically, this chapter provides a process that any individual can follow when considering the development of a career or a career change. Being able to complete a self-assessment, including the use of the Strong Interest Inventory and the Myers-Briggs Type Indicator, and many other types of assessment tools is an essential aspect of knowing more about self before initiating a job search. Learning about the career of choice and how to prepare for that choice is also important.

To learn about how to prepare for the career of choice depends on understanding four properties of the career creation process: the shape and direction of the preparation; the pathway to pursue, which includes eight steps; identity change; and whether the approach is opportunistic or humanistic. Being able to master these four steps should provide the career seeker with the tools for a successful career pursuit. The chapters that follow present more in-depth information about the career creation process, which includes the four aspects outlined in this chapter.

REFERENCES

Arthur, M.B., Claman, P.H., & DeFillippi, R.J. (1995). Intelligent enterprise, intelligent careers. *Academy of Management Executive*, *9*, 7-20.

Austin, A. (2002). Explore your possibilities: Change is the only constant. From time to time, you may need to reinvent yourself to keep up (Brief Article). *Career World,* Feb-Mar issue, p. 2 of 2-available on-line April 8, 2003 at http://www.findarticles.com/cf_0/m0HUV/5...4780/pl/article.jhtml?term=career+change.

Bolles, R.N. (2003). *What color is your parachute? A practical manual for job-hunters and career-changers* (2003 ed.). Berkeley, CA: Ten Speed Press.

Brown, D. (1988). *Life-role development and counseling.* Paper presented at the meeting of the National Career Development Association, Orlando, FL.

Case, B. (1996). *Career planning for nurses.* Albany, NY: Delmar.

Farmer, H.S. (1995). *Gender differences in adolescent career exploration.* Greensboro, NC: ERIC Clearinghouse on Counseling and Student Services.

Greenhaus, J.H., Callahan, G.A., & Godshalk, V.M. (2000). *Career management* (3rd ed.). Fort Worth, TX: The Dryden Press.

Hall, D.T. (1990). Career development in organizations. In D. Brown & L. Brooks (Eds.), *Career choice and development: Applying contemporary theories to practice* (pp. 422-454). San Francisco, CA: Jossey-Bass.

Harris-Tuck, L., Price, A., & Robertson, M. (2000). *Career patterns: A kaleidoscope of possibilities.* Upper Saddle River, NJ: Prentice-Hall.

Haylock, P.J. (2003). Charting the course of your nursing career. *American Journal of Nursing 2003 Career Guide*, pp. 33-36.

Hefferin, E.A., & Kleinknecht, M.K. (1986). Development of the nursing career preference inventory. *Nursing Research, 35*(1), 44-48.

Henchley, N. (1978). Making sense of the future. *Alternatives,* 7, 24.

Heydman, A.M., & Madsen, N. (1989). Career ladders for nurse retention. In T.F. Moore & E.A. Simendinger (Eds.). *Managing the nursing shortage: A Guide to recruitment and retention* (pp. 117-132). Rockville, MD: Aspen.

Katz, J.R., Carter, C., Bishop, J., & Kravits, S.L. (2001). *Keys to nursing success.* Upper Saddle River, NJ: Prentice-Hall.

McCloskey Dochterman, J., & Grace, H.K. (2001). *Current issues in nursing* (6th ed.). St. Louis, MO: Mosby.

Miller, T.W. (1991). The career creation process of persons with previous college degrees pursuing nursing as a career change. Dissertation, University of Texas, Austin.

Morrison, R.S., & Zebelman, E. (1982). The career concept in nursing. *Nursing Administration Quarterly, 7*(1), 60-68.

Osiprow, S.H., & Fitzgerald, L.F. (1996). *Theories of career development* (4th ed.). Boston, MA: Allyn & Bacon.

Parsons, F. (1909). *Choosing a vocation.* Boston, MA: Houghton Mifflin.

Perlmutter-Bloch, D.P., & Richmond, L.J. (1997). *Connections between spirit and work in career development.* Palo Alto, CA: Consulting Psychologists Press.

Robinson-Smith, G. (1984). Alternative careers in nursing. *Imprint, 30*(5), 23-24.

Schulenberg, J.E., Vondracek, F.W., & Crouter, A.C. (1984). The influence of the family on vocational development. *Journal of Marriage and the Family, 46*(1), 129-143.

Slaney, R.B., & Russell, J.E.A. (1987). Perspectives on vocational behavior, 1986: A review. *Journal of Vocational Behavior, 31*(2), 111-173.

Statland, B.E. (2002). Is it time for a career renewal? *Medical Laboratory Observer.* May issue, p. 1 of 6- available on-line April 8, 2003 at http://www.findarticles.com/cf_0/m3230/5_32/624450730/...4780/print/jhtml?.

Sukiennik, D., Bendat, W., & Raufman, L. (2001). *The career fitness program: Exercising your options* (6th ed.). Upper Saddle River, NJ: Prentice-Hall.

Sundal-Hansen, L.S., & Hansen, L.S. (1996). *Integrative life planning*. San Francisco, CA: Jossey-Bass.

Super, D.E. (1990). A life-span, life-space approach to career development. In D. Brown & L. Brooks (Eds.), *Career choice and development: Applying contemporary theories to practice* (pp. 197-261). San Francisco, CA: Jossey-Bass.

Vondracek, F.W., & Lerner, R.M. (1982). Vocational role development in adolescence. In B. B. Wolman (Ed.), *Handbook of developmental psychology*. Englewood Cliffs, NJ: Prentice-Hall.

Vondracek, F.W., Lerner, R.M., & Schulenberg, J.E. (1983). The concept of development in vocational theory and intervention. *Journal of Vocational Behavior, 23*, 179-202.

Chapter 3

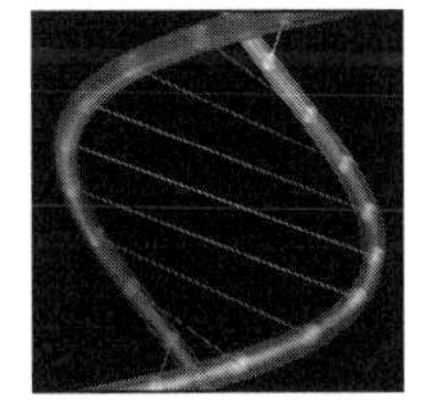

Shape and Direction

by Terry W. Miller

If there was a simple formula for success and it was easy to follow, everybody would be doing it (Edward C. Johnson, III).

INTRODUCTION

Careers have shape and direction. The shape and direction of the career creation process is driven by the way the career seeker responds to certain conditions, such as education, practice, support, finances, time, role models, exposure, availability and convenience. Further, the individual consciously or unconsciously determines the extent to which others influence the shape and direction of the career creation process, as well as its success.

Responses to conditions are determined predominantly by the individual affected and by input from others. Some individuals seldom question the advice and suggestions of others believed to have more knowledge, authority or experience. They let others who do not have the ability to be mentors direct and shape their work lives. Regardless of the extent a career choice is influenced by others, the consequences for the career decision rest with the person making the decision. Blaming others for a career failure or lack of career success, anytime during the career creation process, will not improve the shape or direction of the career. Basically, a person has three options in an unsatisfactory work situation: to resolve to accept it, to work to change it, or to leave the position.

As with any passage to a higher level of self-awareness and professional competence, change occurs. Often the process of change is painful for the individual undergoing it. It is nearly always difficult. Although no single theory or body of research adequately describes the influences on career-related behavior throughout the lifespan, what does exist can help the person to make better decisions and experience a more satisfying career. Ultimately, the career creation process is the identification, clarification and validation of values spread over a lifetime of work.

Influences that Shape and Direct a Career

The literature indicates there are several factors that significantly influence the shape and direction of the career creation process. These factors are:

- The family
- Gender
- Culture
- Motivation

Influence of Family on the Shape and Direction of a Career

The shape and direction of a career starts even before the individual chooses any occupation or line of work. The first role models for the interpretation of work and career are those available in childhood. The family is the first source for learning how to interpret reality (Way & Rossman, 1996). How parents define and relate to their work at home and elsewhere affect the child's understanding of work life (Santrock, 1995). This understanding includes beliefs about what is categorized as a successful career or an unsuccessful career and even whether a career should be attempted.

Several research studies have shown that family plays a significant role in career choices, particularly about the decision to pursue or not to pursue entrepreneurial activities or be self-employed (Whitlock & Masters, 1996). For nearly 50 years, research studies have demonstrated familial factors are especially critical to women's careers (O'Brien & Fassinger, 1993; Betz & Fitzgerald, 1987; Roe, 1956). Family characteristics, such as parental employment, education and nontraditional attitudes, are positively related to the career development of women (Rainey & Borders, 1992; Betz & Fitzgerald, 1987). Various family experiences also impact women's careers (Fisher & Padmawijaja, 1999; Altman, 1997; MacGregor & Cochran,

1988), such as critical life events and a stressful family environment. In addition, women's career development is affected by family relationships, whether parent-child, sibling or the family as a whole (Altman, 1997; O'Brien & Fassinger, 1993; Pennick & Jepson, 1992).

Overall, research findings demonstrate that there is a significant association between one's family-of-origin and career development. Findings also indicate overall family functioning (parental support and guidance, positive or negative environmental influences, and interaction styles among family members) has a greater influence on career development than either family structure or parents' educational and occupational status (Altman, 1997; Fisher & Griggs, 1994; Trusty, Watts, & Erdman, 1997). Integral to successful career planning is appreciating the impact of the family (past, present and projected) on the pursuit of any career path.

Influence of Gender on the Shape and Direction of a Career

> *[There is] a major difference in the way men and women approach their work. Men plan their careers years ahead of time. While applying for their very first job, most men will already be thinking how long they will stay there, what they will learn, where that job will lead them, and what they want to achieve by age 35, 45 and 55. Women tend to limit themselves by looking at the positives and negatives of only that one job, while they are with it* (Cherne, n.d.).

An internalization of gender role stereotypes and cultural expectations of women and men (Bartholomew & Schnorr,1994) can cause a person to make career decisions based on gender stereotypes more than other factors, such as ability, skills and educational opportunities. Many myths exist about women in careers predominantly filled by males. Myths also exist about men in careers predominantly filled by females. Nursing offers a remarkable example of how myths may negatively influence career development and decision-making because of misinformation about the profession.

A review of history demonstrates men were the first nurses to undergo large-scale formal training in the Western world. Some historians who have analyzed the works of Hippocrates of Cos believe the first formally trained nurses appeared during the period 460-370 BC. Furthermore, nursing care "was undoubtedly performed chiefly by men and almost always under the supervision of men" (Levine & Levine, 1965, p. 86). While this knowledge is quite controversial, the appearance of formally trained male nurses during the Crusades of the 11th century is not.

Historians such as Dolan (1973), Jameson (1966) and Kaufman (1976) have described the significance of nursing care by men during the Middle Ages and the Renaissance period. Few nurses, much less the public, are aware one-half the nursing care in the 11th, 12th and 13th centuries was provided by men. People forget the Knights Hospitalers, Teutonic Knights, Franciscans and other male religious orders provided the esteemed nursing care of their eras (Miller, 1989). Regardless of whether this documented history is characterized as a case in which "men recognized only men in history," the fact remains that 1,000 years ago, many men proclaimed themselves to be nurses.

Sometimes, myths exist because old data and research findings are used to support a perception that is not accurate or correct. Such misinformation can have serious consequences for the person pursuing any career path. For example, some people continue to believe it is not as important for women to attain a baccalaureate or higher degree as men and that relatively few women pursue college degrees. Yet, it has been clear for the past few years that female enrollments in undergraduate college programs have surpassed those of men (*Chronicle of Higher Education*, 2002). The report *Trends in Educational Equity of Girls and Women* (Bae, 2000) has concluded women are more likely than their male peers in the United States to hold higher educational aspirations, to enroll in college and to persist to degree attainment. Another recent report indicates men's and women's enrollments in undergraduate programs continue to vary widely by age, race, ethnicity and socioeconomic class (King, 2000).

Regardless of a person's gender, career success often depends upon ability, that is, the ability to work well with others of the opposite sex, as well as with others of the same gender. Both men and women often fail to recognize their contributions to a sexist situation or comment. Some people "play along" with comments and jokes and buy into a characterization of others not based in reality. Sometimes, considerable pressure is exerted on an individual to support the stereotyping. Part of career development is developing an understanding of how people relate to each other with a level of awareness and sensitivity that avoids and downplays sexist behavior and communications.

Influence of Culture on the Shape and Direction of a Career

As career development theories are tested using a variety of different populations, a complex picture emerges. The research findings suggest career choice and development are influenced by multiple factors, such as racial/cultural identity, worldview and socialization.

Although expressions of culture are primarily unconscious, they have a profound effect on an individual's interactions and responses to conditions (Catalano, 2003).

Individuals making wise career decisions understand their personal values in relation to the values of the present culture, as well as the culture of origin. A person's *culture of origin* consists of patterns of behavior and belief systems learned from the family. However, cultural orientation and worldview change over time with increasing exposure to a "bigger world." Thus, a person's *present culture* includes personal history, language, religion, education, interests, travel experiences, hygiene practices, sexual orientation, lifestyle, work and even dietary habits. Values form the core of a culture (Andrews & Boyle, 1999).

Most everyone is part of several evolving subcultures. One of these evolving subcultures is the work group and the workplace. It is useful to understand the appropriate and desired behavior in the workplace. For example, the cultural norms of nursing and of the hospital exert pressure on the individual to conform. Conflict arises when a person's cultural orientation differs significantly from the cultural norms of the profession or the work environment.

A simple effort to diminish the discomfort associated with conflict between personal values and the values of others is accommodation. Accommodation is not resolution, and it is not professionally transformative (Kritek, 2001). Most people have not been educated nor trained to live in a pluralistic world without certainty, fraught with ambiguity and awash in social constructs where they are unable to locate the constructors of their work and take them to task for their products (or values). For the person pursuing a career in the future, it is important to develop a high level of self-awareness about the context of work. The context not only includes the person's immediate educational or work environment, but also includes local, regional, national, international and global environments as well (Kritek, 2001).

The demographics of Western countries are changing at an increasing rate. No longer is the cultural portrait of the United States predominantly Western European. Currently, ethnic minorities constitute about 28 percent of the U.S. population, and during this decade, non-Hispanic Whites will contribute only one-quarter of the total U.S. population growth (U.S. Bureau of Labor Statistics, 1998). By 2010, people of color, Caucasian women and immigrants will account for 85 percent of the net growth in the nation's labor force (Judy & D'Amico, 1997; Wentling, 2001). African Americans, Asian Americans, Hispanic (Latino/Latina) Americans and Native American Indians constitute the major ethnic minority groups in the United States. Contrary to the uniformity suggested by their labels, each of these groups subsumes a highly heterogeneous mix of peoples and subcultures, and each is growing faster than the majority population, with the implication that the U.S. workplace is becoming increasingly diverse and will continue to do so (Osiprow & Fitzgerald, 1996).

Changes in values accompany demographic shifts. It is predicted future career success will be linked to diversity and the person's ability to understand multiple perspectives. One of the greatest challenges facing the United States (and increasingly other countries) is to determine how ethnic minority students and families "can gain access to the full range of careers commensurate with their abilities and equitable opportunities for promotion and economic reward" (Gelso & Fretz, 2001, p. 385). At the organizational level, "managing diversity means changing the culture, that is, the standard operating procedures. It requires data, experimentation and the discovery of the procedures that work best for each cultural group" (Triandis, Kurowski, & Gelfand, 1994, p. 773).

To attain the desired goal of eliminating the barriers to successful career development will increasingly require cultural competence. Cultural competence can be developed by continually expanding the capability to respond appropriately and effectively to the cultural history, norms, values and needs of others. The reason people choose to explain or to justify a point of view about their career goals and work situations is because their goals are inextricably related to their assumptions about work and careers in general. Perhaps nothing does more than culture to interpret whether or not a work experience or career objective is desirable and, therefore, supportable.

Influence of Motivation on the Shape and Direction of a Career

Motivation requires two conditions—value to the person and the expectation of success. How individuals define success varies and is dependent upon their personal value system. For example, a person may value materialism more than leisure time such that success is defined by the individual's acquisition of material goods rather than having time off from work. "No one wants to do something he or she sees as worthless" (Biggs, 1999, p. 56).

Motivation or lack of it is connected to how the individual views achievement, affiliation and power. *Achievement* (accomplishments through effort), *affiliation* (associations and relationships with others), and *power* (ability to influence others) are interrelated. All three can be positive attributes of a person's personality or can lead to highly destructive behavior. Affiliation and power needs are predominantly *interpersonal*; whereas, the need for achievement is predominantly *intrapersonal*, motivated by a personal conviction of capability and competence. People with high achievement needs tend to rely on themselves to get things done. Consequently, they expend a lot of energy by focusing on improving their personal skills and learning new things (Miller, 2003).

The answer to the question "Do I want to be the best?" can best be answered by having the career seeker understand how achievement is viewed. Whether or not the person enjoys meeting and associating with people who are successful indicates whether the person values and is ready for affiliation. And, to the extent the career seeker feels in control of situations indicates his or her need for power. A person has motives when s/he wants to be the best, enjoys meeting and associating with successful people, and wants more control or autonomy. In career terms, motives are apparent when the person has a desire for personal achievement in the chosen career, positive affiliation with professional peers and seeks power through work situations (Grasha, 1995).

Biggs (1999) describes four types of motivation that can help the career seeker understand motives. The extrinsically motivated person does something because the expected outcome has value. For example, if a student believes hard work will produce good grades and good grades are valued, then the student will work hard. Good grades are the expected outcomes and have value to the student. Although the student may want to learn, the value of the grade may overshadow the actual attainment of knowledge or skill. Positive and negative reinforcement drive this type of motivation.

Social motivation is described by Biggs (1999) as the desire to impress or be liked by those the person values. A student who is socially motivated may choose to do poor academic work if the valued peer group does not value or demonstrate good academic performance.

Achievement motivation is driven by a person's attempts to enhance her or his ego. This type of motivation is driven by the desire to feel good about self. Students who seek opportunities to compete against others in order to out perform them represent achievement motivation.

The fourth type of motivation is described by Biggs (1999) as intrinsic and is driven by the process of doing, more than competing. Students who are intrinsically motivated appear to be self-starters and less concerned about external rewards or recognition from others. They succeed in what they do because they are internally driven. They feel good about themselves when they achieve above others.

Beginning a career path is somewhat analogous to beginning childhood. Children are egocentric, quickly respond to rewards and punishments, and have a need to be recognized by others for their achievements. As they mature, they become more capable of acting and learning with less external pressure or manipulation. Their actions become self-directed for causes greater than being recognized by significant others. Similarly, when a person begins a career path, there is a need for recognition and validation from others. As the person matures, intrinsic or more intrapersonal motives overtake the other forms of motivation, so the person is able to pursue career development and personal goals without external assistance and can even reach to help others with their goals and career pathway.

SHAPE AND DIRECTION OF A PROFESSIONAL CAREER

People sometimes define themselves as professionals in a professional career without understanding what differentiates a profession from a non-profession or a professional from a non-professional. There is more status generally attributed to being a professional in a professional career (Moloney, 1992; Habenstein, 1963; Hughes, 1965). However, whether the line of work or the position is professional bears close examination. Moloney (1992) and others (Goode, 1960) claim those occupations that have succeeded in the struggle to obtain professionalism have demonstrated a vested interest in drawing a line between what is deemed professional from non-professional, because they have successfully made the case that a profession has more status and prestige

Professions, compared to non-professions, have more rigorous processes, mechanisms and structures governing the requirements for involvement and membership. Professions are defined and regulated by state laws with the intent to protect the public. Also, there are external accrediting bodies of educational programs leading to professional membership. Whereas professions require market awareness and demand good business practices to be sustainable, the profit motive is usually viewed as secondary to what the profession ideally represents.

Several authors and researchers have attempted to articulate what defines a profession and a professional (Moloney, 1992; Styles, 1982; Cogan, 1953; Carr-Saunders & Wilson, 1933; Flexner, 1930). In most cases, professions are described as having a rigorous, systematic educational program; a code of ethics; research and theory development; and a high level of commitment to social values that goes beyond an individual's economic welfare. Less reference is found to define the professional and professionalism. However, the professional has been described as having a set of values and attributes, such as a commitment to work and an orientation toward service over personal profit, self-regulatory behavior, and support of peer review. Ultimately, professionalism implies a high level of accountability and responsibility directly connected to the occupied role (Styles, 1982).

The important thing for the individual pursuing a career to understand is that professional careers typically have greater educational requirements, often including significant graduate study beyond an initial baccalaureate degree. Also, there is an expectation that the professional accept a level of accountability for work that exceeds a job description or a particular employment situation. A professional is expected to work to improve the conditions of others, even without pay. This service comes in many forms such as contributions to professional organizations, mentoring others into the profession, and volunteering services to the community when needed. Inherently, the professional demonstrates leadership in the community that extends well beyond the boundaries of the salaried job.

Whereas professional careers may require more of the individual for entry and advancement, they tend to greatly enhance a person's earning potential, degree of career related autonomy and mobility, and social status. These rewards are not characteristic of non-professional work or most part-time work. It is a wonderful time for the job seeker who is professionally oriented and committed to improving the health of individuals, families and communities to enter nursing. However, pursuing nursing can be accomplished with either a professional orientation or a non-professional orientation. If the career seeker wants to reap the full benefits of a profession, there must be a professional orientation.

PLANNING THE SHAPE AND DIRECTION OF ONE'S CAREER

In the early phases of the career creation process, the person does a realistic self-assessment, identifies career interests and career options, and learns more about the career or careers of interest. The culmination of these efforts is a career focus, and it is highly beneficial to develop a career plan at this time. A career plan provides direction for the career by outlining the steps needed to reach a career goal and a time frame for reaching that goal. A well-crafted career plan keeps the career seeker career oriented and goal directed.

A well-developed career plan is analogous to a travel itinerary with a map. The itinerary and map enable the traveler to get to the desired destination in a timely manner. Although a person may rigidly adhere to a travel itinerary and follow the map very closely, surprises are often encountered. Some of the surprises are discouraging, such as detours, delays, cancelled flights or extra expenses. However, some of the surprises are enjoyable, such as unexpected hospitality, new friends or an extra-special meal. Longer and more global travel in unfamiliar territory greatly increases the number of unanticipated travel experiences. Yet, it is the surprise that makes the trip most memorable and enlightening to the adventurous person. Similarly, the career seeker with a well-developed career plan encounters surprises and unanticipated challenges. The conditions encountered are often dynamic in nature and seldom predictable to the extent anticipated.

A good way to begin developing a career plan is to ask the question "Am I sincerely interested in becoming the best in my chosen career field?" A "yes" answer suggests the person has motives for a professional level of achievement and should cause the individual to plan accordingly. A professional level of achievement requires careful long-term planning in terms of educational preparation, work experiences and professional affiliations. Less-challenging career goals take less planning and tend to be driven by immediate circumstances.

There are several sources that provide methods and suggestions for developing a career plan. The commonly identified eight steps are listed below and include:

1. Determining what will be required for entering the career field of choice using primary sources. For example, if a person has interest in nursing, it is best to contact an admissions counselor of a baccalaureate nursing program or the state board of nursing for information.
2. Identifying education, training and work history needed for the chosen career. Often meeting the minimal requirements for entry into a career field limits the ability to get the best or more desirable jobs. For example, anyone entering nursing who desires professional advancement will need more than a baccalaureate degree in nursing. If a person chooses to enter nursing with an associate degree, it means returning to school for a baccalaureate degree before pursuing a graduate degree. If possible, it would be better to enter the nursing field at the baccalaureate level, although it exceeds minimal requirements leading to licensure as a registered nurse.
3. Outlining the requirements for the chosen career path by determining the educational requirements, necessary credentials and whether there is any required work experience. For example, the major steps for the pursuit of a nursing career might include earning the bachelor of science degree in nursing (BSN); successful completion of the national licensure examination for RN licensure (NCLEX-RN); applying and interviewing for a first-level, professional entry position; one to two years of practice in a professional setting; selection and application to a master's degree program; completion of the master's degree; applying and interviewing for second professional position; and so forth.
4. Assigning realistic time limits to each of the major steps. For example, if work is required while attending school, the time frame

for obtaining a degree may need to be extended. Failing to do the best when pursuing a degree or working at a job has negative consequences. Although a person may "get through it," poor academic showing or less than satisfactory employer evaluations can seriously affect the next step in the career plan.

5. Breaking down each major step into smaller parts. For example, a major step is completing the BSN in four to five years. One way to create smaller steps is to locate all the accredited BSN programs in the state on the computer and then contact each one for information regarding the admission requirements, the curriculum, and so forth. For the first one or two years in nursing practice, reading a resource like *From Novice to Expert* (Benner, 1984) would help a nurse understand the stages a person goes through to become an expert clinician. Reading this book would also help the nurse layout further steps in pursuit of a career.
6. Sharing the career plan with significant others and people who are connected with the career for every major and minor step. This is where the career seeker is most likely to connect with a mentor for guidance and support.
7. Documenting actions and updating the career plan to stay focused on the career goals and revising the career plan as new information is gained and changing conditions occur. This step should be approached systematically with input from others. A mentor, academic advisor, work supervisor and/or significant other can validate progress and identify areas needing extra work. This part of the planning process can be done too often, as well as too seldom. For example, a growing child who measures his height every week is often frustrated because there appears to be no change from week to week. Having an adult take a measurement every six months is better and more satisfying. Similarly, assessing progress through the career plan to stay on course is encouraged and should occur at timely junctures and not by weeks or months.
8. Celebrating the successful completion of each major step in the career plan. Celebrations serve as markers for the career seeker and the other people involved. During a celebration, the career seeker has the opportunity to show appreciation to the others who have made the success possible.

A well-developed career plan is comprehensive and long-term; although it will change, there is progression through each step of the plan. The best career plans focus on structures, processes, and consequences or outcomes. Institutions, such as universities and hospitals, have elaborate organizational structures and sophisticated processes for achieving goals. Increasingly, learning and work are being defined in terms of outcome measures. As the career seeker enters into any learning or work situation, it is critical to know the expected outcomes, not only for self but also for others, such as teachers and employers.

EDUCATION AND THE CAREER

The most crucial and perhaps mysterious part of the career path is the process of learning. Learning encompasses more than gaining the prerequisite knowledge to do the job. It involves acquiring a perspective of work and career goals beyond any particular employment situation. The mechanisms and structures for a career vary by occupation, as well as by individual circumstances. The former is often very difficult to change as a person attempts to enter a career field. The latter is where an individual has the greatest potential for change and improvement.

Formative evaluation of a person's experience through the career process is valuable but limited by what the individual knows and understands at that point in time. For example, nursing students often react negatively to aspects of their nursing programs because of their inability to connect the content and experience in a semester or in a course to what they believe nursing to be. It is also common for the same nursing students to reflect on these experiences positively after graduating and working for a year or two.

Moloney (1992) states education is the essence of a legitimate profession. Most professional careers for men and women require a baccalaureate or higher degree. Those failing to earn college degrees find themselves at a great disadvantage at entry and throughout the life of their careers. Over the past four plus decades, the total number of college degrees awarded has increased by more than 325% (Hollenshead & Miller, 2001). It should also be noted the "traditional" 18- to 21-year-old college student is being overtaken by older, more diverse adult learners on many, if not the majority, of college campuses. In other words, age has become much less of a deterrent for attempting to enter college for the first time or to return to college after a significant time period. What is critical for anyone pursuing a career is that the person makes every effort to obtain the best and highest level of education possible in order to enter and sustain the chosen career field.

Working at Jobs to Support Career Goals

Most people work at some job(s) while attending college. This can be a positive or negative experience that either supports the attainment of the career objectives or delays or even prevents the fulfillment of real career goals. While part-time work may be created to retain valued workers with family commitments, part-time work may be destructive or prevent a person from fulfilling career goals. "Secondary" part-time work receives its primary impetus from employers' drive for flexibility in a competitive market. It creates numerical flexibility, intensifies work and reduces cost. For workers, it fails to provide employment security, benefits or a living wage (Kahn, 1998).

For the individual who must work at secondary jobs while pursuing a career path, long-term financial planning becomes even more crucial. Sometimes, it is difficult for the individual, and the significant others, to understand a significant investment in the career at the onset may be necessary. This investment is not defined in terms of money alone, but includes time, living arrangements, delayed gratification and study. Priority setting with others is critical to success. Discussing career plans with family members is relevant and should be a part of anyone's career planning. Without the support of others, pursuing a career path becomes more difficult.

Work-Study Programs

One approach for addressing the need of an individual to work while going to school has been the Federal Work-Study Program. This program was created to provide jobs for undergraduate and graduate students with financial need attending eligible postsecondary schools. This program allows students to earn money to pay educational expenses. Work-study programs help students fulfill the American tradition of "working your way through school." Pay is based on federal minimum wage standards but varies with job requirements, skill and experience levels. When a student applies for federal financial aid by completing the Free Application for

Federal Student Aid (FAFSA), the student indicates a desire for work-study assistance.

EMPLOYING A CAREER COUNSELOR

Career counseling is an interpersonal process, designed to assist individuals with career development problems, as well as with the process of choosing, entering, adjusting to and advancing in an occupation (Brown & Brooks, 1990). It may involve only a few meetings or many sessions throughout the life of a career.

Career development proceeds whether or not career guidance and career counseling are used. Thus, career development is not an intervention but the object of an intervention (Herr & Cramer, 1996). Career development is the total constellation of psychological, sociological, educational, physical, economic and chance factors that combine to shape the career of any given individual over the life span (Sears, 1982).

Before committing to a professional relationship with a career counselor, an assessment of the counselor's qualifications and theoretical perspective is needed. Career counselors use a repertoire of synergistic strategies (Herring, 1997) based on career development and decision-making theories to assist the career seeker. A qualified career counselor can help the individual to better understand the career creation process; to explore career possibilities; to determine interests, skills and aptitudes; and to make more informed career decisions. Usually, career counseling focuses on identifying and acting on the person's goals to help generate self-understanding, option availability and feasibility, and informed decision-making. The successful recipient of career counseling becomes more aware, more strategic and more responsible for the career path.

Most people can benefit from the services of a qualified career counselor. One caveat to avoid is the career counselor who treats "different as deficient," whether it be in terms of gender, age, race, religion, ethnicity or disability. Everyone becomes more vulnerable at certain times as a result of transitions in life (e.g., death in the family or peer group, unanticipated pregnancy, illness, lawsuit, loss of job and acts of nature). Although such conditions may not be fixed, they can nevertheless cause serious career problems such that career guidance and counseling can be helpful (Herring, 1998).

Individuals face different barriers to career creation and the attainment of their career goals. A professional career counselor can help the individual recognize the primary barriers and how best to address them. A person's dominant culture can cause a risk in some ways and create advantages in other ways, compared to other cultures. "Risk factors are attributes of the person or of the person's relation to the environment that are associated with a higher-than-average probability of experiencing the types of problems under consideration" (Gottfredson, 1986, p. 143).

Gottfredson's (1996) work helps determine whether there is a need for a career counselor by identifying three categories of need, distinguishable by risk factors. They are:

- Factors that cause the person to be different from the general population (e.g., poverty, low intelligence, cultural segregation, low self-esteem)
- Factors involving differences within a person's own social group (e.g., having nontraditional interests for one's gender, social class or ethnic group)
- Factors involving family responsibilities (e.g., being a primary caregiver or primary economic provider)

This "at-risk" framework is essentially intended to identify the barriers to free career choice. For example, a person estimated to be at risk regarding economic responsibilities is less free to seek self-fulfillment in other roles that do not produce income.

UNANTICIPATED CHANGES IN SHAPE AND DIRECTION

Everyone will experience a career transition, whether self-initiated because of a mismatch or caused by a change in the economic scene. Most professionals will change direction several times during their careers or even transform their careers completely (Rosen, 2000-2002).

Many factors can cause the individual to change career plans. Whereas the individual may define self in terms of the future, the reality of being in the full-time workforce tends to turn future orientation into a more "this is now" one. Fellow workers and professional peers expect and judge performance in the present. Even if the new graduate works during the educational path to a chosen career, none of the jobs have the seriousness that the ones after formal entry into the career field do.

Unfortunately, people with well-developed career plans may still experience a level of frustration and anger that causes them to redirect their career efforts. The idea that a person chooses a career and exits that career 30 to 40 years later is seldom true. More and more adults are finding their careers in direct collision with their former expectations. Many adults become dislocated workers or face major career shifts because of changes in workforce requirements beyond their immediate control. These adults are caught in career shock and are being forced to refocus, to restructure and to change careers with little real insight, direction, information or workable strategies. For many of these individuals, who were already unhappy in their chosen careers, this reality presents an opportunity to choose a career they will enjoy—provoking them to ask themselves the question "How can I go about finding and pursuing a career that I will like?" (Sukiennik, Dendat, & Raufman, 2001).

People aspire to career roles that provide desired levels of status and power. The social context for achieving a career role also is a factor because career transitions depend upon decisions made by others, such as educators, employers and licensing personnel. There is reason to be optimistic about career aspirations and making career transitions when one or more conditions exist. These conditions include: (1) when the career role being sought is readily available, (2) when few competitors for the career role exist, (3) when investment in the career role is significant and ongoing, (4) when authorities governing or employing the career role are eager to fill the position, and (5) when the authorities are receiving information the role aspirant is a fitting candidate for the position. On the other hand, aspirations are threatened or even terminated when the career roles are not available, when authorities neglect the role (e.g., role of the clinical nurse specialist in the late 1980s), or when authorities receive no information about the career aspirant or when they receive information disqualifying the career aspirant (Heise, 1990). These conditions shift over time as exemplified by the growing demand for clinical nurse specialists today.

CONCLUSION

Careers can be viewed both as cultural structures that unfold in accordance with institutional rule systems (Heise, 1990) and as individual work histories. The career seeker can build a career with individualistic flair. But as Heise suggests, most people do so "largely by voyaging along standard career trajectories in idiosyncratic combinations" (pp. 59-60). This is because career decision-making is correlated with factors the person has little control over, such as family, gender and culture of origin.

A significant part of the career creation process is planning, considering family and cultural background. Being aware of how the values of others influence career decision-making is key to understanding a person's responses in any situation and to any condition. A high level of self-awareness coupled with professional maturity and a growing pattern of career success enables the individual to change processes, structures and outcomes that traditionally direct and shape a career path.

A mismatch between personal values and the values of the work site creates conflict. Unresolved conflict leads to career discontent. This mismatch causes career discontent because accommodation alone does not transform the individual, nor does it change a person's values. A career mismatch causes discouragement, because despite the greater expenditure of effort in attempts to appear motivated, the person is still faced with the mismatch.

Power from one's career is closely linked to how an individual perceives power, how others perceive the individual in terms of his or her work, and the extent to which an individual can cause something to happen because of his or her work. There is power associated with transforming career plans into action. Strategic actions describe what one needs to do, how one is going to do it, who will be responsible, when it will occur (the timing or time frame), where it will occur (if relevant), and the resources needed to carry out the actions (Wells, 1998, p. 197).

REFERENCES

Altman, J.H. (1997). Career development in the context of family experiences. In H.S. Farmer (Ed.), *Diversity and women's career development: From adolescence to adulthood* (pp. 229-242). Thousand Oaks, CA: Sage.

Andrews, M.M., & Boyle, J.S. (1999). *Transcultural concepts in nursing.* Philadelphia: Lippincott.

Bae, Y., et. al. (2000). *Trends in educational equity of girls and women* (National Center for Education Statistics-NCES 2000-030), Washington, DC: USGPO.

Bartholomew, C.G., & Schnorr, D.L. (1994). Gender equity: Educational problems and possibilities for female students. *The Journal for the Professional Counselor, 92*(2), 59-71.

Benner, P. (1984). *From novice to expert: Excellence and power in clinical nursing practice*. Menlo Park, CA: Addison-Wesley.

Betz, N.E., & Fitzgerald, L.F. (1987). *The career psychology of women.* Orlando, FL: Academic Press.

Biggs, J. (1999). *Teaching for quality learning at university*. Buckingham, England: Society for Research in Higher Education & Open University Press.

Brown, D. & Brooks, L. (1990). *Career choice and development* (3rd ed.). San Francisco, CA: Jossey-Bass.

Carr-Saunders, A., & Wilson, P. (1933). *The professions.* Oxford: Clarendon Press.

Catalano, J.T. (2003). *Nursing now! Today's issues, tomorrow's trends* (3rd ed.). Philadelphia, PA: Davis.

Cherne, F. (n.d.) *Job versus career: Are you really doing what it takes to make it? IMDiversity.com Women's Village*, Retrieved November 8, 2002, from http://www.imdiversity.com/villages/woman/Article_Detail.asp?Article_ID-2327.

Cogan, M. (1953). Toward a definition of profession. *Harvard Educational Review, 23,* 49.

Chronicle of Higher Education (2002). *Almanac 2002.* Washington, DC: Author.

Dolan, J.A. (1973). *Nursing in a society: A historical perspective.* Philadelphia, PA: Saunders.

Fisher, T.A., & Griggs, M.B. (April, 1994). *Factors that influence the career development of African-American and Latino youth.* Paper presented at the Annual Meeting of the American Educational Research Association (AERA), New Orleans, LA.

Fisher, T.A., & Padmawijaja, I. (1999). Parental influences on career development perceived by American-American and Mexican-American college students. *Journal of Multicultural Counseling and Development, 27*, 136-152.

Flexner, A. (1930). *Universities: American, English, German.* New York: Oxford University Press.

Gelso, C.J., & Fretz, B.R. (2001). *Counseling psychology*. Fort Worth, Texas: Harcourt Brace.

Goode, W. (1960). Encroachment, charlatanism, and the emerging profession: Psychology, sociology, and medicine. *American Sociological Review,* 25, 902.

Gottfredson, L.S. (1986). Special groups and the beneficial use of vocational interest inventories. In W.B. Walsh & S. Osiprow (Eds.), *Advances in vocational psychology: The assessment of interests* (pp. 127-128). Hillsdale, NJ: Erlbaum.

Gottfredson, L.S. (1996). Gottfredson's theory of circumscription and compromise. In D. Brown & L. Brooks (Eds.), *Career choice and development* (3rd ed., pp. 179-232). San Francisco, CA: Jossey-Bass.

Grasha, A.F. (1995). *Practical applications of psychology* (4th ed.). Menlo Park: CA: Addison-Wesley.

Habenstein, K. (1963). Critique of profession as a sociological category. *Sociological Quarterly, 4*, 290-295.

Heise, D.R. (1990). Careers, career trajectories and the self. In J. Rodin, C. Schooler, & K.W. Schale (Eds.), *Self-directedness: Cause and effects throughout the life course* (pp. 59-84). Hillsdale, NJ: Lawrence Erlbaum Associates.

Herr, E.L., & Cramer, S.H. (1996). *Career guidance and counseling through the lifespan: Systematic approaches* (5th ed.). New York, NY: Harper Collins.

Herring, R.D. (1997). *Multicultural counseling in schools: A synergetic approach*. Alexandria, VA: American Counseling Association.

Herring, R.D. (1998). Career counseling in schools: Multicultural and developmental perspectives. *American Counseling Association*, 1(17), 1-10.

Hollenshead, C.S., & Miller, J.E. (2001, Spring). Diversity workshops: Gender equity—A closer look. *Diversity Digest* (pp. 1-4). Retrieved November 7, 2002, from http://www.diversityweb.org/digest/spo1/reserch2.html.

Hughes, E. (1965). Professions. In K.S. Lynn and the editors of Daedalus, *The professions in America* (p. 3). Boston: Houghton/Mifflin.

Jameson, E.M. (1966). *Trends in nursing history: Their social intervention and ethical relationships* (6th ed.). Philadelphia, PA: Saunders.

Johnson, E.C. (1996). Adventures of a contrarian. *Daedalus: Journal of the American Academy of Arts and Sciences, 125*(2), 67-183.

Judy, R.W., & D'Amico, C. (1997). *Workforce 2020: Work and workers in the 21st century*. Indianapolis, IN: Hudson Institute.

Kahn, P. (1998). *Time and money: Women workers, unions, and the political economy.* Retrieved February 18, 2002, from http://www.umich.edu/cew/pubs/hahn98.

Kaufman, C. (1976). *Tamers of death: The history of the Alexian brothers.* New York, NY: Seabury Press.

King, J.E. (2000). *Equity in higher education*. Washington, DC: American Council on Education, Center for Policy Analysis.

Kritek, P.B. (2001). Some reflections on conflict resolution in nursing: Implications of negotiating at an uneven table. In J. McCloskey Dochterman, & H.K. Grace (Eds.), *Current Issues in Nursing* (pp. 473-479). St. Louis, MO: Mosby.

Levine, E.B., & Levine, M.E. (1965). Hippocrates. Father of nursing, too? *American Journal of Nursing,* 65(12), 86-88.

MacGregor, A., & Cochran, L. (1988). Work as enactment of family drama. *Career Development Quarterly, 37,* 138-148.

Miller, T.W. (1989). Men in nursing. *California Nursing Review, 11*(2), 10-12; 14; 16; 33-36.

Miller, T.W. (1991). *The career creation process of persons with previous college degrees pursuing nursing as a career change.* Dissertation, University of Texas, Austin.

Miller, T.W. (2003). Power. In P. Kelly-Heidenthal (Ed.), *Nursing leadership and management* (pp. 347-359). New York, NY: Thomson-Delmar Learning.

Moloney, M.M. (1992). *Professionalization of nursing: Current issues and trends* (2nd ed.). Philadelphia, PA: Lippincott.

O'Brien, K.M., & Fassinger, R.E. (1993). A causal model of the career orientation and career choice of adolescent women. *Journal of Counseling Psychology, 40*, 456-469.

Osiprow, S.H., & Fitzgerald, L.F. (1996). *Theories of career development* (4th ed.). Boston, MA: Allyn & Bacon.

Pennick, N.I., & & Jepson, D.A. (1992). Family functioning and adolescent career development. *Career Development Quarterly, 40*, 208-222.

Rainey, L.M., & Borders, L.D. (1992). Influential factors in the career orientation and career aspiration of early adolescent girls. *Journal of Counseling Psychology, 44*, 160-172.

Roe, A. (1956). *The psychology of occupations*. New York, NY: Wiley.

Rosen, S. (2000-2002). Making healthy career transitions & choice. *Career changeability.* Retrieved November 8, 2002, from http://www.careerchangeability.com/doctors/articles/healthy.html, pp. 1-4.

Santrock, J.W. (1995). *Child development: An introduction* (2nd ed.). Madison, WI: Brown & Benchmark.

Sears, S. (1982). A definition of career guidance terms: A national vocational guidance perspective. *Vocational Guidance Quarterly, 31*, 137-143.

Sukiennik, D., Dendat, W., & Raufman, L. (2001). *The career fitness program: Exercising your options* (6th ed.). Upper Saddle River, NJ: Prentice-Hall.

Styles, M. (1982). *On nursing: Toward a new endowment*. St. Louis, MO: Mosby.

Triandis, H.C., Kurowski, L.L., & Gelfand, M.J. (1994). Workforce diversity. In H.C. Triandis, M.D. Dunnette, & L.M. Hough (Eds.), *Handbook of industrial and organizational psychology* (2nd ed., pp. 769-827). Palo Alto, CA: Consulting Psychologists Press.

Trusty, J., Watts, R.E., & Erdman, P. (1997). Predictors of parents' involvement in their teens' career development. *Journal of Career Development, 23*(3), 189-201.

U.S. Bureau of Labor Statistics. (1998). *Statistical report on employment* (pp. 9-30). Washington, DC: Department of Commerce.

Way, W.L., & Rossman, M.M. (1996). *Lessons form life's first teacher: The role of the family in adolescent and adult readiness for school-to-work transition.* Berkeley, CA: National Center for Research in Vocational Education.

Wells, S. (1998). *Choosing the future: The power of strategic thinking*. Boston: Butterworth-Heinemann.

Wentling, R.M. (2001). *Diversity in the workforce: The highlight zone: Research@work* Number 4. National Centers for Career and Technical Education. Retrieved November 8, 2002, from http://www.nccte.org/publications/info.

Whitlock, D.W., & Masters, R.J. (1996). Influences on business students' decisions to pursue entrepreneurial opportunities or traditional career paths. Retrieved November 10, 2002, from http://www.sbaer.uca.edu/Research/1996/SBIDA/96sbi039.htm.

Chapter 4

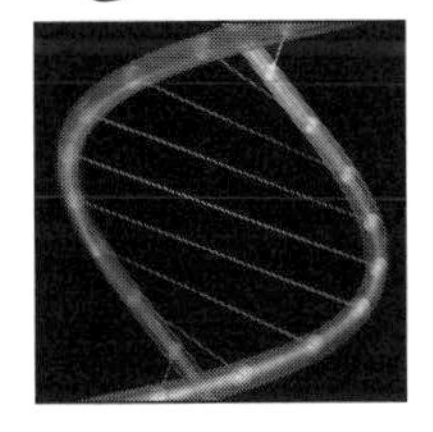

Stages of Careers

by Terry W. Miller

Do careers also unfold in orderly stages of development? The answer seems to be yes, although there is still disagreement about the exact nature and timing of the career stages (Greenhaus, Callahan, & Godshalk, 2000).

INTRODUCTION

The second property of the career creation process is that it has a pathway, better described as a trajectory that extends beyond qualifying for and entering the career-related workforce. A nursing career trajectory initially can be broken down into the eight stages presented in Chapter 2. The first stage of the career creation process, identifying a strong interest, entails discovering one's occupational interests. The second stage, exploring how to pursue a career, involves making an occupational choice. The third stage, fulfilling requirements for entry, is often described as career entry. Yet, these three stages are only the beginning to a career.

Developmental theorists recognize that adulthood, similar to childhood, has developmental tasks that need to be completed successfully by every individual. Understanding adult development enables career counselors to provide people with assistance as they move through career stages or life events that shape their careers. More specifically, each career stage is defined by a set of tasks the person must complete before advancing to the next stage. Not being able to successfully complete the tasks that define a career stage often leads to career discontent or career failure.

Whereas some people do a remarkable job of assuring the best for themselves through the first three stages of a career, they underplay the significance of the subsequent stages. Too many people in human service professions fail to successfully reach their career goals, and they leave their profession of choice within a few years after entry. People who fail to identify personal values in the context of the values inherent to a career path are very likely to experience career discontent and leave the career (Miller, 1991). An adult who does not intellectually and emotionally mature through the stages of adulthood will be challenged to have a successful career. Many careers require a high level of personal accountability and teamwork that are externally validated by professional peers and the public that is served.

People may enter a nursing career in one of several ways. For instance, today nurses constitute the largest single division of healthcare providers and as a division are quite segmented (Camilleri, 2001, p. 90). This segmentation begins with multiple entry points into nursing practice. Nurses with basic preparation entering professional practice can find themselves sandwiched between those with advanced credentials and those with limited credentials that restrict their nursing practice by legal definition, if not institutional setting.

To enter the nursing profession under the best terms, it is critical to choose the best nursing program available and to take the time necessary for assuring a desirable future beyond entry into an early career, a middle career and even a late career. The purpose of defining career stages is to better understand how a nursing career unfolds and how work relates to different periods of a nurse's life in the workforce. Defining the stages in terms of psychological and sociological transitions along a career trajectory, as opposed to the chronological aging of an individual, removes many of the problems inherent to any career staging model.

EARLY CAREER

The three stages or tasks that a person needs to successfully complete early in a career, to be successful and remain highly motivated, are identifying personal values in the context of the values inherent to the career, recognizing career-life linkages, and making nursing self-linkages. Kelly and Joel (1996) use a variation of Hardy and Conway's (1988) role theory to offer some valid suggestions for this period of a career. They believe that new nurses must re-socialize themselves into the work setting, as contrasted with the educational setting. They also believe that nurses will need to re-socialize themselves many times during their career lives.

Whereas students may define themselves in terms of the future, the reality of being college graduates and in the full-time workforce tends to turn a future orientation into a more "this is now" one. Fellow workers, college graduates or not, expect and judge performance in the present. Students have spent years being socialized in educational settings; now re-socialization into the work world is necessary.

Even if the new graduate works during the educational path to a career, none of the jobs have the seriousness the ones after graduation do. In the educational setting, the student is recognized for presenting an analysis of action more than action itself. Even if one believes the socialization process for a career is one continuum throughout a person's work life, people entering the workforce for the first time are likely to experience reality shock. This shock results from a recognition that the actual work is significantly different than what the person imagined or believed it would be. As Kramer (1974) pointed out years ago, reality shock occurs when the individual's perceptions and beliefs are threatened by the expectations of others in a job or career transition.

When people are unable to cope successfully with reality shock, job frustration develops. Job frustration is a stressful condition caused by not being able to perform in the work setting as anticipated or expected by self or others. Actions for dealing with job frustration, other than quitting the job, include negotiation, rationalization, counseling, escapism and therapy. If these actions do not limit or sufficiently reduce the level of job frustration, the consequence is career discontent. Therefore, the conditions of reality shock and job frustration are precursors to career discontent.

It is important to enter a profession with realistic expectations. If a person enters a career believing performance can be at the same level of understanding and competence as an experienced person, failure is probable. Further, it is important for a person, especially at career entry or in a new job, to discern the difference between valid criticism and suggestions for improvement from inappropriate or destructive criticism.

Nursing is a challenge and requires professional maturity that seldom comes quickly or easily for anyone. Unfortunately, some people do not understand this requirement. Occupations that do not promote lifelong learning and place few demands upon individuals who pursue them become monotonous. Nurses entering practice as new registered nurses need to have time to assimilate their knowledge and skills as a new nurse, regardless of educational background and previous work experience. It is during this time the new nurse takes on a new role and leaves behind the student role.

Early Career Success

Research findings have identified four phases in one's first position in an organization such as a healthcare agency, with each phase having different but related tasks for the new person and the employing agency. These four phases are:

- Recruitment
- Selection
- Orientation
- Socialization (Greenhaus, Callahan, & Godshalk, 2000)

All four of these phases cost both parties money and time, and they should be approached as an investment requiring careful planning and a formal commitment of resources. A successful approach to each phase can offer tremendous rewards to both the employing agencies and the nurses seeking employment in these agencies. The best agencies and employers understand the correlation between this investment and return in employee satisfaction, retention and productivity. Similarly, the most successful career seeker understands the correlation between careful planning and commitment of resources to finding the best employment opportunities and getting better jobs.

Recruitment

Recruitment of nurses has expanded, in the past few years, to overseas because of the growing nursing shortage. Many, if not most new nurse graduates, have formal positions waiting for them at the time of graduation or at least upon successful completion of the examination for registered nurse licensure (NCLEX-RN). Unfortunately, some of these graduates prematurely accept positions or do not take the time to explore the many career opportunities available to them. It is important to recognize that recruitment is a process with the intent of finding a fit or match between person (the nurse) and the organization (the employing agency).

Recognizing the implications of how and when an agency recruits for a position reveals much about the agency's regard for and commitment to the position. Is recruitment an episodic approach that relies on "tricks," such as recruitment bonuses and special offers, or is it a well-planned approach that addresses the need for an employee as a long-term investment? The former is more of a sales approach that implies the agency is either desperate or devalues the employee who has a career-orientation.

Selection

In many ways, finding the first position after graduation parallels what the person does in the first three stages of the career creation process. Selection works in two directions, because both the nurse and the organization are determining whether to choose each other. Selection usually involves applications, job interviews and ultimately making a decision among job offers. It is to the nurse's advantage to use every one of these elements to learn more, even if the position is not a fit.

A person selecting any position for employment, especially at career entry, needs to assess more than salary at the time of entry. Benefits can be more valuable than actual salary, depending upon a person's age, career status, family situation, goals for continuing education, need for orientation and professional development, such as long-term career goals. Most people enter nursing with the understanding that it is a practice discipline. As such, most nurses identify nursing practice as one of, if not the most, relevant aspects of successful nursing career development.

New nurse graduates are more likely to select positions that meet their career expectations if they complete a study of the employer with a focus on the area, unit or division in which they want to work. If an agency focuses on new graduates and does not address the needs of older, more experienced employees, the agency relies heavily on "fresh meat" to fill open positions and is thus likely to have a high turnover. Most people expect to have their salaries and benefits improve as they gain experience, knowledge and skills. If the employer fails to recognize or reward an employee's growth needs in a position, salary and benefits usually remain flat or even decrease over time.

The presentation of an agency's policies for recruitment, orientation and promotion means little if they are not official policies available to the job seeker in writing. These policies provide protection to both the employer and the agency, assure the protection of civil rights and help establish realistic expectations. Often, inexperienced job seekers do not take the time to ask about the policies or to ask to see them in writing before committing to a position or signing a contract. Frequently, the written policies can be obtained from the department of human resources of most institutions or can be located on the Web page of the organization.

Finally, anyone seeking employment needs to be flexible and to focus on finding an employer or position that is a match. The key for creating a match is to determine what is essential and what is less critical. The value placed on these two criteria varies with each individual. Salary and benefits, such as vacation time, are often considered essential on first examination. However, the organizational climate, median age of the workforce, possibilities for advancement, commuting time and gender distribution may be very important over time but not so obvious at first to the job seeker.

Orientation

Orientation is the period of initial adjustment for the individual in an organization or new work role. Orientation has many functions, such as introduction to the organization or agency, review of important policies and practices, review of benefits and services, benefit plan enrollment, completion of employment forms, review of expectations and development of an employee, introduction to peers and facilities, and introduction to the new job.

Orientation sets the tone, as well as the expectations, for a person's employment in an agency. A successful orientation to an agency reveals how the agency operates and how the new nurse is to operate in the agency to be successful. It clarifies what the organization values by exposing what is rewarded and what is ignored or punished. It is during orientation that the person attempts to fit in, learn his or her agency role and responsibilities, achieve a desirable degree of independence in the work role, and seek validation from peers and the person(s) over them.

Typically, people with less work experience need a longer, more structured orientation. However, a good orientation often makes the difference between success and failure for any employee entering a complex work environment, such as a hospital.

Socialization

The socialization process for a career in nursing begins long before the graduating nurse enters the paid workforce as a registered nurse. This socialization process creates a set of expectations in the person that causes him or her to anticipate the future and how to enter the next career stage. The better and more realistic the socialization process, the more likely career expectations will be validated with the next career stage. However, when an individual pursues a career that requires rapid professional growth under difficult and challenging circumstances, reality shock remains a possibility.

New nurse graduates and employers of new nurses can benefit from identifying distinct levels of competency in nursing practice, such as Benner's (1984) levels, which are novice, advanced beginner, competent practitioner, proficient practitioner and expert. A new nurse does not enter a nursing position as a proficient practitioner or as an expert. Subsequently, it is critical employers and established peers in the institutional setting working with or depending upon the new nurse have realistic expectations regarding the new nurse's competency level. Benner states, "Any nurse entering a clinical setting where she or he has not had experience with the patient population may be limited to the novice level of performance if the goals and tools of patient care are unfamiliar" (p. 21).

IDENTIFYING PERSONAL VALUES INHERENT TO PROFESSIONAL NURSING

According to Roy (2000), historically, nursing values have been the basis for the development and use of scientific knowledge to promote health. Many believe identifying personal values inherent to professional nursing must occur during the basic educational program. However, the conflict and reality shock experienced by many nurses indicate this stage of professional development is not complete at graduation. This stage of career creation consists of three phases: (1) values identification, (2) values clarification and (3) values reconstruction.

It is difficult for an individual to determine the degree of congruence between personal values and a career course realistically at the beginning of a career for several reasons. Naiveté, immaturity, being misled, reacting and/or being directed by others may be the factors that get in the way of a valid assessment of the congruence of the job with the person's values. When a person does not realize his or her values, others, such as peers in the work setting, are able to exert considerable influence on defining the values. This susceptibility to professional peer pressure or the lack of it, is analogous to the role of peer pressure among adolescents.

Values identification can be the consequence of pursuing a particular career course or quitting a career course. Values identification involves a conscious reflection upon what is wanted or needed in a job. The values identification stage takes time; the amount varies significantly from one individual to another.

After going through a values identification, the values still may need to be culturally defined, more than personally determined. Most people do not recognize what is needed other than what the dominant culture deems as desirable. When a person distinguishes between what is wanted and what is needed, in terms of values, the true nature of the values is clarified.

Values reconstruction occurs when three things occur:

- There is a realization of the extent the values have been influenced by others
- The culture of origin may be influencing the values on an unconscious level, as well as on a conscious level
- There is a recognition of the need to live one's values versus merely acting a role

Ultimately the result and responsibility of personal choice and decision-making rest with the individual. People in this phase confirm what they believe to have value and priority, or they attempt to redefine their values because of changes in perspective on what has value and priority.

Values reconstruction is the process whereby individuals begin to understand the impact that socialization and external forces have had upon their ability to make a decision and to take action. During values reconstruction, people discover to what extent they have been "playing" a role, versus "living" a role. During this process, people gain an awareness of how interaction is both structured and personally determined. They become conscious of how their actions and decisions are being defined by meeting the needs of others. The perceived outcome of values reconstruction is that people feel actions and decisions are authentically motivated, perhaps for the first time.

Several values have been identified as core to nursing. These include service to others and caregiving (Weis & Schank, 2000), as well as values attributed to professions in general, such as autonomy, accountability, responsibility, extensive educational preparation and unique body of knowledge (Styles, 1982). Killeen (1985) states, "The profession's values give direction and meaning to its members, guide nursing behaviors, are instrumental in clinical decision-making and influence how nurses think about themselves. Although skills change and evolve over time, core values of nursing persist and are communicated through the professional publications of nursing.

RECOGNIZING CAREER-LIFE LINKAGE

Regardless of whether or not a person pursuing a career experiences a reconstruction of values or merely identifies values associated with the career, it is a condition for recognizing the relationship between a person's life and having a career. When a person recognizes the importance of having a career, the need to have career goals becomes personally motivated. It is during this stage that the impact of career upon the individual becomes evident in terms of lifestyle, health and personal values.

Many theories regarding what motivates individuals to have careers have been advanced. These theories have attempted to explain the reasons why individuals make decisions and act the way they do. What appears to be a common thread among the theories is that people are motivated by themselves; however, circumstances or conditions in work, education and personal life can be arranged to foster a person's self-motivation (Moloney, 1992).

A person's life work is linked to individual and family status, as well as survival in modern society. Career has taken on the connotation of commitment, personal success and autonomy over "job." Having a career has come to imply greater socioeconomic status and personal control. Up to this stage in the career creation process, there may have been some uncertainty about whether a career is really wanted. It is in this stage of the process that the person overcomes ambivalent feelings about pursuing a career. It is also at this time that the individual realizes that non-work activities can be unfulfilling when not complemented with satisfactory work experiences.

Therefore, recognizing the ties between one's personal well-being and work life is what is called "making a career-life linkage." It is understood any segregation of work and personal life is illusory. One affects the other to such a degree that even valuing one or the other will not eliminate work-life conflicts. The issue becomes how much the individual is willing to accept a job-oriented work life in place of a career-oriented work life.

Making a career-life linkage becomes a condition for making a nursing self-linkage. Otherwise, the pursuit of nursing represents another job and not a career per se.

Making Nursing Self-Linkage

When a nursing self-linkage is established, there is an enhanced awareness of the field beyond basic educational preparation, reality shock and orientation to the first paid position. There is a new determination that requires a more reflective evaluation of nursing in the context of one's life work. The outcome, if the person decides nursing remains the career of choice, is a new and greater level of commitment. It is this linking of nursing to the self that eventually makes the individual determined to have a career in nursing. At this stage, personal values reflect the professional values of nursing, with career decisions made and actions taken accordingly.

Becoming Career Hopeful

Being career hopeful means the individual has made a commitment to pursue a career and feels success is probable. Obstacles, real or otherwise, are viewed as surmountable. In other words, the person is on the career course that is deliberately chosen. This is not to say, however, the person is cognizant of every step or variation of the course. Instead, being on track is a sense of direction that is acceptably congruent with the person's career expectations.

Motivation is especially important at this stage of the career creation process. This is so for two reasons. The motivation to take action depends considerably upon the level of trust the career seeker has for those people who exert pressure on him or her in relation to the career path chosen. The greater the trust, the less perceived are the risks the career path may display. Fewer perceived risks are also related to a greater sense of career security because of an earlier positive career experience.

Motivation has sociological as well as psychological dimensions in that a person's career path is externally evaluated. For example, nurses are charged by state legislatures to protect the public from unqualified, unsafe and unethical behavior. Nurses believed to be unsafe, unethical or incompetent can be denied licensure or have their license revoked.

It is highly beneficial to understand the sociological dimensions, as well as the psychological implications, of career-life linkage in general, and nursing-self linkage in particular. Following a traditional career path is one strategy for career creation. A consequence of this strategy is a reduction in social risks because societal norms are being maintained.

Ultimately, the success of the career creation process depends upon the level of trust the person has in his or her own decision-making.

Having a career plan means the individual defines and hopes to control the career as much as possible. In this sense, success in the career creation process is equated with being on track or off track. "On track" is defined as the course consciously selected as the career of choice and what is believed to be necessary to achieve success in that career.

Career satisfaction in the early part of a nursing career comes when the new nurse is able to internalize the nursing career as fulfilling. The nurse's expectations of the nursing career not only match the reality of the work inherent to nursing, they are validated by peers in the work setting. If an individual's personal values match the values promulgated by a particular career or job, career satisfaction is possible. Without this match, career discontent is probable.

MIDDLE CAREER

Typically, the middle career corresponds with middle adulthood for most people, if middle career is the period 10 to 15 years into the career trajectory, after meeting the educational conditions for entering the career field. However, career advancement occurs more in sociological time than in the number of years in the job. This means career transitions are marked by status transitions during the career course, and subsequently, all of the social-psychological phenomena of (most) careers might be found anywhere along the lifespan of the individual (Heise, 1990). This should provide reassurance to anyone entering a career field later in life or making a career change.

Erik Erickson (1963) labeled middle adulthood the seventh stage of human development. During this stage, the generativity or guiding the next generation becomes crucial. Using his model, the focus of the middle career is to generate and share what is generated with others. For nursing, it is the stage of providing expert nursing care as a clinician, expert teaching as a nurse educator and expert management as an administrator. Failure at this time of a career brings feelings of stagnation and the inability to feel productive or help others. Nurses in mid-career who fail to guide others run the risk of finding little new to explore and often find themselves on a career plateau.

In American society, it is not uncommon for people to begin a difficult, if not painful, re-evaluation of their lives during middle adulthood that includes work. According to Greenhaus, Callahan and Godshalk (2000), the middle career years pose two major career-life tasks. These are

(1) confronting the mid-life transition and (2) remaining productive. However, with nursing careers, it is the middle career when the successful nurse has achieved the level of professional competence and confidence that allows for mentoring others into the role of professional nurse.

Practically everyone experiences "flat" work or personal life periods. Such periods can become a career plateau if the potential for further career achievement or professional advancement becomes unlikely. "Two mid-career experiences, plateauing and obsolescence, can affect mid-career productivity and trigger feelings of stress" (Greenhaus, Callahan, & Godshalk, 2000, p. 221).

Obsolescence can be defined as how much a worker or a professional lacks the necessary knowledge or skills required for performing effectively in either current and/or future work roles. The possibility of obsolescence grows with rapid organizational change, technological advances and lack of continued education. Whereas, successful professional nurses incorporate new developments in healthcare into their practices throughout the lifetime of their careers. They return to college, read about the most current applications and are involved in professional organizations. They continually adapt, innovate and become mentors for others.

Career satisfaction in the middle years of a nursing career comes when the nurse is able to share the value of the nursing career with others, as well as help them to develop into professional nurses. The nurse's expectations of the nursing career not only match the reality of the work inherent to nursing, they now validate the work of others in the work setting. "Unless mid-career obsolescence is prevented or reduced, the situation can only get worse during the late career" (Greenhaus, Callahan, & Godshalk, 2000, p. 235).

LATE CAREER

No society can afford to cast off or take for granted older workers. Yet, it is difficult to imagine being in the late stage of a career until it arrives. The American workforce continues to mature as the baby boomer generation ages. With increases in life expectancy and better management of chronic conditions, more workers are staying longer in the workforce. It is not uncommon for an American to work into the late sixties or even the early seventies. This is all the more reason to develop a career path that is personally fulfilling.

Changes in the nature of work (e.g., contract versus lifetime positions), rapid technological advances, management styles and organizational structures pose a threat of obsolescence, especially to older workers with limited education and skills.

At least three developmental tasks must be accomplished during the late phase of a career. Hopefully, a significant number of late career workers prepare themselves for senior leadership roles. These people are also the mentors of a new generation of workers, as well as a balance to thoughtless change and unrealistic innovations coming from inadequate experience and a lack of a broader, longer perspective. The primary needs for the late career phase is to maintain productivity and to prepare for effective retirement (Greenhaus, Callahan, & Godshalk, 2000).

Retirement represents a lifestyle transition, more than the cessation of a work life. For those people who do not plan for it, there may be many unattractive surprises, such as unanticipated financial difficulties, lowering of lifestyle standards, and inability to travel or pursue retirement goals. Patty Hawken and Ann Hillestad (2000), two highly successful career nurses, have offered a mental framework for retirement planning, and they emphasize that it is written for oneself and not others. The framework includes foundational principles, priorities, opportunities, lifestyle changes, potential problems and conventional planning.

Several value-related questions need to be addressed under foundational principles governing a retirement plan. For example, "What gives me a sense of self-worth, what causes me to feel valuable and valued by others, and how will retirement affect my self-concept and relationship with others?" Hawken and Hillestad (2000) state, "For those who have had careers instead of jobs, much of what we think about ourselves and our value has been professionally based" (2000, p. 102) and, therefore, defined in a professional context by professional peers.

Far more opportunities exist today for the retired person because of the work of many organizations such as the American Association of Retired Persons (AARP). What seems most critical is that the retired person pursue an active retirement life focused on activities and service that sustain a sense of personal value and self-worth in relation to other people. Defining and seizing opportunities means the retired person seeks out others and stays active in some supportive social sphere (e.g., staying active in professional organizations, volunteering for a service organization, taking a college course or engaging in a sport (even if it is for the first time).

Setting priorities becomes easier if a person's personal values, in relation to the values of other people in the work environment and at home, are clearly defined. Without this understanding, setting realistic priorities may be especially difficult during retirement. People who have not retired are still connected to the priorities of the work place. The retired person who has held a position of authority and supervised the work of other people may have a difficult time understanding the implications of losing that authority and priority in the lives of others. Even the new family role of the retired person can be a challenge to other family members because of incongruent priority setting. Understanding what is most important and how it can be achieved are critical to retirement success.

Retirement automatically encompasses a lifestyle change. Hawken and Hillestad (2000) assert, "True professionals [must] make it as easy for their successors and for people in their organizations as possible. They [must] not second-guess decisions that are made; they [must] not see change as criticism. Even though most of one's activities, social as well as professional, may have included professional colleagues, time to develop extraprofessional activities and friends may have been limited" (2000, p. 104). Retiring from a successful career should lead to a desirable lifestyle presenting new opportunities for personal growth and ongoing development. Lifestyle changes involve realignment or even redefinition of friendships among those connected with work and those who may have had nothing to do with the preceding career. A positive lifestyle change can offer the time for developing new or even stronger relationships with people.

The physical reality of aging creates a host of potential problems for the retiree. Whereas aging is a normal process that extends throughout the life span, consideration should be given to the inevitable loss of physical and mental abilities. Fortunately, people pursuing healthy, active lifestyles before and after retirement are likely to have many years to enjoy the benefits of a successful career and the rewards it offers to the retiring professional. Planning for the possibility of increasing physical dependence is necessary, as well as having realistic expectations for social interaction, family support, and personal reaction to illness and some loss of control over one's living arrangements.

By now, it should be evident that conventional planning for retirement is only a small part of a big process. Unfortunately, many people do not have a realistic understanding of expenses in relation to a fixed income. "Since it is axiomatic that income and expenses at least need to come out even, it will be helpful to know what expenses are prior to retirement and calculate how much change is expected" (Hawken & Hillestad, 2000, p. 105). The fiscal planning for retirement actually begins with the person's first job. Those who set aside monetary resources, albeit small amounts beginning early in the career, find themselves in a far more comfortable position in the late stage of their careers. What is certain for everyone in the United States is that social security and Medicare benefits alone at age 68 will not be enough to sustain even a lower middle-class lifestyle.

CONCLUSION

This chapter contained an exploration of the stages that must be mastered in order to be successful in a career. Career stages vary in duration, depending upon the individual and the conditions influencing his or her actions. The redefinition of work in today's world has greatly challenged orderly progression through these career stages. An increasing number of people experience career discontent and become what is known as "career changers." Their career trajectory can be staged as (1) experiencing career discontent, (2) quitting the job representing the previous career, (3) identifying personal values, (4) recognizing career-life linkage, (6) returning to college or school, and (7) becoming new career hopeful. However, the most likely period for a person experiencing career discontent that results in a career change is in the early stages of the career.

Careers have stages that unfold in accordance with the life stages of individuals. The career seeker can build a career that has moved smoothly from stage to stage, but most people do so "largely by voyaging along standard career trajectories in idiosyncratic combinations" (Heise, p. 60). A mismatch between personal values and the values of the work site creates conflict. Unresolved conflict leads to career discontent. This mismatch causes career discontent, because accommodation alone does not transform the individual, nor does it change personal values. A career mismatch causes discouragement, because despite the greater expenditure of effort in an attempt to appear motivated, the person still faces a mismatch.

Any model or discussion of career staging would be inadequate or misleading if the impact of change on career staging was not addressed. The nature of work in general is changing, and the nature of nursing is changing as well. Hospitals continue to employ a majority of working registered nurses, but this percentage is projected to decline to 52.8% by 2008

(U.S. Bureau of Labor Statistics, 2000), as more nurses choose many other kinds of employment and entrepreneurial opportunities. The present shortage of registered nurses in the United States is projected to grow through the next decade to reach over one-half million unfilled nursing positions throughout the healthcare system.

Nurses are assuming a greater responsibility, and therefore a level of accountability, for patients and clients regardless of the work environment. Grando (2001) writes, "Nurses are caring for sicker, often older patients for shorter periods of time with ever more sophisticated technology" (p. 16). In response to increased responsibilities, "many nurses are becoming certified in their specialty area and taking the next educational step to becoming advanced practice nurses, including both clinical nurse specialists and acute care nurse practitioners" (p. 16).

The American Nurses Association (1996) claims specialization is "a mark of the advancement of the nursing profession" (p. 21). Specialization has resulted in certification as a form of regulation and recognition of nurses in advanced practice. The two significant areas of advanced practice to date are the clinical nurse specialist (CNS) and the nurse practitioner (NP). These two groups are differentiated further by practice specialization, i.e., the CNS in psychiatric/mental health or the family nurse practitioner (FNP). Barriers to NP and CNS practice can be substantial because of competition and a possible overlap between medical and nursing roles. Other specialized roles requiring advanced degrees and certifications include certified nurse midwives (CNM) and certified nurse anesthetists (CNA).

It has become a cliché to say that healthcare organizations, like others, will have to become leaner, flatter and more flexible to survive in an increasingly competitive, market-driven environment. The professional nurse will have to address change in the work environment in new ways. The shift from retrospective to prospective payment systems for healthcare services in the 1980s to managed care systems in the 1990s illustrates how the healthcare work environment has changed. The one certainty is the concern for healthcare costs will not go away. This concern can do much to position the professional nurse for a greater, more accountable role in the future. Research findings increasingly support the perspective that professional nursing services produce better healthcare outcomes for less cost than those provided by other competing healthcare providers (Monarch, 2003, p. 30).

In addition to the changing nature of work itself, many other influences are likely to affect a person's career creation process. These include the potential, if not the demand, for multiple job changes; an economy that is increasingly global; expanding technology; organizational innovations in structures and processes; a more culturally diverse workforce; and work's relationship to family life. Greenhaus, Callahan, and Godshalk (2000) claim, "The world is changing rapidly and dramatically, and these changes—economic, political, technological and cultural—are having profound effects on the world of work. Accompanying these changes is a level of uncertainty that is playing havoc with people's careers and lives" (p. 4).

The nurse who plans a career understands well the concept of change and change processes. Instead of becoming a victim of change, the professional nurse can orchestrate career moves with changes in educational requirements, work environments and job changes. Understanding the career creation process and career staging enables the nurse to plan better and minimize the potential for disappointment and failure. The professional nurse builds bridges to the next opportunity, instead of "burning" bridges to the past. The nurse who plans a career also understands the possibility of returning to an old job in a new role.

Learning to accept criticism in a way that benefits a career is a major task to be achieved early in the career. People who are professionally immature may have a very difficult time accepting even valid criticism or suggestions from others to help them improve their performance. How a person reacts to evaluation during nursing school can offer insight to how well the same person will fare in early clinical practice.

A socialization process for a career in nursing begins long before the graduating nurse enters the paid workforce as a registered nurse. This socialization process creates a set of expectations that cause the person to anticipate the future and how to enter the next career stage. The better and more realistic the socialization process, the more likely career expectations will be validated with the next career stage.

REFERENCES

American Nurses Association. (1996). *Standards of nursing practice.* Washington, DC:Author.

Benner, P. (1984). *From novice to expert: Excellence and power in clinical nursing practice.* Menlo Park, CA: Addison-Wesley.

Camilleri, D. (2001). The century ahead: Old traditions and new challenges for nursing education. In J. McCloskey Dochterman & H.K. Grace, *Current issues in nursing* (6th ed.). St. Louis, MO: Mosby.

Erikson, E.H. (1963). *Childhood and society*. New York, NY: Norton.

Grando, V.T. (2001). Staff nurses working in hospitals: Who are they, what do they do and what challenges do they face? In J. McCloskey Dochterman, & H.K. Grace, *Current issues in nursing* (6th ed., pp. 14-18). St. Louis, MO: Mosby.

Greenhaus, J.H., Callahan, G.A., & Godshalk, V.M. (2000). *Career management* (3rd ed.). Orlando, FL: Dryden Press/Harcourt.

Hardy, M.E., & Conway, M.E. (1988). *Role theory*. Norwalk, CT: Appleton & Lange.

Hawken, P.L., & Hillestad, E.A. (2000). Retirement: A job in itself. *Nursing Administration Quarterly, 25*(1), 102-106.

Heise, D.R. (1990). Careers, career trajectories and the self. In J. Rodin, C. Schooler, & K.W. Schale (Eds.), *Self-directiveness: Cause and effects throughout the life course*. Hillsdale, NJ: Lawrence Erlbaum Associates.

Kelly, L.Y., & Joel, L.A. (1996). *The nursing experience: Trends, challenges, and transitions* (3rd ed.). New York, NY: McGraw-Hill.

Killeen, M.L. (2001). Socialization to professional nursing. In J.L. Creasia & B. Parker, *Conceptual Foundations: The bridge to professional nursing practice* (3rd ed.). St. Louis, MO: Mosby.

Kramer, M. (1974). *Reality shock*. St. Louis, MO: Mosby.

Miller, T.W. (1991). *The career creation process of persons with previous college degrees pursuing nursing as a career change*. Dissertation, University of Texas, Austin.

Moloney, M.M. (1992). *Professionalization of nursing: Current issues and trends*. Philadelphia, PA: Lippincott.

Monarch, K. (2003). Making informed employment decisions. *American Journal of Nursing Career Guide, Part 2*. New York, NY: Lippincott/ Williams & Wilkins.

Roy, C. (2000). The visible and invisible fields that shape the future of the nursing care system. *Nursing Administration Quarterly, 25*(1), 119-131.

Styles, M. (1982). *On nursing: Toward a new endowment*. St. Louis, MO: Mosby.

U.S. Bureau of Labor Statistics (2000). *National industry-occupational employment matrix*. Retrieved November 8, 2002, from http://stats.bls.gov/oep/nioem/empiohm.asp.

Weis, D., & Schank, M.J. (2000). Professionalism and the evolution of nursing as a discipline: A feminist perspective. *Journal of Professional Nursing, 10*, 357-367.

Chapter 5

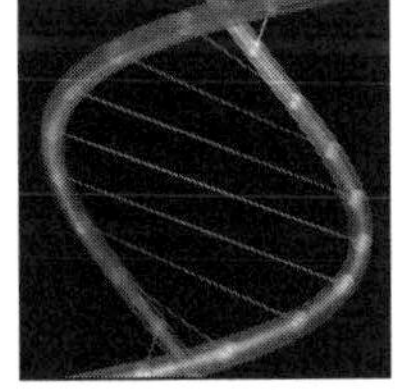

Change at the Personal Level

by Patsy Maloney

It is never too late to become what you might have been (George Eliot).

INTRODUCTION

The process of discovering a new direction in a present career or a totally new career involves a thorough personal and environmental assessment, an action plan, the implementation of the plan, an evaluation, and celebration of the change. In order to implement change, a sense of personal power is required. LeBrun (1999) defines personal power as the ability to create a desired life. Too often power is perceived as that which exists outside oneself. Everyone else has the power. In order "to become what you might have been," you must find within yourself the power to become. According to Williams (2000) the ways to this power are:

- The acknowledgment and application of personal strengths and resilience,
- The shaping of opportunities to develop and demonstrate competencies and skills,
- The creation of a satisfying and nourishing personal life, and
- The continual movement toward an ideal vision of oneself.

THEORETICAL BACKGROUND

Self-Efficacy

The belief that one's own actions can produce desired outcomes is referred to as self-efficacy (Bandura, 1977). "Self-efficacy beliefs provide the foundation for human motivation, well-being, and personal accomplishment. This is because unless people believe that their actions can produce the outcomes they desire, they have little incentive to act or to persevere in the face of difficulties" (Pajares, 2001, p.1). Of course, other factors influence human motivation to act in new ways or change a career. The daily experience with success and failure, as daily tasks are performed, affects one's choices. An individual's motivation, actions and emotional state are based more on what is believed to be true than on "what is objectively true" (Bandura, 1997, p. 2). Given this, it is often easier to predict individuals' behaviors based on their beliefs about their capabilities rather than their actual capabilities, because most individuals' perceptions of self-efficacy aid in determining what individuals will do with the knowledge and skills they have. This theory assists in explaining why two individuals with similar knowledge and skills enact roles very differently. Reality and beliefs are rarely matched. An individual is more likely to be guided by beliefs. Therefore, an individual's self-efficacy beliefs are better predictors of future career attainment than knowledge, skills or previous accomplishments. Of course, a sense of personal power and confidence cannot make up for a total lack of knowledge and skills (Pajares, 2001).

Self-Efficacy and Career Choice/Change

Brown (1999) examines ways of applying self-efficacy beliefs toward career development and expansion. Self-efficacy beliefs, relating to careers, have been defined by Betz and Hackett (1997) as an individual's personal beliefs regarding "career-related behaviors, educational and occupational choice, and performance and persistence in the implementation of those choices" (p. 383). When an individual suffers low self-efficacy expectations, he or she is apt to limit participation in a career activity and is more likely to surrender at the first difficulty. Such low self-efficacy beliefs serve as barriers to an individual's career development. For example, women's low self-efficacy beliefs have been attributed to the disadvantaged position women have in the workplace (Hackett & Betz, 1981).

Acquiring Self-Efficacy

The four ways of acquiring self-efficacy are performance accomplishments (mastery), vicarious learning (modeling), verbal persuasion and physical/affective status (Bandura, 1997).

Performance accomplishments are believed to have the greatest influence on one's self-efficacy. If an individual experiences success and positive feedback, he or she begins to expect success and positive feedback. The contrary is also true. When an individual experiences continued failure and negative feedback, he or she begins to expect failure and can develop a low self-efficacy or a sense of decreased personal power. In the work environment, sexism and unrealistic work expectations can also work to decrease a person's sense of self-efficacy (Brown, 1999). Whether failures and negative reinforcement actually succeed in promoting low self-efficacy depends on one's perceptions and whether or not the person is able to eventually succeed in spite of the initial negative experiences (Swanson & Woitke, 1997).

Vicarious learning of self-efficacy occurs while observing and interpreting the behavior of others. Individuals who have learned vicariously through observing others can reflect upon those observations and apply them to new situations. However, when they have a limited range of models, their behavior and perceived career options become limited (Brown, 1999). The converse is true. The more career models people are exposed to, the more options are perceived. But according to Pajares (2001) all models are not equally influential. If individuals have limited experience or are unsure of their abilities, then they become more sensitive to the effects. The power of vicarious experience is even greater when they notice the model has similar attributes to theirs. For instance, the perception that the model and the individual have similarities in common might lead to the belief that they have similar abilities, so if the model is successful, the individual's self-efficacy is increased. But to the contrary, if the model is unsuccessful, the individual's self-efficacy can decrease. If a model is not similar to the individual, the model's effect is minimized (Pajares, 2001)

The influence of verbal persuasion on self-efficacy is through the message of others. When family, teachers and friends convey messages of support and encouragement, self-efficacy is promoted. When criticism is the primary message received, low self-efficacy can result. Significant others can unintentionally limit or change career progression with verbal or nonverbal messages (Brown, 1999). These messages can be as simple as not believing that an individual is capable of career progression—even when unsaid. Instead of verbal persuasion, Pajares (2001) has termed this behavior as social persuasion, which seems to be a more accurate description of this kind of influence than verbal persuasion.

Physical/affective status refers to the physical and emotional state of an individual. If a person is anxious about performing a task and is overwhelmed with negative feelings, these emotions can lower self-efficacy and result in poor performance. By improving physical and emotional well-being, self-efficacy can be enhanced (Pajares, 2001).

All the sources of self-efficacy do not directly influence one's judgment of competence. The results of events are interpreted, and these interpretations form the foundation on which judgments of competence are made. Therefore, an individual's judgment of self-efficacy is dependent upon the "selection, integration, interpretation, and recollection of information" (Pajares, 2001, p.1).

Application of Self-Efficacy Theory

Growing up in a poor and broken family with a grammar-school-educated mother who worked as a waitress, Cherie heard negative messages that she was not smart and could never go to college (social persuasion leading to low self-efficacy). She was a below-average to average student who scored below average on standardized tests (lack of performance accomplishment leading toward low self-efficacy). Cherie's dream was to become a nurse. When she talked to the high school counselor, she received the same message, that she was not smart enough to go to college and become a registered nurse (social persuasion toward low self-efficacy). She decided to go to the local technical college and become a licensed practical nurse. She worked nights as a nursing assistant and went to school during the day. She did well in school in spite of her full-time employment (performance accomplishment toward greater self-efficacy). She worked as a licensed practical nurse for a few years, married and had a family. When her children were older, she found herself growing irritable and feeling trapped. Her sister, who had been an outstanding high school student and attended college on a full scholarship, suggested that she revisit her dream of becoming a registered nurse (vicarious learning toward increased self-efficacy). She said that there wasn't enough money for her to go to school. Her sister, not taking no for an answer, stated that she would loan her the money to return to school (social persuasion toward greater self-efficacy). Cherie's husband fully supported her return to school (social persuasion toward greater self-efficacy). Cherie enrolled in courses as a step toward her dream. Her sister encouraged her to go to a four-year university program.

With her dream in sight, Cherie worked very hard and continually surprised herself with outstanding grades (performance accomplishment toward greater self-efficacy). She earned scholarships that allowed her to finish her degree before her 44th birthday. Cherie earned a 4.0 grade point average and received the leadership award from the university nursing program upon graduation (performance accomplishment toward greater self-efficacy). She stated, "I wish my high school counselor could see me now." According to Cherie, the highlight of her academic career was not the perfect grade point average, nor even the leadership award, but her induction into Sigma Theta Tau, the nursing honorary society, because she remembered her sister's induction 26 years earlier (vicarious learning toward increased self-efficacy). She had arrived, or so she thought. With the encouragement of the nursing school faculty and her sister, she entered the graduate program (social persuasion toward greater self-efficacy).

Cherie initially did not recognize her personal power due to childhood negative messages. As the positive messages increased—vicarious learning from her sister, the initial social persuasion by her husband and sister, followed by her own highly rewarded performance accomplishments and the social support of the nursing school faculty—so did Cherie's self-efficacy. She was out of school only a year before returning to graduate school. The once-reserved and almost shy woman radiated confidence and a "can-do" attitude. The change in Cherie's life could not have occurred without her recognizing the power that resided within her.

So much for theory and Cherie's life, but how do you get started with the change in your career direction? Kanchier (2002) shared some life changing tips—he proposes first know yourself, plan and then change. These activities can easily be translated into the more familiar and more thorough nursing process—assessment (first know yourself), plan, implement (change) and evaluate.

THE CHANGE PROCESS

Personal and Environmental Assessment

As one begins a personal assessment, the first step is to think of self-efficacy. Consider what accomplishments are worth notice. Is there a history of completing what was started? What activities were really enjoyed? Why? Who were the role models? How were they like you? How were they different? Have they been successful? What were the messages received from the family while growing up? What were the messages received from others? What messages are received now from significant others? What could be done if there was no fear of failure or no need for money? If death occurred today, what would be regretted? Take some time and answer these questions. What are the results? The results may include the darkest moments, as well as life's triumphs. LeBrun (1999) states that in decoding these messages and finding the themes, we encounter a personal power, which is our birthright. What are your themes? Kanchier (2002) says the themes reveal your purpose. Your purpose should give direction to your life and your change.

Once life's purpose has been established and the sources of self-efficacy have been examined, there is a need to assess well-being. Bryan (1997) states life is comprised of several parts that all work together for optimal well-being. She believes these parts are physical, mental, emotional, philosophical, social and career/recreational. Bryan's concepts can be reduced to this square (see Figure 5.1).

In the figure, *physical* depicts the healthy body acquired from nutritious food, water, exercise, shelter and a safe environment. *Mental* equates with cognitive functioning. *Social/emotional* covers the positive feelings, a sense of belonging, the sense of security. *Spiritual* stands for authenticity, meaning, relating to something greater than self. According to Bandura (1997), self-efficacy is affected by the physical and emotional status of the individual. The questions to be answered: Are you a perfect square? Are you healthy and balanced?

Bryan (1997) states that prior to considering a change of career, there is a need to assess one's strengths and competencies, values, and obligations

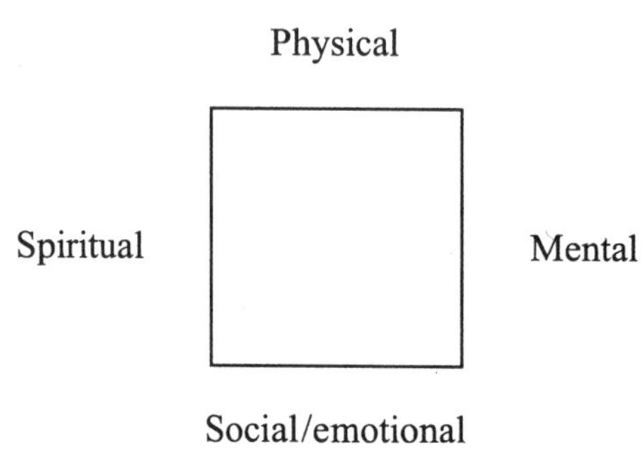

Figure 5.1 *The Perfect Square*

to others, as well as to look at what might have to be done, which really depends on marketplace opportunities. The following questions are offered as a way to assess what needs to be accomplished, what is desired and how it should be implemented.

- What are your strengths?
- What are your knowledge and skills?
- What do you really want to do? (Review your purpose.)
- What are your obligations to family or friends?
- Do you need to work full time or part time?
- Do you need to be home in the evenings?
- Do you need a flexible schedule?

Hieronymus & Geil (2002) suggest there is a need to consider income requirements, whether income can vary from month to month, and whether or not there is a need for healthcare coverage. Berlinger (1998) recommends a review of past work habits to determine whether there was a limitation of oneself. There are self-sabotaging behaviors that can hold one back. For example, was it the over-emphasis of caregiving (known as the caregiving syndrome), mistaking friendly for friendship or being caught up in passive-aggressive behavior that held me back?

The caregiving syndrome is described as taking care of and enabling others even when it means over-committing and using the limited resource of time on rescuing, fixing and being endlessly available to others without accomplishing personal established goals. Nurses suffering from the caregiving syndrome often forfeit personal growth and change for the endless pursuit of perfection (Berlinger, 1998). Are you a caregiver who spends so much time caring for others that you lose sight of your own life goals? Are you a perfectionist? Do you have difficulty holding yourself and others accountable for choices and outcomes? If you answered yes to any of the above questions, Berlinger's (1998) advice to you is:

- Realize that you cannot make others happy.
- Hold yourself and others accountable for behaviors and outcomes.
- Seek growth and not perfection.

Mistaking friendly behavior for friendship occurs when an individual's colleagues are friendly and kind, but this is mistaken for friendship, allowing the nurse to share intimate details of his or her life prematurely and inappropriately. Friendships do develop in a work situation, but they take time

(Berlinger, 1998). Thinking back, have there been instances when you felt betrayed by others because you prematurely considered them friends?

Passive-aggressive behavior occurs when an individual deals with feelings of anger and frustration by eliciting these feelings in others and as a result becomes a victim. Instead of directly dealing with anger the individual believes s/he is not entitled to, the resultant behavior is procrastination, forgetting, not completing tasks, complaining and/or generalized irritability. A passive-aggressive individual will say yes, when no is the appropriate response. Such an individual may become angry, because while knowing no is the correct response, there is a feeling there is no choice. Do you feel that you have no choice but to say yes to demands? Once you have agreed, do you feel like a victim and have trouble completing the tasks in a timely manner? If you answer yes to these questions, practice saying no without guilt. Practice viewing your supervisor as an individual like yourself trying to get the job done the best way possible. Learning to thoughtfully and honestly discuss controversial issues with the boss, while taking responsibility for one's own thoughts, feelings and decisions, is important. Having answered questions concerning self-sabotaging behaviors, the next step is to assess the environment for opportunities.

Environmental Assessment

What are the opportunities in nursing ? Awareness of all the possible career options that a nursing career offers is essential for career advancement and often career satisfaction. Opportunities in nursing are abundant and can be categorized by practice setting, specialty and function. The practice settings include acute care; extended care (nursing homes, assisted living, adult day care); community (public health offices, schools, churches, homes and work places); ambulatory care (physician's office or ambulatory care center); health insurance companies; pharmaceutical businesses; architectural agencies; book publishers; and universities. Most nurses are more familiar with the common clinical specialties than with the settings. The clinical specialties include medical-surgical (orthopedic, oncology, urology, etc.), gerontological, pediatric, obstetric, perioperative, emergency, psychiatric, neonatal and critical care. In addition to setting and clinical specialties, nurses can serve in a variety of roles—direct bedside care provider, nurse manager, nurse educator, clinical nurse specialist, nurse practitioner, nurse informaticist, case/care manager, nurse executive, nurse researcher (nurse scientist), nurse attorney, nurse consultant, etc. There are advanced practice roles, such as nurse midwifery and nurse anesthesia, in which nurses have a long history of outstanding performance. There are newer roles, such as utilization managers, quality managers, legal consultants, forensic nurses, nurse entrepreneurs, occupational nurses and many more. It is difficult to imagine with all the opportunities in nursing that a nurse would have trouble finding a fit within the profession.

Kanchier (2002) suggests it is helpful to consult with a good friend or associate, to take a look at all the possible opportunities. He urges us not to let a lack of education or money, the existence of a disability, or advancing age interfere with brainstorming possibilities. He suggests we come up with three possibilities for further exploration and take a closer look at each option. By reviewing nursing journals, calling the local hospital's human resources department, and speaking to a nurse manager, nurse educator or clinical nurse specialist in the area of your interest, it is possible to learn a lot about what is available. And it is important not to forget to check out Internet sites (Don't undersell, 2000). Kanchier also suggests volunteering, attending conferences, interviewing others in the specialty of interest and shadowing the professionals are useful.

After this assessment of opportunities, it is important to assess your knowledge and skills to determine a match. See Table 5.1 for an example of how to do the assessment. Please note that if there is a lack of knowledge,

Table 5.1
Required Competencies and Attributes

	Option 1	Option 2	Option 3	You Possess
Knowledge				
Skills				
Personality traits such as risk-taking, logical, friendly, confident, quiet, out-going, attentive-to-detail				
Other experience or activity				

Table 5.2
Required Activities

	Choice	Assessment	Deficit	Necessary Action (School, training, temporary job, internship, volunteer, independent study)
Knowledge				
Skills				
Experience				

skills or experience for one of the preferred options, it is possible to acquire them. But if the preferred option requires a different personality or set of attributes, then another option should be selected.

Once an option is selected, the next step is to determine what needs to be done to turn that option into a viable possibility. See Table 5.2 for assistance in determining what education, training or experience is necessary to pursue that new career. Having discovered the necessary action for the desired career, the next step will be to develop an action plan with measurable short-term and long-term outcomes.

Action Plan

Short-term goals may include education, followed by a practicum. Often an individual resists getting more education. "I won't make more money. In the past, nurses did this without advanced education." Mee (2001) acknowledges it is unlikely immediate financial advantages will occur upon completing additional education, but over time, advanced education opens the door to opportunities that eventually result in pay increases. The real advantage of an advanced education is "a different pot of gold" (p. 8). She describes this "different pot of gold" as renewed energy, creativity, knowledge, friends and increased confidence and believes that advanced education often changes one's entire life. Of course, even the goals of an education and a practicum might have to be broken down into smaller steps, such as exploring educational programs, deciding on one, applying, moving, enrolling, matriculating, etc.

Once the goals are established, what are the obstacles to these goals? Writing them down and outlining the ways to overcome the obstacles helps (Kanchier, 2002) (see Table 5.3). It is important to not let the obstacles block the goal of becoming what is desired and possible. There are always ways around, through or over any obstacle.

Table 5.3
Obstacles to Goal Attainment

Obstacles (money, time, lack of support, distance)	**Strategies to Overcome (scholarships, loans, request for help, build support, relocate or travel buddy)**

Implementation of the Plan

As mentioned earlier, the implementation of the long-term change begins with the completion of short-term objectives that are reduced to smaller steps. Putting these steps on the calendar helps as does monitoring progress and, if necessary, modifying the plan (Kanchier, 2002). Throughout the process, there is a need to maintain a positive attitude, which is reinforced by keeping a diary of positive experiences and staying with positive people who support each other toward the desired goals (Hieronymus & Geil, 2002).

As a goal appears to be near, it is important to develop a career identity. According to Chope (2000), career identity represents the totality of one's knowledge, skills, experience, values, personality and attributes. Most people cannot describe their career identity or who they are in the work world. But after doing a personal and environmental assessment, determining the actions needed to take on an ideal career, and having moved toward that career, it should not be difficult to articulate a career identity. This well-articulated identity helps one maintain excitement while pursuing a position in a new career field. Six approaches to clarifying this identity have been proposed by Chope. These approaches are similar to work already completed during the assessment and the action planning process yet serve to bring the process to completion.

The first approach is to create a career genogram. The career genogram resembles a family tree and shows where the desired career choice fits into the career choices of other family members. This genogram serves as a starting place to understand the family's judgments and expectations concerning a successful career. The individual can actually see how the desired personal career choices fit the family's expectations and how these expectations affected the choices (Chope, 2000).

In order to construct a genogram, draw your family tree on a pad of unlined paper. Father is represented by a square and mother by a circle, and, if married, a straight line with the marriage date connects them (See Figure 5.2). The parents are centered at the top of the page. Instead of your parents' names, place their careers within their symbols. Add lines perpendicular to the marriage line to identify the other children and their careers. Squares represent male family members, and circles represent females. Add the other extended family members to include grandparents, aunts, uncles and cousins. Instead of names, place the careers/occupations in the symbols for each family member (Chambers, 2002). For each of

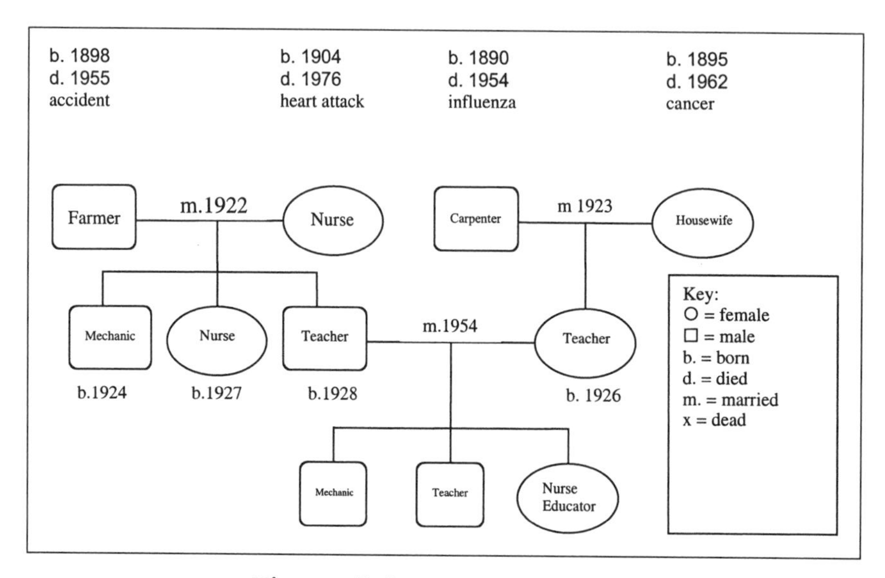

Figure 5.2 *Genogram Example*

your important models, place his or her income range with the career and describe the range of social status. Describe how your family modeled such behaviors as security vs. risk-taking, career orientation vs. job orientation, leisure vs. work. Describe the effect of gender on work roles of your family members. Elaborate on how your family's career choices and attitudes affected your career decisions.

After creating the career genogram, review your life, looking at factors that influenced you toward your career choice and those that moved you in other directions. Think about what your idea of an ideal career was as a child, as an adolescent, as a young adult and now. What events influenced your ideal or fantasy career? Ideal or fantasy careers often model the ideal self. The more narrow the divide between the ideal self and the real self, the greater the possibility of a satisfying life (Chope, 2000).

The next approach really follows the articulation of the development of an ideal career. It is discovering and telling your career story. You merely need to tape or write your career journey. You start at your first memories and move forward, discussing your interests and dreams as you grew up, and then as you developed as a mature adult. You can take all the time you need to develop the story and even give it the ideal ending.

The fourth approach really gets at your values. If you won a lottery, providing you with all the money that you would ever need, what would you do with it and with whom? (Chope, 2000; Kanchier, 2002).

The next step is to name your ideal position. The naming process requires you to have investigated the nursing job market using the Internet, journals, conference brochures and networking to find work that fits your life purpose, talents, competencies and preparation.

The final step is to develop an advertising sound bite of approximately 30 seconds that describes you to potential employers and others who might be able to help you find your dream position. Once the sound bite is created, you need to practice it until if flows easily and can be confidently shared with others.

Once the sound bite is developed, what you might do, can do, want to do and should do is evident. You have an action plan developed and the sound bite is the marketing tool. Once you have enacted the plan by obtaining education, training and/or new experiences, you are ready for the final action—the new career.

Celebration of Change

You have arrived. Take some time out and celebrate your goal accomplishment with your supporters. You deserve to take some time to celebrate. But remember, this is a beginning and not the end.

Evaluation of the Plan

Since the end is really the beginning, your new career will require constant evaluation. Are you happy? Are you learning and growing? Do you have a sense of accomplishment? When you wake up, are you eager and enthusiastic to go to work? Does your work provide you with a sense of worth? Would you continue this job in some capacity even if you won the lottery? If things are not going as well as you would like, what needs to be done to make things right? Is it time to move in a different direction? Bryan (1997) suggests a review be done periodically using the questions provided in Table 5.4. Do any themes emerge that indicate a need for (a) a big change? (b) a minor change? (c) congratulations for goal achievement? If you decide that you are in for a big change, go back to the beginning with assessment.

Lifelong Learning and Change

Change is constant and pervasive. An individual must keep pace with ongoing change. In order to keep up, learning and growth must be continuous, which requires constant updating of knowledge and skills. Motivation for this constant updating can be the result of increased opportunities, increased job satisfaction, increased compensation and increased personal satisfaction. There are many ways to update and grow, such as (a) participating in training opportunities at your workplace; (b) self-study with audio/video tapes, computer-assisted instruction, Internet-based instruction or printed materials; and (c) courses offered by educational institutions. An investment of time and money in lifelong learning should not be taken lightly. Be sure to investigate all possible paths to growth considering the quality and suitability of the activity. You might want to ask about the graduates of the programs/courses and the positions and salaries of the graduates.

Bryan (1997) proposes the four C's of conquest: challenge, commitment, control and connection can guide lifelong learning. In order to grow, you must be **c**hallenged to stretch your current capabilities. You need to

Table 5.4
Evaluation Questions

Evaluation Questions
Do you understand your role in the big picture of the organization?
Does supervision acknowledge your contributions?
Do you continue to expect greatness from yourself and others? Are you an integral part of an outstanding work group?
Are your assignments challenging and exposing you to a variety of experiences that develop you personally and professionally?
Are you contributing to continuous improvement, team building, conflict management and the professional development of others?
Are your growth and advancement stunted?
Are you feeling that you are not fitting in your current workplace and may need to move within your organization or move to another organization?
If you are self-employed, is it time to seek employment? If employed, is it time to look at entrepreneurial opportunities?
Do you daily face problems instead of challenges? If your answer is yes, check out your attitude.
Are you coming up with creative ideas?
Do you feel like an innocent victim of rampant change in your organization and world?
Has politics or the need for expediency affected your decisions?
Do you feel that it is difficult to do what is right? Do you regularly face ethical conflicts?
Are you encouraged to continue your professional development? (time off, financial reimbursement, verbal encouragement and advice)
Do you have a relationship with a mentor? Is the relationship helpful? Are you ready and willing to mentor someone else?
Are you earning your salary? In other words, are your efforts and accomplishments worth what you are being paid?
Do you feel that your efforts and accomplishments should receive more compensation than you are currently receiving?
Where does your work fit in comparison to other life priorities? Is your work affecting your health either negatively or positively? Is your work affecting your relationships?

make a total commitment to continued growth in order to sustain when the going gets tough. You must control the process by seeking out experiences and educational opportunities instead of being a passive recipient of institutional training. Further, growth is not a solitary task. A connection with colleagues and family for support and sustenance is essential.

The "high five" of career development, according to Redekopp, Day and Robb (1995), is very similar to Bryan's (1997) four C's. These five points are: (a) change is constant, (b) follow your heart, (c) focus on the journey, (d) stay learning and (e) be an ally. The common elements of lifelong learning or lifelong career development are connecting with others by being an ally and owning the process by taking control of your own career and learning opportunities as opposed to being at others' whims.

CONCLUSION

LeBrun (1999) believes personal power is our birthright. We are born with it. Yet, many of us grow up believing that we do not have personal power to change our lives and influence our world. Covey (1990) revisited the concept of the "circle of control." He tells us to define our circle of control—things we can control belong within the circle, while the things we cannot control belong outside the circle. Many of us spend our lives fighting outside our circle, trying to gain control of what can never be controlled and failing to control that which we can control—our personal growth and change, our choices, and how we respond to others and our world. We cannot control other people. They are accountable for their own choices, responses and happiness.

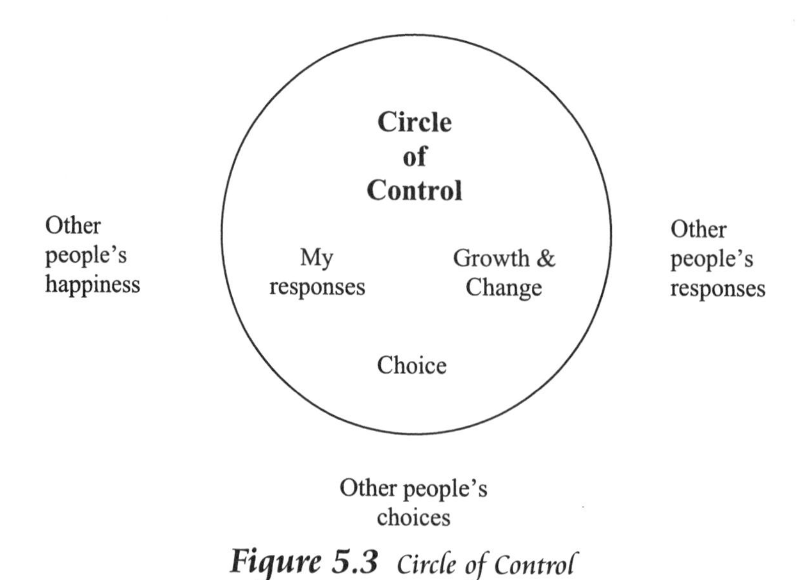

Figure 5.3 Circle of Control

Each of us has the personal power to change our lives. Please join Cherie in becoming "what you might have been"... "It is never too late." You have the power and the control.

REFERENCES

Bandura, A. (1977). Self-efficacy: Toward a unifying theory of behavioral change. *Psychological Review, 84,* 191-215.

Bandura, A. (1997). *Self-efficacy: The exercise of control.* New York: Freeman.

Berlinger, J. (1998). Sweeping away stereotypes. *Nursing98, 28*(9), 61-62.

Betz, N.E., & Hackett, G. (1997). Applications of self-efficacy theory to the career assessment of women. *Journal of Career Assessment, 5*(4), 383-402.

Brown, B.L. (1999). Self-efficacy beliefs and career development. *ERIC Clearinghouse on Adult, Career, and Vocational Education.* Retrieved January 10, 2002, from http://icdl.uncg.edu/ft/062000-08.html.

Bryan, M. (1997). *Career development manual* (2nd ed.). Waterloo, Ontario, Canada: Career Services, University of Waterloo.

Chambers, C. (2002). Enhancing communication with family. Nursing Spectrum Career Fitness *Online.* Retrieved January 31, 2002, from http://nsweb.nursingspectrum.com/ce/ce78.htm.

Chope, R.C. (2000). *Dancing naked: Breaking through the emotional limits that keep you from the job you want.* Oakland, CA: New Harbinger Publications.

Covey, S.R. (1990). *The 7 habits of highly effective people.* New York: Simon & Schuster.

Don't undersell yourself when returning to work. (2000). *Nursing, 3*(12), 70.

Hackett, G., & Betz, N. (1981). A self-efficacy approach to the career development of women. *Journal of Vocational Behavior, 18*(3), 326-39.

Hieronymus, L., & Geil, P. (2002). Taking the leap of faith. *Excellence in Nursing Administration, 3*(1), 2.

Kanchier, C. (2002, January). Life-changing tips from a psychologist. *USA Weekend*, pp. 11-13, 18.

LeBrun, L. (1999). *Pathways to personal power.* Retrieved January 10, 2002, from http://icdl.edu/pdf.042800-01.pdf.

Mee, C.L. (2001). Going for the gold. *Nursing2001, 31*(3), 8.

Pajares, F. (2001). *Overview of self-efficacy.* Emory University. Retrieved January 29, 2002, from http://www.emory.edu/EDUCATION/mfp/eff.html.

Redekopp, D.E., Day, B., & Robb, M. (1995). The "high five" of career development. *ERIC Clearinghouse on Counseling and Student Services*, Canadian Guidance and Counseling Foundation, Ottawa (Ontario).

Swanson, J.L., & Woitke, M.B. (1997). Theory into practice in career assessment for women: Assessment and interventions regarding perceived career barriers. *Journal of Career Assessment, 5*(4), 443-462.

Williams, C.P. (2000, November). *Helping women shape a career path and a life that works*. Presented at the International Career Development Conference 17th Annual California Career Conference.

Chapter 6

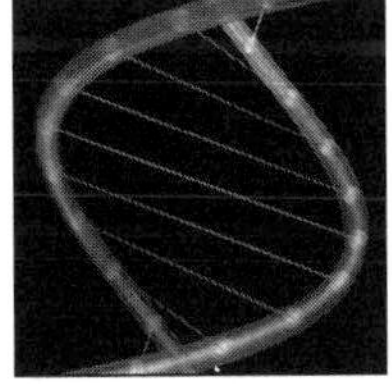

Career Opportunities

by Arthur Wallace

Understanding Your Strengths and Weaknesses + A Dose of Risk-Taking + Boldly Taking the Next Step = Grasping an Opportunity

I shall be telling this with a sigh
Somewhere ages and ages hence:
Two roads diverged in a wood, and I—
I took the one less traveled by,
And that has made all the difference.

Robert Frost (1874-1963)

This timeless passage from Robert Frost's famous poem captures the ageless uncertainty we all face when confronted with the following questions: What do I do next? Should I try something new in nursing? Do I want to take risks at this stage in my life? At some future date, will I have a sense of fulfillment or missed opportunity? Informed or impulsive decisions about our career result in the consequences that form the building blocks of: "who we are," "what we are capable of doing" and "where we are capable of going."

Today, more than ever, nursing is a profession that is in demand and caught between meeting traditional roles and expectations . . . and a future that has unlimited opportunities in a broad array of career choices and work settings. The projected supply of RNs will grow 1.5% per year for the next eight years; yet, the demand rate will be 21% per year. The current session of the U.S. Congress is already exploring the concept of awarding Nurse Corps scholarships in exchange for service in critical nursing shortages (AAMA, 2002). Employers are being challenged to restructure workload, improve compensation and working conditions, and subsidize continuing education for new roles and opportunities (U.S. Bureau of Labor Statistics, 2002). With these dramatic contemporary market developments as a backdrop, we will examine at a personal and practical level the key factors that nurses should consider when contemplating *where they are today and where they want to be in the future.*

This chapter contains "pearls of wisdom" that have applications to today's job market rich with interesting career opportunities limited only by your education, demonstrated potential, skills and where you're willing to relocate! Throughout the discussion are anecdotal stories from the personal nursing career history of the author that reinforce lessons learned with the ingredients that you should consider adding to your personal career roadmap when contemplating new career opportunities. These "ingredients" are:

- Know thyself.
- Seek mentors and wise people.
- Take risks.
- Never stop learning . . . and understand the business of healthcare.
- Get involved in community/professional organizations and network.
- Understand cultural diversity.
- Be an effective communicator . . . speak, write, listen.
- Always set short- and long-term goals . . . and strive to achieve them.

These ingredients played a key role in sustaining my nursing focus and job fulfillment and contributed to my 26-year career odyssey of discovery through an assortment of positions that included hospital nurse's aide, medical-surgical and ICU staff nurse, head nurse, clinical instructor, burn unit and emergency room staff and head nurse, White House nurse supporting Presidents Bush (Sr.) and Clinton, Emergency Nurses Association certification exam item writer and developer, adjunct college faculty, hospital education coordinator, chief nursing officer (in Alabama and South Korea), and chief executive officer (Hospital Commander in Kansas).

In 1979, I was faced with my first career opportunity. I had been a medical-surgical staff nurse in a rural community hospital for one year. I had graduated with a BSN in 1978 through an Army scholarship program. My head nurse encouraged me to begin cross-training in the intensive care unit. My eagerness to learn new competencies and skills had caught her attention; thus, my first nursing career opportunity arose from a first-line manager who recognized potential and offered clinical advancement avenues to her staff members.

Know Thyself

The shift from being a learner, acquiring basic core nursing knowledge while in school or in your first salaried or volunteer position, to that of a staff nurse or first-time manager, applying these new skills with confidence, is a gradual and sometimes traumatic one. But, over time, you develop an understanding of your underlying strengths and weaknesses (areas that may need further education, guidance and training). Establishing a baseline self-assessment and early goal-setting skills are critical in order to "thrive on opportunities created" that allow one to "grow with change rather than merely react against it" (Donner & Wheeler, 2001). My decision to accept my head nurse's invitation to transfer to the ICU was based on my medical-surgical core competencies and the nurse manager's confidence in my basic nursing and interpersonal skills. Such a move also required a commitment to obtain additional education to prepare for critical care competency requirements. Participation with the local American Association of Critical Care Nurses chapter and Advanced Cardiac Life Support (ACLS) training were essential preliminary steps that were valuable later in my career. It validated my faith in a system that provides positive feedback, recognizes good performance via an offered incentive, and offers a potential career opportunity in critical care.

In 1981, I was offered a position as a clinical instructor with emergency medical technicians and, later, a project officer position to develop a concentrated 16-week course that trained military combat medics with paramedic-level skills. This opportunity arose because I had been active as an instructor with BCLS, ACLS and the local Red Cross chapter. The rewarding experience of teaching, dealing with students' trials and tribulations, and enjoying it are personal revelations that contribute to career development in clinical and administrative positions.

Seek Mentors and Wise People

Any organization that has nurse leaders who lead by example and enthusiastically coach/guide/mentor their subordinates (and colleagues!) while developing their strengths and innate talents, will empower our profession with positive leadership and direction. According to a recent leadership best-seller by the Gallup Organization, *Now, Discover Your Strengths* (Buckingham & Clifton, 2001), the best managers (and mentors) follow two underlying assumptions:

1. Each person's talents are enduring and unique.
2. Each person's greatest room for growth is in the area of his or her greatest strength.

Whether it was my superior's recognition and nurturing of my teaching interests or another nurse's demonstrated expertise with clinical informatics, visionary and wise leaders are crucial players in keeping nurses interested, motivated and vested in a career with diverse opportunities. It's truly a sound investment in our profession *and our future* if we can portray nursing as a lifelong career of talents recognized and opportunities afforded instead of the same job for many years. Nursing leadership and education must establish the right attitude and mind-set in new nurses by shaping a future filled with opportunities for diversity and growth and not an "assembly line" healthcare job.

After completing graduate school in 1984, I was offered a position as a staff nurse at a nationally known burn center. In my mind, it was a "step down" after obtaining my Master's degree, but I was assured that there would be leadership opportunities opening in the future. There was some risk involved with this "tepid career enhancing opportunity"! I took the position and, after 15 months, became head nurse of the Step Down/Rehab Unit and co-authored a research project presented at the annual Burn Association meeting.

Take Risks

Inherent in any career or job change is risk-taking and a large dose of trust in your current leadership or future employer. But as Frost's poem indicated at the beginning of this chapter, "taking the road less traveled" made all the difference. My opportunity at the burn unit was taken after I evaluated the benefits of learning additional skills in a unique environment and my conversations with the leadership. Trust in what they told me (and my commitment to meeting their expectations) played a major role in my decision.

The current healthy market for nurse employment is shifting the burden of individual risk-taking to one of elevating the appeal of new opportunities by desperate employers, particularly hospitals. In the recent Health Care Advisory Board (2001) publication *Competing for Talent, Recovering America's Hospital Workforce,* a key point is that "the task ahead is one of rebuilding the appeal of our institutions to our current and future staffs one by one, from the bottom up" (p. 14). This doesn't eliminate risk by a nurse seeking new opportunities, but in the supply-and-demand nursing marketplace, it does create a climate where the employer is trying to find the "right recipe" of working conditions and incentives to accommodate and retain key staff and a broader range of job seekers.

In 1987, I moved to Hawaii hoping to obtain a leadership role in a cardiothoracic ICU. Unfortunately, the lead surgeon departed and, with him, the job. I worked in an urgent care clinic for one year and then was offered a position at a medical center emergency room where I was senior clinical nurse and, eventually, head nurse. Sustaining focus and enthusiasm while working evenings and nights was a challenge, but family and friends made a difference. In 1989, I was nominated for a position at the White House on the Presidential Medical Team; my background in ICU, burns and ER played a key role. After nerve-wracking interviews and background screens, I was accepted, and a new, unexpected opportunity and honor lay before me.

Never Stop Learning and Understand the Business of Healthcare

It cannot be overemphasized that as nurses we must never stop acquiring new information and understanding the *larger stage* (local nursing issues, healthcare policy and its local implications, etc.) that provides insights into future career opportunities and possibilities. Despite my disappointment with an unexpected change in jobs upon my arrival in Hawaii, I plunged myself into meeting local emergency medicine and nursing leaders, who provided suggestions on projects I could pursue at my level of interest and influence. Through the local Emergency Nurses' Association chapter and Sigma Theta Tau International, I found my career being enriched by new friends and a broader understanding of vital nursing issues. This exposure, along with varied leader mentors and my diverse critical care background, contributed to the unexpected nomination to the White House position.

Consumer demands on the healthcare marketplace are reshaping healthcare delivery and access. Nurses must understand the changes and where their influence can be asserted. As Stutz (1996) predicted, "Never before have so many opportunities existed for nurses to take a leadership position in the evolutionary process of our healthcare industry" (p. 6). The migration of healthcare to outpatient and ambulatory surgery centers, the sophisticated technology encountered in home care (geriatric and home post-operative care), and the new medical surveillance systems monitored increasingly by nurses and technicians contribute to complex new roles and interesting entrepreneurial business ventures. Amidst this evolutionary new environment is the crucial need to retain and prepare a cohort of nurses to sustain patient care, health education and disease management priorities.

Since 1987, my participation in professional nursing organizations, honorary societies, community organizations (ranging from American Youth Soccer Organization to Rotary) and healthcare organizations has contributed to my growth as a senior nurse executive and healthcare administrator. By balancing the concerns of nursing, medical and ancillary staff with the need to market to and educate the external community, I discovered that nurse leaders must always achieve a balance between the internal (inside the hospital or business) and external (community and user) populations. For example, how we addressed issues related to indigent and geriatric user populations had a direct impact on the staff's opinion of who we were and what we represented as an organization. In addition, active participation with local community groups facilitated education outreach programs in the rapidly changing medical benefit, insurance and primary care/specialty care marketplace.

Get Involved in Community/Professional Organizations and Network

The importance of joining and participating in both community and professional organizations that reflect your professional, political, social and recreational interests cannot be overemphasized. Occasionally, the information obtained on a potential position opening or opportunity is discovered due to your presence at a meeting where colleagues and administrators with similar interests are eager to find an applicant. Regular attendance and presence at such meetings may indeed be part of the screening process! In the job hunter's classic reference *What Color is Your Parachute?,* Richard Bolles (2002) emphasizes that most employers prefer the following methods when seeking new applicants:

- Hiring from within their organization
- Hiring unknown applicants who have demonstrated evidence that they are qualified
- Obtaining a recommendation from a friend or business colleague
- Using an ad or a placement agency
- Reading a resume received in the mail or from a job board

If you attend any meeting, always remember that you represent the organization where you are currently employed. An outsider's opinion or perception of a hospital or organization may be formed based upon your stated remarks and opinions and the way you conduct yourself at the meeting.

If you are exploring new career opportunities outside of your current specialty area, seek out gatherings of specialty groups reflecting a potential area of interest. For instance, unique areas of interest like nurse paralegals, forensic nursing, occupational health nursing, pharmaceutical sales, nurse practitioners, etc. can be researched by contacting a nurse currently employed in that field and asking when and where the local chapter will meet. You can only blame yourself if you do not actively seek opportunities to observe and interact with nurses who are active in these interesting new frontiers of nursing.

In the past 20 years, the importance of understanding multicultural diversity unique to my hospital's catchment area and the predominant cultural, socioeconomic and language demographic groups within my staff and our patient populations cannot be overemphasized. Nursing education programs cannot always anticipate the multicultural diversity that their students will encounter. Thus, it becomes incumbent on the workplace leadership to establish local cultural competence programs. From ensuring patient education and advanced directives are available in multiple languages and that interpreters are accessible in high-traffic areas, to emphasizing that various cultural, ethnic and religious norms are understood are essential foundations that must be acknowledged when seeking career opportunities in many urban and agricultural rural areas.

Understand Cultural Diversity

For nursing to be appealing as a profession and successful in providing care to the increasing diversity within the U.S. population, the demographic mix of nurses ideally should reflect the patient populations that are serviced by our institutions (Tanner, 1996). Patients are comfortable when they receive care from nurses who respect their culture and language. Some career opportunities (family nurse practitioner, nurse midwife, ER nurse practitioner, etc.) are advocating bilingual skills when applying for employment in certain border and urban areas. Otherwise, you will encounter frustration with communicating details to patients and liability concerns during patient education breakdowns. Be prepared for screening questions when interviewing for positions in areas where cultural and gender norms are different from a euro-centric curriculum and school setting.

In the past 10 years, I have served as a director, Hospital Education and Training Service; chief nurse executive at two hospitals; and a chief executive officer. The tremendous value of being able to listen, speak and write well and in clear, concise terms cannot be overemphasized. When interfacing with senior trustees, community leaders and departmental chiefs, it is imperative that complex information is communicated in terms that can be understood by a diverse audience that usually dislikes business and medical terminology and acronyms! Healthcare is a conservative culture, so conforming your dress code to your audience (or interviewer!) is important. When I speak with elderly groups, I always wear a suit or a uniform. When using visual presentations or slides, it is often wise to present the "bottom line up front" and then provide supporting information to reinforce your position. One of my other "pearls of wisdom" is to always research your audience before you meet with them. It will save you from potential embarrassment and remarks that are "off the mark."

Be an Effective Communicator

A healthcare marketplace that is desperately short of qualified applicants tends to waive the requirement that you are an effective communicator. This is unfortunate and short-sighted. However, possessing written and verbal communication skills is often a discriminator during interviews if you plan to pursue opportunities in education, management and other leadership positions where you interface frequently with key hospital staff and/or the public. As hospitals rely more on traveling nurse services and agency nurses, the requirement to be licensed, trained and competent will be the "bottom line."

For the nurse who wants to maximize his or her exposure to a broad range of job opportunities, the value of being articulate with your career vision and aspirations on your resume and in person remain powerful discriminators when seeking unique positions. Any self marketing plan must include networking, mentoring, written and verbal skills that address clinical competence, expert knowledge, and an ability to be creative and flexible.

The most important advice I was ever given during my 26-year nursing career is to set short- and long-term goals and strive to achieve them. Without a "blueprint" and vision for your future, you are just working and earning a paycheck. The motivation to establish such goals must be based on a self-assessment of your current commitment and degree of fulfillment in your profession. If you are comfortable with your profession but would like a job change, then setting goals with a budget and timelines is crucial. In my career, my lifecycle goals were based on a decision to apply for graduate school after working for at least five years. My assumption was that I would know my areas of nursing interest after at least two different nursing positions following graduation from nursing school. While in graduate school, I specialized in burns and trauma because these were interest areas developed during my assignments in the surgical ward and ICU. My decision to apply and migrate to positions as a senior nurse executive and chief executive officer was based upon my exposure to healthcare administration and nursing management areas of responsibility. In the military, rank promotion based on recognized potential also qualifies you to be screened for senior leadership opportunities. However, none of this can be accomplished without an awareness and commitment to a career plan.

Set Short- and Long-Term Goals . . . and Strive to Achieve Them

The evolution of nursing from a devalued profession in the hospital hierarchy in the early 20th century to one that is autonomous and occupied by well-educated and career-orientated individuals has been impressive (Donner & Wheeler, 2001). Nurses today have unlimited horizons restricted only by their education, imagination and motivation. The concept of nursing today as a lifelong career is forcing new approaches to career counseling and planning by mentors, nursing faculties and professional associations. Information is readily available in libraries and on the Internet referring to fascinating and varied career options within nursing; it's critical that the unlimited opportunities available to nurses be used to re-examine the way we define and market future career planning and retention initiatives.

The nursing profession must also *reinvigorate the cultivation of future roles that appeal to men and women.* Outside of independent practice and entrepreneurial roles, hospital and outpatient nursing has evolved very little in the past 50 years with the exception of the high-technology resources that monitor, track and regulate patient care and education. In the absence of a creative expansion of career clinical nursing opportunities appealing to future young Americans (Staiger, Auerbach, & Buerhaus, 2000), there has been a 40% drop, since 1975, of college freshmen who indicated nursing among their top career choices. Implications for nursing may include a reality that the current aging nursing workforce exodus will be replaced by agency or part-time nurses and a potential increase in the number of immigrant and foreign nurses. This has significant implications, as the information management era in healthcare has increased dramatically the requirement that nurses are comfortable using computers and virtual systems while promoting patient safety and being advocates of quality healthcare. The nurse's role in becoming a consumer consultant will undoubtedly increase in the 21st century (Malone, 1996). Entrepreneurial nurses have been the risk-takers in the profession. Unfortunately, hospital-based nurses have seen their inpatient nursing model evolve very little; thus, low risk-taking has resulted in stop-gap measures that are facing the growing "baby-boomer" patient population.

CONCLUSION

Career opportunities abound within nursing. The need for visionary nurse leaders who are willing to provide leadership for the future evolution of nursing is crucial. Market demands should not detract from the need to better define and market the profession to the next generation. The current generation of working nurses must be proud enough of their profession to convince their children to follow them. Nurse educators and leaders must define what the healthcare marketplace is looking for in the future and evolve programs that produce graduates with those future skills, services and talents that will sustain the profession's appeal. This will demand an economic, educational and political process that needs articulate leaders who understand nursing and what it means if attractive opportunities are not cultivated in the future.

REFERENCES

American Academy of Medical Administrators. (2002, Winter). *Newsletter*. Report from 107th Congress.

Bolles, R. (2002). *What color is your parachute?* Berkeley, CA: Ten Speed Press.

Buckingham, M. & Clifton D. (2001). *Now, discover your strengths.* New York, NY: Free Press.

Donner, G. & Wheeler, M. (2001). Career planning and development for nurses: The time has come. *International Nursing Review, 48*(2), 79-85.

Health Care Advisory Board. (2001). *Competing for talent, recovering America's hospital workforce.* Washington, DC: Author.

Healthcare workforce shortage getting worse. Retrieved February 28, 2002, from ACHE-news@ache.org.

Malone, B. (1996, November/December). President's perspective. *The American Nurse* (p. 6). Washington, DC: ANA.

Staiger, D., Auerbach, D., & Buerhaus, P. (2000). Expanding career opportunities for women and the declining interest in nursing as a career. *Nursing Economics 18*(5), 230-236.

Stutz, L. (1996, November/December). The evolution of managed care: New jobs for nurses in the 21st century. *The American Nurse* (p. 6). Washington, DC: ANA.

Tanner, C. (1996). Cultural diversity in nursing education. *Journal of Nursing Education, 35*(7), 291-292.

U.S. Bureau of Labor Statistics, Department of Labor. (2002). Registered nurses. *Occupational Outlook Handbook, 2002.*

Van Allen, G. (1996, July-September). Career options: The increasing demand for courtroom nurses. *Oklahoma Nurse,* p. 31.

Unit II
Developing a Career

Chapter 7

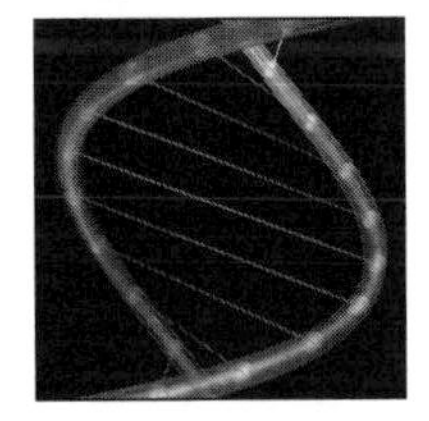

The Humanistic Career Pathway

by Fay L. Bower & Robinetta Wheeler

There was but one person in England that I know of who would be capable of organizing and superintending such a scheme. . . . Your own personal values, your knowledge and your power of administration . . . give you the advantages in such a work which no other person possesses (Statement about Florence Nightingale by Woodham-Smith, 1951, 87-89).

INTRODUCTION

Many individuals seek a career based on humanistic values. They plan the career based on what appeals to them because it fits a modern humanistic philosophy. Humanism is for those people who think for themselves, for there is no area of thought a humanist is afraid to challenge or explore. Humanistic values are based on intuitive feelings, hunches, speculation, flashes of inspiration, emotion, altered states of consciousness and even religious experience. Humanism is a philosophy of the here and now and is based on the human experience (Edwords, 1989).

In this chapter, the authors discuss how a framework of humanism is sometimes used as a springboard for accepting a position or for taking one direction rather than another when building or maintaining a career. It is also a way of viewing the job market that is quite different than the way an opportunistic individual would view it. Clearly, there are risks to using humanism as a framework for establishing a career, but it could be argued that given the job market of today (and probably the future) there are no guarantees any particular framework is better than another.

The authors of this chapter are not suggesting a humanism approach is any better than an opportunistic approach when seeking and building a career. Their intent is to show the ways people pursue career development and that there are at least two frameworks for that activity.

WHAT IS A HUMANISTIC APPROACH TO CAREER DEVELOPMENT?

Generally, individuals pursue a career by planning and by locating positions that fit into a step-by-step progression of jobs that lead to an ultimate outcome. For instance, nurses usually start their careers in hospitals moving from staff nurses to managers before they start to look outside the institution for work in the community. Most career-oriented nurses return to school during that time to prepare themselves for a greater array of nurse positions. Some stay in the field; others move into education, move into the corporate world, or even establish their own businesses. This movement from one job to another is influenced by a variety of considerations. Such things as working hours, autonomy, location and salary determine whether the position is "right" or will move them forward to bigger and better opportunities.

Some nurses, on the other hand, seek new positions because they are bored or unhappy or have a work-related disability. However, there are nurses who seek a change because an opportunity surfaces or they have a "calling" to do something different. Some change their work life because it is their nature to accept a challenge, explore new adventures or seek new knowledge. It is this third kind of individual this chapter describes.

Definition of Humanism

Edwords (1989) has listed the qualities of a humanist (whether religious or secular) in the following manner:

1. Humanism is one of the philosophies for people who think for themselves. A humanist is not afraid to challenge and explore.
2. Humanism is a philosophy focused on human means for comprehending reality. Humanists make no claims to possess or have access to supposed transcendent knowledge.
3. Humanism is a philosophy of reason and science in the pursuit of knowledge. Therefore, when it comes to the question of the most valid means of acquiring knowledge of the world, human-

ists reject arbitrary faith, authority, revelation and altered states of consciousness.

4. Humanism is a philosophy of imagination. Humanists recognize that intuitive feelings, hunches, speculation, flashes of inspiration, emotion, altered states of consciousness and even religious experience, while not valid means to acquire knowledge, remain useful sources of ideas that can lead us to new ways of looking at the world. After rationally assessing these ideas for their usefulness, they can then be put to work, often as alternate approaches for solving a problem.
5. Humanism is a philosophy for the here and now. Humanists regard human values as making sense only in the context of human life rather than in the promise of a supposed life after death.
6. Humanism is a philosophy of compassion. Humanist ethics is solely concerned with meeting human needs and answering human problems—for both the individual and society—and devotes no attention to the satisfaction of the desires of supposed theological entities.
7. Humanists recognize the existence of moral dilemmas and the need for careful consideration of immediate and future consequences in moral decision-making.
8. Humanism is in tune with the science of today. Humanists, therefore, recognize that we live in a natural universe of great size and age, that we evolved on this planet over a long period of time, and that human beings have certain built-in needs that effectively form the basis for any human-oriented value system.
9. Humanism is in tune with today's enlightened social thought. Humanists are committed to civil liberties; human rights; church-state separation; the extension of participatory democracy, not only in government but in the workplace and education; an expansion of global consciousness and exchange of products and ideas internationally.
10. Humanism is in tune with new technological developments. Humanists are willing to take part in emerging scientific and technological discoveries in order to exercise their moral influence on these revolutions as they come about, especially in the interest of protecting the environment.

11. Humanists take responsibility for their own lives and relish the adventure of being part of new discoveries, seeking knowledge, exploring new options (Edwords, 1989, p. 7)

In summary, humanists are in love with life. Though some would suggest those who claim to follow a humanist pathway are limited and eccentric, history indicates otherwise. Among the modern adherents of humanism are Margaret Sanger, the founder of Planned Parenthood, Carl Rogers, Abraham Maslow and Albert Einstein.

How Does Humanism Look?

The best way to think about humanism is to look at who has been proclaimed a humanist and what they have accomplished. For example, in 1962 the Humanist of the Year Award went to the first director of UNESCO (the UN organization promoting education, science and culture), Julian Huxley, who drafted UNESCO's charter by himself. Brock Chrisholm, the first director-general of WHO, was the 1959 Humanist of the Year. One of this organization's greatest accomplishments was the eradication of small pox from the face of the earth. Betty Friedan's and Gloria Steinem's fights for women's rights, Mathilde Krim's battle against the AIDS epidemic and Margaret Atwood's advocacy for literary freedom are all good examples of Humanists.

Even though this list of humanists and their accomplishments is awesome, it must be remembered that many others in small and simple ways are also doing incredible things for others and for the betterment of mankind. They are doing it because of their love of others, because of the challenge it presents and because it is just common nature to do so. Further, it brings personal meaning to them and inspiration to others.

Is there a risk to being a humanist? Probably, but because these people are self-directed and move on hunches and intuition, they are able to defend their right to choose other ways, to speak and write freely, and to live their lives according to their own beliefs. Could we imagine the world today without the contributions of Margaret Sanger, who was imprisoned for her activities, or without the knowledge surfaced by Maslow and Carl Rogers, or the insight and discoveries generated by Einstein? Probably not!

HOW DOES THE HUMANISTIC APPROACH FIT INTO THE CAREER CREATION PROCESS?

A return to Chapter 4 provides the framework for seeing how being a humanist or an opportunist fits into career building. While many consider the shape and direction of a career and learn more about it, most humanists simply move into something because they are drawn by interest, desire or a passion for the work. Clearly, Margaret Sanger had a passion to see women and children experience a better life after she witnessed so much misery, sickness and ignorance of women who could not adequately care for their children. She was also drawn forward to create change because there was such a need for education. Did she consider a career pathway? Probably not, but she devoted a lifetime to seeing that things changed. Was it easy? Not in the least, for she fought a society that did not want women educated about contraception and the control of births. She only knew she wanted to see things improve for women so they could, through education, determine their own life pathway.

Being a humanist does not mean a career cannot be developed, maintained or changed. It simply means the approach to doing the above is driven by a distinct but personal reason. Unlike those who seek a job because of opportunity or salary, the humanist seeks to fulfill self by helping others or humanity. A distinct pathway is pursued, change in the individual occurs, and balance between work and play must be considered. While it might not be fair to say there is no balance, humanistic approaches to career building often consume the individual as the passion for seeing change often becomes a major part of the self.

Determining Readiness for Change Using a Humanistic Approach

Because today's humanists are in tune with social thought, readiness is often determined by what happens and what is needed in the world. They seem to have a sixth sense about what is needed and are willing to expend considerable energy in the pursuit of that quest. The story of a nurse in Chapter 12 is a good example of how a nurse has been drawn into positions and has pursued an education dependent on what was going on in the environment and in the world and what grabbed his attention and interest. His current interest in those "crossing the border" is a good example of how a career can move one into different and needed areas because of the individual's openness to seeing or creating change.

It appears readiness for change for a humanist is related to what is available and what activities they value. Clearly, Margaret Sanger is a good example and so are the lives and passions of Clara Barton and Florence Nightingale. All three women devoted their lives to seeing the health of the various populations improved.

Searching for a Humanistic Position

It is hard to imagine a humanist searching for a position. They often create positions or take on positions others find too difficult or too demanding because they demonstrate a societal need. Yet, it surely demands alertness and a link with others in the field to know what is needed and where to go to find the opportunities. Those with humanistic approaches need some of the same search skills used by others. As the nurse in Chapter 12 described, moving to New Mexico was not in search of a position that offered humanistic opportunities. It was after he had been there awhile that he noted the need for certain things to happen for the Mexicans trying to cross the border. Since that realization, he has been deeply involved in the education of Mexicans and in helping them gain access to the U.S. Nearly every professional move he has made was the result of something happening in his life that touched his values and moved him into activities that he has a passion for.

CHARACTERISTICS NEEDED TO SUCCEED WHEN USING HUMANISTIC APPROACHES

In the last few years, with the instability of the work world, a new model of work called "career self-reliance" has been adopted. Originally it was defined as "the attitude of being self-employed, whether inside or outside an organization." This definition was later modified to make it more palatable to the consumer as "the ability to actively manage one's work life and learning in a rapidly changing environment" (Collard, Epperheimer, & Saign, 1996). In either definition, the underlying assumption is that the individual must think of self as his own corporation. As Scott Cook, chairman of Intuit and champion of self-reliance, has stated, "Workers should no longer expect their employers to take care of them, but now must take personal responsibility for managing their work lives" (Cook, 1996).

Career self-reliance contains some useful principles that work especially well for those who pursue work from a humanistic framework. The principles are:

- The individual is the primary architect of his or her work life. Responsibility for the design and direction of the career is in the hands of the individual.
- Continuous learning is necessary in order to stay current.
- Workers must be willing to stretch beyond the boundaries of what is needed and be willing to take on more and new tasks. Flexibility and adaptation to change are paramount (Waterman, Waterman, & Collard, 1994).

Primary Architect of the Job

A basic principle that all people who approach work from a humanist perspective know is that their work is their responsibility. Taking personal responsibility fosters feelings of competence and control over one's life. It also encourages active thinking about what kind of work would be satisfying while stimulating a synthesis of unique kinds of work. Clearly, the work of Margaret Sanger, Florence Nightingale and Gloria Steinem was unique, satisfying and different. So much so that they angered others, fought battles to support their ideals and expectations, and took responsibility for whatever occurred.

While not an easy road to travel, taking responsibility for the job also has the potential for strengthening the individual who may need to fight many battles, justify actions and, as Sanger did, spend some time in jail. Florence Nightingale was a stronger woman and a more powerful leader as the result of her adventures in the Crimean War. The nurse in Chapter 12 will undoubtedly be a more knowledgeable, stronger advocate as the result of his actions on the border.

Continuous Learning

Regardless of the approach to a job change, one must continue to keep abreast of the fast and ever-changing workplace. As certain careers become more specialized, it is wise for workers to stay current in their fields through continuing education classes, certification and degree programs, and relationships with mentors. In addition, learning today is so much easier with online courses and distance education methodologies. Whether the approach is humanistic or opportunistic, the worker must continue to stay current.

Flexibility in Managing One's Work Life

The greatest value of a humanistic approach to work is that the individual usually understands the value and need for flexibility. Being able to stretch beyond the boundaries of the job and take on new and different tasks are essential, for the individual may find him/herself in a leadership role or be faced with more than was expected. With work no longer predictable and societal needs expanding, the individual must be ready for the changing needs of an employer while keeping a clear sense of self and direction. The worker of today must be able to adapt to change.

The "values-driven" tenet of career self-reliance helps workers discern their priorities, and they can use this information to determine the appropriate work content and work setting. In 1909, the prevailing career-counseling model was the "trait and factor" approach developed by Frank Parsons (Brown, Brooks, & Associates, 1990). This model was based on the belief that workers and jobs each had a unique set of characteristics or traits. Career counselors tried to match workers with the appropriate job. The closer the match between personal characteristics and job requirements, the greater the likelihood of worker satisfaction and work productivity. In the 1990s, values clarification was strongly emphasized in order to match the worker with a suitable occupation. Today, the model is suggesting something different, the ability to move from this job to that one and to adapt to either using one's own skills, whether new or old.

According to Byster (n.d.), rather than being a new paradigm, career self-reliance is a collection of old useful approaches, repackaged to help individuals cope with a looser social contract between the employer and the worker. The model is criticized for creating isolation for the employee, forcing the employee to take blame for failure when so many factors are out of the control of the individual, and dismissing the value of loyalty between worker and employer. Some also believe there is a double message in the model.

> *The career self-reliance model emphasizes finding one's core values. Yet, why would employees discern their core values if they are simultaneously expected to change themselves continuously to thrive in the*

marketplace? According to career self-reliance, the top performers will be those who can adapt to the employer's changing needs. The model issues contradictory instructions. "Find out who you are, then ignore these insights and mold yourself to the employer's needs" (Waterman, Waterman, & Collard, 1994, pp. 89-90).

Even with these criticisms, the self-reliance model seems to fit the person who approaches a job from a humanistic perspective, because these individuals function from a strong sense of who they are, select positions responsive to their values, and are flexible and able to cope with change. Rather than a career pathway, they create careers. Sometimes the careers complement one another and sometimes they are quite different.

CONCLUSION

In this chapter, the authors attempted to describe a humanistic approach to career development. In retrospect, this direction may not have adequately accomplished the task. It is hard to see self as a Florence Nightingale or a Gloria Steinem or a Margaret Sanger, but if we were to roll back time, we could easily identify with these individuals as they began their quest for change. They knew what they wanted, and they had the knowledge and skill to pursue their goals. But on the way, they had to elicit the help of many others, and this is where it is easy to see how they were able to pursue a dream, take the flack they did and still keep going. Getting help must not be understated, for it takes more than one to do what they did.

It is this ability to elicit help from others that made these pioneers for equality and a better life able to accomplish what now looks like a tremendous set of events. But it was all based on their ability to move with their values and to never lose sight of what they wanted to accomplish. It was their humanistic perspective and approaches that drove them forward and kept them focused when times became difficult.

REFERENCES

Brown, D., Brooks, L. & Associates. (1990). *Career choice and development* (2nd ed.). San Francisco, CA: Jossey-Bass.

Byster, D. (n.d.). *A critique of career self-reliance.* Retrieved January 13, 2003, from byster@best.com;http://www.best.com/-byster.

Collard, B.A., Epperheimer, J.W., & Saign, D. (1996). *Career resilience in a changing workplace.* Adapted from Information Series #366. Washington, DC: ERIC Clearinghouse on Adult, Career and Vocational Educational Center on Education and Training for Employment.

Cook, S. (1996). *Self-reliance is the new reality of work, competition, companies and life.* Edited transcript of speech by Scott Cook at the 14th Annual Pinnacle Luncheon sponsored by the Career Action Center.

Edwords, F. (1989). *What is humanism?* Presentation given to various audiences over the years. Available from American Humanist Association, P.O. Box 1188, Amherst, NY 14226-7188

Maslow, A. (1987). *Motivation and personality* (3rd ed.). New York, NY: Harper & Row.

Waterman, R.H., Waterman, J.A., & Collard, B.A. (1994). Toward a career-resilient workforce. *Harvard Business Review*, pp. 87-95.

Chapter 8

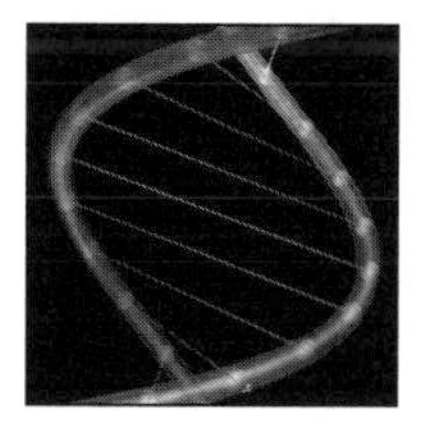

The Opportunistic Career Pathway

by Fay L. Bower & Robinetta Wheeler

INTRODUCTION

How individuals are socialized to a profession is important. Benner (2001) has described the process of socialization from novice to expert, but little is available about the pre-socialization process. What attracts a person to a specific profession or career? How does one know about careers or vocational choices? Often it is happenstance, as a result of personal contacts. Or it may be by way of a portrayal of someone in the profession, such as an autobiographical work. Writers such as Studs Terkel (1997) introduced us to the lives of workers in numerous professions. It may be the result of a horrific event such as "9/11" when the heroic acts of firefighters and others were placed forefront by the news media. Finally, we may be exposed to being a professional, like a nurse, at a time of illness, our own or a family member or friend.

Accounts of why people seek or accept a job can be categorized into opportunistic or humanistic approaches. This chapter is devoted to a discussion about opportunity as an approach to a career. The authors provide definitions, characteristics, and the advantages and disadvantages for an opportunistic pathway to a career. While the opportunistic approach is different from a humanistic approach, there are times when the job seeker may use one or the other; however, the literature suggests the approach used has a lot to do with the person and what that person values and believes about self and life.

DEFINITION OF OPPORTUNISTIC APPROACHES

According to the Oxford Dictionary and Thesaurus (Oxford University Press, 1996), opportunity is defined as "a chance or opening offered by circumstances" (p. 1045). A job and even a career can be the result of an opportunity that occurred by chance or is the outcome of certain circumstances. For instance,

> *I never knew what I wanted to be ... [after high school graduation]. It did not take many days working as a waitress to decide "waiting on tables" wasn't for me. Then one day I heard a nurse telling the clerk at the supermarket about her activities in the Peace Corps. She told him they were looking for nurses. I asked her how I could become a nurse, and four years later, I found myself in Guatamala doing what I do today, nursing.*

While this story is an example of how certain circumstances helped a young woman make a career decision, there are many, many stories about how people find their career using opportunistic strategies. But let's look further at the characteristics of opportunistic approaches and their advantages and disadvantages.

WHAT IS AN OPPORTUNISTIC APPROACH TO A CAREER?

Hemsley-Brown and Foskett (1999), in their article titled *Gambling in the Careers Lottery: A Consumer Approach to Career Choice*, proclaim after extensive study that complex processes and perspectives are at work in career decision-making. "The macro-scale character of the labor market can be seen as the sum of long- and short-term decision making by individuals" (p. 421). They found the assumption that young people make choices based on need to acquire the skills most in demand in the labor market was not supported. They also discovered most young people do not seek a job because of their parents' history as workers, but because they are ambitious for themselves and seek to maximize personal fulfillment and an enhanced lifestyle. They categorized young people's career choices based on the intrinsic characteristics of the jobs chosen and named them:

- Lottery jobs
- High-status jobs
- Customary jobs

Lottery Jobs

These occupations are unusual jobs that rely on luck, chance and being "talent spotted." Such occupations include sportsmen/women, famous actors and actresses, and rare or unusual jobs such as a TV news reader. Many, if not all, lottery jobs are high-status jobs in the sports and the arts. From the job seeker's perspective, these jobs offer substantial financial rewards and high status. Potential entrants to these jobs are able to remain hopeful that they might "win" a top job without going through the formal rejection and selection processes associated with higher education.

High-Status Jobs

Jobs in this category are typically among the professions, such as physicians, dentists and lawyers, and usually require academic qualifications. Based on the analysis of Hemsley-Brown and Foskett (1997), it would be accurate to assume that people in this category will find themselves actually doing the job they have chosen for themselves. Even though the labor market may change in the next century with a focus on service jobs, these jobs will still be available and popular for those who pursue them.

Customary Jobs

Customary jobs are occupations that most people have. They include service jobs, clerical jobs, computing jobs, teachers, nurses, managers, etc. These jobs are occupations that are most likely to be available in the labor market. A majority of the workforce occupy these jobs.

Given what we know about the job market today and how it is likely to change in the future, and using these categories as a framework for differentiating humanistic from opportunistic approaches, it would appear that customary and lottery jobs are subject to opportunistic behavior. Given the possibility that the intent and devotion to humanistic values were not present, some of those in high-status jobs could also be considered opportunistic job seekers.

CHARACTERISTICS OF OPPORTUNITY AS AN APPROACH TO JOB SELECTION

Opportunity has many faces. It is often characterized, like the story above, as a result of certain circumstances, or it can occur because of timing, rewards and/or advancement. For example, the present nursing shortage offers many opportunities that are related to timing and to rewards. The time for opportunity could not be better. This means the individual, prone to making job decisions based on opportunity, has many options to consider before accepting a job. The story below illustrates how timing can be a determinant of opportunity even when the present job is satisfying:

> *I wasn't really interested in leaving my present job. I liked my colleagues, and I really loved the work. But, I was offered a chance to see the world as a "travel nurse" if I accepted the position. I did accept the offer, and I am glad I did because I have had an incredible experience and have learned so much about different areas of the globe and the different cultures in those areas. It is going to be hard for me to return to what I did, so I will just wait for the next good opportunity.*

This story also demonstrates how travel nursing, one of the many solutions to the nurse shortage, has become an opportunity that was not available before the nurse shortage.

Benefits have always been a part of opportunity. Benefits can also have many faces. In the world of healthcare today, benefits come in the form of bonuses, educational reimbursement, forgiveable loans, flexible hours, better retirement, etc. Nurses are bombarded daily with opportunities to work hours that are more flexible, return to school at the expense of the employer if they will return the offer with a promise to work longer at the present site, and offers of huge bonuses if they will move from the present site to another. The issue is not about having opportunities but knowing which one to accept.

Another characteristic of opportunity is the chance for advancement. Some people accept opportunities because they will advance their careers. "I went back to school to get my BSN so I could do public health work, something I hadn't thought about until money was available for school costs. As a result of that school experience, I am now working on my master's degree as a family nurse practitioner."

Advantages of Using Opportunity as a Pathway to a Career

The biggest advantage of using an opportunistic approach to job acceptance is the availability of positions now available for nurses. The slow but continuing move of healthcare from the hospital into the community has created a plethora of nurse opportunities. Nurses now work in homes, clinics, hospice, industry, insurance companies; with book publishers and architectural firms; and for themselves. Opportunities abound if the nurse is educationally prepared and open to change.

The second advantage of using an opportunistic approach to job selection is the chance to experience a variety of jobs. Generally speaking, those people who pursue a humanistic approach follow a career of similar events, while an opportunistic approach allows for whatever is available and acceptable to the individual. For instance:

> *Over the last 10 years, I have had a variety of jobs. I started as a staff nurse and then moved to another hospital as a charge nurse. Then I functioned as a hospice nurse. While doing that job, I had the opportunity to do some part-time teaching, which I loved so much I went back to school to get a master's degree. Now I am working for an insurance company doing case management. I plan on going back to school for a doctoral degree and then into research. All of these jobs came to me as opportunities I just couldn't reject.*

The third advantage of using opportunity as a way of seeking positions is the sense one gets of being current and employable. After having a variety of jobs that were pursued as the result of opportunity, the job seeker usually has acquired a number of skills and gained an understanding of a variety of care problems and solutions. This accumulation of variety and new knowledge just makes a person more marketable and hungry for more activity.

Disadvantages of Using Opportunity as a Pathway to a Career

Like every activity, there are disadvantages to procuring a job using opportunistic methods. The major problem with opportunistic decision-making is what is known as "defaulting." Defaulting is a process whereby the individual revises his or her career aspiration (usually downward) (Hemsley-Brown & Foskett, 1999). Because of an opportunity, the individual accepts something that is not as satisfying over time or is beneath what they can do. It is possible these career decisions are made in a haphazard manner rather than in an entirely economically rational way, and it is clear that the issue of who makes the "default" decision, when and why is tied to complex issues of personal history, personality and responsiveness to "environmental signals" (Hodkinson & Sparkes, 1997).

Another disadvantage of opportunistic decision-making about a job is the risk of accepting a position because it is considered a good place to work, given what the recruiter says, when in fact it is not. Opportunities in healthcare abound but, they all are suffering from like problems. To accept a position without careful assessment is nothing more than trading sites.

And while employers do not reject a resume with frequent job shifts, if there is more than one applicant for the position, the one with a more stable work history will have the advantage.

Frequent job shifts based on opportunity can be detrimental if a career in a selected area is desired. There is lot to say about staying in the same speciality area and working "up the ladder." Known as "job migrating," frequent shifting from job to job because of opportunity can create a string of jobs rather than a career (Michaels, Handfield-Jones, & Axelrod, 2001).

HOW DOES THE OPPORTUNISTIC APPROACH FIT INTO THE CAREER CREATION PROCESS

Most opportunistic job seekers "back" into their careers. Because they are not actively seeking a position and planning but instead "reacting to an offer," their approach to the career creation process is to let it develop. In addition, unlike their counterparts, the humanists, who are passionately pursuing what interests them, which often drives them to change, opportunistic job seekers are willing to move on if a better job offer comes their way.

Being an opportunistic job seeker does not mean a career cannot be developed or maintained. A career can be created, but it is motivated by what is available and attractive and not by what one values as a way to fulfill self by helping others. The career is more likely to unfold than to be created. In addition, as for balance, opportunists can be just as involved in the job as the humanists, but in the opportunists' case, the involvement is usually because of external reward rather than an internal one.

Determining Readiness for Change Using an Opportunistic Approach

The best way to explain opportunistic readiness is by the story below of a nurse who had an incredible offer she should not have accepted.

> *I was a critical care nurse and loved my job. It was during an evaluation of my performance that my manager asked me to take her job. She had talked about retiring, but no one thought she would do so. I was flattered and said sure. It wasn't long before I discovered I knew nothing about being a manager. I was overwhelmed and hated to go to work. When a nurse manager across town offered me a job in the CCU, I took the opportunity to move on. Boy did I learn a lesson! I should have thought about getting prepared for the job by going back to school. But since I do not want more schooling, I returned to what I do best.*

Readiness for change, whether the job is the same or different, must be assessed. No matter how good the offer, it is imperative the individual think about what is needed for quality performance. Unfortunately, many opportunists are swayed and enticed into jobs because the salary is good or the bonuses are extreme or they are unhappy with the current position. This inability to determine readiness is one of the downsides of being an opportunist. There will always be opportunities. The trick is to be able to select the one that is right and that will provide an opportunity for success.

CHARACTERISTICS NEEDED TO SUCCEED WHEN USING OPPORTUNISTIC APPROACHES

Probably the best way to avoid the kind of experience the nurse had in the story above is to balance opportunity with readiness. Not every opportunity is a good choice. In addition, salary is but one kind of expectation. The ability to evaluate self to meet the requirements of the opportunity is a learned skill and one that involves an evaluation of the following:

- What skills and knowledge are necessary for completing the responsibilities of the job?
- Do I need additional schooling?
- What amount of time will the new position demand?
- What kind of support do I have during the transition from one job to the other?
- What help is available for me at the new position?
- Will my life in this new position have balance, that is, will there be time for family and friends?
- What rewards will this new job provide?
- How will I be oriented to this job?
- Are the demands of the job worth the rewards gained?

Clearly, such an evaluation requires input from others and an opportunity to think about the answers before accepting the job. Sometimes the opportunity is so enticing the job seeker forgets to step back and review the answers to these questions before giving a response.

CONCLUSION

In this chapter, the authors described an opportunistic approach to the development of a career. Nurse stories were used to illustrate the points. A framework developed by Hemsley-Brown and Foskett (1999) was used to describe the kinds of careers that are often offered to opportunists. To complete this chapter, the authors want to provide another perspective as the most useful way to use opportunistic hiring in a world of change.

In the book *The War for Talent,* Michaels, Handfield-Jones and Axelrod (2001) offer the following about opportunistic hiring, which has implications for those interested in an opportunistic approach to career development.

> *Opportunistic hiring may seem a little strange, but we've found three ways to make it work. First, identify the kind of job a candidate would fit and court that person until one of those jobs becomes available.*
>
> *Second, hire the person with a specific position in mind, even though the slot is not currently open. While the person is waiting for that position, he or she can be doing special projects and get to know the organization. Third, create or earmark certain jobs that are suitable for mid-to-senior-level hires. . . . Keep people in these intake jobs only for a short time so they are vacated for the next incoming hire (p. 8).*

Given these steps, the individual who is inclined to accept an opportunity for a job can feel more comfortable when making the decision to accept the job knowing that employers are trying various ways to make opportunistic career development work.

REFERENCES

Benner, P. (2001). *From novice to expert: Excellence and power in clinical nursing practice.* Upper Saddle River, NJ: Prentice Hall.

Hemsley-Brown, J., & Foskett, N.H. (1999). *Higher education awareness among year 6 pupils in Hampshire Schools.* Southhampton, United Kingdom: Heist Publications.

Hodkinson, P. & Sparkes, A. (1997). Careership: A sociological theory of career decision-making. *British Journal of Sociology of Education,* 18, 29-44.

Michaels, E., Handfield-Jones, H., & Axelrod, B. (2001). T*he war for talent.* New York, NY: McGraw-Hill.

Oxford University Press. (1996, American Edition). *The Oxford dictionary and thesaurus.* New York, NY: Author.

Terkel, S. (1997). *Working: People talk about what they do all day and how they feel about what they do.* New York, NY: New Press, University of New York.

Chapter 9

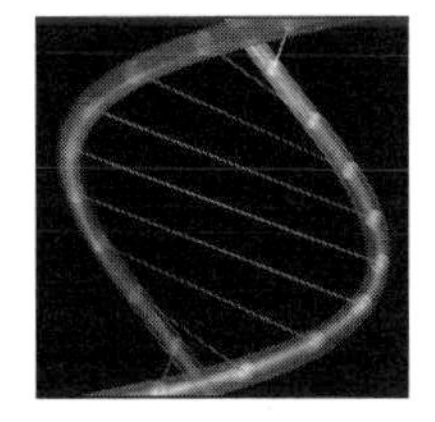

Achieving Balance

by Fay L. Bower

How many people on their deathbed wish they'd spent more time at the office? (Covey, Merrill, & Merrill, 1996).

INTRODUCTION

Career/personal life balance is achieved differently by everyone. The previous two chapters covered two different ways to approach the development or change of a career (opportunistic or humanistic). Clearly, the career builder does not use one or the other approach but often balances the approach against other issues. This chapter covers one of those other issues: specifically the balance of work time with personal time. Like approach, the ability to select a position that will provide balance between work and personal time is important. The following discussion focuses on a definition of balance, why balance is important, how work/personal life balance was born, a model for balance, what makes achieving balance hard, and what to do to develop or change a career that will help balance work with personal life.

DEFINITION OF BALANCE

Balance is defined in many ways, but for the purposes of this discussion it is "to bring into or keep in equilibrium" "the ability to strike a happy medium" (Oxford University Press, 1996, p. 101). According to Epstein (2002a), balance has several characteristics, such as:

- It is not a constant, it comes and goes as things change in life.
- It has to be worked at.

- The process of seeking balance can be stimulating and a true learning experience about what is important.

These characteristics suggest it takes work to stay balanced and that it does not necessarily have to be a feared or negative process.

WHY IS BALANCE IMPORTANT?

The events of September 11, 2001, and the declining economy that followed have changed how people think and feel. Since that tragic event, many people are looking for greater meaning in their lives, and that includes greater flexibility in their work lives, which might entail working from home or having more personal days or more vacation days or just more time with family and friends.

Uncertain times make everyone more introspective and more focused on things that really matter. And the one value Americans are talking about today is quality time for themselves and their families. Employers are also concerned. Though most businesses, governments and nonprofit organizations are focusing on how to save money, they are also concerned about how to recruit new staff and retain their best workers who often make up the skeleton staff of workers after massive layoffs and downsizing. According to Kleiman (2002), a survey by Metlife determined 58% of employers see programs that help workers achieve balance as one of their most important strategies for retention of employees.

HOW WORK/PERSONAL LIFE BALANCE WAS BORN

The focus on balance of work and personal life began in the 1970s when women entered the workforce in great numbers. Men had long had the advantage of having a spouse at home full time to care for all household and family responsibilities. However, the huge number of women working full time or part time changed that situation. The women's movement that swept the country in the 1970s forced attention to be placed on issues such as child care, flexible hours and sharing family responsibilities in the home.

Men have also become sensitized to the fact that children need fathers, so they began to ask for flexible hours and time off to attend parent-teacher meetings, be soccer dads, enjoy their children's children, and relax a bit themselves. Since this movement toward time with family, work/personal life balance has become a way of life for women and men alike.

This attitude and value for work/personal life balance is also held important by other groups. A majority of undergraduates name it as their top career goal; single people say they have a right to it; and Generation Y, the 29 million Americans born from 1981 and on, are extremely vocal about their desire to have the demands of work fit the demands for personal time. Even executives want a life. According to Kleiman (2002), 82% of marketing directors struggle to get balance between their professional and private lives.

Appelbaum, Bailey, Berg and Kalleberg (2002) claim workplaces in the U.S., while trying to make change, are in a "time warp." Their research indicates the way work is scheduled and done in the U.S. is drastically out of step with the reality of workers' lives. In the book *Manufacturing Advantage: Why High-Performance Work Systems Pay Off,* the authors describe how work in other countries fits better with the lives of the people.

MODEL FOR WORK/PERSONAL LIFE BALANCE

One way to characterize balance is to contrast two powerful tools that direct us: the clock and the compass (Covey, Merrill, & Merrill, 1996). The clock represents commitment, appointments, schedules, goals and activities—what is done and how time is managed. The compass represents our vision, values, principles, mission, conscience and direction—what is deemed important and how life is pursued. The struggle begins when there is a gap between the clock and the compass—when what is accomplished doesn't contribute to what is most important as determined by the individual.

For some, this gap is intense. There is a feeling of being trapped, controlled by the job to be done or others' expectations. There is constant need to "get it done." It feels like life is being defined by others. For others, the pain is a vague discomfort. There is an inability to pull things together, that is, to do what should be done, what one wants to do and what is actually done. There is guilt over what is done, so there is no joy in what is accomplished.

Some just feel empty. Happiness is defined solely in terms of professional or financial achievement, and the success reached does not bring the satisfaction it was supposed to deliver. It is like climbing the ladder of success rung by rung—the diploma, the late nights, the promotions—only to discover at the top of the ladder that it is leaning against the wrong wall. Absorbed in the ascent, a trail of shattered relationships or missed moments of deep and rich living are left in the wake of an intense, over-focused effort.

Others feel disoriented or confused. There is no real sense of what comes first. Time is spent completing one thing and then another automatically. Life becomes mechanical. Real meaning is lost. Every now and then, there is a search for the meaning of what is happening.

WHAT MAKES IT HARD TO ACHIEVE CLOCK/COMPASS BALANCE?

While the clock/compass paradigm explains the way balance can be achieved, there are many who find it hard to alter their behavior to comply with the paradigm. The following list provides a few of the reasons:

- Inability to say "no"
- Work is pleasure
- Financial need
- Need for recognition
- Inability to delegate

Inability to Say "No"

There are some people who find pleasure in helping others to the point of harming themselves. These are the people who cannot say "no" when asked to take a job or complete a task. Sometimes their saying "yes" gets them into situations that take more time than they had envisioned, and they find themselves in a "workaholic" mode. While it would seem obvious they need to do something to relieve the work load, they simply cannot for two reasons: (1) they enjoy what they are doing and (2) they cannot bring themselves to disappoint others. They complain, fret and sometimes get sick with too much time spent on work when they would rather spend it in play. The problem is they like what they do but find it using too much of their personal time.

Work is Pleasure

A real trap that engulfs many is the job that is so enjoyable it takes up most of one's time. Getting balance between work and personal time when the job is fun or rewarding is hard to accomplish. In fact, having a job that is pleasurable is hard to limit, particularly if the pleasure of the job overrides the pleasure of personal time. Even so, these people also complain about having no personal time and are vocal about wanting the day to be more than 24 hours so they can have more time for the family. One would have to question if more time is the solution or whether a re-examination of values is the best way for these people to reach a better balance.

Financial Need

The biggest reason, as determined by many surveys, for a lack of balance between work and personal time is money. Single parents, low-income families, and people with little education or skills simply cannot pay their bills unless they devote much time to work. Work for them is often not just one job but two or three jobs to "make ends meet." The rising cost of living and the need to pay for child care has created a work life that consumes most of their time.

Recognition

There are some people who work long hours and have little personal time because their jobs provide the recognition they cannot acquire elsewhere. Feeling important, being rewarded for a good job and having a need for attention keep these people "on the job" for many hours. In many ways, the job becomes the focus of their lives and provides for the family or friends they may not have. However, they too complain of having no time for self. Frequently, these people create a surrogate family of the people they work with and while at work are happy. Yet, they realize work should not become one's life, so they too seek ways to find personal time, not for family or friends, but to seek solitude or other adventures.

Inability to Delegate

A common problem for some people that makes their work life consuming is the inability to delegate. People who do not delegate often have a need to control or have a lack of trust in their subordinates, so jobs that could be accomplished by others are done by them. Being able to delegate means the work tasks are assigned to those who can best do the job. However, there are people who find it hard to assign tasks, because they doubt the abilities of others or are forced to do the tasks, because they have no one who can do the tasks in a satisfactory way. For these people to get more personal time would mean an evaluation of tasks based on employee talents, which might result in changes in who does what.

Wake-Up Calls

Some people know they are out of balance but do not have confidence in the alternatives. Others are afraid to try something else, or they feel the cost of change is too great. Sometimes the lack of balance is rudely brought to their attention by such events as illness, the death of a family member, a teenager found on drugs, company downsizing, notification of one's own impending death, or a divorce. Some crises bring an awareness that what has been going on with time use does not match one's values.

In the absence of a "wake-up call," many never really confront the critical issues of life. Instead of looking for deep chronic causes, quick-fixes are used to treat the acute pain. Fortified by temporary relief, the individual gets busier doing things and never even stops to ask if what is being done really matters.

WAYS TO ACHIEVE CLOCK/COMPASS BALANCE

Anything less than a conscious commitment to the important is an unconscious commitment to the unimportant (Anonymous).

Time Management

In an effort to close the gap between the clock and the compass, aside from changing jobs and/or evaluating whether the time spent is in line with one's values, many people turn to time management. According to Covey, Merrill and Merrill (1996), there are three generations of time management. Each one builds on the one before it and moves toward greater efficiency.

First Generation Time Management

First generation time managers organize time with reminders. They are characterized by notes and checklists. They try to keep track of time by listing tasks that need to be accomplished, such as prepare a Power Point, attend the undergraduate council meeting, prepare the graduate announcements, call the vet for an appointment for the dog, rent a Halloween costume, etc. At the end of the day, the list is reviewed to determine if all the tasks were accomplished.

Second Generation Time Management

Second generation time managers are characterized by calendars, appointment books and palm computers. Efficiency, personal responsibility and achievement of goals are valued by second generation time managers. Goal setting, planning ahead and scheduling future events are the focus. People in this generation make appointments, write down commitments, identify deadlines and note where they should be at certain times.

Third Generation Time Management

Third generation time managers are characterized as planners, prioritizers and controllers. Values are clarified and prioritized by asking, "What do I want?" Long-, medium- and short-range goals are set to meet these values. All of this is done on a daily basis by electronic means, as well as on paper.

In many ways, these three generations of time managers have brought us a long way toward increased efficiency and a balance of the clock and compass paradigm. However, a gap still remains between what is deeply important to each individual and the way time is spent. In many cases the gap has been exacerbated—we are getting more done in less time, but the rich relationships, the inner peace, the balance, the confidence that we are doing what matters most is still missing.

Workplace Benefits

Finding the proper balance between work and personal time often depends on what the workplace offers. Many employers offer an array of benefits that include those that help the worker perform at the highest level while not impinging on personal time.

Child care, elder care, optional hours, advancement, wellness programs and fitness centers, and sabbaticals are the kinds of benefits the worker should expect if balance between work and personal time is to occur.

A company that has on-site child care or child care off-site for its employees clearly understands the value of providing incentives. Child care can be provided in four ways: (1) on-site child care, which is the most expensive even when the employee pays; (2) paid or partially paid child care at an outside facility that the company might have a vested interest in; (3) child-care referral services that help workers find quality, low-cost and convenient child-care services; or (4) pre-tax dollars for child care, which signals a company's interest in the workers and their needs.

Elder care is becoming increasingly important for baby boomers and their children and Generation Xers who have elderly parents who need care. On-site elder care, help with paying for elder care at an outside facility and elder care referral services are extremely important and helpful. Employees in the sandwich generation, caught between children who need day care and parents who need elder care, find these responsibilities are completely different. Elder care is far more demanding and stressful, because it is usually so unpredictable. Employers who recognize and provide some kind of child and elder care help are most likely to have productive employees, because these services relieve employee anxiety and allow for more attention to the job.

Many companies are clearly moving toward offering employees a selection of "work-day possibilities." Flex hours, job sharing and part-time professionals allow people to select the hours they want to devote to work. Employee choice is an important aspect of governing the clock/compass balance.

Many employees want to know if the company provides advancement and how one qualifies for "moving up." Companies that have women advancing through the ranks are companies that are generally open to the balancing needs most women have. And given the changes in the ways a family functions, it is also something men are interested in, that is, advancing while devoting time to family.

On-site wellness programs and fitness facilities or paid or partially paid memberships in outside programs/facilities are very popular benefits savvy companies are offering to relieve worker stress and to keep them in good health. Most workers are enthusiastic about having a place to workout or swim, because it is what they like to do and it keeps them fit.

Sabbaticals, a feature of college and university life for professors, are now being offered by private organizations and businesses. A sabbatical is most often offered to employees who have been with the company for five years or more and are usually a paid leave of from three months to one year. It's a time of renewal and even recovery for exhausted workers who typically return to work after the absence with renewed vigor and commitment.

Today's employers are open to creative solutions that help employees successfully juggle all the elements of their lives. Some of the innovations include:

- Ability to "buy" and "sell" vacation days
- Discounted travel arrangements

- Tickets for theater and sporting events
- Dry cleaning services
- Auto tune-ups and car washing at reduced rates
- Transportation and commuting discounts
- Massages in the office at the worker's desk
- Catering services
- Pets brought to the workplace
- Financial and retirement planning
- Rooms to relax in

It appears that work/personal life benefits are here to stay. Even during times of increased unemployment, employers are reluctant to cut back on flexibility, because it does not cost them anything. What might take a hit are the benefits that the company pays for in full or in part. Many of these benefits are the things the wife used to do at home when the husband was the sole support of the family. They include child care, elder care, referral services, and taking kids to and from school.

Although many consulting firms are trying to help employers offer programs that help replace so-called "women's work," these programs are not expected to expand in a slow economy. But flexible scheduling, which is viewed as directly contributing to the bottom line, isn't expected to suffer at all. Instead, flexible hours and self-scheduling might even be expanded to relieve stress felt by the remaining and overworked staff at downsized companies and industries, like nursing, where there is a critical shortage.

Protective Laws and Work Arrangements

Fortunately, there are a variety of options to bring balance into the worker's life without losing or changing jobs. The Family and Medical Leave Act, part-time work, travel nurses and telecommuting are just a few of the opportunities available.

Family and Medical Leave Legislation

The Family and Medical Leave Act is probably the most important employment legislation passed in recent years. In 1993, the act was signed into law. It mandates entitlement of 12 weeks of unpaid leave each year for employees (men and women) who work for organizations with 50 or more employees. To qualify, the employee must have worked for the organization for 1,250 hours or more. There are employee advocates who are trying to change the "unpaid" to "paid" and the "50" to "15" or more employees (Kleiman, 2002).

The law guarantees the employee will have the job when s/he returns from caring for a newborn, adopted child or sick family member or from a health problem that prevented work. Healthcare and other benefits, as well as seniority, are protected while the employee is on leave. These protections mean the employee's financial and job status are secured.

Part-time Work

Reducing the work week to part time has long been a viable solution for people who do not want to work full time. In a slow economy, part-time work is plentiful because these jobs usually do not include health-care insurance or other benefits. Still, part-time work, particularly through a temporary agency, is an important option for those who want to continue earning some income, keep their skills up-to-date, and have time for other interests and responsibilities.

Travel Nurses

A popular and innovative way to balance work with fun is to be a travel nurse. Travel nurses work Monday through Friday, have weekends off and travel from one area of the country to another every 13 weeks. This work schedule allows the nurse to tour on the weekends and to see many areas of the country while maintaining a 40 hour/week position.

Telecommuting

Working from home is not only prevalent, it is a well-established way of life. And it has been possible because of new technology that adds to the advantage of having a telephone to communicate with clients, colleagues and managers with the extra advantage of using fax machines, computers, cell phones, beepers, lap tops, e-mail, Internet access, duplicating machines and scanners.

Many technology professionals say, "Why spend hours in travel to and from work when the work can be completed at home?" According to *Recruiting Trends*, "A whopping 96% of 1,953 techies surveyed indicated they want to work from home at least a few hours every week, and 39% say they would take a pay cut to be able to telecommute" (Kleiman, 2002, pp.143-144). Since September 11, 2001, virtual offices and virtual teams have become popular because more workers want to work in a safer place than in a highly visible office and they want more time with the family.

Working at home also saves time and money because there is no need to dress up and spend hours on the road. It also allows for getting the kids off to school and being there when they return. Shopping can be accomplished when the stores are not crowded, and healthcare appointments can be scheduled during the day. And the job can be completed because it is not confined to an 8 to 5 schedule.

Clearly, there are many ways to schedule work/personal life balance, but the real issue may be balancing the clock/compass phenomena, which demands an alignment of values against time. Even when the job is at home, it can consume life unless there is an assessment of what is important and how to adjust work to fit it. The next section presents ways the worker can establish this kind of balance.

WAYS TO ESTABLISH CLOCK/COMPASS BALANCE

Knowing what to do to stay balanced is important even when there are workplace benefits and laws and flexible schedules or innovative programs. Epstein (2002a) offers a list of the "top 10" ways to establish balance based on what can be done to match values with time.

1. Recognize that balancing roles is truly work in itself.
2. Take time to think about balance and how to get it this week.
3. Apply the best analytical and creative thinking to solving the task.
4. Identify needs, wants and what creates happiness—this is the ultimate barometer of balance.
5. Have faith there is a way—do not put barriers in front of possibilities.
6. Know the signs of imbalance, including resentment, fatigue, depression, dissatisfaction.
7. Flexibility is important—what worked this week may be out of whack next week—stay open to new solutions.
8. Revisit core values and live them, know what is important today.

9. Remove or delegate the things that interfere with the important stuff.
10. Find joy in the process.

This list clearly indicates gaining balance is consciously planned work. It means taking time to assess wants, needs and what creates happiness. It means knowing when balance is missing by tuning into the symptoms of imbalance. It means being able to delegate, eliminate and readjust work. Above all, it means being able to identify core values and to commit to doing what is consistent with them. And it means the process need not be negative but a positive, productive one.

Townsend (1999) has surveyed working mothers to determine the biggest work/family dilemmas. He was able to get them to identify four challenges and has provided some tips on how to solve them. The challenges identified by the mothers were:

- Needing to be in two places at once
- Getting to school and work on time
- Never having enough time
- Getting it all done

Needing to be in two places at once. Townsend suggests we should let technology work for us when it comes to being in more than one place at a time. He points out by 2004 more people will tap into the Internet through Web-based cell phones and other mobile devices rather than through personal computers. And as early as 2002, more Internet-connected wireless phones, TV set top boxes, handheld computers, network computers, Web pads and other devices were sold than personal computers.

Getting to school on time. He also suggests, as mothers did years ago, that preparation the night before is essential to avoid the hassles and fear of being late that occur when lunches must be prepared, clothes organized and backpacks organized each morning. One solution proposed was to have the children sleep in the clothes they would wear to school the next day. While the clothes may be wrinkled, the children would not be late for school. This option may seem silly, but it demonstrates what parents will do to meet deadlines or get what needs to be accomplished done on time.

Never having enough time. Having enough time means some things will have to wait or standards will need to be lowered. For instance, if the children and work are the priority, then household responsibilities will need to be done by others or not be done until there is time. That could mean lowering standards and being able to accept a little mess and a less than spotless environment.

Getting it all done. To get it all done means delegation of tasks. This might mean an assignment of tasks for mom and others for dad or the development of a support system whereby friends and family help with the tasks. It also means getting the children to help or to hire help when needed and to accept that things may not be perfect.

CONCLUSION

Reaching balance between work and personal time depends on several processes. First, balance depends on the individual wanting it. Second, it rests on the individual's ability to define a commitment to certain values. Third, it is determined by the individual's position with its demands and the identified values. And finally, it rests on the individual's ability to balance the demands with the commitment to values. This process may seem simple, but a review of the conditions and barriers to its achievement makes it a process that one has to work on. And while it may not seem worth the effort, those who have taken the time to wrestle with the clock/compass paradigm have found it worth the time it took. As Epstein (2002b) pointed out, it is up to the employee to learn about what is possible and to determine whether the effort to make what seems like a fruitless and difficult task a really worthwhile and positive experience is justified.

REFERENCES

Appelbaum, E., Bailey, T., Berg, P., & Kalleberg, A.L. (2002). *Manufacturing advantage: Why high-performance work systems pay off.* New York, NY: Cornell University Press.

Covey, S.R., Merrill, A.R., & Merrill. R.R. (1996). *First things first: To live, to love, to learn, to leave a legacy*. New York, NY: Fireside.

Epstein, S. (2002a). *What is work and family balance? And how do I get it?* Retrieved on September 28, 2002, from http://www.bluesuitmom.com/career/balance/finding blance.html.

Epstein, S. (2002b). *What does a working mom need? Support and a road to getting it*. Retrieved on September 28, 2002, from http://bluesuitmom.com/career/balance/support.html.

Kleiman, C. (2002). *Winning the game. The new rules for finding and keeping a job you want.* New York, NY: Wiley.

Oxford University Press. (1996). *The Oxford dictionary and thesaurus.* New York, NY: Author.

Townsend, L. (1999). *Top work/family challenges and solutions.* Indianapolis, IN: Jist Publishing.

Chapter 10

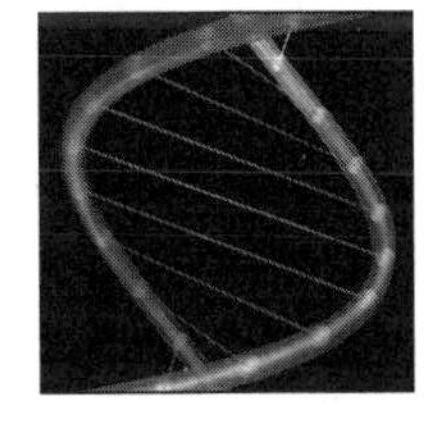

Marketplace, Culture, Politics and Timing

by Cyndi McCullough & Barbara Pille

INTRODUCTION

Job opportunities for nurses in today's marketplace are plentiful. As a matter of fact, healthcare is cited as one of the top 10 occupations to have the largest number of new jobs (Kleiman, 2002). However, if career development is the goal, looking for a job is short-sighted. Even if a job change is the goal, there are several issues to consider. Too often, individuals jump at opportunities before assessing the:

- Marketplace
- Culture and politics of the institution where the job resides
- Timing of the search

Currently, the healthcare marketplace offers many opportunities and likely will remain that way for several years. However, before accepting a position or considering making a change, the nurse should consider whether the move would provide options for growth or simply be another stressful experience in another place or at a different level. Do the culture and politics of the institution where the job resides support change, recognize talent and reward it, and promote team effort and individual initiative? Where will the new position be in the future? Is this the best time for a change? These and other questions need to be raised and answered.

This chapter contains discussions on the marketplace, culture, politics and timing as a framework for decision-making related to career/job change. Pitfalls and things to avoid, as well as recommendations for movement forward, are also provided.

MARKETPLACE

What is Happening in Healthcare?

Healthcare professionals are facing increasing demands to care for patients who are very sick, with a diminishing number of nurses and technicians and fewer financial resources. Hospital administrators are looking for ways to reduce cost and lower length of stay while increasing the ratio of patients to nurses. At the same time, consumers are concerned about medical incidents and are looking for hospitals that are more family-centered and offer easy accessibility, convenience and privacy. Professionals are looking for better patient-to-nurse ratios and better work environments.

For-profit hospitals are actively addressing these dichotomous goals, while not-for-profit hospitals are struggling. Increases in medical errors, labor costs, union activities, costs of new technologies and facility renovations are but a few of the challenges facing healthcare executives (Goe, 2001).

Specialty hospitals of years ago have been reinstituted mostly to compete with the for-profit companies and physician joint ventures that have siphoned profitable service lines from traditional nonprofit hospitals. Traditional hospitals have created specialty centers in free-standing clinics or incorporated them within a hospital in order to compete. Because of these changes, nurse demand is particularly acute for BSN nurses and advanced practitioners (nurse practitioners and clinical nurse specialists) in key areas like critical care, neonatal nursing, emergency, surgery, and labor and delivery.

Driven by a need for control over healthcare decisions and more involvement in care, consumers are pursuing control of their healthcare choice from managed care companies. Consumers are aligning with providers who deliver the quality, access and convenience that meet their needs. The success of programs for smoking cessation, exercise, healthy diet and stress reduction has reduced the chance of death by chronic disease, which has resulted in less need for inpatient hospital stays and more intervention at the community level (Goe, 2001).

Affiliations and Mergers

The number of hospital acquisitions and mergers in the healthcare industry has increased. Factors forcing hospitals to seek affiliation with other institutions include:

- Financial and competitive pressures resulting from managed care
- Prospective payment methodologies and selective contracting initiatives
- Growth of alternative delivery systems
- Cost of technological advances
- Numbers of excess or underutilized hospital beds
- Increased competition

While mergers and acquisitions have occurred, in many instances they have not worked. In some cases, the hospitals have continued to function independently of each other, which has led to increased cost and staffing shortages. Attempts to combine distinctly different cultures takes time and effort, distracting the administrators from the original purpose of the merger—to achieve economies of scale and/or increased market share.

Evolving Changes that Affect Healthcare Services

No single trend has impacted healthcare like the growth of ambulatory care. This growth over the past 15 years has resulted from advances in technology, payment incentives, and consumer acceptance and demand. The development of safe forms of conscious sedation and the invention of endoscopes and scoping video systems has allowed many surgical procedures to be safely performed on an outpatient basis. Today, 70% of surgeries are performed on an outpatient basis nationwide. Outpatient business accounts for 45% of hospital revenue. There continues to be a shift from inpatient business to outpatient business in areas such as orthopedics, urology, gynecology and general surgery (Goe, 2001).

While small outpatient diagnostic or ambulatory surgery centers experienced growth during the '80s and '90s, the trend today, in response to the demand for more comprehensive care in a less-costly environment, appears to be the development of comprehensive complexes developed by hospitals with physicians, such as neighborhood health villages. History has proven that when ambulatory services have moved out of the hospital setting, there have been significant savings in operating costs. These savings have been attributed to several things:

- Decreased staffing costs due to streamlined processes and consolidation of functions
- Standardization of supplies
- Reduced building costs because of less-strict building codes

In addition to physician partners, hospital administrators are also exploring the development of relationships with pharmacies, supermarkets, department stores, shopping malls, schools and housing developments in order to capture more of the market. Clearly, consumer demand for technology, convenience and easy access is driving the movement to more ambulatory care.

A relatively new trend affecting the delivery of healthcare is alternative (complementary) therapies. Alternative therapies include such services as herbal remedies, massage, acupuncture, chiropractic medicine, aroma therapy, guided imagery and traditional Chinese medicine. Reasons for the increased popularity and demand for alternative therapies are:

- Consumers' desire to consider a broader range of options for effectively managing their healthcare budgets
- Desire for and expectation of wellness among the "baby boomer" generation
- Desire to decrease the side effects of medication
- Increased awareness of medical practices from other cultures
- Progression of scientific literature suggesting links among disease, nutrition, emotion and lifestyle (The Advisory Board, 2000)

Americans are now spending more money on these alternative therapies than on primary physician visits (Eisenberg et al., 1998). The demand from consumers, the proliferation of free-standing providers, the growing number of insurance companies funding such services, not to mention the enormous cash business associated with these therapies, have captured the attention of hospital administrators.

With the introduction of age-reversal drugs, genomic therapies, bioengineered organs, artificial organs and tissues, and new vaccines and antibiotics, healthcare is changing. The expectations and preferences of the baby boomers and Generation X will also transform care. Generation Xers (those people born between 1963 and 1977) comprise between 10% and 15% of the current nurse workforce. The management of this workforce is primarily from those in the baby boomer generation (those born between 1943 and 1960). Creating harmony between these two groups is a big challenge for healthcare leadership (Cordeniz, 2002).

It is predicted that in 2010, chronic disease will affect at least 45% of Americans, with 80% of all hospital stays due to chronic illness. When genomics and bioengineered organs can't fix the problem, the hospital stay will be extended. Chronic disease and the conditions that accompany the aging process are by nature incurable. The functionality and quality of life for those individuals can be improved by using available palliative measures. The aging population and the longer survival of patients with chronic diseases will shift greater attention to the use of palliative interventions (Grosel, Hamilton, Koyano, & Eastwood, 2000).

The implications of these changes indicate healthcare will be different than it is today. Much of the care will be delivered in the home with vital functions monitored and managed remotely by experts. The chronic diseases not at the critical level will be cared for in assisted living facilities or a similar home-like setting. Chronic diseases will be managed by computer protocols monitored by nurse care coordinators. Only the very ill and those dying will be hospitalized and not for long.

Who will provide this care whether it be inpatient or outpatient? The declining birth rate in the U.S. indicates there will not be enough young to care for the sick.

Change from Cure to Prevention

Led by health-conscious individuals and pushed by cost and a generation of baby boomers, healthcare is moving beyond the curative model to one that preserves health and prevents illness (Grosel, Hamilton, Koyano, & Eastwood, 2000). For many years, there has been discussion about the value of prevention rather than cure. The World Health Organization has included prevention goals in proposals since its establishment in 1948 (World Health Organization, 2002). Recently, with the escalating cost of healthcare, it has become apparent we have no choice. Our efforts and money must be dedicated to prevention.

What is Happening in Nursing?

Nursing is the nation's largest healthcare industry. Currently, there are 2.5 million nurses nationwide (Kleiman, 2002). Two-thirds of nurses work in the hospital setting. Reports from federal studies indicate if current trends continue, by 2015, the rising demand for nurses will outweigh the supply of RNs. Ernst & Young report nursing shortages at hospitals and clinics will exceed 500,000 positions by 2020 (New nurses, 2002).

The causes of the nursing shortage include:

- A nurse workforce that is aging and near retirement

- Impacted status of nursing education programs because of a shortage of nursing faculty (AACN, 2002)
- Many career opportunities for women (who comprise the largest number of nurses)

Nurses' roles range from directing patient care to case management, from establishing practice standards and developing quality assurance procedures to directing complex nursing care systems. The hospital setting is where 60% of nurses are employed, but the following areas of healthcare practice are growing and in need of nurses:

- Private physician practices
- Public health agencies
- Primary care clinics
- Home health agencies
- Outpatient surgery centers
- Insurance and managed-care companies
- Nursing homes
- Schools
- Mental health agencies
- Hospices
- The military
- Industry
- Colleges/universities
- Research institutions

New employment opportunities for nurses can also be found in biopharmaceutical companies, architectural firms, book publishing companies, fitness centers and in personally owned businesses.

The BSN nurse is prepared to practice in all healthcare settings and thus has the greatest employment flexibility of any entry-level RN. All projections forecast an accelerating demand for nursing care and for nurses with expanded education and skills. Many nurses are searching for an entrepreneurial and creative environment that is more flexible (New nurses, 2002).

Employers are keenly aware of the nursing shortage and are seeking nurses prepared at the bachelor's and graduate degree level from all over the globe who can deliver the complex care required for a variety of acute care, primary care and community health settings, as well as provide other needed services such as case management, health promotion and disease prevention. The words "BSN preferred" are frequently appearing in advertisements for nurses.

Wireless technology has significantly improved the delivery of nursing care and will continue to do so in the future. Wireless telemetry transforms any patient room to a telemetry room. Wireless technology also transforms the traditional nursing station to a mobile unit. Small, handheld wireless computers can now allow nurses to access the Internet from almost anywhere. This connectivity allows a nurse to receive and transmit information to a physician's office or to the patient's/family's home. With paperless medical records, robots and remote devices, the time the nurse is able to spend with patients is increased (Goe, 2001).

Healthcare employers are continuing to look for ways for nurses to be more efficient. Mobile workstations, task consolidation, cross-training, and the maximum use of technology solutions and automation to reduce the number of vacancies have been implemented so staff spend more time with patients.

The use of robots in healthcare will offer more options for the location of care. Robotic surgical applications are currently being used. Robots deliver medications and supplies to patient areas in many facilities. These applications integrated with information technology provide a new platform for care delivery and documentation.

CULTURE

Frequently, the job seeker's emphasis when looking for new employment opportunities is focused on the job itself and its associated benefits. While money and benefits may keep someone satisfied with a job for a while, these reasons are rarely connected with enjoyment of the job. Employees tend to identify their manager, co-workers and the organizational environment as the reasons they remain in a position.

Every organization has a culture that permeates the work environment. Deal and Kennedy (1982) published a landmark book, *Corporate Cultures*, based on their research about the social fabric that exists in organizations. They described distinct types of cultures that evolve within companies and the impact of culture on the organization's performance. Peters and Waterman (1988) described *In Search for Excellence* many successful organizations and attributed most, if not all, of their respective business success to a strong corporate culture. Although it is sometimes very subtle, the corporate culture does "set the stage" and does impact every employee.

The culture of an organization may not be the desired, planned or cultivated one, but every organization has a distinct culture that penetrates every aspect of the organization. It is alive and can be felt. Job seekers should inquire about the culture and ask, Does the culture feel right? Is it cold or inviting? Are employees smiling or frowning? Are phone conversations light and cheery or strained? Does the receptionist greet visitors or ignore them? Do staff members hustle around or take a moment to greet and acknowledge visitors? Is there any laughter? Does the atmosphere feel comfortable or grating? The larger question for job seekers might be whether the culture fits or whether it is so foreign they want to run in the opposite direction.

When assessing an organization, the first step is to obtain a copy of the company's mission statement and its corporate values. They are the basic framework from which the culture evolves. Each department or section may implement it differently, but the core culture is the same. One organization, for example, lists its core values in what it calls "Leadership Principles," The seven principles are:

1. Leaders maintain a never-ending focus on the mission and the pursuit of excellence.
2. Leaders create an environment where staff members feel proud of their company and know the company is proud of them.
3. Leaders work hard to help staff be successful at work and in life.
4. Leaders protect the right of good staff to work with good staff.
5. Leaders encourage and promote open discussion and analysis as a predicate to decision-making.
6. Leaders deal promptly with conflict.
7. Leaders encourage others to enjoy their work.

If these principles were truly implemented, the corporate culture of this company would be very inviting to most employees.

Determine if the mission is alive and implemented. Ask for examples of how the mission and values have been brought to life. A tour of the organization and watching what happens as staff members interact with customers and each other always helps. Look for consistency.

The next step is to determine if the mission and values of the organization are congruent with those of the job seeker. If the answer is yes, then the job seeker must determine if the implementation of mission and values of the organization, by the employees, is congruent with the mission and values of the organization and acceptable to the job seeker. It is not uncommon for employees to be ignorant of the mission and core values or to have their own way of executing those values. Reading the mission and core values is not enough. The job seeker needs to determine how the employees function, that is, how the organization's culture, the people, function. The following questions might be asked to determine the nature of the culture:

- What opportunities are there to develop new ideas?
- Is the organization bureaucratic, matrix, flat or a hybrid?
- How is information disseminated?
- How is good work rewarded?
- What is the nurse's clinical authority?
- What is the nurse's scope of practice?
- What is the nurse's role in relation to the patient?
- Is employee satisfaction measured, and what are the results? What department has the highest satisfaction and why? Is there an action plan to address concerns?
- How are managers selected? Are they promoted from within? Is there a management track?
- Does the climate encourage employees to be creative with customer delivery? Are the employees having fun?
- Are there opportunities for teamwork as well as individual projects?
- Is the relationship between nurses and physicians collaborative?

An example of how matching personal values with the organizational culture is necessary is exemplified by a story about Mary. Mary was doomed for failure because she failed to assess her values to see if they matched the culture of the organization.

Mary accepted a management position in an organization that functioned with self-directed work teams. Mary's previous experiences had been in top-down, bureaucratic organizations. Instead of learning about the new organization, Mary tried to impose her management style and values on a very autonomous staff. Mary did not want to learn a new style of management and imposed her values on staff. This obvious mismatch made life miserable for both the staff and Mary. After a year, Mary was asked to leave.

Taking time to evaluate the culture of the organization and her own work style would have saved Mary from a bad career move.

POLITICS

Corporate politics is a fact of life. Corporate politics is based on the power and influence within an organization. It is what people do to get their way. Politics in organizations involves going outside the usual, formally sanctioned channels. The handshake deal made in the backroom before a board meeting involves politics, as does the promotion received because of personal connections. Real political moves are the ones not documented anywhere, they are just known. Over time, these political moves can become part of the corporate culture. They give rise to the games people play to build power bases, defeat rivals and promote in-group members rather than choose someone from outside the group.

Understanding politics is important. Knowing what is acceptable or not acceptable and having the correct timing are important to maneuver within a political arena. Knowing what to say and when to say it are equally important. How should someone approach a difficult situation? When should an individual take forceful action to stand up for personal beliefs? Which battle is worth fighting? Who will be the ally or enemy in the process? All these questions are part of surviving and succeeding in the organization.

Being politically naïve may spell the death of a career. Attacking a senior manager is not a good place to begin experimenting with the political arena. Neither is being a maverick. It is important to understand the political environment within an organization before taking that first step. Achieving success in a political environment requires collaboration, cooperation and diplomacy. While being professionally competent may open the door to a desired position, being politically astute will most likely assure survival in that position and facilitate advancement within the organization.

How does someone learn about the organization's political climate? The best answer is to look, listen, network and find a mentor. Developing political shrewdness takes time. It also requires good people skills.

Learning negotiating skills can be helpful when attempting to break the political barrier. It also helps to be well read and well informed on the debated subject and to anticipate the arguments, both pro and con. Being able to defend a position from all sides is critical. Always think like the opponent and anticipate the next move. Rally allies to bolster and defend the position and establish a sound political base.

Being naïve and accepting an offer without evaluating the situation could have allowed Jane to make a career move that was not in her best interest.

Jane is an RN who works for a biomedical company. She and her husband have three children under the age of 10. Jane loves her job and travels 2½ weeks each month. Her in-laws live close by and help her husband with the children when Jane is out of town. One day, Jane's boss suggested Jane might want to take a position in sales in another state. This would be a promotion for Jane with a slight salary increase, but she would have to move her family, and her husband would have to find a new job. They no longer would have the help and support from the in-laws. At first, Jane was flattered by the offer, and if she did not have children to consider, she probably would have accepted the job immediately. But, because she did have a family, she and her husband decided to visit the new city and look at housing and schools. At the same time, Jane started to take inventory of the reasons she liked her current job and what she really wanted in a career. She discovered that the new job did not involve travel (something she loved). While at a company dinner, Jane made an important discovery. She discovered a physician who was being recruited by the group she worked with had accepted the job with the contingency that his friend would be hired into Jane's position. Since there was not enough work for two Janes, the plan was to get Jane to move to another territory and accept a different position. Jane felt betrayed. What she thought was a promotion was really a ploy to attract a new physician. Had she not done some homework, Jane would probably be in a job she didn't like and would probably fail. Taking the time to assess the situation and consider what she really wanted in a career saved Jane from a bad career move.

TIMING

Timing for the job searcher is twofold. There is the right time to seek a new position, and there is the right time to accept a new position. The job seeker must determine if the current job is not worth keeping and if the new position is worth accepting given the effort, energy and change it will demand. Many times the new job looks better than the old one. However, after the change, the job seeker discovers the new job is not better and is, in fact, even worse than the old job. Why does this happen? Most often, it is because the job seeker did not do the research necessary to determine if timing was an issue. Perhaps the old job was not as bad as it seemed if the job seeker had waited and worked at making the changes that were needed.

Timing is also an issue when a new position is considered. Many healthcare organizations are undergoing massive change. To accept a position when the organization is changing might not be wise. Waiting awhile for the changes to be implemented will provide the job seeker with a clear view of the position. Too many people jump from one position to another because the "grass always looks greener" when, in fact, it is often just the "same old brown grass" as the job they already have.

Sometimes the job seeker elects to seek a position at a particular time, because a job offer appears to be more attractive than it is. For example, a nursing assistant was ready to make a move from her current position with a local nursing home to another position across the city for an additional $1/hour in pay. When her supervisor asked if she had considered how much the move would cost her, she replied no. The supervisor decided to demonstrate how a move across town might affect the decision.

Income:	**Company A**	**Company B**
Salary: $8.00/hr vs. $9.00 (26 wks)	$ 8,320	$ 9,360
Salary increase: 3%@6 mos vs. 0%		
$8.24/hr vs. $9.00 (26 wks)	$ 8,570	$ 9,360
Overtime: $12.00/hr vs. $13.50 (4 hrs/wk)—6 mos	$ 1,248	$ 1,404
$12.36/hr vs. $13.50 (4 hrs/wk)—6 mos	$ 1,285	$ 1,404
Bonus:	$ 500	$ 0
Pension Plan: 4% vs. 2% company contribution	$ 665	$ 375
Total Annual Income:	$20,588	$21,903
Salary increase: 3%@6 mos vs. 0%		
4%@1 yr vs. 3%	$ 686	$ 561
Expenses:		
Cost of Uniforms: 0 vs. $30/uniform × 3 uniforms	$ 0	$ 90/yr
Shoes: 0 vs. $40/pair	$ 0	$ 40/yr
Meals: meals provided vs. $4.00/meal/day	$ 0	$ 1,000

Benefits:		
Health insurance: $15/pay period vs. $20	$ 390	$ 520
Dental insurance: $6/pay period vs. $17	$ 156	$ 442
Total Annual Expenses:	$ 546	$ 2,092
Net Income:	$20,042	$19,811

This analysis indicates there is a net loss of $231 the first year. Of course, the nursing assistant may recover this loss over time . . . but moving only for increased salary may not result in increased income.

This example demonstrates how easy it is to be pulled toward what appears to be a higher income and why so many people move from job to job. However, if the nursing assistant had thought about the best time for a move instead of what appeared to be a better salary, she might have moved in a very different direction. If she had decided to go back to school to obtain a BSN, which would bring her substantially increased income, she would have put off a job change until the degree had been earned. This just wasn't the right move to make, nor was it the right time for a change.

CONCLUSION

A shortage of qualified workers, an aging population and new technologies have created many opportunities for nurses. However, matching the needs of nurses with those of an organization is not an easy task. Because individuals want and value different aspects of their positions and organizations offer such different opportunities, the process of matching desire with offer is a very dynamic one. The primary responsibility of career seekers is to understand themselves and be able to clearly communicate their wants and needs. The better they know their skills, abilities and values, the better prepared they will be to sell themselves to the employer of choice. On the other hand, employers who are seeking new hires must be very clear about what they need and be able to create flexible career paths with attractive incentives and reward systems.

Career seekers must understand what is happening in healthcare and how that knowledge might impact nursing and take the time to find out about the culture and politics of the organization that is offering a position. They must also consider whether it is the best time to make a change. Bonuses, promises of better benefits and flexibility are not always the only criteria when considering a new position. Timing and the workplace environment should also be considered.

While knowing the marketplace, the culture and politics of the organization, and the best time to make a move are important, the nurse should think first about whether the move fits into a career pathway. There are plenty of jobs in nursing and there are plenty of career pathways. The important issue is to make the job decision based on a career pathway so there is progression, advancement and financial growth throughout one's professional life.

REFERENCES

AACN. (2002). *Your nursing career: A look at the facts*. Retrieved August 3, 2002, from http:www.aacn.nche.edu/education/Careerhtm.

Cordeniz, J.A. (2002). Recruitment, retention, and management of Generation X: A focus on nursing professionals. *Journal of Healthcare Management, 47*(4), 236-249.

Deal, T.E. & Kennedy, A.A. (1982). *Corporate cultures. The rites and rituals of corporate life.* Reading, MA: Perseus.

Eisenberg, D.M., Davis, R.B., Ettner, S.L., Appel, S., Wilkey, S., Van Rompay, M., & Kessler, R.C. (1998). Trends in alternative medicine use in the United States 1990-1997. *Journal of the American Medical Association, 280*(18), 1569-1575.

Goe, S. (2001). Healthcare delivery in the future. In C.S. McCullough (Ed.), *Creating responsive solutions to healthcare change* (pp. 235-264). Indianapolis, IN: Center Nursing Press.

Grosel, C., Hamilton, M., Koyano, J., & Eastwood, S. (2000). *Health and healthcare 2010: The forecast, the challenge*. San Francisco, CA: Jossey-Bass.

Kleiman, C. (2002). *Winning the job game: The new rules for finding and keeping the job you want.* New York, NY: Wiley.

New nurses shift to biotech or other health-related jobs. (2002, October 14). *The Omaha World Herald,* p. 21.

Peters, T. & Waterman, R.H. (1988). *In search of excellence: Lessons from America's best-run companies*. New York, NY: Harper & Row.

The Advisory Board. (2000). *Current status of complementary and alternative medicine: Research in brief.* Washington, DC: Author.

World Health Organization. (2002). Retrieved November 22, 2002, from http://www.who.int/about/en/.

Unit III
Changing a Career

Chapter 11

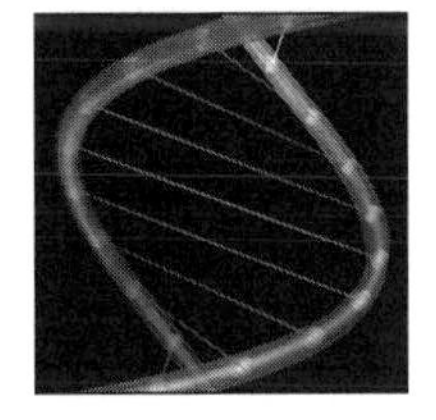

Experiencing Career Discontent

by Michelle T. Renaud

It was the best of times, it was the worst of times, it was the age of wisdom, it was the age of foolishness, it was the epoch of incredulity, it was the season of Light, it was the season of Darkness, it was the spring of hope, it was the winter of despair (Dickens, 1859).

INTRODUCTION

The current and future viability of nursing as a profession depends on a continuous pool of career-oriented nurses who remain in the profession through both periods of discontent and periods of satisfaction. Registered nurses currently constitute the largest group of healthcare professionals in the country, with over 2 million RNs employed in healthcare (Buerhaus, 2000). However, the U.S. Bureau of Labor Statistics (1998) has projected between 1998 and 2008, the healthcare system will have 400,000 to 800,000 vacant RN positions. By the year 2020, we will have 20% fewer nurses than needed to fill open nursing positions, and the supply of nurses will be about the same as it is currently (Buerhaus, 2000). Nurses whose careers span the years of 1995-2025 will be caught up in one of the most significant nursing shortages in history.

Historically, there have been cycles where nursing faced shortages, and the daily work became a bigger challenge. Availability of adequate resources, including personnel shortages and lack of experienced nurses trained in various areas, has been cited as a correlate to job discontent. On any given hospital unit, the average severity of illness is greater than ever before; nearly every patient requires intensive monitoring and care; and close to 20% of hospitalized patients have adverse events during their hospitalizations. Federal statistics suggest the increasing complexity of acute care will result in a 36% greater need for RNs in hospitals by the year 2020. Several recent studies have demonstrated the RN-to-patient ratio to be the single most important factor explaining the differing success rates for outcomes of patients who experience serious adverse events. For example, Kovner and Gergen (1998) found a significant inverse relationship between the number of nurses on the staff and post-surgical urinary tract infections, pneumonia, thrombosis and pulmonary compromise.

At the same time as hospitals experience a heightening need for acute care nurses, the shift in healthcare services to primary care and home-based settings brings an increasing need for community-based nurses—nurses in home care, in clinics and in long-term care facilities (U.S. Bureau of Labor Statistics, 2001).

As demand for nurses intensifies, the supply of new nurses across all levels of education continues to decline. The nation's nursing workforce is aging; the average age of all RNs is now 44.3 years, with only 31.7% of working RNs under the age of 40. Approximately 50% of the current workforce will reach retirement age in the next 10 to 15 years (HRSA, 2001); the average age of RNs at that time will be 50 years. Meanwhile, enrollments in baccalaureate nursing programs have dropped steadily over the last five years; the American Association of Colleges of Nursing estimates this five-year enrollment decline at −15% (AACN, 2002).

The shortage of nurses across all levels manifests itself not only in hospital and community-based nursing practice, but also in a growing shortage of nurse faculty and academic nursing leaders. Currently, while the average age of nursing faculty rises, new faculty members are not entering academic nursing in numbers sufficient to replace those retiring. AACN (2001) reported the average age of nursing faculty was 50.2 years. A need thus exists for strategies to not only attract new nurses to the profession but, more essentially, to retain the current pool of experienced nurses who can assist newer nurses with transition from their education into clinical practice, academia and research.

The issue of career discontent is important to address at any time but with the current projections and shortages discussed above, the coming decades are a time when satisfaction and retention are important to the health of the profession. What, then, are some of the issues that result in career discontent among nursing professionals?

CAREER EVOLUTION AND FACTORS OF DISCONTENT

Career Evolution

Any career evolves and progresses through phases, and often the phases repeat throughout the course of the career. McNeese-Smith (2000) queried 412 hospital-based nurses using a framework developed by Graham that articulated three major career stages: entry, mastery and disengagement. The entry phase includes role assimilation, skill development, and idealism or dreaming. Mastery is a broad process and includes moving through beginner skills toward expertise in the career. There is a movement away from earlier idealism toward more egocentrism and identity. During the final stage, disengagement, there is indifference toward the career, no satisfaction, boredom and declining performance. The employee literally disengages from the career, and there is no meaning in the work. In her research, McNeese-Smith (2000) related that disengagement is related to longevity. The importance of this finding is that just when nurses are achieving mastery in their careers, they feel the most disengaged. If this is true, interventions and incentives should be directed at long-term nurses, as well as beginning nurses.

Key Factors Affecting Career Satisfaction

Nursing Education Versus Nursing Reality: Unmet Expectations

There is a critical period during and in the immediate period following formal professional education at each level. This is a time when the ideas and knowledge generated within the academic environment come into contact with the realities of the nursing practice context. The literature has referred to this as a "reality" check, although a person might ask where the reality of the nursing future lies, with long-standing and traditional practice models or with the evidence-based practice of recently educated graduates? New initiatives in nursing education are needed to blend academic teaching and clinical outcomes in realistic care environments.

Images of Professionalism or Images of Servitude

Nurses have had little accurate media representation until very recently (Stewart, 1999). Images of nurses have been present in sitcoms or other venues where professionalism was not depicted. A study of doctorally prepared nurses using a stratified sample of 842 Sigma Theta Tau International members revealed that professionalism is critical to career satisfaction (Gurney, Mueller, & Price, 1997). The researchers reported the factors related to job satisfaction and employer loyalty were professional values such as autonomy, variety and justice, career ladders, and adequate resources. These researchers reported pay was not an important issue for their doctorally prepared participants. Perhaps this lack of interest in pay as an aspect of job satisfaction was due to their likely higher than normative income.

Sense of Purpose

In a survey design study of 10,000 hospital nurses in Missouri, it was reported most nurses entered nursing for patient care rewards and chose to remain in nursing for the same reason (Mills & Blaesing, 2000). The story below supports this finding.

> *When I graduated from my BSN program in 1972, I was very idealistic and recall the energy I felt at every new opportunity. I entered the Army NurseCorps while still in school and soon after graduation began what was to be a 25-year Army nursing career. It is likely that the reason I lasted as long as I did as an Army nurse was the constant challenge of new assignments every 2-3 years, the multiple roles I was able to experience, and the sense of purpose that came from my belief that I was doing something worthwhile and for a common good. This sense of purpose is similar to that described by McNeese-Smith (2000) as key to nursing job satisfaction.*

Other authors report the factors related to dissatisfaction include the organizational climate, patient care reward, environmental conditions, nursing position or job held, salary, hours of work, geographical location, and years in nursing (Bakker, Kilmer, Siegrist, & Schaufeli, 2000; Mills & Blaesing, 2000; Takase, Kershaw, & Burt, 2001).

Nursing career discontent is complex, multifaceted and often insidious. What appears to be a satisfying job can evolve into a mediocre and unchallenging existence if the numerous factors above, combined with a personal lack of challenge and frustration, occur over time. A career can become "flat," void of challenge or of reward, perhaps in part due to an inability to recognize the onset of a combined menu of overwork, scattered commitments and lack of positive thinking. Nursing is a difficult profession, and over the course of a long career, frustration can easily overshadow benefits.

One of the major realizations a person needs to watch for is the recognition that it is easy to push out conflicts and adopt a sense of futility. The long history of oppression within and external to nursing can create a vision that there will never be change and that the tales of drudgery and tradition will suppress any creativity and new direction. For one nurse, this sense of frustration was altered.

Once in my doctoral program, I became much more open and aware of these thoughts and recognized my own anger that nursing would never move forward because those within held the profession back. What developed for me was a framework for nursing based on critical theory, with an eye for the influences of oppression and social injustice upon a profession that strives to provide health and preventive care for a myriad of people within an impossibly complex and underserving healthcare system.

NURSING WITHIN A CRITICAL THEORY CONTEXT

Critical theory can serve as a framework for understanding some of the issues related to career discontent within nursing. It also can provide some solutions for the individual dealing with the unrest of an unfulfilling career. A critical theorist assumes human experience is constructed through social and historical interactions, lending a unity and coherence to multitudinous human lives. Critical theory is based on an understanding of the influence of oppression and power upon individuals or groups within a particular society. Critical theory is the collective term for a variety of theories that attempts to understand how power and oppression operate within a society and, in doing so, provide people with knowledge that can be used to promote social change (Agger, 1998; Fay, 1987; Kincheloe & McClaren, 1994). A goal of critical theory is emancipation from the forces of domination and oppression. Fay (1987) explained that emancipation could be achieved through the processes of enlightenment, education and empowerment.

Enlightenment implies developing an awareness of the rules and constraints that operate to oppress people within current society and involves an understanding of relationships between power and daily activity, revealing the contradictions of life (Fay, 1987).

Education involves changing people's self-understandings by liberating them from social processes that cause oppression. The power to oppress and control people is dependent upon the ignorance of the people in question (Fay, 1987). The development of critical consciousness occurs through stimulation of learners' creativity and questioning ability (Freire, 1970). One important consideration that Fay discussed was the need to translate the knowledge or theory into ordinary language and ground it in the participants' self-understanding.

Fay (1987) described empowerment as a practical force that seeks to mobilize its audience into socially transformative action. People are able to take action and gain mastery over their lives. Young (1997) further explained empowerment as "a process in which individual[s], relatively powerless people, engage in dialogue with each other and thereby come to understand the social sources of their powerlessness and see the possibility of acting collectively to change their social environment" (p. 91).

The profession of nursing is caught up in a healthcare system full of oppression and domination. The influences of critical theory can be seen in the way that people have not been educated, enlightened or emancipated by the medical regimes to which they become subject. Traditional thinking disempowers both the patients and many of the nurses who are caring for them. For example:

> *I will always remember a family whose baby was in the NICU in which I was working in the early 1970s. The infant had been placed on antibiotics, a fairly common occurrence with premature infants. When the parents visited, they asked me some questions about the antibiotics, and I answered. These were not complex questions, but the following day, the physician and head nurse both counseled me that this was the doctor's role and not for me to discuss. Parents in that unit knew very little about their babies' treatment plans and certainly had no part in decisions. It is likely that would not happen today, and parents would be invited to hear the plans for their child, but it serves as an example of the attitudes and traditions of nursing that are part of the profession and its history.*

The concepts and components of critical theory can also provide insight into the everyday lives of nurses and the ways in which they experience oppression and domination through the United States social systems. Furthermore, an understanding of social injustice and its effects upon social groups can shed some light onto possible ways in which nurses in the United States have historically been viewed as a lesser profession, which in turn affects the public image of nursing and individual professionals' self-esteem. Takase, Kershaw and Burt (2001) discuss how stereotypical images of nursing create an oppressive environment for practicing nurses. Prior work has suggested that nurses practice as an oppressed group in part due to class, gender, history, and lack of confidence and autonomy (Fulton, 1997).

A continued and long-standing tension between medicine and nursing and a domination of nursing by the medical profession add to the dilemma of nursing professionals who are professionals in their own right but often defer to the medical model of practice. Since multiple authors have articulated that self-esteem and professional image are factors enhancing career satisfaction, these issues are essential in dealing with career discontent in nursing.

Part of the issue with thinking about nursing career discontent is the tendency to look at nursing without considering all of the context and social ramifications that influence the profession widely, as well as the self-esteem and satisfaction of those who choose a nursing career. Stewart (1999) refers to the lack of nursing presence in the media, indicating that physicians are often contacted about healthcare issues, while nurses are less comfortable in the spotlight. The tendency to equate healthcare expertise with physicians rather than nurses is the broader problem and is reinforced continually in all venues of the media. Recent efforts to portray a positive image of nursing are encouraging, although nurse educators need to include these issues in the curriculum and teach young nurses the skills needed to portray their profession in a positive and dynamic manner. Pride in profession cannot but help enhance pride in self and thus perhaps provide some counter to the forces that discourage and disengage nurses.

One of the barometers of future success with nursing recruitment and retention is the perceived desirability of nursing as a career by youth. Recent campaigns portraying positive images of nursing aimed at youth might be followed with continued efforts by the public to encourage nursing as a career choice.

Moving Within or Moving On

When faced with the dilemma and angst of irreconcilable career discontent with the current job at some time during a nursing career, there are several possible options. There may be times when the best choice is to change professions totally, but other alternatives include focusing the career path in a different direction, going to part time or a more flexible work schedule, and increasing the effort to balance work with family life.

Grandinetti and Brand (2001) describe how changing one's position can increase self-esteem and bring back the sense of purpose that enhances professional satisfaction. Nursing as a profession has the benefit of offering varied job opportunities that are expanding over time, giving nurses options to change the job and keep the career. Some of the many possibilities include:

- Relocating to a different geographical area
- Moving in or out of the hospital setting
- Pursuing forensic nursing, parish nursing or consulting
- Seeking a faculty position
- Conducting research
- Going back to school for further education

After the realization that I was facing discontent, burnout and disinterest in nursing, I decided that a change might revitalize my previous energy and enthusiasm for the profession. My current job was a good one, with people I enjoyed and students I respected. Perhaps my feelings were in part due to returning to the same job after achieving the hurdle of a rigorous PhD program and feeling like I was viewed as the same person, when I clearly felt I was not. My family was also ready for a change and a new geographical location. I was grappling with these and other issues when I was offered the opportunity to do something totally different while remaining in nursing. I currently direct an accelerated BSN program for people from other careers who elect to move into nursing. I find this ironic in that rather than moving away from my chosen profession, I am bringing others from varied backgrounds to nursing. I am still in a time of discontent with nursing in general, but I have a definite sense of purpose and hope that over time I will be able to contribute to nursing through the students in this program. My own nursing career is now into its 30th year. Hopefully, as I move toward retirement, the youth of the profession will carry it to a new and better level.

CONCLUSION

Career discontent is not unusual. What is unusual is staying in the career and not understanding the source of the discontent and not being able to move on. Using critical theory, the source of the discontent, as exemplified in this chapter, can be located. Once the source is understood, the individual can determine the next step. Choices for what to do about discontent are available—but without an understanding of what the discontent is all about, the individual is likely to step into another job and experience the same kind of discontent.

While the healthcare industry is experiencing the worse nurse shortage in history, nurses are experiencing opportunities unlike any in the past. Historically, most nurses have worked in hospitals. Today, nurses are able to work in a variety of roles. Nurses manage their own businesses and function as consultants to lawyers, doctors, architectural firms, pharmaceutical operations and computer industries. They also function as marketers for hospital equipment firms and publishing companies. They work for city, state and national governments. They are lawyers, CEOs, government officials and college presidents. There is no reason for the nurse to be discontent when there are so many diverse ways to practice nursing.

Clearly, the issue is to recognize career discontent and to know how to locate the source and how to move on. No nurse should feel trapped. No nurse should feel at a loss for what to do to relieve discontent. And no nurse should feel the need to abandon the profession when there are so many ways to be a nurse. As Dickens pointed out at the beginning of this chapter, with discontent comes hope IF the nurse has the courage and fortitude to pursue ways to alter the situation or move from it.

REFERENCES

American Association of Colleges of Nursing. (2001, July). Amid nursing shortage schools employ strategies to boost enrollment. *AACN Issue Bulletin* (pp. 1, 2). Washington, DC: Author.

American Association of Colleges of Nursing. (2002, February). Effective strategies for increasing diversity in nursing programs. *AACN Issue Bulletin* (pp. 1, 2). Washington, DC: Author.

Agger, B. (1998). *Critical social theory: An introduction.* Boulder, CO: Westview Press.

Bakker, A.B., Kilmer, C.H., Siegrist, J., & Schaufeli, W.B. (2000). Effort-reward imbalance and burnout among nurses. *Journal of Advanced Nursing, 31*(4), 884-891.

Buerhaus, P. (2000). Implications of an aging registered nurse workforce. *Journal of the American Medical Association, 283*(22), 2948-2954.

Dickens, C. (1859). *A tale of two cities.* London, England: Chapman & Hall.

Fay, B. (1987). *Critical social science: Liberation and its limits*. Ithica, NY: Cornell University.

Freire, P. (1970). *Pedogogy of the oppressed*. New York, NY: Continuum Publishing.

Fullerton, H.N., & Toosai, M. (2001). Labor force projections to 2010: Steady growth and changing composition. *Monthly Labor Review, 124*(11), Need page nos.____.

Fulton, Y. (1997). Nurses' views on empowerment: A critical social theory perspective. *Journal of Advanced Nursing, 26*(3), 529-536.

Grandinetti, D., & Brand, J. (2001). Stuck midstream? Change horses. *Medical Economics*, 2, 72.

Gurney, C., Mueller, C., & Price, J.L. (1997). Job satisfaction and organizational attachment of nurses holding doctoral degrees. *Nursing Research, 46*(3), 163-171.

Health Resources and Services Administration. (2000, July). *Projected supply and demand and shortages of registered nurses: 2000-2020*. Washington, DC: National Center for Health Workforce Analysis.

Hemsley-Brown, J., & Foskett, N. (1999). Career desirability: Young people's perceptions of nursing as a career. *Journal of Advanced Nursing, 29*(6), 1342-1350.

Kincheloe, J., & McClaren, P. (1994). Rethinking critical theory and qualitative research. In N. Denzin & Y. Lincoln (Eds.), *Handbook of qualitative research*. Thousand Oaks, CA: Sage.

Kovner, C., & Gergen, P.J. (1998). Nursing staffing levels and adverse events following surgery in U.S. hospitals. *Image: Journal of Nursing Scholarship, 30*(4), 315-321.

McNeese-Smith, D. (2000). Job stages of entry, mastery and disengagement among nurses. *Journal of Nursing Administration, 30*(3), 140-147.

Mills, A. & , Blaesing, S. (2000). A lesson from the last nursing shortage: The influence of work values on career satisfaction with nursing. *Journal of Nursing Administration, 30*(6), 309-315.

Stewart, M. (1999). ANA puts nursing in media spotlight. *American Journal of Nursing, 99*(5), 56-57, 59.

Takase, M., Kershaw, E., & Burt, L. (2001). Nurse environment misfit and nursing practice. *Journal of Advanced Nursing, 35*(6), 819-826.

U.S. Bureau of Labor Statistics. (1998, May 8). *Occupations with the largest job growth, 1996-2006*. Washington, DC: Author.

Young, I. (1997). *Intersecting voices: Dilemmas of gender, political philosophy and policy*. Princeton, NY: Princeton University Press.

Chapter 12

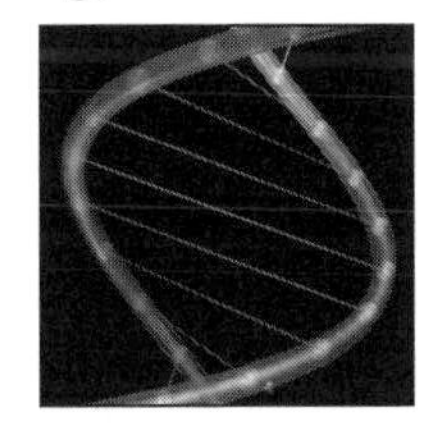

Personal Values and Identity: Basis for Career Change

by Wendell Oderkirk

INTRODUCTION: A CASE STUDY

A successful nursing career can take many forms. Usually the career evolves; in some instances it is planned. This chapter focuses on career development based on personal values and identity, that is, how a career can evolve based on the person's values rather than on opportunities or planned directions. For example, the following statement demonstrates how one person defined his evolving career in nursing.

> *I am satisfied with my career to this point, although it does not reach a standard of success as measured by, say, the American Academy of Nursing. I have published little of significance. I have not garnered large grants. I do not hold an advanced practice credential. My doctoral degree is not in nursing. My master's degree in nursing actually came after my doctoral degree, and I earned it to meet a National League for Nursing requirement. Before that I had earned a master's degree in urban education. I most recently added a bachelor of arts in Spanish to my preparation, because it seemed to be the most useful "advanced practice certification" I could have where I live, on the U.S.-Mexican border. My career looks like the unplanned hodgepodge that it is. My career has not contributed to the larger issues and movements in nursing, in my opinion, but to me this meandering career has been successful.*

What is notable about this statement is not the individual's recognition of the evolution of the career, but his acknowledgement that the career for him has been successful. In the following statement, he clearly defines what he means by successful and outlines how his personal values have driven his decisions.

> *Had I used a focused career plan, I undoubtedly would be able to list more publications, present a more consistent record of research production, and could point to a higher salary. But I did not make a career plan. Rather, my career has lurched through a series of goals I wanted to explore for personal reasons. My hope was that my professional work would not interfere with my personal goals. I recognized that using personal values to shape my career was not an efficient way to manage a career conducive to consistency, production and advancement. But consistency, production and advancement were not values for me. I have not based my career on an "opportunistic" model either, a plan that would have me moving from university to university or hospital to hospital simply for higher income or better promotion opportunities. Were I using the opportunistic model, I would likely be working at a much higher salary level and likely not be working in nursing education.*

It is not uncommon to base one's decisions on what is valued. We do that everyday. What is different, though, for this individual is his differentiation between personal values and professional values and how his personal values have provided direction or have affected his professional path.

> *I purposely failed to put much thought into career planning because my personal goals often crowded my professional goals. My basis for career planning has been my personal values, and, yes, personal values do change. However, my personal values have generally been consistent. If I were to use a formal career plan, I would list my core values as wanting to learn new things, be independent, live in different places, teach others, live with mixed cultures and be personally fit (I weigh what I weighed in high school, and I have run at least five miles daily for more than 30 years). I do not enjoy supervising others, although I have been an interim department chair in two schools of nursing, and I am regularly bored at faculty meetings. Personal recognition and financial gain have never been important. I am the oldest*

of six children from a lower-middle-class family. I have worked since I was 9 (I had early morning paper routes between ages 9 and 16). I fully expect to work the rest of my life. I do not "know" where my career is headed, but I'm not anxious about that.

Finding the reasons for one's behavior is often a way of explaining why we do what we do. For this gentleman, being a male nurse in a world of women nurses seems to be an important factor.

Some of my reluctance to have a career plan may be related to the fact that I am a man in nursing. Even after many years, it is hard to say how being a man in nursing has affected my career in nursing. For sure, the social implications of being a male in nursing created internal and external barriers I had to manage before, during and after my basic degree program. I can still vividly recall the shock of entering my first nursing course as the only male student in a class of some 50 women. From my beginnings in nursing, however, I have been accepted, or at least tolerated, by women nurses.

In nursing, I have experienced something of how it feels to be a minority. I am Anglo, but in nursing, I am clearly a minority in a world dominated by the women who have taught me, hired me and supervised me. I rarely saw other men in my BSN or MSN degree programs. On the job, my designation as a nurse tended to exclude me from socializing with other males, such as physicians. I was like an immigrant to a world where I had to learn new languages (the languages of medicine and nursing), new social behaviors and new skills. What I felt, but could not have articulated at the time, was that I was a minority creating new identities as I crossed into the occupational worlds of healthcare and nursing. My self-identity would change whether or not I wanted it changed. Over the years, I have become comfortable reestablishing my personal "identity" as I have moved into other new areas of life and learning.

Identity and Personal Values

Personal values can move a nurse through a series of career changes. Such career changes can be considered new "identities" one creates during a career. The use of personal values as a basis for career decisions may be especially useful for the 10 percent of women in nursing who are ethnic minorities, as well as for men in nursing. Minorities and men in nursing have had to deal with "identity" many times in their careers. Minorities and men are not part of the 90% of Anglo women who dominate the profession. Perhaps identity issues, particularly those related to nursing, are not as common for Anglo women nurses as they are for minorities and men. Career planning may work better for Anglo female nurses since their experiences are shared by nearly 90% of all nurses.

For me, identity changes occurred when my personal values and interests led me to move into other experiences. My personal values have usually mixed well with my professional values, which has helped me stay in the nursing profession. I believe nursing is a near ideal occupation for those who want to "try on" various identities yet remain in the same profession.

The concepts of self-identity and identity change are familiar to nurses. The nursing profession has a long history of "identity" concerns. The journals, textbooks and theorists reflect decades of hand-wringing about the nature of the profession. We also routinely use the concept of identity in common ways daily. We validate the identity of our patients by looking at wrist bands. Patients identify us by looking at our identity badges. We worry about "identity theft" on the Internet and we have PIN numbers (personal identification numbers) to prevent such theft. We hear that a friend is having an "identity crisis." We also know establishing a new identity requires self-reflection.

We know there is a North American Nursing Diagnosis Association (NANDA) diagnosis related to identity, although it is not very useful in this context. It is one of several varieties of "self-concept disturbance," which includes "self-esteem disturbance" and "body image disturbance," among others. The diagnosis, "personal identity disturbance," is described as:

. . . an organizing principle of the personality for the unity, continuity, consistency and uniqueness of the individual. It connotes autonomy and includes self-perceptions of sexuality. . . . Identity formation begins in infancy and proceeds throughout life, but it is the major task of the adolescent period (Carpenito, 1999, p. 783).

Carpenito believes *personal identity* can be marked by disturbance in the perception of self, which is best captured by the phrase, "Who am I?" (p. 784). The concept of "identity" socially links individuals to family, neighborhoods, culture, state and nation. As a result of September 11, 2001, our nation is struggling to find a new identity. One's identity as a human is associated with basic human rights. Millions across the world base their identity on religious creeds. Identity includes ideas about clothing and food, about the nature of time, and about health beliefs, including life and death. In the United States, identity most importantly includes our skin color and gender. In other parts of the world, one's most important identity marker may be the language one speaks. But no matter the order, language, gender and skin color of an individual shape human destinies by establishing one's basic identity.

One's culture, one's identity, and one's language are inseparable. For example:

Where I live, I have come to see language as the most basic part of culture. A simple thing such as learning a second language has led to internal confusion about my identity as an American nurse. Language has changed my personal values. I frequently ask myself, "Who am I?" My thinking is carried on in daily self dialogues that move back and forth between English and Spanish. I have also learned, gratefully, that this question of identity ("Who am I?") is part of a normal process one engages in when one is a minority interacting with other cultures. In my case, my questions have arisen in my professional work with people who do not speak my primary language but who seek healthcare and health information. In trying to meet that other culture as much as possible on its own terms, I've questioned my past assumptions and understandings about how the world "is." As my internal identity has changed, so have my values and so have my nursing practice and interests.

Identity, Personal Values, "Place" and Loss

Some personal values change throughout one's career. For some, they stay the same. Where one lives is sometimes a very important part of one's identity. And what happens to the family is another important variable that affects one's identity.

Where I live has consistently been an important value for me, one that has helped shape my identity. I see the place where I live as a major determinant for living an interesting life. "Place" has consistently driven my career choices. I was born in Glendale, California, but raised as a youngster in North Dakota, very near the U.S.-Canada border. My family often shopped in Canada, and I vividly recall these early crossings of an international boundary. After high school in Iowa,

I left home, independent, at age 19 and moved to the Los Angeles area. I enjoyed its mix of cultures, especially the sounds of Spanish where I worked. I attended classes at a community college at night and was employed as a meat cutter by day.

Traumatic amputation of my four right-hand fingers at the second joint marked a change in both self-identity and career. Suddenly, there were things I could not physically accomplish. I continued my community college courses by learning to write with my left hand during recovery. A year after losing my fingers, I completed the business degree at the community college. We moved the same month, with a 3-year-old daughter, to Alaska, a place that had attracted me for several years. The romance of Alaska was captured by that state's identity as the "Last Frontier." In moving to Alaska, I moved to another world. In almost every way, life in Alaska was strangely separated from the other United States, and I very much liked that strangeness. It is not surprising to me that I now live in another kind of "frontier," that of the U.S.-Mexico border.

The death of a parent, spouse, child and/or a sibling can significantly affect one's sense of identity. Loss of a loved one puts in question our own existence and when we also will need to face death ourselves. It also heightens our awareness of things we often take for granted.

Such an identity change occurred shortly after moving to Alaska, when my mother died of cancer at age 44. My father's death four years later, from cancer at age 49, was even more painful. My identity as a person, formed by my parents' traditional values, was shaken by their deaths. I did not understand what the doctors and nurses were telling me about my parents. I tried to read about their diseases, but I literally could not understand what I was reading. Self-reconstruction of my identity started six months after my father died, when I entered a nursing program.

Until my parents died, I had never thought about healthcare as a career, not even during months of exposure to healthcare workers rehabilitating my right hand. My immediate goal to enter a nursing program was quite personal: I wanted to understand how, and why, my parents died. I needed to find an occupation that allowed me to work without a strong right hand. I was also looking for an occupation that promised good employment opportunities. I had not yet thought about the social implications of being identified as a nurse. I was preoccupied by the loss of my parents when I entered my nursing program. On the other hand, had my parents not died young and had my identity and values not been so strongly affected by those deaths, I doubt I ever would have thought about nursing as my career.

Identity in a Basic Nursing Program and Graduate School

Identity continues to change as we encounter different experiences. These changes, over time, also affect our career directions. Identity also influences what we think we can do and what we ultimately pursue. In addition, various unexpected instances also have an impact on our choices.

I knew nothing about nursing before I entered my BSN program. I was a 29-year-old father of two, newly returned to the mainland after six years in Alaska, whose major personal goal was to understand how his parents had died. I related "nursing" to doctors and to hospitals and that was the extent of my "knowledge" of nursing. I selected a BSN program, not because I was knowledgeable about differences among types of nursing programs, but because I had a transcript with two years of academic credit from an associate degree program. With those credits, I could complete the BSN in about three years.

Besides one's identity, there are times when certain opportunities change our values and thus the directions we take. In fact, it is not unusual for a career to take a side-step or be altered by a positive and inspiring event. Such events often have the ability to make an impression that is sustained over our lives and occur without a plan. These events alter our directions and provide a reward that is hard not to accept. They also open our vision of what we can become.

My self-identity significantly changed in the nursing program. I did well in my basic science courses. I learned I was a good student when self-motivated. My self-concept came to include the identity of "student" and I enjoyed the new role. I could feel inside that I was being changed by my studies. I was asked by the nursing program director to be a student lab assistant in human anatomy, an experience that lasted two years. (My program in a small private Catholic college had nursing students dissecting cadavers.) I minored in philosophy, something nursing students did not do. I began to trust my self-motivation to carry me into new experiences. It did not hurt that I was named the nursing department's "Outstanding Graduate" in 1976. My sense of changing self-identity and the learning of new values was personal and shared with few. But changes had occurred. By the end of my program, I realized two new values that remain to this day: I wanted to be in places of learning, and I liked teaching.

How one relates to colleagues and what motivates also influence the career directions taken. It is interesting to note the reason for pursuing an education can change as the experience brings meaning to our awareness. For instance, the following continuing story highlights how our protagonist, the nurse, moves forward in his career as events and people affect his trajectory, and all without a plan. His story also underscores how being different can affect a person (whether good or bad) and how it either motivates or dampens interest. His discovery of a new identity and purpose, which leads to career decisions, is also apparent as he tells his story.

My interactions with the female nursing students were in classes, laboratories and hospitals. My self-consciousness about being the only man in the program diminished, although some of that has never disappeared. (I am still the only man in the department of nursing where I work, and I still notice it.) I did not feel left out by the other nursing students. But it was clear to me and to them that my motivations for attending college were different from what I heard the women students saying. I was also 10 years older than most of the other nursing students, and they mostly lived on campus, while I was married living off campus. I did not participate in many college-wide activities, because I studied hard and I usually had a part-time job. My identity as a nursing student was accepted by my classmates and by my instructors so far as I could tell. I had no sense of being discriminated against in my undergraduate program, but I did sense the strangeness of being the only man. In the three years of my bachelor's program, I acquired a new identity, mostly through my own efforts to understand relationships between what I was studying and my parents' deaths. Although I did not have a career plan, I was also ready to move on.

Changing Values in Graduate School

We read brochures about how education can change our lives and create avenues for career opportunities. Surely, there have been questions by many regarding these statements. However, for some it is true but not for the usual reasons. For many, it is who inspired the student, for others it is what happened in their personal lives that made the difference. For some, it is both of these issues.

In my experience as a nursing educator, I have seen how graduate school can often dramatically change students' values and career plans. In my undergraduate program, the only freedom I had from nursing was in my philosophy courses. The freedom to choose to study what I wanted to became an essential value in graduate school that I have continued to follow throughout my career. For a few weeks after graduation, I thought about enrolling in medical school, but the graduate nursing program at the University of Iowa also beckoned with federal traineeships for graduate students. I accepted the traineeship and realized the original goal, to return to Alaska, was no longer so important. I started a master's in nursing program at the University of Iowa but did not finish it, again for personal reasons. I withdrew lacking three courses and the thesis. Part of the reason was that my wife had received an excellent promotion and a significant salary increase upon moving to Nebraska. I could have arranged to finish the MSN without attending the University of Iowa campus full time, but I was not sufficiently motivated to stay in the program because of personal changes. Perhaps the fact that I was still a minority as a male in graduate school was a bit of a factor. I now consider my failure to finish at the University of Iowa to be the biggest "mistake" made in my nursing career. A "real" career plan might have saved the situation. However, my action was entirely consistent with my reliance on personal values as the vehicle directing my career. It was personal values and another death that drove my decision to resume graduate education. At the University of Iowa, I was a graduate teaching assistant to Dr. Teresa E. Christy. Dr. Christy's enthusiasm about the history of nursing was highly contagious. She was a genuine inspiration. She usually wore a piece of jewelry engraved with the words, "You have the freedom to be yourself, now and forever," and I have not forgotten those words. When I learned that Dr. Christy had died, I resolved to become a nursing educator.

As part of the search for identity and its effect on one's career, the choice of education becomes important. If the career pathway is planned, the selection of preparation is based on that plan. However, if personal values are the basis for the selection of an education, the selection process and outcomes are different and often determined by other considerations.

I completed a master's degree in education at the University of Nebraska at Omaha and went straight to the doctoral program at the University of Nebraska (Lincoln), where I enrolled in the Psychological and Cultural Studies program in Teachers College. My major was in the Social Foundations of Education. My program reflected my personal interests in both history and culture. My interest in history was still strong, and I again felt the genuine pleasure of learning things that I wanted to learn. My PhD certainly was not a very practical degree considered in the context of doctoral degrees in nursing. My decision to obtain a doctoral degree in a college of education rather than in nursing was again much more personal than professional. I wanted to study history but did not want to be a professional historian, that is a PhD in history. University departments of history were assuring history majors there were no jobs for PhDs except in secondary schools. At Teachers College I could pursue history and education courses in the history department. I could link my interest in history to my professional goals, because the history of nursing has always been accepted in the profession. I eventually completed a dissertation of some 500, well-documented pages covering the history of Nebraska nursing education between 1888 and 1941.

My interest in history continued after my dissertation and led to a contract to write a centennial history for a leading school of nursing in Nebraska. I believe both my dissertation and the centennial history are good examples of my capacity to do scholarly work in the history of nursing. I also believe that because nursing is such a broad discipline, the profession should encourage and recognize scholars who seek cross-disciplinary doctoral degrees. Such scholars can help nursing maintain contact with other disciplines and bring new ideas to the profession. It was in my doctoral program that I first saw the value of having some nurses take graduate degrees outside the discipline of nursing. Completing the doctoral degree (and my other five degrees), by the way, was never a great high. The value of education for me is in the learning. I have never framed or displayed my degrees.

Identity in Nursing

Identity and self-concept are related. If we are normal, we can describe who we are, at least to ourselves. We can also describe things like our cognitive and physical abilities. For example,

> *I can identify myself as a heterosexual man, over 50, a student, a teacher, a nurse. My identity includes an internal locus of control, although that is changing given my exposure to populations that see the world as full of external loci of control. I have made several role transitions in my career, and my identity now is such that I expect to function and perform well in new roles. There are still many things I cannot do well, especially things that require manual dexterity and fine motor skills. I knew my identity included "heterosexual man" before I entered nursing school. My social identity as a man who is a nurse, however, sometimes causes others to wonder about my gender identity. Obviously, I did not need to work in what are stereotypical men's jobs to maintain my identity as a male. The existing stereotypes about men and nursing did not keep me from entering the profession, although such stereotypes still function as a "border" to be crossed by any man who enters the nursing profession. In social settings, when other men ask me, "And what do you do?" I have experienced dead silence to my response that I am a nurse. I have always taken the point of view that if someone has a problem with my occupation, it's their problem not mine. Still, the biases exist. They existed in my undergraduate program, for example, where I could not attend the labor and delivery room even though I was the married father of two daughters. In terms of career choices and career values, I think it an absolute prerequisite that a man in nursing be comfortable working with women, and especially with "taking orders" from women. This has not been an issue for me, but it is for some men, and I occasionally see it in men who are nursing students. Because only about nine percent of registered nurses are men, the stereotypes about men doing "women's work" will not be erased during my lifetime.*

Identity on the Border

With age and experience, values change. So do the rewards received for "work" to the point that payment for work is not always the reason a position is pursued or accepted. Personal values, in the form of "place," have led some to resign from a well-paying job. Personal values and their accompanying rewards have helped many find their places in the world of work. And for professionals, there is always someone who needs a qualified professor and one who is willing to "start again." At least these experiences and their resultant outcomes are true for the male nurse telling his story in this chapter.

> *My interest in the history of nursing was one peak in my nursing career. I was active in the American Association for the History of Nursing, a group of specialists in nursing history. I had support from my employing institution to continue that work, including support to teach a nursing history class. But I had lived in Iowa and Nebraska for over 15 years. I was bored by life in the same place for so many years. An almost mythic American value is the freedom to move to other places and restart a life. I looked again to moving to Alaska, where my younger daughter attended the university, and again to Los Angeles. I had visited every state east of the Mississippi, and I had sisters in Connecticut and Florida, but the East has never captured me. Long ago I determined that for me, "place" meant west of the Rocky Mountains. After a particularly bad Nebraska winter, I looked to the Southwest.*
>
> *I left Nebraska where I was a full professor in a private school of nursing. I decided I wanted to reinvent myself in southern New Mexico, a place as exotic in its own way as Alaska. Once again, I had no career plan to save me from such an ill-advised career move. There were absolutely no incentives at the new university. I took a significant salary cut (it took six years to regain my Nebraska salary level). Even worse, I lost an academic rank and had to restart the tenure track. No career plan would have suggested I leave a well-paid position and lose academic rank to move to the poorest of places in the United States. In retrospect, I am glad I did not have a career plan to prevent me from making such a foolish change. My lack of career planning led me to career renewal in completely unexpected ways. Nothing that has happened in the last seven years would have developed, including a Fulbright Scholarship, if I had followed a normal career plan. I had only my personal values as guides. The result is I created a nursing career in a very unique place. I now live on the U.S.-Mexico border,*

specifically in the region formed by southern New Mexico-El Paso-Ciudad Juárez. I knew nothing of the language or culture when I moved there. At first in my community health nursing clinical, I felt incompetent and lost without interpreters. After almost seven years, I am more competent and more confident about what I do, including my efforts to work with schools of nursing on the Mexico side of the border. My identity and values continue to evolve. I do not, for example, regard myself as being from New Mexico; I now say I'm from "the Border," because that better captures my thinking and feelings about this region. The borderlands are neither part of the United States nor part of Mexico. The border region is its own place, not readily described in words. It is better to see, hear and smell it. Hundreds of thousands of people cross that border every year and every year 250 or more, including women and children, die trying to cross. How can one not be changed in such a place?

The downside of taking direction from your values is that there is no one to blame if things do not work out except yourself. The upside, however, is the unexpected, wonderful outcome that results because your values have directed you to what turns out to be rewarding and growth producing. Perhaps this is always the case, because your values are the essence of you and cannot be translated into a plan that is designed to be right for you. This is not to say a plan could not be built on values! It is just difficult if values change as they did for this young man.

I am learning a second language. It is a little like learning about nursing; there is no end to the learning. At first, learning Spanish seemed the obvious thing to do given my nursing specialty of community health. Several years later, however, the language has changed my identity. I am again asking, "Who am I?" In my first year in New Mexico, I learned I could not accomplish much in community health without being able to speak with clients and patients in their preferred language. My self-diagnosis was clear and so was my intervention: I started to learn Spanish. Something unexpected happened, something for which no career plan would account.

My increasing knowledge of Spanish and Mexican cultures has led me to ask questions about healthcare and nursing in those cultures. The more I have learned, the more I wanted to learn. Spanish, now a personal value, has been driving my career and personal life in the past three years. I have been much affected also by international nursing experiences I have had as a direct result of learning Spanish. I received a Fulbright-Garcia Robles Senior Scholar award to Mexico in 1999. I have also made numerous trips to university-based nursing programs in the states of Guanajuato and Chihuahua, as well as attended nursing conferences in Mexico. I speak Spanish daily in my personal and professional lives. It is a good feeling to be able to connect directly with my Spanish-speaking nursing students. Learning a second language has been like learning any new nursing skill. At first it is difficult, then it is easier, then it is comfortable. For me, Spanish is a value, a tool, a project, a process and a self-identity marker that did not exist before I came to the border. The ability to work directly with non-English speaking patients is a personal and professional value that has changed my career.

The Future

It is not surprising that my reference peer groups are changing. Making new peer groups is consistent with identity change based on theories and research from literature about second language learning and cultural issues (Ogulnick, 2000; González, 2001; Norton, 2000, Peirce, 1995; Rouse, 1995). My peers are no longer composed mostly of Anglo nurses. My reference groups, that is, people I seek out and who seek me out, are composed of bilingual public health employees (some are nurses) and a second group, which is a mixture of monolingual Spanish speakers learning English and some professors and graduate students interested in language issues. Some of my peers live in Mexico. That I am a nurse, or even a man in nursing, has not seemed relevant to these two groups. I may be drifting somewhat from my Anglo nursing peers, if only because we see different worlds when we look at the same non-English speaking patients. Perhaps I will focus more on international nursing in the future. But I still do not have a career plan. Cultural differences in the southern New Mexico-El Paso-Cd. Juárez region have affected my values. I have also been introduced to new ways of looking at health and nursing by my peers in Mexico. My personal and professional identity for the near future involve living in Mexico for extended periods, with an immersion into the nursing and health promotion mod-

els there. Becoming acculturated to Mexico's health systems might inform my future work with Mexicans and with Mexican-Americans on the U.S. side of the border. With such experience and knowledge, I could also bring change to nursing education on the U.S. side.

What the future holds for nurses interested in career change is variable and dependent on each person's framework. The story told in this chapter exemplifies how values can influence one's professional selections. It also highlights the important issues a career plan must consider, that is, the reason change over time must be considered. Of major importance is the role "place" played for the young man in this story. As his geographic place changed, so did his opportunities and, ultimately, his values. This tells us how important geography can be and must be considered when a change in location (at least of the magnitude of this story) is considered. The globalization of nursing warrants more attention by U.S. nursing as nursing education faces the next quarter century. The lack of cultural diversity in American nursing must also be addressed. In the future, it may take nurses of color who speak other languages to help American nurses learn to personally value cultural and ethnic diversity.

CONCLUSION

Pursuing a career solely based on personal values is tricky and sometimes has its drawbacks. However, the person telling this story was able to accomplish many things he valued, such as:

- Freedom to choose
- Freedom to be himself
- Freedom to implement personal values

He was also able to turn what appears to be a lack of planning into positive outcomes. And while he never let professional work interfere with his personal values, he was able to pursue a professional path that has been productive and satisfying for him.

REFERENCES

Carpenito, L.J. (1999). *Nursing care plans & documentation: Nursing diagnosis and collaborative problems.* Philadelphia, PA: Lippincott.

González, N. (2001). I am my language: *Discourses of women and children in the borderlands.* Tucson, AZ: University of Arizona Press.

Ogulnick, K.L. (2000) (Ed.). *Language crossings: Negotiating the self in a multicultural world.* New York, NY: Teachers College Press.

Norton, B. (2000). *Identity and language learning: Gender, ethnicity and educational change.* Edinburgh Gate, Essex, England: Pearson Education.

Peirce, B. (1995). Social identity, investment, and language learning. *TESOL Quarterly, 29*(1), 9-31.

Rouse, R. (1995). Questions of identity: Personhood and collectivity in transnational migration to the United States. *Critique of Anthropology, 15*(4), 351-380.

Chapter 13

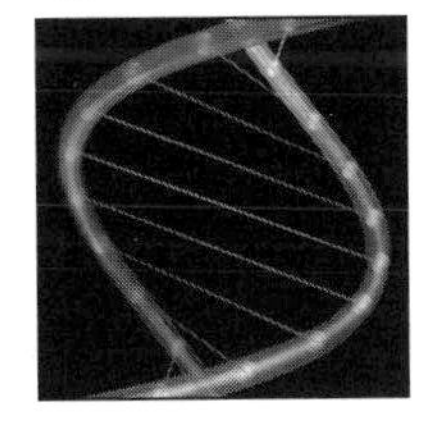

Crossing Borders: International Careers in Nursing

by Wendell Oderkirk

INTRODUCTION

This chapter contains an exploration of nursing opportunities available for nurses interested in learning about the challenges associated with international nursing, which can include working with both patients and nurses who are recent immigrants to the United States. Discussions regarding the effects on personal and professional career decisions, as a result of "crossing a border," are presented. Terms are defined and cultural differences and their effects on those who risk crossing borders are also described. Opportunities, with their inherent problems, are discussed with startling documentation.

BORDERS AND BOUNDARY LINES

By nature, borders and borderlands are in-between places, neither here nor there places. Sometimes, the boundary is obvious, as with an international border. But most borders are not so obvious. A "border" can be defined as "the outer edge of something" (Webster, 1965). A dress can have a border. We may use flowers and stones to make borders on a sidewalk. Book pages have border margins, and picture frames have borders. In many cities, train tracks mark a social boundary that serves as a divider between the poor side of town and the "better" side of town. Freeways serve a similar border function.

"Boundary line" is a related term. State and international borders mark actual lines put on the ground to mark where one place ends and another begins.

The words "border," "edge," and "boundary," thus signify limits, beyond which one crosses into something very different. Anzaldua (1987) writes "Borderlands are physically present wherever two or more cultures edge each other, where people of different races occupy the same territory, where under, lower, middle, and upper classes touch, where the space between two individuals shrinks with intimacy" (preface).

Borderlines exist to divide and separate. They separate the alien from the citizen, the black and brown from the Anglo, rich from poor, powerful from weak, and sick from well. Some borderlines can be hard or impossible to cross. Language and cultural differences constitute another powerful example of borderlines not readily crossed. Borderlines are always in flux, are often tense and are always being tested. The concept of borderlands also suggests the "fringe element," something peripheral, on the margin. In the case of crossing an international boundary, one is usually very aware of "crossing the line."

In the case of nurses following a career trajectory, the lines to be crossed may not be so evident. However, personal and/or career development goals sooner or later will require a nurse to cross boundaries. Whether those boundaries are international borders or whether they are boundaries within a current employment situation, such as crossing into (or out of) a position of authority, the effort to make the crossing may be challenging and the results not at all guaranteed. The nurse who crosses borderlines will be an "alien," at least for a while, when a newcomer to a hospital, another state or a nation. Any nurse making career changes will reach the borderline. Once at the borderline, the nurse will make a decision to cross into that new and different place or stay home on "my own side," of the border.

Border crossings can be risky. Those who attempt to cross borders without proper documents (for example, a state nursing license valid in the state in which the nurse is practicing) will meet with a strong "NO!" from those hired to prevent border crossings. The nurse who lacks a valid license will be frustrated and perhaps disillusioned about whether to cross or not. For others trying to cross international borders without proper documents, death is sometimes the result. For example, in the case of Mexican and

Canadian borders, border crossers meet a strong commitment by the U.S. Border Patrol; officials look at all documents and examine every vehicle, from engine to trunk. The U.S. Border Patrol covers the almost 2,000-mile-long Mexican borderline with 9,100 agents, roughly one agent for each 1,000 feet. On the Canadian border, the border patrol recently added 22 agents to the 331 already posted along a 5,525-mile border separating the United States and Canada, about 16 miles of border for each agent. Clearly, the commitment to prevent people from entering the U.S. is very strong on the United States' southern border (Malone, 2002). Even so, more than 250 people die annually trying to cross the U.S.-Mexico border.

CULTURAL COMPETENCY, LANGUAGE AND CAREER CHOICES

Skin color and gender create another kind of unchangeable border. The language one speaks is almost as solidly fixed as skin color and gender. Religious beliefs create other borders and barriers. Efforts to reduce minority population barriers to healthcare access have developed in professional nursing during the last decade under the rubrics of "diversity" and "cultural competence." As an example, a two-issue roundtable discussion in the *American Journal of Nursing* (Lester, 1998a; 1998b) demonstrated the difficulties of trying to prepare nurses with "cultural competency." As one participant stated, "We all have prejudices. It's essential to know what these areas are. [But] can you change them? .... This requires a dedication beyond what some people bring to their professional life because it means making a huge commitment both professionally and personally to be a different person" (p. 33).

The rich dialogue among the experienced nurses already committed to giving patients excellent, culturally competent care suggests nursing education has not yet been successful in operationalizing "cultural competency." Articles such as this two-issue series provide insights and help for individual nurses who want to seek nursing career challenges associated with international nursing, as well as with patients who have crossed international borders into the U.S.

Most nurses who have a second language know firsthand the challenges associated with learning a second language. These nurses, through their own experiences of working in two languages, can readily identify with patients and families who lack English language proficiency. These nurses are also more likely to understand the difficulties immigrants experience trying to find English-as-a-Second Language (ESL) classes. Nurses looking to expand their knowledge and skills for the coming 25 years are strongly advised to add a second language to their nursing skill set. Be warned, it is not easy. If it were, everyone would speak two (or more languages), and all immigrants would quickly learn English (Oderkirk, 1999).

Perhaps a better skill set for nurses looking to career advancement without having to learn a second language is to learn how to work with a certified interpreter. What is clear to staff nurses, nursing students and patients is that patients want to be spoken to in their own language when making important health decisions for themselves or their family. For this to happen, the patient's nurse must speak and understand the patient's language or be able to efficiently work with a certified interpreter. However, certified healthcare interpreters are scarce. For example, the Washington State Department of Social and Health Services (DSHS) prepares certified interpreters and translators, which is one response to an Office for Civil Rights complaint and a class-action suit against DSHS in the early 1990s. The result is that DSHS has created an excellent interpreter certification program. It certifies interpreters and translators in Spanish, Russian, Vietnamese, Mandarin Chinese, Cantonese Chinese, Korean, Cambodian and Laotian and qualifies interpreters in other languages (DSHS, 2002). Most states have nothing similar.

Nursing education has a special responsibility in this area. Because nursing instructors are 90% Anglo women, nursing education programs will not adequately prepare culturally competent nurses until schools attract, and admit, substantial numbers of minority students. Requiring second-language training equivalent of two years of college-level foreign language before admission to a nursing program may be one method to increase minority applicants. Giving students with a second language a higher admissions ranking might also help. Communication with the patient in the patient's preferred language may be more useful to practicing nurses than two semesters of college chemistry.

A medical school is trying to lead the way. The Wake Forest School of Medicine is requiring fourth-year medical students to complete an hour of intensive Spanish everyday for a four-week period. Students who already have basic Spanish take lessons from a retired neurosurgeon who speaks Spanish (Wake Forest, 2002). Elsewhere, language-frustrated physicians are finding other ways to learn Spanish (Glabman, 2002). These efforts appear almost trivial. They are certainly naïve about language learning. But the examples do demonstrate a genuine frustration on the part of physicians who lack access to certified interpreters.

Within the past two years, significant change has occurred in federal government regulation concerning a patient's right to be spoken to by healthcare providers who can address the patient in the patient's preferred language. Receiving translated documents such as permission forms and patient education material in the patient's preferred language is also part of the new regulations. Nurses looking for a unique career niche might consider becoming the Culturally and Linguistically Appropriate Materials (CLAMs) expert in their facility (Smith, 2000). The Department of Justice's (DOJ) "Guidance to Federal Financial Assistance Recipients Regarding Title VI Prohibition Against National Origin Discrimination Affecting Limited English Proficient Persons" describes how healthcare agencies can meet these new requirements (DOJ, 2002; Ensuring linguistic access, 2001).

Hospitals in most states are also not ready to meet the Office for Civil Rights standards related to patients who cannot speak and/or read English. The absence of training programs for interpreters and translators creates an unusual opportunity for qualified nurses to practice independently. Certified legal (court) interpreters have been required in courthouses for decades. Training for this work requires near native proficiency in both languages and in all four language domains (understanding spoken language, speaking, writing and reading). Nurse entrepreneurs, however, who can readily organize and manage such programs need not be particularly fluent in languages. Also, interpreter trainees need skill training in medical terminology and in the common, everyday words patients use related to health. These roles, as well as teaching interpreter ethics, are within the scope of nursing at this time (Avery, 2002).

Nurses Crossing International Borders

Nurses from foreign countries are increasingly moving across international borders, not only by coming to the United States, but by going to other nations around the world. With the exceptions of travel nurses, nurses on missionary work and military nurses, few registered nurses from the United States will ever seek practice in another country. After all, most foreign nurses come to the United States for professional advancement and a better salary. The most likely international nursing experience most American nurses will have in their careers will be rubbing elbows with immigrant nurses and caring for immigrant patients.

Nurses in the past have crossed international borders. Florence Nightingale and Margaret Higgins Sanger took social and personal risks to create change. Nightingale crossed enormous social barriers to become a nurse. She communicated extensively with emerging hospitals and public health movements around the world. Sanger traveled extensively in Europe and Japan to spread information about birth control. She was subject to prison and social rejection. She even acquired a thick FBI file (Oderkirk, 2002). Potential border crossers need look no further than Nightingale and Sanger for inspiration. Modern-day border crossers certainly exist.

> *Matt Bording, RN, received $350 a month plus room and board to work for a year in a children's hospital in rural Cambodia. Earlier travels in Asia had taken him past the stage of the culture-shocked tourist, but even so he was not ready for the nursing situation he encountered. His critical care knowledge was of little value. Nursing and medical conditions were sometimes substandard. He contracted dengue. He taught nursing students who had no texts. And, yes, language was a barrier. His advice is that nurses should travel and work in Third World nations.*

Bording would agree that crossing such borders changes one's life (Coates, 2002). Sibbald (1997) gives other examples of nurses' working beyond North American borders in *The Canadian Nurse*.

Nurse Immigration

Katie Morgan is a 27-year-old British-educated nurse who doubled her salary by moving to Phoenix about two years ago. Her small flat and rusting car in Great Britain were left behind as she acquired a large house (with pool) and a new car. According to the *Guardian* (Browne, 2001), Morgan has joined an exodus of British nurses deserting the U.K. because of poor pay and poor working conditions. Browne claims that Britain's "brain drain" is forcing the country to recruit thousands of nurses from poor African and Asian countries. In the past, Canadian and Australian nurses regularly migrated to Britain, but in recent years, the number has decreased by half. The government has brought in thousands of replacements from Zambia, Botswana, Zimbabwe and Malawi, countries where health services are failing because of the AIDS epidemic (Browne, 2001). On the U.S. side, British nurses immigrating to the United States are being promised help with immigration issues, including green cards for family members. According to the article in the *Guardian*, Kate Morgan says she will not go back to the U.K.

In Great Britain, the entry of foreign nurses by the thousands, including nurses from the Philippines, India, Nigeria and Ghana in addition to the countries mentioned above, has created problems for hospital administrators, staff nurses and patients concerned about immigrant nurses' poor English skills. Foreign nurses are now required to pass an English proficiency examination before seeking practice privileges (Carvel, 2002). Great Britain has also signed agreements to import as many as 5,000 nurses from Spain, with English-language classes added as part of the program (Hernández, 2000). More recently, the number of immigrating nurses to the U.K. from the European Union has also declined, and language differences are given as the key factor. The National Health Service recently claimed it is no longer actively recruiting nurses from developing countries, because international nursing recruitment can no longer be seen as a short-term solution to nursing shortages (Royal College of Nursing, 2002).

Another example of the international movement of nurses is offered by Tenet Healthcare Corp., which recently signed a two-year accord with the International University of Barcelona to recruit Spanish nurses to the United States. In September 2002, the Barcelona program was to offer academic courses to assure English language skills and familiarity with English language clinical terminology. The nurses from Spain will likely work in Tenet hospitals in Texas, Florida and Southern California, areas with high concentrations of Spanish-speaking populations. The nurses' salaries may start at $45,000 and, depending on experience and specialty, could reach $77,000 annually. When the nurses return to Spain, they will be integrated into an existing Tenet facility. The company has had some success with similar programs for nurses from Canada, Australia, New Zealand, the United Kingdom, Ireland, Switzerland, Norway and Denmark (Red hospitalaria de EEUU, 2002; Palma de Mallorca, 2002). There will be new career opportunities for American nurses to help immigrant nurses get settled in their new countries.

International movement of nurses to the United States has never been easy. As a result, immigrant nurses in America have never numbered more than about one percent of practicing nurses in the United States (Davis & Maroun, 1997). That said, the increasing international movement of nurses has challenged existing immigration regulations and certification processes for immigrant nurses moving to the United States. After waiting almost three years for immigrant visas, nurses to be certified by the Immigration and Naturalization Service (INS) received new rules in December 1998. (The American Immigration Law Foundation finally sued the INS to produce the Section 343 nursing rules, pending since the passage of the 1996 Illegal Immigration Reform and Immigrant Responsibility Act [IIRIRA]). Subsequent rules were issued in April 1999 and January 2001. INS recently selected the Commission on Graduates of Foreign Nursing Schools (CGFNS) to continue managing the certification process for nursing while adding a number of other healthcare professions to CGFNS processing, excluding physicians. (The CGFNS was formed by the American Nurses Association, the National League for Nursing, the U.S. Department of Labor and the INS in 1977 to address issues related to immigrant nurses.) The new rules may also apply to non-immigrant and immigrant nurses, including the (mostly) Canadian and (very few) Mexican nurses coming to the United States under the relatively easy process of the TN (NAFTA) visa (CGFNS, 2002; Xu, Xu, & Zhang, 1999).

The history of admitting immigrant nurses to practice in the United States is convoluted (Xu, Xu, & Zhang, 1999; Davis & Maroun, 1997). Despite successes in the past, the future of the Commission on Graduates of Foreign Nursing Schools is not so clear. The purpose of the CGFNS is, in part, to serve the INS and the Department of Labor. Its scope now includes certifying several other health-related professions. The new credentialing process for foreign nurses might well add to the CGFNS workload. As the nursing shortage deepens, it is possible that complaints about the slowness of the certification process will increase.

INS immigrant processing has also significantly slowed since September 11, 2001. For example, INS Texas Service Center processing times for most types of visas has slowed, including visas for work permits and relatives. The delays reportedly reflect as much as 85% of employees in some INS areas have less than one year in their jobs (Murthy, 2002). The CGFNS qualifying exam itself may come under criticism for modeling the NCLEX-RN, which reflects linguistic and cultural understandings of American nursing students. A more culturally and linguistically neutral mechanism for international nursing certification warrants study. A nursing career opportunity exists here.

There may also be nurse consultant opportunities related to nurse immigration into the United States, regardless of visa types. Few, if any, countries have such an extensive credentialing process for immigrant nurses as does the United States. Immigration lawyers dominate the field, but they do not know nursing. Also, few boards of nursing are likely to regularly consult attorneys who are immigration specialists. In the past, the CGFNS process has functioned well for managing the relatively small number of immigrant nurses seen by state boards of nursing. But as more nurses continue to immigrate, boards of nursing (and nurse employers) may balk at the slowness of INS and CGFNS processes. Boards of nursing may welcome nurse-driven advisement related to INS regulations and visa issues as well as help for foreign nurses in locating nursing programs friendly to foreign students.

Globalization

A question to be asked is "Who, or what, is driving international processes to endorse or certify nurses?" Those who believe that globalization offers opportunities for nurses are not merely dreamers or visionaries. They are pragmatic observers of the nursing environment who believe that everything in healthcare, from international viruses to international terrorism, can and should be addressed on an international basis. "Globalization mandates that the nursing profession be internationalized," argues Xu (2000, p. 39). Regulation of nursing practice and nursing licensure on an international level is slowly developing under the International Council of Nurses (ICN). Gathering information about nursing education models and nursing practices throughout the world probably should not be the undertaking for the CGFNS, although CGFNS experience could be valuable.

The ICN, perhaps best known to American nurses for its International Code for Nurses, also addresses standards of practice that can be accepted by nurses around the world. The ICN is interested in nursing regulation, nurse credentialing, and occupational health and safety for nurses everywhere in the world. The ICN is interested in a unified language for nursing. The International Classification for Nursing Practice aims to establish a common language for nursing that can be used by local nursing practices across all spoken languages and specialty areas. ICN position statements are of universal interest to practicing nurses, educators and students. From women's health to social issues, such as cloning and torture, the ICN has taken positions appropriate for nursing roles.

The ICN has also taken a position on nurses crossing borders for employment. Concerned in part by the aggressive recruitment of nurses and cases of nurse exploitation, the ICN has issued a five-page position statement titled "Ethical Nurse Recruitment." Good faith contracting, freedom of international movement for nurses, access to grievance procedures, safe work environments and regulation of recruitment are among their areas of concern. The statement also references related ICN position statements such as *Nurse Retention, Transfer and Migration*; *Career Mobility and Nursing*; *and International Trade Agreements*. Nearly all information on the ICN Web site (http://www.icn.org) is available in Spanish, French and English. The ICN could play a significant role in the internationalization of nursing education and practice, especially if Sigma Theta Tau International continues to emphasize to American nurses the value of international nursing. The ICN is certainly aware of ethical issues surrounding international nurse migration. The "brain and skills drain" tends to move nurses from poor countries to nursing in rich countries, not the other way around. The balance point hovers on recognizing individual nurses' rights to migrate vs. concern for a nation's health when that nation is losing nurses (Kingma, 2001).

Two other organizations of interest to nurses who cross borders are the Pan-American Health Organization (http://www.paho.org/) and the World Health Organization (http://www.who.int/en/ in English.) Most American nurses have at least heard of the World Health Organization, but few have consulted with the WHO, let alone PAHO. Both are excellent organizations able to help practicing nurses and students enhance cultural competency on an international basis. Nurses and students interested in crossing international borders will want to actively use ICN, WHO and PAHO resources. Nursing career opportunities related to transnational nursing in North America, under NAFTA, may become more likely in the future, although language (Spanish in the U.S. and French in Quebec) will remain as barriers for United States nurses.

Foreign Students

International nursing education for foreign students in American nursing programs offers nurses, and especially nurse educators, opportunities to internationalize their work via exchange programs. Arguably, students who come to the United States face the more difficult situation; they often experience months or even years of document processing to enter the U.S., and they are more likely to come alone. American students going to another country can readily obtain a U.S. passport and, depending on the country, a permit or entry visa. Americans are also more likely to have sufficient funds to manage their lives in another country. Foreign students who come to the United States, regardless of native language or skin color, will sense they are marginalized (Hall, Stevens, & Meleis, 1994), a concept that applies to most border crossers. Re-entry to the home country is another area of concern (Weaver,1994).

Certainly, nursing educators are interested in helping foreign graduate and undergraduate students meet success in nursing education programs. Not surprisingly, language barriers are the greatest challenge for most students (Ryan, Markowski, Ura, & Chong-Yeu Liu-Chiang, 1998; Gay, Edgil, & Stullenbarger, 1993). Faculty without personal experience learning a second language as an adult may subconsciously blame the student for failing to communicate well. Unless faculty spend significant time working with an international graduate student, they may not realize that an international student actually takes two courses for every one course the American graduate student takes. The second course for international students is the heavy use of a foreign-language-to-English-language dictionary. Using this method to learn English consumes hours when a foreign student tries to read nursing textbooks.

Malu and Figlear (1998) have perfectly captured the reality of the foreign graduate students' dilemma: The students appear to speak English fairly well because their ESL courses have helped them learn to navigate the relatively simple aspects of daily living in the United States. What ESL cannot possibly do is concentrate five-to-seven years of *formal* language learning into two or three semesters of ESL. For graduate students to understand the high "register" of English that appears in graduate-level textbooks, six years or more of *formal* English language study is required. Nurse educators should not be surprised. Even native-born, English-speaking graduate students are seen struggling with the high "fog level" of nursing textbooks.

Qualitative research evidence from extensive work with adult students of ESL suggests they have fears about not being able to learn English, about changes in self-identity, and about verbal and nonverbal slights from Americans (Norton, 2000). One way nursing instructors can help a student cross language barriers is to investigate the available literature within nursing about language learning and the limits of ESL (Julian, Keene, & Davidson, 1999). Outside of nursing, the literature on foreign language learning, whether ESL or formal language learning, is extensive. Of course, reading about language learning is not the same as learning another language.

Foreign graduate students will likely be more common in our universities in the future. The faculty member who decides to learn about the learning needs and anxieties of foreign graduate students will not only be helping students and the nursing program, but also will be managing a new career experience.

American Nurse Scholars and Students in Foreign Countries

Few American nurses seem interested in working in other nations. In a survey of university nursing professors who traveled internationally as part of their careers, Lash, Lusk and Nelson (2000) reported that only 27% of academic nurses reported international activity during the decade 1985 to 1995, a disappointingly low percentage. Interestingly, about half of the nurse educators who did go to foreign countries spoke a second language. The fact that more than half of the professors spoke a foreign language suggests foreign language ability made it easier to meet people from, and in, other countries. Where the nurse educators conducted their international activities is also revealing: The countries most frequently visited over the 10-year period were the United Kingdom (86), China (50), Canada (49), Japan (45) and Australia (39).

Nursing education programs must aggressively create opportunities for student experiences in international nursing. Schools that have crossed international borders to see how nursing and healthcare are conducted on the other side are leading the way. Duquesne University has modeled a sister school program in Nicaragua (Ross, 2000). Michigan State University's College of Nursing conducted its first semester-long, study-abroad program for senior nursing students in 1998. The program is based in Celaya, Guanajuato, Mexico. Students have at least two semesters of U.S.-based, college-level Spanish before spending almost a month studying only Spanish at the university. They receive full academic credit for both Spanish and community health theory and clinicals (Currier, Momar, Talarczyk, & Guerrero, 2000). Although the programs' goals are different, each school is far ahead in helping students and faculty learn about international health realities. Nursing educators who want to cross borders to expand international nursing opportunities for their students have, in these two cases, evidence of successful models. Other reports have had similar results (Haloburdo & Thompson, 1998).

Although the International Council of Nurses has carried the banner for international nursing for more than 100 years, it has not captured much attention from American nurses. This may change with the increasing international movement of nurses worldwide. In the United States, Sigma Theta Tau International (STTI) has sparked interest in international nursing for the last several years. It is the only major American nursing association to consistently stress that American nursing adopt global understandings of international health and health resources. STTI articles in *Reflections on Nursing Leadership* and the *Journal of Nursing Scholarship* give sustained attention to international nursing. *Leadership* always carries articles about international nurses and nursing achievements. *Scholarship* publishes (in English) scholarly research conducted by nurses from non-English speaking countries.

Another journal that supports international nursing is *The Canadian Nurse.* This national journal for nurses is bilingual. Canada has published article abstracts and often complete articles in both French and English for decades. Canadian nurses are more comfortable working in a bilingual country (and internationally) than are Americans. Nurses in the United States could emulate the Canadians. Just as Canadians have adapted to being a bilingual nation, so can the United States. By 2025, the United States will be home to the world's second largest national population of Spanish-speaking individuals. Every Spanish-speaking nation except Mexico will have fewer Spanish-speaking individuals than does the U.S. Spanish is NOT a foreign language in the United States. It is, de facto, the nation's second language, just as French is Canada's second language. (New Mexico is the only U.S. state that has a state constitution requiring two official state languages, Spanish and English.)

CONCLUSION

The rapidly changing demographics in the U.S. merit much, much more support for American minorities and more support for immigrant nurses and foreign nursing students, especially at the graduate level.

American nursing's 90% Anglo, female, monolingual hegemony is not serving the country, let alone the profession. As for international nursing, it IS the future. The ICN can drive changes around international nursing language issues and international certification and standardization. American nursing career opportunities abound for bilingual nurses, regardless of the second language.

REFERENCES

Anzaldua, G. (1987). *Borderlands/La Frontera: The new Mestiza.* San Francisco: Spinters-Aunt Lute.

Avery, J.M. (2002). The role of a health-care interpreter: An evolving dialogue. *The National Council on Interpreting in Health-care.* Retrieved March 15, 2002, from http://www.ncihc.org/.

Browne, A. (2001, August 19). Nurses desert NHS for good life. *Guardian Unlimited.* Retrieved November 5, 2002, from http://society.guardian.co.uk/NHSstaff/comment/0,8005,539642,00.html.

Carvel, J. (2002, March 8). Foreign nurses to sit for English tests. *Guardian Unlimited.* Retrieved November 5, 2002, from http://society.guardian.co.uk/NHSstaff/story/0,7991,664132,00.html.

CGFNS. (2002). *Status of Regulations Regarding Section 343 of the Illegal Immigration Reform and Immigrant Responsibility Act (IIRIRA).* Retrieved October 27, 2002, from http://www.cgfns.org/ICHP/interpre.htm.

Coates, G. (2002, August 12). Culture shock. *NurseWeek*, pp. 30-33.

Currier, C., Momar, M., Talarczyk, G., & Guerrero, R. (2000). Development and implementation of a semester program in Mexico for senior nursing students. *Journal of Professional Nursing, 16*(5), 293-299.

Davis, C., & Maroun, V. (1997). Immigrant nursing personnel: The view from CGFNS. In *Cultural diversity in nursing: Issues, strategies, and outcomes.* Washington, DC: American Academy of Nursing.

CGFNS. In *Cultural diversity in nursing: Issues, strategies, and outcomes.* Washington, DC: American Academy of Nursing.

DOJ. (2002). Department of Justice. Guidance to Federal Financial Assistance Recipients Regarding Title VI Prohibition Against National Origin Discrimination Affecting Limited English Proficient Persons. Retrieved November 5, 2002, from http://www.usdoj.gov/crt/cor/lep/dojrecipguid.htm.

DSHS. (2002). *Washington State Department of Social and Health Services.* Retrieved October 27, 2002, from http://www.dshs.wa.gov/trial/msa/ltc/index.html.

Ensuring linguistic access. (2001). *Federal Register,* 66(10), 3833-3848. Retrieved October 27, 2002, from http://www.ojp.usdoj.gov/ocr/lep.htm.

Gay, J., Edgil, A., & Stullenbarger, E. (1993). Graduate education for nursing students who have English as a second language. *Journal of Professional Nursing, 9*(2), 104-109.

Glabman, M. (2002). Doctors take crash courses in Spanish to meet rising need. *Physician's Financial News, 20*(1), 1, 21.

Hall, J., Stevens, P., & Meleis, A. (1994). Marginalization: A guiding concept for valuing diversity in nursing knowledge development. *Advances in Nursing Science, 16*(4), 23-41.

Haloburdo, E. & Thompson, A. (1998), A comparison of international learning experiences for baccalaureate nursing students: Developed and developing countries. *Journal of Nursing Education, 37*(3), 13-21.

Hernández, I. (2000). La sanidad britanica contratara a 5.000 enfermeras espanoles. *Sociedad.* Retrieved November 9, 2002, from http://www.el-mundo.es/2000/11/08/sociedad/08N0073.html.

Julian, M., Keene, A., & Davidson, K. (1999). Language plus for international graduate students in nursing. *Image: Journal of Nursing Scholarship 31*(3), 289-293.

Kingma, M. (2001). Nursing migration: Global treasure hunt or disaster-in-the-making? *Nursing Inquiry, 8*(4), 205-212.

Lash, A., Lusk, B., & Nelson, M. (2000). American nursing scholars abroad, 1985 to 1995. *Journal of Nursing Scholarship, 32*(4), 415-420.

Lester, N. (1998a). Cultural competence: A nursing dialogue: Part I. *American Journal of Nursing, 98*(8), 26-33.

Lester, N. (1998b). Cultural competence: A nursing dialogue: Part II. *American Journal of Nursing, 98*(9), 36-42.

Malone, J. (2002, July 29). Only 22 agents added to Canadian border despite call for more security. *Seattle Post-Intelligencer.* Retrieved October 27, 2002, from http://seattlepi.nwsource.com/national/80389_borders29.shtml.

Malu, K. & Figlear, M. (1998). Enhancing the language development of immigrant ESL nursing students: A case study with recommendations for action. *Nurse Educator, 23*(2), 43-46.

Murthy, S. (2002). *Texas service center: Latest processing information.* Retrieved October 23, 2002, from http://murthy.com/Udtsclat.html.

Norton, B. (2000). *Identity and language learning: Gender, ethnicity and educational change.* England: Pearson Education Limited.

Oderkirk, W. (1999). Challenging Spanish: Ways for nurses to become bilingual. *The Journal of Continuing Education in Nursing, 30*(2), 88-93.

Oderkirk, W. (2000). Personal copies of Sanger's FBI file.

Palma de Mallorca. (2002). *Un nuevo curso de la UIC para enviar a enfermeras Españoles a trabajar a hospitales de Estados Unidos.* Retrieved September 20, 2002, from http://www.terra.es/educacion/articulo/html/edu5868.htm.

Red hospitalaria de EEUU recluta a enfermeras de Espana. (2002, julio 31). Retrieved November 20, 2002, from http://noticias.espanol.yahoo.com/ 020731/2/ckjn.html.

Ross, C. (2000). Building bridges to promote globalization in nursing: The development of a hermanamiento. *Journal of Transcultural Nursing, 11*(1), 64-67.

Royal College of Nursing. (2002, July 17). Government called on to ensure nurses are not recruited from developing countries. *RCN News Online.* Retrieved October 22, 2002, from http://www.rcn.org.uk/news/printpage.php3?ID=85.

Ryan, D., Markowski, K., Ura, D., & Chong-Yeu Liu-Chiang. (1998). International nursing education: Challenges and strategies for success. *Journal of Professional Nursing, 14*(2), 69-77.

Sibbald, B. (1997, May). Beyond our borders: How to get involved in international development. *The Canadian Nurse,* pp. 24-30.

Smith, S. (2000). All health plans need CLAMS. *Healthplan,* 41(5). Retrieved January 15, 2002, from http://www.prenatalEd.com/CLAMS.htm.

Wake Forest University requires Spanish classes for would-be doctors. Retrieved April 24, 2002, from http://www.wral.com/News/1416347/detail.html.

Weaver, G. (1994). The process of reentry. *The Advising Quarterly, 27,* 1-8

Webster's Seventh New Collegiate Dictionary (7th ed.) (1965). Springfield, MA.

Xu, Y. (2000). Said another way: On an international nursing license. *Nursing Forum, 35*(4), 39-40.

Xu, Y., Xu, Z., & Zhang, J. (1999). International credentialing and immigration of nurses: CGFNS. *Nursing Economics 17*(6), 325-331.

Chapter 14

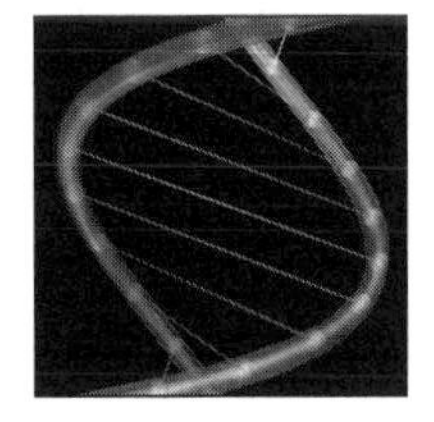

Assessing Readiness for Job/Career Change

by Fay L. Bower & Edith Jenkins-Weinrub

INTRODUCTION

Making a career change is more than simply moving from one office to another or from one building or city to another. And while the promises and benefits of a new position may seem very tempting, unless the individual seeking a career move is ready for many personal and interpersonal changes, the move could be very traumatic. Like any change, assessment, preparation and strategy planning are needed (Bower, 2000).

This chapter contains discussions and recommendations about ways to assess and prepare for a change. Much has been written about change. Change theories, concepts and processes have been outlined, debated and critiqued in the literature for years. Some of these theories will be discussed in this chapter and then used to help the job seeker prepare for a career move. However, most of this chapter is devoted to a process of assessing readiness for change and what needs to occur to maximize readiness and minimize barriers so the change is smooth, productive and free of horrendous anxiety.

Assessing Readiness for Change

Most people know something about assessment. Health professionals know a great deal about assessing health problems. However, doing an assessment of self is quite different, especially if the process is used when the individual is stressed, excited or depressed over a decision about changing positions. Most people change jobs when they are discontent with the present one, regardless of their state of mind. Others face a change in job because they were part of a downsizing or because they became bored. Some change their positions because of a fantastic offer or a new opportunity. However, changing jobs without an assessment of readiness, regardless of the reason for the move, is a not a good idea, particularly if the job does not fit into the career pathway.

What is Self-Assessment?

Self-assessment is a process of learning about oneself. It is a process of gathering information that is multidimensional and multi-layered. It includes information about one's personality, interpersonal styles, interests, knowledge, technical competencies, personal needs and motivation. The process of gaining this information depends on how much energy the job seeker wants to put into the assessment, for there are many tools and resources available. For example, the Myers-Briggs Type Indicator or the Keirsey Temperament Sorter could provide information about a person's personality and interpersonal style. Reading about Howard Gardner's theory of multiple intelligences (verbal/linguistic, musical/rhythmic, visual/spatial, logical/mathematical, etc.) or about the research conducted by Daniel Goleman, who has written extensively about emotional intelligence, could provide valuable knowledge about oneself. Priorities, goals and ambitions, and ideals and values could be assessed by using Maslow's Hierarchy of Needs or Herzberg's Theory of Motivation. Holland's Code, Sigi Plus or the Strong-Campbell Interest Inventory could provide information about vocational interests. Careerleader, developed by the Harvard Business School and normed on over 25,000 students and clients, could provide information for those interested in the business arena. Clearly there are many, many tools for assessing self.

With knowledge about self, the person interested in a job change is in charge of career planning, strategy and development. Understanding and appreciating the key elements of one's personality and interpersonal style, as well as needs, values, interests and skills pertinent to the job search, keep the person fresh and ready as the marketplace changes. With this information, the job seeker can approach employers with competence and the confidence of well-considered goals.

All of the above resources provide the job seeker with valuable information about self. However, there is one other element, which will be discussed at length in this chapter, that is equally important, and this is the *readiness* to make the move or change.

In this chapter, three frameworks are presented as ways to assess readiness for a change, particularly a change of a job or a career direction. Using Herzberg's Theory of Motivation, risk-taking theory and change theory, the case is made that by using these tools individuals can determine, with certainty, if they are ready and able to pursue a job/career change.

Assessing Motivation/Dissatisfaction

Herzberg's Theory of Motivation is built on the belief that employees can be motivated by the work itself and that there is an internal or personal need to meet organizational goals (Sullivan & Decker, 2000). Herzberg found in his research that the factors causing job satisfaction (and presumably motivation) were different from those causing job dissatisfaction. This distinction between what he called hygiene or maintenance factors (salary, supervision, job security, positive working conditions, personal life and interpersonal relations/peers) and motivator factors (achievement, recognition, work itself, responsibility, advancement, possibility for growth, company policy and status) is called the motivation-hygienic theory or two-factor theory (Syptak, Marsland, & Ulmer, 2002).

Herzberg maintained motivators or job satisfiers are present in work itself; they give people the desire to work and to do that work well. Hygiene or maintenance factors keep employees from being dissatisfied or de-motivated but do not in and of themselves act as real motivators. However, the opposite of dissatisfaction is not necessarily satisfaction. When hygiene factors are met, there is a lack of dissatisfaction, not an existence of satisfaction. Likewise, the absence of motivation does not necessarily cause dissatisfaction. For example, salary is a hygiene factor. Although it does not motivate in itself, when used in conjunction with other motivators, such as recognition or advancement, it can be a powerful motivator. If, however, salary is a deficit, employee dissatisfaction can result. Some have argued that money is a powerful motivator as evidenced by those who work insufferable hours at jobs they truly do not enjoy. However, others have argued that money may be taking the place of some other unconscious need (Marquis & Huston, 1996).

So what does this all mean when a person is interested in making a job change?

It means the individual must look seriously at the two-factor theory as it relates to what motivates and what is dissatisfying about the present position and what will be done if the same conditions are present in the new or potential job. It means several questions should be answered before a step forward into something new or different is attempted, such as:

1. Am I satisfied with my work performance?
2. Do I expect recognition beyond the paycheck?
3. Do I enjoy the work I do?
4. Have I been responsible? Have I met my commitments?
5. Have I learned while on the job?
6. Have I grown professionally in the present position?

Answers to these questions should be positive, as they are the motivators and indicate the person is satisfied with self as a result of the work itself and is likely to succeed in a new position if the work is similar. If the answers to these questions were negative, it could mean the person should seek a different kind of position or return to the job and look for the barriers to motivation and thus satisfaction. Having negative answers does not necessarily mean the person is not ready for change. It could mean exactly the opposite—that the present job is not motivating and thus performance could be better. However, the job seeker will need to look carefully at the next position so a repeat of the present behavior is not inevitable in the new position.

An assessment of the hygiene factors would also be necessary to determine what in the present position is dissatisfying. For example:

1. Does company policy create dissatisfaction?
2. Is supervision a problem?
3. Is the relationship with the boss a good one?
4. Are the working conditions satisfactory?
5. Is the salary adequate for the time, effort and energy expended?
6. Are relations with peers positive and rewarding?

Again, affirmative answers to these questions suggest the workplace is compatible with the employee's values and expectations and is a good indication of the type of environment the job seeker should be looking for. Negative answers also indicate what aspects of the next environment should be avoided so there is satisfaction on the new job. Too many negative answers could mean the worker should move on but not before assessments of work expectations and of oneself are accomplished. While the hygiene factors are work related, dissatisfied workers are often unhappy because they expect something that is impossible in the present or perhaps other environments. In these cases, the worker should accept responsibility and adjust the expectations. This is to say, we sometimes make are own difficulties because we expect things that are not possible or even appropriate given the time, place and potential of the employer.

Herzberg's theory suggests the employer must attend to the hygiene and maintenance factors and to the motivating climate by including the employee. The worker must be offered challenges, greater responsibility and recognition for work accomplished. While hygiene factors do not motivate, they are needed to create an environment that encourages the worker to move on to higher level needs. The job seeker must be cognizant of these factors when looking for a new position as part of the self-assessment for readiness to change.

Assessing Risk-Taking

Changing a job or accepting a new one contains a certain amount of risk. One never really knows whether the decision to accept an offer is the right one, but there are some actions that can be taken to reduce the risk of making a bad decision. It also helps to know the level of risk that is acceptable for the individual and exactly how much risk can be tolerated. Risk is defined as the "chance or possibility of danger, loss, or injury or other adverse consequences" (Oxford University Press, 2000). For the job seeker, risk could mean letting a good job go for one that appeared better. It could also mean taking a job that is later "wiped out." It usually means the job doesn't work out as expected.

Victor Vroom, another motivational theorist, has developed the expectancy model, which is one way to assess one's risk ratio (Marquis & Huston, 1996). His theory examines the individual's valence or preferences based on social values. When contrasted with operant conditioning, which focuses on observable behaviors, the expectancy model focuses on a person's expectations about the environment or a certain event that will influence behavior. Actions are judged as having a cause and effect with the effect being immediate or delayed. However, a reward, inherent in the behavior, exists to motivate risk-taking. In Vroom's theory, people make conscious decisions in anticipation of rewards. In other words, the individual takes the risk if the consequences appear better than not taking the risk.

The job seeker has two kinds of risks to evaluate: the risk of the decision itself and the level of risk the individual is willing to take. There are several ways of evaluating risks. One way is to ask the "Why?" question five times. This is referred to as the "five-why" technique (Marquis & Huston, 1996). For example:

1. Why am I unhappy with my present job?
2. Why have I not considered doing something about my discontent with my current job?
3. If I am not unhappy, why would I consider leaving my current job?
4. Why should I consider the new job?
5. Why would I want to move to another organization, city or state?

The five-why technique is helpful for discovering the underlying issues that a cursory overview might miss.

There is also a technique known as triangulation. This technique involves using a variety of data sources and data collection techniques. Quantitative methods, such as the yes/no answers, merged with qualitative data, such as descriptions, are good sources of information about the risks of the potential job. While triangulation takes more time, it provides a broader perspective than just using one method. For instance, the job seeker may ask questions of the potential employer and may also seek information on the Web about the organization.

Measuring the risk factors for the individual interested in seeking a new position involves a look at several issues, such as:

- Present responsibilities
- Ability to make a move if needed
- Ability to take a salary cut
- Time it would take to get prepared for the job

Present Responsibilities

How much risk the job seeker can tolerate often depends on the extent of support s/he must provide. Single individuals without a family can take more risk because they do not have to provide food, housing, clothing, school costs, etc. for others. If the job seeker has a sizable debt, whether married or not, the risk rises and may deter him or her from taking a new position even if it looks like a pretty stable and predictable position.

Ability to Make a Move

Again, the risk of a move for a new job is small if the job seeker has no family. However, when the job seeker has children, interrupting a school year may be too risky. Young children can usually make the adjustment, but school-age children often have a difficult time making new friends if they are moved from what they know into something new. The job seeker also has to think about the cost of a move. If the new employer is ready to pay for the move, the risk is low. If the job seeker has to pay, the risk becomes higher, especially if the job doesn't work out. According to the stress scale, moving is the second highest stressor of all events that cause stress in our lives, so making a move, even if the job works out, is a very stressful event and one many people would rather avoid.

Ability to Take a Salary Cut

There are times when a new position is so attractive and promising, even a salary cut is worth the move. However, again the risk is higher if the applicant has dependents who need support. It would also be important for the new salary to be sufficient to cover expenses. Sometimes, the person takes the position and the lower salary with the idea that advancement would bring an increase and that both would occur in a short period of time. If these expectations are not part of the agreement at the time of hire, the risk may be higher than anticipated.

Time to Get Prepared for the Job

Sometimes, the new position demands new skills. And while the opportunity may exist for the acquisition of these new skills, there is always the possibility they cannot be obtained in the time allowed. The risk of this potential is generally small, but it should be considered when the risk assessment is made.

Clearly, there are risks when making job shifts and when seeking a first position. The prudent job seeker takes the time to assess the risks of the position and of self before taking the leap, even when the risk appears to be low.

Assessing the Ability to Change

Change is the newest buzz term, for it appears the pace of change has accelerated with the birth of information technology. However, change is an important aspect to think about, and while we all like to believe we can handle change, the fact is, change is resisted by most everyone. As Williamson (2002) has said "people enjoy the sense of security that comes from doing the same things each day—preferably with the same people, at the same time, and in the same place" (p. 3).

Change is the process or condition of transforming to a completely different form or appearance (Pickett, 2002, p. 240). According to Lancaster (1999), there are four types of change. The first type of change is haphazard. Haphazard change often is random with no advance preparation. The second type of change is coercive. Coercive change involves forces and intimidation by someone with power toward a non-mutually agreed upon goal. The third type of change is developmental. Developmental change occurs through the results of experience and sequence of events. The fourth type of change is planned changed. Planned change is intentional and deliberate and involves the exploration of several possibilities in advance of the proposed change.

There are several ways of assessing readiness for change. Lewin's Force-Field Analysis (1951) or his Three Stages of Change (1947) are excellent models for making a decision about a change. While different, both frameworks are excellent ways to assess whether a leap forward into a new job is right or whether postponing the change is appropriate or whether the individual is ready for the change.

Force-Field Analysis

Using Force-Field Analysis, it can be determined whether it is the right move or the right time for the move. By looking at the forces that push the decision and the forces that push against the decision, it is easy to determine which force is dominant. For example, let's imagine a job is open that has great appeal. However, the position currently held is also good and right on track with the career plan. Using force-field analysis, the decision would look like this:

Forces for acceptance of the position:

1. Long-term opportunities
2. Better benefits
3. Family move is not necessary
4. Same skills needed as used presently

Forces against acceptance of the position:

1. Good current environment and no knowledge of the new work environment
2. No salary increase
3. Understanding of the expectations of the current boss and no knowledge of the expectations of the new boss
4. Great current co-workers and no knowledge of the new colleagues

An evaluation of the forces for and the forces against reveals there are two issues: many of the forces against the change are unknowns and the forces that push for change are related to opportunity, benefits and good working conditions. The best course to take before a decision can be made would be to find out more about the unknowns. If this is not possible, it would appear the forces for change may outweigh the forces against change because they are tangible, positive and opportunistic. The diagram below illustrates the process.

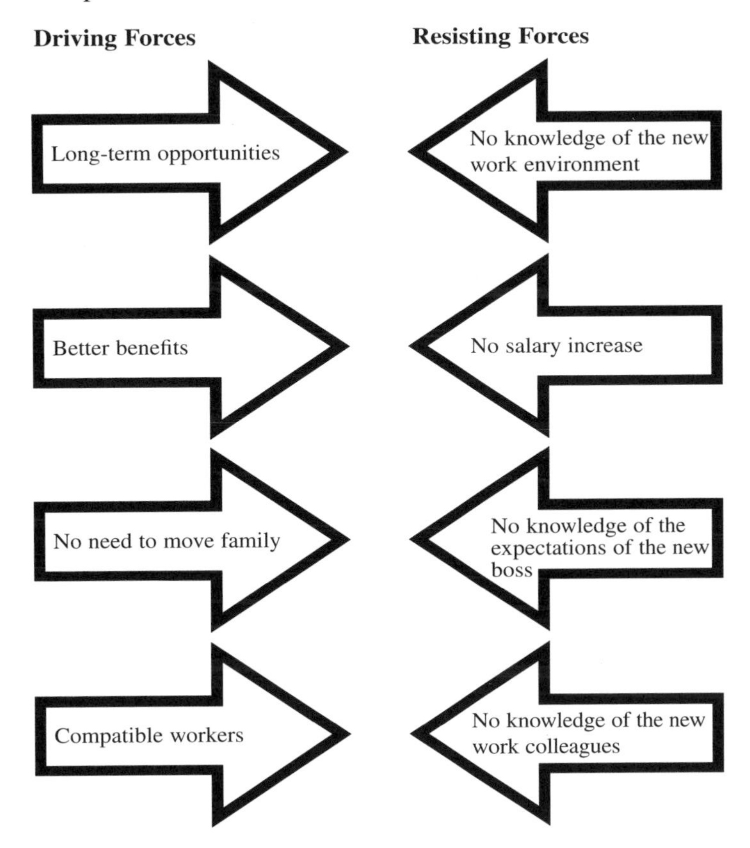

Lewin's Change Process

Kurt Lewin (1947) claims change is a process that involves three basic phases: unfreezing, experiencing the change and refreezing. The first phase is unfreezing. Unfreezing involves thawing or questioning the current situation causing uneasiness or imbalance so change can occur. The second phase is moving or making a change. This second phase involves changing the current state of equilibrium and transforming it to another state that may involve changing behavior and attitudes. The third phase is refreezing. Once the change has taken place, the focus is on maintaining the change. The refreezing occurs by focusing on the goals and objectives related to the change.

In the unfreezing phase, the worker must let go of current activities, relationships and work conditions and accept new ones. The focus becomes one of looking forward to a different situation with different players and thus different expectations. It is a process of releasing self from the known for the unknown. It includes bringing closure to the present and being ready to accept what is available in the new position, both in the role and those things that support the role.

The second phase, the changing phase, often involves changes in terms of expectations, behavior and outcomes. The individual must be able to function in a different way, in a different place and perhaps at a different time. New relationships with new people are needed, and this often involves trying to fit into an already-formed group. Knowing what to expect may not be clear, so in the changing phase, there is often a lack of clarity and some confusion until the individual is able to establish a place in the new environment.

The final phase, the refreezing phase, is when the individual works to maintain the changes. This statement may seem simple, but it is not unusual for people to try to create the old and familiar way in the new environment. If anything is likely to make the change a tragedy, it is when the new hire begins to talk about how it was in the last job and how it would be better to change to that way. Being accepted into the new environment and as a member of the new team will not happen if a person cannot let go of the past. It takes energy, effort, commitment and resolve to accept and maintain the changes that are necessary in the new environment with the new co-workers.

If the individual considering a job change cannot "unfreeze," that is, let go of what is; move forward; and refreeze and accept what could be, readiness for a new position may not be present. Without readiness, the job seeker is likely to be unable to adjust to the new position or will do so and be miserable. Moreover, because one unhappy worker tends to make others uncomfortable, before long, the entire workforce could become unhappy, a situation no employer wants.

Resistance to Change

Lancaster (1999) suggests there are two types of resistance to change: resistance because of the nature of the proposed change and resistance resulting from misconceptions and inaccurate information about what the change will mean. Resistance to change is an attempt to maintain the status quo when there are efforts being made to alter the current situation. It is a human instinct to resist, especially when there is limited information about the change.

Change that is resisted usually creates strong emotions, such as fear, anger, chaos, depression, perceived loss of power, insecurity or feelings of being uncomfortable. As seen in the example presented, if there are many unknowns in the decision to make a job change, the emotions listed above could occur, which is an indication the time may not be right for a change or the individual is not ready for a change. Emotions tend to be a barometer of one's readiness for change, so it is a good idea to keep in touch with them.

CONCLUSION

Being ready for change is an important aspect of making the move to accept a new position. It is a major aspect of any successful change. While there are many ways to measure readiness, the models presented in this chapter are offered as concrete ways to determine if the conditions necessary for a successful change are present.

An important aspect of change is that it takes time to become accustomed to the new while letting go of the old. If readiness is not a condition of the process, it could take more time to adjust and more effort to complete the transition. Whether the decision to make a job change is based on Lewin's Force-Field Analysis or his Three Stages of Change, the change will create a need for constant attention to what it takes to make the transition complete. Having a support system, such as family or friends, makes that transition easier.

REFERENCES

Bower, F. (2000). *Nurses taking the lead: Personal qualities of effective leadership.* Philadelphia, PA: Saunders.

Lancaster, J. (1999). *Nursing issuses in leading and managing change.* St. Louis, MO: Mosby.

Lewin, K. (1947, June). Frontiers in group dynamics: Concept, method, and reality in social science; social equilibria and social change. *Human Relations, 1*(1), 5-41.

Lewin, K. (1951). *Field theory in social science.* New York, NY: Harper & Row.

Marquis, B.L. & Huston, C.J. (1996). *Leadership roles and management functions in nursing: Theory and application.* Philadelphia, PA: Lippincott.

Oxford University Press (2000). *Oxford dictionary and thesaurus.* New York, NY: Author.

Pickett, J. (2002). *American heritage college dictionary.* New York, NY: Houghton Mifflin.

Sullivan, E. & Decker, P.J. (2000). *Effective leadership and management in nursing* (5th ed.). Upper Saddle River, NJ: Addison-Wesley.

Syptak, J.M., Marsland, D.V., & Ulmer, D. (2002). *Job satisfaction: Putting theory into practice.* Retrieved November 20, 2002, from http://www.aafp.org/fpm/991000fm/26.html.

Yoder Wise, P.S. (1995). *Leading and managing in nursing.* St. Louis, MO: Mosby.

Williamson, E.P. (2002). *Career fitness.* Retrieved November 20, 2002, from http://nsweb.nursingspectrum.com/efforms/GuestLecture/PickUpSticks.cfm.

Chapter 15

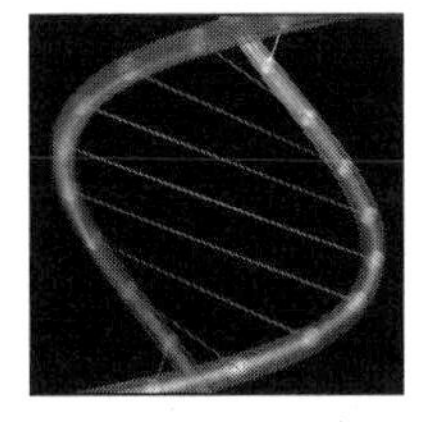

A New Mission with New Career Goals

by Cyndi McCullough

There is no security on this earth: There is only opportunity (Douglas McArthur, 1964).

Some people labor in their jobs when they are bored or not satisfied. They complain, often reject help and do only what is necessary. One could ask, why would someone stay in a position that was boring and not satisfying? Perhaps it is because they do not know what is available, or they don't believe they can do anything else, or they do not have the courage to change and get out of the work environment until their employer makes departure a necessity. When a nurse finally breaks free of these bonds, it is hard to consider other opportunities or perhaps a different career. Changing one's work environment, even when it is unsatisfactory, can be unnerving. Although uncomfortable, discovering a new career can also be very stimulating. By simply planning to change a career, one shows creativity and a willingness to take risks. Having a strategy for finding a new career may make it more energizing while at the same time minimizing the risk.

This chapter contains some clues about what a person needs to know to make the transition. For example, knowing about self, what to do to determine a career pathway, and how to maintain focus on the course of finding the new career are essential items when considering a career change. Changing careers can mean changing the job within the same profession, changing how current skills are used in another profession or changing the profession. No matter what direction the change takes, establishing a new mission for oneself and creating career goals begins with a self-assessment, which may lead to developing new skills.

Knowing Self

Reaching career satisfaction requires the individual think about a variety of issues; it begins with a self-assessment so the individual clearly knows what motivates, what satisfies and what gets in the way of satisfaction. The self-assessment begins with the following four questions: (1) Why was the current profession selected? (2) Why does the present job feel so uncomfortable? (3) What are the reasons for remaining in the current position? and (4) What motivates and what does one really want to do? The more one knows about self, the more likely action and change can occur. When you know who you are, you can never really be lost. Knowledge of self becomes the inner compass that directs a person to the most desirable path in life.

Understanding why the current profession was selected in the first place is an important step in the self-assessment phase. If the reasons are not clear, the following are some common ones that may help start the process.

- It's what my parents/family wanted me to do. Parents/family often suggest careers for their children/loved ones when they see them struggling to determine what career to pursue. This may have a positive result; however, unless the career searcher shares the same desires, selecting a career to please others usually doesn't work. However, before ruling out the career suggested by parents/family, the career searcher should find out about it. Interviewing someone who currently has that job/career and volunteering and/or observing/shadowing someone who is doing that job are good ways to begin to understand a particular career.
- It's what the results of a career test suggested. Career tests can help identify what preferences to pursue. While taking several different career tests will be more valid than only one, the results should be treated as suggestions only.
- There was a great demand for those skills. Demand for certain skills at a certain time doesn't mean that the demand will always be

there. Healthcare and high-tech industries, for example, have certainly seen their share of shortages and oversupply of professionals. Selecting a career that one has a passion for and then developing skills that are transferable will offer the most flexibility.

- It would assure security. Often individuals rely on achieving job security alone. They go back to school to get a degree in the field that shows the most promise. Unfortunately, there isn't always a job/career that corresponds with the degree. Again, taking the time to research the desired career/job and understand how that field has changed historically and how the experts think it will change in the future will help avoid this pitfall.
- It required minimal effort. Sometimes, an individual has information about a desired career but doesn't have the money and/or time to acquire the necessary skills. The person who wants to pursue a nursing career often falls into this trap. An individual who doesn't want to spend four years to get a nursing degree may decide to become a licensed practical nurse, which only requires one year of schooling, or they may opt for an associate's degree in nursing that only takes two years. That way, the individual can work while they finish the four-year degree. Even if the intent is to ultimately receive the four-year degree, the difference in salary is so minimal that some feel it is not worth the effort and, therefore, never complete the career of choice.
- It would yield the greatest income. The fact that a career will guarantee a certain income doesn't mean a thing unless the job is what one is interested in doing. If the career that yields the greatest income involves working with people and the individual has no people skills and prefers to work with technology, no matter how much money they make, they will never be happy.

In addition to understanding why a certain job/career was chosen, what makes an individual uncomfortable in his or her current job should also be examined. The factors that make the present job uncomfortable must be identified, for they may well be the same in other environments/jobs. A demanding boss, fluctuating schedules, low salary, high expectations and a lack of rewards are often the reasons for dissatisfaction in the job. Many jobs have difficult schedules and low salaries but are great places to work because the people are supportive and the rewards for good performance are available. But when low salaries and poor scheduling are joined by demanding bosses and few rewards, the job is not appealing and often dreaded. Before considering a change, it helps to determine what in the job environment is acceptable and what is not so the next selection of a position doesn't end up being the same as the one discarded.

The third part of self-assessment is to determine why the present unsatisfying job is not discarded and a new one pursued. The following list contains some of the most common reasons people stay in a position that is not satisfying:

- Never worked anywhere else
- Afraid to try something new
- Don't know how to locate another job
- Have a salary that can't be matched elsewhere
- Have rank that can't be matched elsewhere
- Waiting for the boss to change

Note that a couple of these factors are speculative, and two indicate a loss if a change is made. One indicates a lack of knowledge about what to do, and one suggests a fear. These reasons point out that there are gains and losses in career changes. An assessment of what is important to hold onto and what can be discarded should be attempted. It is also evident that some people stay in unsatisfying jobs because they simply do not know how to move on. This last reason is the easiest to remedy.

The last factors to assess are motivation and desires. Be aware that what you really want to do may be the same as it was when the profession was selected years ago, but what one now wants to do in that profession has changed. The same or different motivating factors may have developed. Given these factors, it is important to know as much about self as possible so a plan of action can be devised. To discover what motivates you, ask the following questions:

- Are rewards for performance expected?
- Is feeling good about self important?
- Is being fired a fear?
- Is doing something useful and good important?
- Is the salary worth the effort?
- Will there be time for family and other activities?

To some degree, everyone is concerned about these issues. Pay level, bonuses, promotions, stock options, medals, letters of commendation, prizes, awards and title changes are all types of recognition. The ideal organization is one that creates flexible career paths and incentive and reward systems that correspond to individuals' need for recognition. Since few organizations offer this flexibility, knowing self and what kind of recognition you seek is an important step in managing a career and finding the organization that best meets your needs.

For many, feeling good about self and doing something that is useful and good drives the search for new opportunities that may require changing organizations. The fear of being fired can limit a person's career. Everyone has certain needs for employment security and stability. Sometimes, this stability involves compromising values and loyalty for job promotion or tenure. Those who are concerned with the quality of their work or their position in the organization are less likely to be fearful of being fired and do not let fear limit the search for new opportunities.

A career that allows for the integration of work, family and personal needs requires compromise and flexibility. A person may refuse a promotion that requires a geographical change in order to be near the ocean for sailing. Another may choose to pay more for benefits in exchange for part-time, flexible working hours. Finding a career situation that provides the flexibility for this integration will most likely require some sacrifice.

To further focus on what one really desires, ask these questions.

- What was I born to do?
- How can I be the most useful?
- What would give me the greatest joy and satisfaction?
- How can I best use my skills/knowledge?

Bolles (2002) suggests that making a list of favorite interests and subjects is a good way to find what you were born to do. Begin by determining what skills are most enjoyable and what vocabulary is associated with the list of favorite interests and subjects. This will lead to the most desired career.

Sometimes a career change is not voluntary. And while most people dread being fired, given these times, it is not uncommon. Some people are removed from the job they loved because economics made it necessary. Others are fired because of poor performance. Whether a new career is being pursued voluntarily, because the current one has been eliminated or because of poor performance, there are a series of steps in the process of discovering a new pathway to a new job/career.

Regardless of the reason, job loss has the following effects: it often makes the job loser feel like a failure, it undermines self-worth and professional ability, and it may create doubt about the ability to do the job. Many emotions occur at this point, including denial, anger and depression. If the search for a new career is due to job loss, the first step is to deal with the emotional fallout. This may take some time depending on the circumstances. Emotional reaction to job loss may even warrant professional counseling. Embarrassment often accompanies the need for counseling, but it should be remembered that job loss ranks high on the scale of life stressors, so seeking help should be viewed as the smart thing to do. It is essential to affirm worth, get over the shock, get through the personal and professional implications, and accept the situation. Whether the job loss was voluntary or forced, it is important to take this time to get grounded and place the past job in history. Only then can an exploration of possibilities of what to do next begin.

Case Examples of Ways to Know Self

Jacquie was a staff nurse on a transplant unit. She was an excellent nurse who knew she wanted to remain at the bedside. For years, she dreamed of working on the obstetrical unit. She finally got the opportunity to fulfill her dream, but after a couple weeks, she appeared in my office begging to return to her old job. She realized she didn't enjoy taking care of well people. She loved the challenge of acute care nursing. I counseled her to give her new job a chance, but she said she was sure she didn't want it, and she didn't want to waste the OB director's time and money on her orientation. I went with her to discuss the situation with the director of the OB unit and by the end of the day had completed all the paper work to transfer her back to her old job. Jacquie was always open about her goals, and she left the unit on good terms. The fact that she made a change and tried something different was very positive. Other staff members who thought they might want to make a change to achieve their goals but were afraid to learned that it was okay. Later, when Jacquie's priorities shifted so she could spend more time with her children, she was able to make a career change to a part-time job in an ambulatory surgery center. She was challenged by the work and at the same time was able to achieve a greater balance in her life.

Three months after Sue graduated from college with a teaching degree, her younger sister, Jean (who had just changed her major to nursing), decided Sue should be a nurse. Sue had never considered a career in nursing and told her sister she was nuts. However, Jean saw something in Sue that Sue didn't see in herself, so she persisted. Jean was convinced Sue would love nursing. She actually contacted nursing school administrators who in turn contacted Sue, and eventually Sue conceded and decided to give it a try. Sue started nursing school and also began a job as a nursing assistant on a medical-surgical unit (her interview consisted of one question—When can you start?) to find out if she really would like nursing. Sue worked every weekend while studying for her degree, and she found out that she did love nursing. Although Sue has had many titles and positions, nursing has been her career for the past 22 years. Since teaching and nursing are both "helping" professions, Sue may have been happy with a teaching career; however, she now knows nursing provided and will continue to provide many options and opportunities.

Kris is a nurse who always dreamed of managing the intensive care unit where she worked most of her career. She eventually was given that opportunity and loved it for four years. Then she became very unhappy with a job she once loved. The work environment changed. The workload left her little time for family and friends. She found she was tired of managing people, doing tedious paper work and not being able to effect change. She discussed her feelings with her immediate supervisor who listened but didn't do anything to help her manage the workload and find meaning in her job. After discussing her feelings with her husband and examining their finances, Kris decided to quit her job, take some time off, and then look for something that didn't involve managing a large number of people. She made a point to schedule an exit interview with the VP of nursing to explain her reasons for leaving. She left on a positive note. She was not unhappy with the organization, only her job. She searched the hospital intranet for possible positions. Within a month, Kris accepted a position in the same organization. She now has more autonomy, less management requirement and less paperwork. Oftentimes, managers who are miserable in their jobs continue to do them because they don't have the courage to change. Kris was wise enough to recognize her unhappiness and the effect it had on her staff and family, and she had the courage to make a change without burning any bridges.

To this point, the discussion has been about the overall assessment of self. However, there are many excellent tools for assessing specifics, such as skills, knowledge, interests, experience and job preferences that are easy to find and easy to complete, so you will know what you are most suited for. Career questionnaires and assessment instruments come in many forms. You can order them on the Internet or get them at a career counselor's office or in career books. Try several of these tests, because one test would or would not validate the other and thus provide a more complete assessment. In any case, a job searcher needs to make an introspective analysis of his or her wants and skills and match them with the wants and needs of the prospective employer.

It is also paramount to know about the industry of choice, that is, the location, work environment, level of responsibility, travel requirements, company culture, salary range and level of autonomy. For example, identify: What was the best part of the most recent job? What was the least satisfying aspect of that job? Then think about the ideal job and determine how the terms just identified regarding the most recent employment would be different. What would change to make the job more fulfilling? What adjustments are needed? Perhaps additional education/training will be needed. Are there limitations such as salary, travel time or geography? If imagining an ideal job is difficult, it might help to ask the following question: "If money and geography were not limitations, what would the ideal job be?"

If the services of an outplacement agency are to be used, the focus should be on self-assessment and moving on. Personnel at the agency can guide that process and can recommend counseling and support groups if needed. If these services are not available or the cost is prohibitive, begin by going to the local bookstore or library and locate the career section. There are many books on finding new careers and dealing with change. Three excellent references that contain self-assessment exercises are:

- Bolles, R.N. (2002). *What color is your parachute? A practical manual for job-hunters and career-changers.* Berkeley, CA: Ten Speed Press.
- Schein, E.H. (1990). *Career anchors. Discovering your real values.* San Francisco, CA: Jossey-Bass/Pfeiffer.
- Burton, M.L., & Wedemeyer, R.A. (1992). *In transitions: From the Harvard Business School Club of New York's Career Management Seminar.* New York, NY: HarperBusiness.

Once the assessment of self and the situation have been completed, the next step is to determine a career path based on what has been established as the ideal work and work environment.

Determine a Career Path

Some people are fortunate because they know what they want to do with their lives and have the means and the opportunity to accomplish their goals. Others need to explore possibilities, weigh options and find the financial means to reach their goals. Changing careers and finding the best job can be expensive and time-consuming. Ultimately, the choice must fit with the desired lifestyle and budget. Further, the job searcher must investigate the ideal position and workplace, develop a support system, assure there are adequate finances, begin the job search, prepare a resume, and prepare for the job interview.

Investigating the Ideal Position

To find the job of your dreams, Bolles (2002) suggests the job searcher consider the following six categories.

- Geography—Is a move for the ideal job possible? If not, list those places where a job search can be accomplished.
- Interests—Is travel an interest? Is teaching or hands-on work preferred? Is management an interest?
- People environments—Is working with curious people an interest? Artistic? Social? Innovative? Detail oriented?
- Values, purposes and goals—Since values guide action, what values are most important? List a few. Goals are what we strive to reach. Perhaps learning a second language, helping people deal with stress or opening an alternative health clinic are goals of interest. List a few.
- Working conditions—What working conditions are desired? Is supervision or self-direction the preferred working arrangement? Is a team environment or working alone preferred?
- Salary and level of responsibility—What level of responsibility is preferred: CEO, manager, staff or team member? What is the desired/needed salary?

Bolles (2002) also suggests it is helpful to make a list of physical, mental and interpersonal skills. For example, how are the following handled: time and promptness, people and emotions, authority and being told what to do, supervision and being told how to do the job, impulsive vs. self-discipline, initiative vs. response, and crises or problems.

Schein (1990) suggests completing a career orientation inventory and participating in a "career anchor" interview. He believes it helps stimulate thoughts about one's areas of competence, motivation and values. Research on "career anchors" reveals that most people see themselves in terms of eight categories:

- Technical/functional competence
- General managerial competence
- Autonomy/independence
- Security/stability
- Entrepreneurial creativity
- Service/dedication to a cause
- Pure challenge
- Lifestyle

The "career anchor," as described by Schein (1990), is that one element in a person's self-concept that will not be given up even in the face of difficult choices. People define their basic self-image in terms of that concern, and it becomes an overriding issue at every stage of their career. Many in the health professions are anchored to a cause category (sense of service/dedication), but not everyone in the service-oriented occupation is motivated by the desire to serve. Some in the health professions may be anchored in the category of technical/functional competence, autonomy or security. Without knowing what anchor is actually operating, the career searcher will not know how to locate the ideal position.

To understand the value and use of "career anchors," the eight categories are summarized below.

Technical/Functional Competence. People who are anchored in the technical/functional category continue to develop their skills to a higher level. They are motivated by a particular kind of work and do not give up the opportunity to apply their skills at a higher level. Work must be challenging. While viewed as a painful experience, these individuals will perform managerial functions if they enable them to seek other areas of expertise. Individuals in this category find reward in a career ladder promotional system or an increase in scope of work.

General Managerial Competence. The people in this group possess analytical, interpersonal/intergroup and emotional competence. They must have some degree of each of these levels of competence. They seek greater levels of responsibility and opportunities for leadership. They enjoy influencing organizational goal achievement. Merit, measured performance and results are reasons for promotion in this group. Members of this group expect to be highly paid and demand internal equity.

Autonomy/Independence. Autonomy anchored individuals don't want to be bound by other people's rules, procedures, working hours, dress codes and other norms. They have an "overriding need to do things their way and at their own pace" (Schein, 1990, p. 26). Consulting, teaching, research and development, and management of geographically remote units are examples of jobs that autonomy-anchored individuals pursue. Merit pay for performance, bonuses and immediate payoffs work well for these individuals. Promotion is equated to greater autonomy. Medals, testimonials, letters of commendation and awards are motivators.

Security/Stability. Security/stability-anchored people often seek jobs in organizations that provide job tenure, have a reputation for avoiding layoffs and have good benefits. These individuals are willing to transfer responsibility for their career management to their employer. Improved pay, working conditions and benefits mean more than job enrichment. These individuals "prefer pay in steady, predictable increments based on length of service" (Schein, 1990, p. 28). A seniority-based promotion system and recognition for loyalty and steady performance are desired.

Entrepreneurial Creativity. Individuals in this group are focused on and obsessed with creating new services or products. Making money is a measure of their success. Members in this group achieve recognition by building fortunes. They are also self-centered and often put their names on products.

Service/Dedication to a Cause. Service/dedication-to-a-cause-anchored people want fair pay for their services and contributions. They tend to move into positions with more influence and freedom to operate autonomously. They want recognition and support from peers and superiors and support for their values. In the absence of that support, "they move to more autonomous professions such as consulting" (Schein, 1990, p. 31).

Pure Challenge. Some people have the need to "conquer anything or anybody" (Schein, 1990, p. 31). Success to them means overcoming impossible obstacles or winning against all odds. Challenge is the one thing that matters most. Easy is equated to boring for this group.

Lifestyle. Lifestyle-anchored individuals integrate the career with total lifestyle. These individuals need flexibility and will choose to work for organizations that provide the options they desire at that particular time. Originally observed more in women, this anchor is becoming more prevalent in men. Lifestyle-anchored individuals identify with how they deal with family and how they develop themselves within a job. Lifestyle-anchored people are reluctant to make a geographical move for their career.

Developing a Support System

A support system is anything that gives support and may include people, pets, things and the environment. Having the support of family, friends and colleagues is essential for making a career change. It is also important to seek out supportive people who encourage new thinking, are good listeners and can be a taskmaster when discipline is needed. Besides family and friends, churches, community services, state employment agencies and career counselors often have job-hunting groups that meet regularly.

A special place in the home or in nature (beach, park, scenic view) can give support by creating a safe and peaceful environment. Pets and objects that contribute to the peaceful environment are also integral parts of a support system.

Take the initiative. Choose and recruit a support group and know what environment contributes to your sense of security.

Assuring Adequate Finances

Transitioning from a job to a search for a new position is difficult and can also be financially devastating. The time needed to locate a new job could be extensive, so having enough money to cover living expenses and the job search is necessary. The best way to begin is by assessing one's financial capabilities/expectations by determining monthly expenditures, which usually include the following:

- A mortgage
- Insurance

- Credit card debt
- Personal loans
- Children's education funds
- Professional dues
- Car payments
- Basic expenses (food, clothing, etc.)
- Household expenses (utilities, phone, association dues, cable costs), repairs, etc.
- Healthcare
- Interview expenses
- Entertainment

Sometimes a severance payment will take care of some of these expenses. Without severance pay, unemployment compensation can help. A part-time position or a full-time, temporary position might be pursued during this period. Loans from family and friends are a common way for individuals to finance a new career. Refinancing a home is also used for this purpose.

The Job Search

There are many job search tools that can be used to locate a new position. Family, those at church, fellow alumni, professional organizations and neighbors are excellent sources of help when looking for a new position. Job placement services are also helpful for they benefit not only the candidate but the agency and the company of placement, so they are particularly anxious to serve a person looking for a position. The goal is to place the best candidate quickly and cost effectively. This service can also be obtained through the Internet.

Some people use search firms to help them locate jobs. However, it is important to note that search firms are usually trying to locate people for specific positions. Remember, the search firm is working for the employer and probably won't consider a career changer or novice. (See Chapter 20 for more information about search firms.)

Newspapers are excellent sources for locating a job. And the Internet is another excellent source when a job in a different state or city is needed. In addition, the Internet is a wonderful resource for learning about companies, message boards, chat rooms and groups if a talk with experts about a particular area of interest is needed/desired. It is even possible to post a resume on the Internet and have a "search engine" find a match. Although this process has been a successful method for some, it shouldn't be the only strategy used. (See Chapter 20 for more information on the use of the Internet to locate a job).

Preparing a Resume

Preparing a resume and tailoring it to a job search can take some time, particularly since a resume for a job is different than a curriculum vitae, which is required by academic institutions. If help is needed to prepare either, experts can be found in the Yellow Pages of the telephone book, or books can be purchased that describe resumes and curricula vitae and how to prepare them. In addition to having an up-to-date resume, an explanation of the reason for termination (if applicable) must be available. (See Chapter 22 for a thorough discussion on resume and curriculum vita preparation.)

Preparing for the Job Interview

In addition to having a resume or curriculum vitae, there will be a need to prepare for the interview once a contact for a position is established. Chapter 22 contains a thorough discussion on how to prepare for an interview, the interview itself and what to expect after the interview.

Case Examples for Determining a Career Path

Allan was terminated from an executive position in a large hospital during a re-organization. He was given a one-year severance pay and the services of an outplacement firm. During the self-assessment exercises, he learned he was entrepreneurial and needed autonomy in his work. He dreamed of starting his own business and being his own boss. Allan's skills included planning and mentoring, and he had a marketing degree. He had a strong desire to help people. Not wanting to uproot his family, Allan began to assess the needs of his community. He found a tremendous need for home care services. Allan was not a nurse and did not know what was really involved in home care so he visited local agencies and used the Internet to learn more. He examined the skills and knowledge he possessed compared to the skills and knowledge he needed. His marketing degree and his skill at writing business plans were pluses, but he decided to go to school to become a certified nurse assistant and then worked for a home care agency so he could learn firsthand about home care. Within a year, Allan had established his own home health business. Today, he is very successful and, more importantly, very happy.

Barb was a VP of nursing at a large Midwest hospital who was terminated because of downsizing. She did not see it coming; it had nothing to do with her performance, but she was devastated. Why her? Even though she received an adequate severance and the services of an outplacement agency, she was traumatized by the change. It took her a couple months to deal with the emotions before she could begin to think about another job. Although she used the outplacement services, Barb's heart wasn't in it. Her friends and colleagues maintained a close relationship with her, and it was through this network that Barb found her new job. She accepted an executive nursing position in an organization with an exceptional work culture. She has built new programs that serve a vital need in her community, and although she works long hours, it is apparent she loves her work. Barb's situation reinforces the need to recover, regenerate and recharge yourself so you can move on.

Deb was a clinical nurse specialist who was getting tired of "taking call" all the time and doing physicians' work and not being paid for it, so she decided to take control of her life. She had just completed a master's degree in nursing and did not want to go to medical school. She enjoyed being autonomous and solving medical problems, so she decided to find out what she needed to do to become a nurse practitioner. She could not afford to quit her job to attend class, so she found a school with a weekend and evening class option. She was able to complete the class work in two years and now is working with a family practice physician and loves the clinic work and her autonomy.

Maintaining Focus

Once the career direction has been established and the strategy for reaching it has been determined, it is now important to stay focused on the search. The exact amount of time the job searcher can devote to the task is crucial, for everything rests on how much time is available before a position must be found. A search can consume several months or be limited to a few weeks, dependent on the financial status of the job seeker. It can also be a trying time no matter how long it lasts. Frequently, job searchers begin to question their worth and may even consider taking a position just to have a job. Staying true to the mission and being able to sustain the search is really important. There are several strategies that can help, such as:

- Establishing a routine
- Concentrating on the future
- Maintaining a positive attitude
- Keeping involved and connected
- Keeping in touch with the support system
- Volunteering to fill the employment gap
- Paying attention to family and their needs
- Persevering, being organized and exercising patience
- Keeping options open
- Networking
- Having fun
- Rewarding yourself

Case Examples of Ways to Maintain Focus

Deb is a nurse who was fired from a job she had for 18 years. Her performance was exemplary, but she got caught in a political debacle. There were signs her dismissal was imminent, but she ignored them and was quite devastated the day she was asked to leave. She was offered an outplacement service and went there every day, but her heart wasn't in it. She didn't have to work, but she wanted something meaningful to do in her life. She enrolled in an art class and spent more time with her family. I think she even started watching soap operas. Deb took time to focus on herself and her family. She didn't seek a new position, but opportunity found her. She was at a social event that she really didn't want to attend because there were people there from her previous job. Since she was still struggling with acceptance of the fact that she lost her job, she didn't think she could face them. Her husband convinced her to go, and she held her head high and suffered through the evening. That night, Deb met an executive who was looking for a nurse with her skills and knowledge to provide leadership in the consulting division in his organization. It was a perfect match for her and one that came about because she had resolved her disappointments and was open to change and focused on doing something different.

Laura, on the other hand, was unhappy with her management job and was actively looking for a staff development job. She was tired of managing people, so she resigned her position and accepted a staff-training position with a large company. She was sure this would be the job of her dreams. After accepting the job, Laura decided to negotiate a higher salary. This move backfired and the company rescinded the offer. She was now out of a job and feeling worthless. She thought she would never find a job, so she foolishly went back to her old job (the one she disliked) because she needed money (security). A few months later, she was terminated. Laura was given three months severance pay and outplacement services where she learned how to do a self-assessment. She learned that she wanted an 8 to 5 staff-development job that required no management of others and allowed her a high degree of autonomy. During this difficult period, Laura maintained her network of friends and met weekly with a group of people who were focused on goal achievement. She set a timeline of three months to find employment, maintained her focus, exercised, renewed her faith in God, and did a lot of soul searching with her husband. She did find the job she loves and is very happy. She has learned to say no to management positions, for she has learned that they make her unhappy and unfulfilled. Additionally, Laura went back to school, so if she decides to make another job change, she will have more options.

CONCLUSION

Many people worry about their careers and never face the real issues that prevent them from being really happy and/or moving ahead. As transitions occur throughout life, individuals will be affected differently, and they will respond differently. During the transition, we might have to say goodbye to things we cherish, and we might have to exert effort we do not want to expend. Understanding change, being prepared for it and welcoming it are important survival skills everyone should possess. Finding that new job/career requires persistence, critical thinking, professionalism, support from family and loved ones, and most importantly—knowing self. Knowing self and being prepared for change will help the individual see the situation more clearly and react more objectively when the time comes.

REFERENCES

Bolles, R.N. (2002). *What color is your parachute? A practical manual for job-hunters and career-changers.* Berkeley, CA: Ten Speed Press:

Schein, E.H. (1990). *Career anchors: Discovering your real values.* San Francisco, CA: Jossey-Bass/Pfeiffer.

SUGGESTED READINGS

Boldt, L.G. (1996). *How to find the work you love.* New York, NY: Penguin Group.

Boldt, L.G. (1999). *Zen and the art of making a living: A practical guide to creative career design.* New York, NY: Penguin Group.

Edwards, P. & Edwards, S. (2001). *Changing directions without losing your way: Managing the six stages of change at work and in life.* New York, NY: Penguin/Putnam.

Harkavy, M. (1999). *101 careers: A guide to the fastest growing opportunities.* New York, NY: Wiley.

Chapter 16

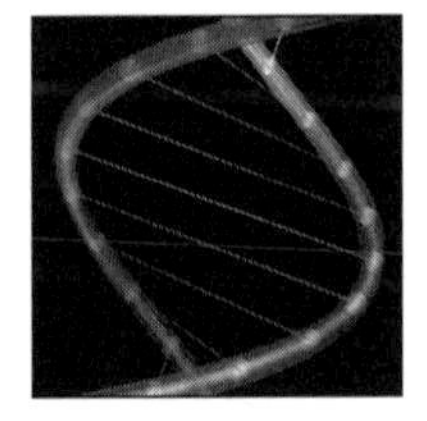

How to Transition: Moving From Where You Were to Where You Want to Be

by Cyndi McCullough

Change is not made without inconvenience, even from worse to better (Richard Hooker).

INTRODUCTION

What is transition? Webster (1997) describes transition as the "passing from one condition, form, stage, activity, place, etc. to another" (p. 1421). Bridges (2000) describes transition as "the necessary psychological process people go through to come to terms with a new situation" (p. 3). Spencer and Adams (1990) state transition is the "passage or adjustment from one situation to another" (p. 9). All of these definitions fit nicely when you consider a job change or career refocus.

The reasons for a transition are varied and are often precipitated by many kinds of change, such as divorce, death, new job/career, retirement, demotion, moving to a new school, implementation of a new process at work, technological advances, having a baby, living on your own for the first time, or moving to a new city. Transitions may be experienced by individuals or groups. The change can happen suddenly or gradually, and it may be chosen or inflicted. Whatever the case, everyone will need or be forced to change sometime and, therefore, will experience transition. Understanding transition and having the skills necessary to deal with it will help make sense of the elation, confusion and pain often experienced.

This chapter contains a discussion on transitions as they relate to individual job/career change. Even when an individual is eager for change, has the skills described in Chapter 17, and has already secured a new job, transition from "what was to what is ahead" is a challenge and must be mastered. Bridges (1980; 2000) and Spencer and Adams (1990) have presented models that help individuals/groups experiencing change make successful transitions. The models focus on the internal struggle people have with change and offer ways to examine the personal attitudes and behaviors that need change when the usual processes no longer work.

BRIDGES' MODEL OF TRANSITION

Bridges (2000), an expert in managerial change, has presented a model of transition that consists of three phases: the ending, the neutral zone and new beginnings. He believes anyone who experiences change will experience these three phases. The following discussion focuses on the three phases with case examples to concretize the concepts.

The Ending Phase

This is the initial phase of transition. According to Bridges (2000), every transition begins with an ending. It consists of "letting go" of an old situation. Even when change is viewed as positive, there is an ending. Endings are significant because letting go of the old way is essential to learning a new way of doing things. It is important to understand what the change involves. What exactly is going to change? What are the secondary consequences that the change will cause? Who will be affected by the change and how? What is over for those experiencing change? Bridges suggests we must acknowledge the losses openly, expect and accept signs of grieving, compensate people for losses, treat the past with respect, communicate well and often, and celebrate the endings. He believes failure to identify and be ready for the ending and losses that change brings is the single, biggest problem individuals and groups experience when faced with transition.

According to Bridges (1980), there are four key aspects of the ending experience: "disengagement, disidentification, disenchantment and disorientation" (p. 92). *Disengagement* occurs when a person is separated from familiar activities, relationships, settings or roles. Disengagement can happen willingly or unwillingly, but either way, the process of change begins.

Disidentification, as described by Bridges (1980), is a loss of self-definition. People in transition may not know who they are. If they lose an important part of their identity, such as a role or title, disidentification can occur. Clearly, an old identity stands in the way of transition. Letting go of who you think you are is essential in order to discover the person you need to become.

Disenchantment sometimes initiates transition. Disenchantment can be a minor disappointment or a major shock. It is the discovery that the world view is no longer what it was. Everyone experiences disenchantment in life. To move on, the disenchanted person needs to recognize the old view was sufficient for its time but unworkable now.

Disorientation is the loss of direction and a time of confusion and emptiness. It's the "I don't know who I am or what I am feeling. Things that used to be important don't seem to matter anymore" (Bridges, 1980, p. 140). As Bridges further states, "Some of our resistance to going into transition comes from our fear of this emptiness. The problem is not that we don't want to give up a job or relationship, or that we can't let go of our identity or our reality; the problem is that before we can find something new, we must deal with a time of nothing" (p. 104).

The Neutral Zone

The second phase of transition is the neutral zone. The neutral zone is that period of time when the old is gone and the new is here, but it hasn't been totally identified or accepted. It is sometimes referred to as a "fallow" period. When the outer situation changes but the inner situation doesn't, the old outlook, old self-image and old value system remain, and change does not occur. Ignoring or resisting change is uncomfortable, but acknowledging it is time to move on must happen. The neutral zone phase is characterized by confusion and discomfort, and since individuals do not "let go" at the same pace, the length of the neutral zone phase is variable. Those who are not adapting well to transition may try seeking help from those who provide guidance and support. Bridges (1980) offers the following tips for groups/individuals who are in the neutral zone:

- Discover new and creative solutions
- Seek opportunities to be part of the solution
- Learn techniques for discovery and innovation
- Try experimentation

- Embrace losses, setbacks or disadvantages to the change
- Look for opportunities to brainstorm new answers to old problems
- Don't push prematurely for certainty and closure

New Beginnings

The third phase of Bridges' (1991) model involves the acceptance of new understandings, values, attitudes and identities. This phase is only possible when "letting go" (phase 1) has been completed. The individual/group is now ready to move forward. Anxiety and turmoil force the need for much communication in this phase. People often have a difficult time accepting the new way. Changing behavior is difficult and does not happen overnight. Transitions are difficult for individuals and even more so for groups. To reinforce new beginnings for groups experiencing change, Bridges suggests the leader of the group (manager, CEO, VP, etc.):

- Be consistent and be a good example
- Reward positive behavior
- Ensure quick success
- Symbolize the new identity
- Celebrate the success

The following story is an example of how Bridges' model of transition supported one nurse as she led her staff through a difficult organizational change. Leading staff through a major change while learning a new job was a task that wouldn't have happened as smoothly as it did without knowledge of transitions.

In an effort to protect the market share, leadership at a tertiary hospital in the Midwest decided to implement several strategies simultaneously. The physical plant change was planned and would occur over several years. The cultural change was drastic but not as well planned.

Although the change was difficult for all employees, the managers seemed to have the most difficulty. The organizational change involved a major renovation of the hospital, implementation of a patient-centered delivery model, and a decrease in the number of formal management positions. The role of the manager was key. It was the manager's responsibility to make the change happen. Strong leadership skills and the ability to both lead and manage were necessary. There was no formal education for managers and many had difficulty determining who they needed to become to survive in this new environment. Managers needed to deal with different issues while leading staff through the same change. The list is not comprehensive, but the following points illustrate the magnitude of the change that occurred.

- The hierarchical structure became flat and staff became self-directed. They were accountable and responsible for the good and the bad.
- The way medications were delivered to the patient and who performed certain skills and tasks changed.
- Patients were registered in their rooms, not in an admitting department.
- Computers were placed in each patient room, and licensed staff were responsible for processing patient orders. There was no clerical staff on the patient unit.
- Staff became responsible for scheduling, interviewing and hiring other staff, peer evaluation, and the financial outcomes of the unit.
- Head nurses and assistant head nurses lost their titles, and along with that, their salaries were decreased.
- Managers gave up some traditional management functions to staff and focused on leading and coaching staff rather than making decisions for them.

Two issues that compounded the stress of this change were: (1) everyone in the organization was not ready for the change and (2) patients were still the priority, and patient care needed to occur in a timely manner no matter how much change occurred.

The managers understood the old way of doing things wasn't working and hadn't been for some time. Knowing the staff shared the same concerns was the impetus needed to make the transition. "Letting go" was actually refreshing. There wasn't a period of doing nothing as sometimes occurs in the transition process. No jobs were eliminated; they just changed dramatically. The new was here and everybody understood that, but not everyone wanted to be a part of it.

The neutral zone was another story. The old was gone, but the new way was not totally identified or accepted by the staff. Everyone had to learn to work in a new environment. Some staff found that so daunting, they resigned and went to work in other institutions. Some staff took the "wait and see" attitude. They adjusted slowly. Even though they didn't like the old environment, they weren't sure they were ready for something new.

Communication was key at this point. Keeping people informed and allowing them to be part of the solution helped the change transition. There was no formal education for managers to understand their new roles. They knew they could not do it alone, so they surrounded themselves with people who would support, challenge and help implement the change. The key people who kept the group focused and informed were a behavioral psychologist who was hired by the organization to help implement change at the physician level, a staff development resource person who helped develop the curriculum to teach staff how to work in the new environment, a graduate school advisor who was available during the transition to study how staff and patients responded to the change, and the physician champion for the organizational change. These people were the sounding board and, when needed, removed barriers and offered suggestions to help staff adapt to the change.

Even though the new way of doing things was a welcomed change, no one understood how difficult the transition would be. Everyone accepted change at a different rate, and all were inefficient for a period of time until the new way was learned. It was easy to slip back to the old, comfortable ways of doing things, so being consistent, rewarding positive behavior and ensuring quick success became the focus of the leader. When there was a busy day and a staff person wanted the manager to settle a conflict with a co-worker, there was a tendency to slip back to that old way of doing things. Instead, the manager took the time to reinforce the new way of doing things and coached the employee through several scenarios to confront the issue. There was a need to move problem-solving to the staff. Although time consuming at first, this was an important accomplishment. Within a few months, the entire staff knew they needed to work on solving interpersonal issues and that the manager would be there only when needed.

Along the way, the group members celebrated their accomplishments. They celebrated when a team implemented a new way of doing things that improved patient outcomes and decreased cost, when staff learned new skills, and always on the anniversary of the implementation of the new model of care. They always invited those who had helped during the transition to the anniversary celebrations.

The staff realized the transition was successful when the worst day in the new environment was far better than the best day in the old environment, and they knew they did not want to return to the old way of doing things. Staff statements like "I knew it would be good but . . . I had no idea it would be this great!" and "Hey, we've gone an entire week without changing anything . . . don't you think we should?" reinforced that the change had been implemented successfully and was now the norm rather than the exception.

The next story is about one nurse's use of Bridges' (2000) model of transition when she was forced to change positions in the same organization. For 11 years, Michaela worked on a gastrointestinal (GI) specialty unit. She was an expert nurse who could assume all positions necessary for the unit to function effectively. The staff and physicians she worked with were exceptional, and they all worked well as a team. The director was a good mentor.

According to Bridges (1980), endings are caused when there is a change. In this case, the ending had nothing to do with Michaela or her job performance. When patient care shifted to the ambulatory setting, there was a decreased need for inpatient hospital beds in the organization. Because it was a smaller unit and since many GI procedures shifted to the outpatient setting, the hospital administration decided to close the GI unit. No one would be terminated, but everybody's job changed and the staff from that unit wouldn't be working together anymore.

Recognizing the need for endings, the staff and physicians planned a party to celebrate their accomplishments and grieve the loss. This was the first step to moving ahead. Michaela chose to transfer to a medical-surgical unit where the inpatient GI patients would reside. She truly believed this transition would be easy. After all, she would be working with similar patients in the same organization. She still had day-shift hours; she didn't need to acquire new skills; and she just moved one floor down from her old unit. How difficult could that be? Understanding the reason for the closure of the unit and celebrating the loss helped with the transition, but Michaela was not prepared for the neutral zone. Nothing was familiar. She was still a nurse working for the same organization, but the culture was very different and the familiar faces of her co-workers were not there. Michaela went from a very team-oriented environment to one where the staff worked individually to get the job done. She also soon learned that working efficiently was rewarded with more work. Once, she was even cautioned to quit working so hard because it was making the rest of the staff look bad. In addition, she found out how much she missed her mentor and former co-workers and realized how important they were to her.

While struggling in this neutral zone, Michaela soon realized she didn't want to adapt to the culture and work ethic of this new department. She was miserable, but she continued to do her job well and make the most of it. She didn't realize how unhappy she was. One day, while still in the neutral zone, Michaela's former boss approached her with a job offer. She was flattered he would consider her, and the job was enticing. It was with the same organization, but this time, the job was very different. Michaela would need to give up her bedside nursing job to manage non-nurses in a business setting. This meant learning new skills, but the schedule would be better for her family life, and since she wasn't happy with her current environment, she decided to consider the offer. This offer made Michaela realize she was holding on to something that wasn't satisfying. She thought learning new skills would be challenging and fun. The difficulty she had was with letting go of her bedside nurse identity. Her successes were within that context, and she could not imagine doing anything different. With the encouragement of her family and friends, Michaela decided to accept the position. This time, there was no party and no formal goodbye, but she was ready for the change. After two days in her new position, Michaela questioned her decision. She wondered why she thought she was capable of this new challenge. She wanted her old, familiar job back even if it meant working in a culture she didn't like. As Bridges (1991) points out, most people expect to move from the old to the new without any problems. But creating a new identity takes time. In Michaela's case, it took a year. What helped her progress through the neutral zone was the relationship she had with a mentor, increased time for her family and personal activities, and the realization that the organization and management skills she used every day in caring for patients were the same skills she needed to manage staff. Later, when Michaela was given the opportunity to develop the patient pre-admission testing service, she knew she was in the "new beginnings" phase. She had unlimited choices, the confidence that she could do anything, and the opportunity to work directly with patients again.

Because of this experience, Michaela discovered work is just one aspect of life. When a job no longer gives enjoyment, it is time to consider something more meaningful. Understanding Bridges' (1980) model has taken the fear out of job change for Michaela.

SPENCER AND ADAMS' MODEL OF TRANSITION

Spencer and Adams (1990) describe a model of transition with seven stages: losing focus, minimizing the impact, the pit, letting go of the past, testing the limits, searching for meaning and integration. Like Bridges, Spencer and Adams believe individuals experience change at different speeds. For example, a person going through a minor transition may experience all seven stages in a few hours, but a significant life change will take much longer, perhaps months. Trying to rush through a stage may cause a person to slip back to the previous stage, and dwelling too long in a stage may make the adjustment more difficult. No matter what the cause of transition, Spencer and Adams believe a good support system is key to a successful transition. The following discussion includes definitions and explanations of each stage.

Losing Focus: Stage 1

Losing focus is the inability to think clearly or keep things in perspective once change occurs. Depending on the individual, this stage may last a few hours to several days. Individuals in this stage have described themselves as feeling fuzzy, numb, completely overwhelmed, frozen by feelings of panic and terror, acting out of character, and out of control with excitement. It is helpful in this stage to be surrounded with things that aren't changing. Having focused activities and/or making a specific "to do" list and following it are ways to facilitate passage through this stage. Support from friends and family who are good listeners helps one stay focused.

Minimizing the Impact: Stage 2

According to Spencer and Adams (1990), this stage is characterized by an urgent need to get back to normal. This stage allows the individual to avoid the full impact of the change. Although it is an important stage, remaining here too long will just make the change more difficult. Those who fail to pass through this stage could resort to dependence on alcohol or drugs and/or become a workaholic.

Finding support in this stage may be difficult because the individual often is sending a message that everything is all right. Some describe this stage as one of "timelessness." Subtle changes in personality and feelings of euphoria are common experiences. Spencer and Adams (1990) suggest telling the truth about the situation, finding help from others to move forward, and exercising and eating right in order to expedite the process. A sense of unrest, emotional discomfort and a hollow sense of loss are signs the individual can no longer pretend things are normal and that they are now ready for stage 3.

The Pit: Stage 3

The pit is described as a period of self-doubt and questioning. It is probably the most difficult stage to handle and also the most painful. The pit can last a few weeks or several months and can range from a short period of depression to the toughest struggle in life. Denial is over and reality sinks in. Feelings such as depression, grief, sadness, powerlessness and anger surface as the individual attempts to recognize what is being lost. Attitudes and behaviors that no longer support the new situation are relinquished in this stage. Avoiding this stage will not work. Understanding how to grieve and recognizing loss facilitate passage through this stage. Often individuals feel lonely, question their self-worth, and have feelings of self-hatred and self-doubt. It is helpful to talk with a trusted friend or counselor. Spending time with nonjudgmental friends and/or a vacation may also help. At this point the individual can no longer live in the past and must focus energy on the future.

Seeing the light at the end of the tunnel, confronting fears, replacing feelings of sadness and anger with optimism, and having the strength to go forward are signs that the individual is ready for stage 4.

Letting Go of the Past: Stage 4

The focus of stage 4 is forgiveness. It is the turning around period that brings a new sense of optimism. Since the new situation is fragile, one may feel great one day and rotten the next. A clear and focused direction is essential. Spending time with friends and colleagues who can assist in creating small success-oriented tasks helps the individual move through this stage. Developing a relationship with a mentor, who is experienced in the area of change or cares a lot about the individual's success, also helps build self-esteem. Rediscovering hobbies or starting new ones also happens in this stage.

Testing the Limits: Stage 5

Stage 5 is described as an active one. The new self is established as the result of trying out new behaviors and developing new skills. Taking charge of the new direction and a new self-confidence make the future seem exciting. Some people have a tendency to appear cocky or filled with bravado. It is important to remain focused on the desired results and to move forward one step at a time. Individuals in this stage begin to develop relationships with those who have the same interests and speak the same language. Recognizing unique success qualities and finding opportunities to use them assure success in trying out new things. Completion of this stage often creates a more relaxed feeling.

Searching for Meaning: Stage 6

Self-reflection and finding meaning for one's life follows the fifth stage. Everything appears to be falling into place, and there is a sense of order and stability. This perspective is often described as the "calm after the storm." It is easier to look at the situation and understand what it means. New skills, new friendships, a reconnection with old friends and the desire to help others who are in the same situation are the outcomes of this stage.

Integration: Stage 7

The final stage, integration, completes the transition. It occurs when there is an understanding of what has occurred and a readiness to share the experience. There is a sense of confidence and happiness and a desire to step out and take a risk. New behaviors occur automatically and confidence prevails.

Case Studies of Transition Using Spencer and Adams' Model

Losing Focus: Stage 1

Cyndi didn't know it at the time, but for four months prior to her departure, she went through the motions of the job but wasn't really there. At some level, she knew she needed a change, but she was so busy holding things together she didn't have the energy to think about a change. She felt out of control, but since her job demanded her attention to the activities of the unit, it appeared everything was normal. Recognizing she had fears about losing her job and discussing those fears with colleagues and friends before it happened helped her prepare and minimize the shock.

Minimizing the Impact: Stage 2

Cyndi passed through this stage rather quickly. She accepted the fact that she would lose her job before it happened. When it did happen, she was upset but immediately told her family, friends and colleagues. Once this reality was out in the open, she felt relieved but anxious about what would happen next. The emotional part of the forced resignation was very painful. Even though she realized she had been holding on to a job she wasn't enjoying, she still couldn't see herself doing anything else.

The Pit: Stage 3

For Cyndi, this stage lasted about two months. She felt depressed, had bouts of elation, self-doubt, self-confidence and anger, sometimes all within the same day. She talked to a couple colleagues who had had similar experiences. It was reassuring to know they had the same feelings. Since they survived, found meaningful work and were very happy, she knew she could do it too. She spent a lot of time reconnecting with family and friends, took a vacation, golfed and exercised everyday, but keeping busy was not enough. During this time, her former staff staged a going away party for her. This was very healing for them, as well as for her. After that, she was ready to move on. Later, several of her staff said they, too, were ready to move on once they saw she was alright. They knew they could make a change. Until that time, they were too afraid to actually do it even though they felt the need for change. Their loyalty to Cyndi prevented them from seriously considering changing jobs/careers.

Letting Go of the Past: Stage 4

During this stage, a good friend became a good mentor. She asked Cyndi to do several projects for her. These activities gave her something to do that was worthwhile, and the success boosted her confidence. No matter how much success she was experiencing at this time, she would occasionally remember she didn't have a full-time job and panic would set in.

Testing the Limits: Stage 5

This stage was easy for Cyndi. Her mentor continued to provide meaningful projects for her to complete, and she also began to work on a project basis with an architectural firm that designed hospitals. She co-wrote several papers that were accepted for professional presentation and contributed to successful marketing efforts for that firm. Others were finding opportunities for her to use her unique skills while she learned new skills. Cyndi had the opportunity to experience the new job and knew she wanted it.

Searching for Meaning: Stage 6

Cyndi had a new job and was happy. She was challenged and ready to accept what happened to her. She was able to help others. This stage happened six months into the process. To signify this milestone, she bought herself an expensive watch to signify it was time for a change. She also donated what was left of her severance pay to the organization where she had volunteered her time. Cyndi was ready to begin a new phase of her career.

Integration: Stage 7

Six months after Cyndi started her new job and one year after the awful event that started the transition, she was ready to share the experience. She now understood what others had seen from the start. She knew it was the best thing that ever happened to her career. She was confident with and challenged by her new job, and she knew she would never again be afraid of changing her job/career.

CONCLUSION

Work is just one aspect of life. When the job/career is no longer enjoyable or satisfying, it is time to consider something different. Understanding transition models that focus on understanding the internal struggle people have with change and talking with others who have had similar experiences helps facilitate the process. Listed below are what can be learned from this experience.

- When the change is something that is wanted rather than mandated, the transition is easier but still involves passage through the same phases/stages.

- When the change involves a group of people, it needs to be carefully orchestrated.
- Seeking advice and help is essential. Developing a mentoring relationship with someone who will both support and challenge is best. Seek out others who have had a similar experience, and find out how they coped.
- Persistence and patience are necessary for a successful transition. Learn how to grieve and let go of the old job/career. Recognize the unique qualities that will support success in new endeavors.
- Never remain in a job that isn't fun, satisfying or challenging. Know when to make a change.

REFERENCES

Bridges, W. (1980). *Transitions: Making sense of life's changes.* Cambridge, MA: Perseus.

Bridges, W. (1991). *Managing transitions: Making the most of change.* Reading, MA: Addison-Wesley.

Bridges, W. (2000). *The way of transition.* Cambridge, MA: Perseus.

Spencer S.A., & Adams, J.D. (1990). *Life changes: Growing through personal transitions.* San Francisco, CA: John Adams.

Webster's New World College Dictionary, 3rd Edition (1997). New York, NY: Simon & Schuster.

Unit IV
Reclaiming a Career

Chapter 17

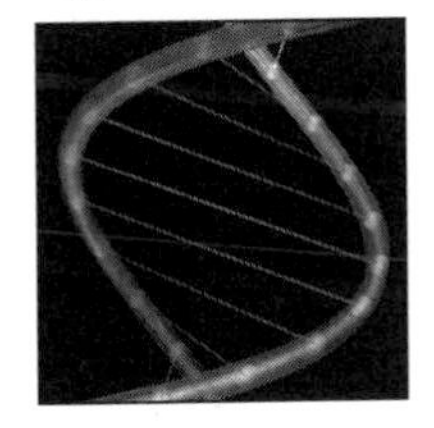

The Stalled/Delayed Career

by Patsy Maloney

Go confidently in the direction of your dreams. Live the life you have imagined (Henry David Thoreau).

LYNN'S STORY

I worked hard to try to balance my family and my career. But of course my family was the most important to me. My career was secondary. I worked as a staff nurse on the night shift to provide for my family. At first, nursing was really tough, and I thought I would never get the hang of it. Then, I grew to love my work. Work even became an escape from my family. Don't get me wrong, my family was my priority. I even gave up opportunities at work because I thought they would require more time than I was willing to give. I believed if I gave most of my energy to rearing the children, being their room mother and their Brownie leader, and taking them on adventures so they would be successful, fulfilled adults—not just people who get by. My children did not turn out as I expected. I dreamed of them going to the best universities and becoming professionals. Now, one is taking forever to get through community college after several failed romances, and the other can't even get through high school. They really are good kids, but they are not what I worked to create. I am so jealous when I read about others with successful children—especially those who did take the challenging and time-demanding jobs. How did they do it—have a family and a career? When I go to work, there is no challenge. I feel like I do the same old thing, and that I don't make a difference. I have done the same job for 20 years. The patients are in and out so fast that I really don't accomplish any more than following the doctors' orders. I feel like such a personal failure that I'm not very nice at work anymore. I see the cup as half empty. Everything is a problem and a drag. Even though I am far more experienced than in those early days, no one is offering me new positions. I'd like to be excited about work and get moving in a positive direction. I can hardly stand to go to work any more. I am a failure as a mother, and my career is stalled—maybe even dead.

INTRODUCTION

Lynn's story is not so different from many other nurses' stories as they approach midlife. They simply do not feel fulfilled. Terms such as dissatisfied, plateaued, unhappy, unfulfilled and suffering from career doldrums are ways to describe a stalled career (Imel, 2000). Although admittedly frustrating, stalls in a career offer a period of time for gaining perspective, which can be followed by a phase of growth (Kreuter, 1993). The nurse in this story and nurses like her do not care about what terms they use to describe their dilemmas and often do not see it as an opportunity for a new perspective followed by career growth. They are living the frustration. They feel the pain. They just want to know how to revitalize their careers and their lives or, more simply put, to jump-start a stalled career.

Prior to one's re-energizing of a stalled career, there must be an awakening to the need for change and renewal. Also required are an exploration of the meaning of work in one's life, to include the acceptance of past negative situations, and the affirmation of one's worth and value as a human and professional. The re-energizing process is very similar to the nursing process of assessment, planning, implementation and evaluation. Assessment begins with discovering one's innermost self, to include natural talents, uniqueness, personal values and interests, and expectations, both realistic and unrealistic (Dutch, 1997). An assessment is needed not only of the individual, but also of the environment to include career opportunities that match the individual. Once the available opportunities are known, a choice is made and strategies are designed for making the choice a reality. When the plan is complete with strategies and outcomes, then the implementation phase begins. Evaluation is the final phase of the process and determines if the outcomes have been achieved. Just as in the nursing process, the re-energizing process is ongoing. A career is not static and requires the individual to continue to learn and grow to maintain a sense of fulfillment and professional satisfaction.

Just like Lynn, most American women's lives are emotionally centered on their families, friends and home, yet the average American worker spends more time at work with co-workers and bosses than with his or her children (Williamson, 2002). Given the time that Americans spend at work, a stalled, unsatisfactory career can lead to a very unhappy life. For far too many, work has become anxiety producing, frustrating, boring and filled with tension. The focus of work and careers needs to be transformed from a material-based focus with all of its emotional and psychological pain (Williamson, 2002). The attacks of September 11, 2001, initiated an inner dialogue within many individuals, with questions like "Am I really living the way I want to live?" (Boyatzis, McKee, & Goleman, 2002, p. 87) and "What am I doing with my life?" (Cannon, 2002, p. 4). Just like Lynn, many people are crying not just for a satisfying career, but a satisfying life. They are seeking self-renewal.

Many people see life as a linear path that one progresses through with perseverance and hard work. Since these individuals believe good, competent work and deeds lead to happiness and success, they are totally unprepared and feel like failures when unexpected events or actions by self and others interfere with their life plan. If an individual views life from a cyclical viewpoint, then there is a time for everything, and patterns are repeated and take on different meanings at different times in life. Life's challenge is to gracefully move through these patterns. Adults must let go of outmoded habits and learn new ways to live (Lankard, 1993). "Adults need not only have knowledge and training to make the changing external world work but self-knowledge and training to make the internal world effective" (Hudson, 1991, p. 44).

How does one prepare for this self-renewal? The answer is through awakening, acceptance and affirmation. First, they must be awakened to the need for renewal. Sometimes, traumatic events like September 11 cause the awakening that leads to renewal; other times, it is more of a gradual, gentle desire for something better. When awakened to discontent, the individual is usually moved to do something. In order to take action toward a new self, the individual must accept the negative happenings in his or her life thus far—disappointments, failures, past wounds and dashed expectations. These should be accepted without excuse or defense. Moving from life's negativity, the individual seeking renewal must affirm the positive, including the meaning and experiences that have come from failures. This affirmation is the celebration of all that is good in life and a commitment to live life fully. The end result of self-renewal does not happen until the inner changes are demonstrated in the outer world (Wong, 2003).

For self-renewal, Lynn must look at her life as a cyclical pattern, not as a line on which her children by now should have entered prestigious schools. Her children have entered the cycles of their lives, and they will have many opportunities to find meaning and success in life. In the cyclical view, there is no point at which life's events must be accomplished. Lynn's dashed expectations for her children's futures and her own personal future have stirred an awakening. She knows that she must change her life and her career. She will now need to accept her children's choices, her past choices, her sadness and her disappointment. She needs to accept the negatives that life brings in order to be ready to affirm the beauty that life holds. After accepting what has gone wrong and what will continue to go wrong, she needs to affirm the good. She says her children are good. She needs to really describe the good, their successes and her successes. And finally, she needs to continuously accept and affirm life's good and bad as she acts to change her life and career.

ASSESSMENT

When an individual has a stalled career, he or she can move forward and do the same thing done before but with a sense of renewed interest and meaning. The individual can move up to a more challenging position, can downshift to a less-demanding position that offers more time for family or personal interests, or can move laterally to an equally demanding and rewarding position in a different area (Hudson, 1997; Imel, 2000). In order to determine which direction to take, the individual with the stalled career will have to do a thorough assessment of self and environment. In his book *Job Shift,* William Bridges (1994) states a career changer needs to ask him/herself four questions to get at desires, abilities, temperament and assets (D.A.T.A.). Essentially the questions are:

1. What do I want?
2. What do I do really well?

3. Who am I as a person and what situations make me productive and satisfied?
4. What education, experiences or personal history could I turn into an advantage?

Bridges believes the answers to these questions allow an individual to establish a core around which to build a work life.

Desires/Dreams/Expectations

Many individuals have spent their lives doing what they are supposed to do or are expected to do—not what they want to do. Some do not even get to do what they want to do on their days off because they are so busy running around doing chores they could not get done on their duty days during their limited time off. Careers are hard enough without choosing one that is not liked (Bridges, 1994).

An individual's present desires are not all that should be explored. Often, career stalls are triggered by non-events. These non-events are really the effect of unmet and unlabeled dreams and expectations. Unmet dreams and expectations are usually related to relationships, legacy, career, family and self-image. These unmet dreams do not fall into tidy categories. A dream about a career can influence all other areas of life. For instance, people who never actualize their dreams often become chronically angry, taking the disappointment out on the family. For some, the dream is not lost, only delayed. This causes a real crisis for some in midlife when they give up hope of making their dreams realities (Schlossberg, 1999). People cannot start with what they want in a career without first working through the unmet needs that might have forced the career stall.

According to Rampersad and Roessel (1995) Langston Hughes once wrote "If dreams die, life is a broken-winged bird that cannot fly" (p. 32). In order to reclaim dreams and fly, dashed hopes and dreams must first be dealt with. The steps for dealing with lost dreams are:

- Discovering and naming the lost dream
- Grieving the loss
- Re-focusing
- Reshaping dreams and expectations for now

Storytelling is a great way to work through the steps of dream reclaiming (Schlossberg, 1999). For example, in naming the dream, Lynn, the nurse described earlier, would need to tell the story about her children's choices not to achieve in school and attend select colleges as if it were her fault. "I was not a good mother. That is why my children didn't get into Ivy League schools and are only marking time." She then needs to retell the story attributing the blame to something else. "My children have minds of their own. They do not want to go to a fancy college. Many successful people don't go to fancy schools." And, finally, she needs to come up with a story that she can tell her friends. "I had different expectations for my children than they have for themselves. I am glad that they are becoming their own people." As you can see, just from retelling the story in these three ways, Lynn is experiencing a transformation.

The second way storytelling can help is by facilitating grieving of the loss of a non-event. Society has rituals for grieving a death, but there is no formalized mechanism to deal with grief over what did not happen, such as a book not written, a marriage not made, a child not conceived or an education not sought. A support group of those grieving a non-event is a great way to share stories. Each person tells about a loss (my children's education), and the group members assist each other in finding ways to help with the grief (Schlossberg, 1999). For Lynn, just realizing that her children's lives were their own, that their lives were not linear but cyclical, and that there was ample time for them to achieve their dreams helped her let go of her own unmet expectations.

The next step is a bit more difficult, because it requires letting go of the old and reframing the non-event. One way this is done is by ritual, just as events like marriages, births and deaths are marked by rituals. A non-event can be marked by a ritual. Rituals can be used as a way of allowing people to separate from the past (Schlossberg, 1999).

Lynn needed a ritual to acknowledge the transfer of her dreams for her children to the children themselves. One ritual Lynn might have used was to copy the Langston Hughes poem "Dreams" on a piece of paper and make two copies. The copies are then tied with a red ribbon and given to each child at dinner as a symbolic way of giving them back their own dreams for their lives.

Finally, the dream must be reshaped or given up. In this exercise, the individual describes a lost dream, decides if there is any hope left to pursue the dream, and if there is, decides what must be done. If there is no hope, the dreamer must modify or delete and replace the dream. In Lynn's case, there was no hope of her realizing her dreams for her children. She finally realized she had been dreaming for them and that she needed a dream to replace her previous dream. This time her dream was for a career of her own that would be successful.

Once past dreams are buried, new dreams must be acknowledged. Bridges (1994) suggests people determine what they really want by asking four questions:

1. What are the first 25 things that come to mind when asked what do you want?
2. Where would you like to live?
3. In 10 years, what would you like to be doing?
4. What is your purpose in life?

When answering these questions, the individual should not judge or seek an acceptable answer. The answers must be real, because these questions help one see desires and dreams clearly.

Bridges (1994) recommends wishes be separated from true desires. A wish list usually contains phrases like "make a lot of money," "win the lottery," "become a country and western singer," and "own an island in the Pacific." Once the wishes have been separated out, each of the remaining desires should be listed on a single notebook page. It is important to look at each page, reflect and write down thoughts. The notebook should then be put away for a day or two before it is reviewed with a fresh pair of eyes, as if it had been written by someone else. What stands out? Are there any patterns? After this exercise, the individual should return to the wishes in search of patterns or a clue to something really important. Perhaps buying an island is not possible, but spending a week on an island every year is very doable.

The second question concerning where you want to live is often given very little consideration, but it is very important. Relocation usually improves the chance of finding the best job. So, considering whether or not to move and where are very important considerations.

The third question requires looking into the future and imagining a day 10 years forward. Bridges (1994) suggests the review be as descriptive as possible and focus on a day in the future. Such questions as: "When do I get up?" "When do I go to bed?" "What would I like to be doing while awake?" be asked and be completed prior to going to bed.

The final question suggested by Bridges (1994) is probably the most important one. For example, "What is my purpose?" "What am I supposed to do with my life?" Some refer to the purpose as a calling, as a vocation.

Hilman (1996) refers to it as the "soul's code" or one's intuitive wisdom or what the heart knows. This question really requires introspection and an examination of one's very being. Techniques for getting at this question are dream recalling, creating a collage of parts of oneself, developing a life line and journaling in an attempt to answer "How do I wish this situation to be? What am I called to express in this world? What's my way of doing it? What do I need to develop in myself to move past this?" (Greenblatt & Greenblatt, 2001, p. 68)

Abilities/Natural Talent

Dutch (1997) asserts that it is very important to separate innate natural talent from learned skills. When young and energetic, it is easy to pursue a career that demands skills and talents outside one's area of expertise. Success and promotion might even occur. But as midlife approaches and energy diminishes, operating on training alone is difficult. It becomes even more difficult as age increases and energy decreases. This principle of natural talent can best be explained by imagining a horse pushing a cart full of tools gained over a lifetime, e.g., speaking and people skills, negotiation skills, etc. When the cart becomes full of skills that are different from the natural talent (the horse), it is impossible for the horse to push the cart. Instead, the natural talent should pull the cart and the acquired skills should complement the natural talent (Dutch, 1997).

Most individuals shape their activities around a cluster of basic abilities or talents. In order to energize a stalled career, it is necessary to discover one's natural talents by thinking about what has been accomplished thus far, starting back at grade school. The question to be asked is: "What have I accomplished over my many roles as employee, family member, citizen, parent?" Once this question is answered, the next question is: "What did I do or know to assist me in my accomplishments?" Or, in other words, "What do I really do well?" (Bridges, 1994). These talents have been described by Gardner (1983; 1993a; 1993b; 1999) as multiple intelligences, and fit into eight categories. The abilities/talents can be verbal/linguistic, logic/mathematical, visual/spatial, intrapersonal/interpersonal, body/kinesthetic, musical/rhythmic and naturalistic. If there are some talents that do not fit into one of these categories, they should just be listed with the others. The list is just a way to examine one's talents to see what can support a career.

Verbal-linguistic intelligence is the talent or ability to use language to express complex ideas and meanings. Linguistic intelligence includes skills such as reading, writing and oral presentations and can be developed (Gardner, 1983). Some individuals seem to have a natural linguistic ability. Nursing is a profession that demands linguistic talent, because one must be able to communicate with patients, families and co-workers. Nurses with a natural talent for linguistics might consider volunteering to teach classes or to write an article for a newsletter to develop their talent even further.

People with *logical-mathematical* abilities can make cause and effect connections and perceive patterns and relationships among objects and/or ideas. They have a natural talent for problem-solving and calculations (Gardner, 1983). Some people are strong in both areas. Nurses with these abilities might be comfortable in administrative positions that require budget and problem-solving or in a nursing or clinical research career.

Spatial ability is the ability to think in images and to accurately perceive visual reality. People with spatial ability can think in three dimensions and recreate visual perceptions through imagination. They can transform an experience into a vision, as well as be handy with instruments (Gardner, 1983). A nurse with strong spatial abilities is likely to find perioperative nursing and "first assisting" a good match.

People with *intrapersonal* abilities are able to understand themselves. They are aware of their personal strengths and weaknesses and can monitor their thoughts and feelings in such a way as to achieve personal efficacy (Gardner, 1983). Such individuals are able to rapidly assess strengths and weaknesses and come up with personal goals for career revitalization. This ability is helpful in all areas of nursing.

Interpersonal abilities are another extremely important talent for a nurse. People who have interpersonal talent are able to understand other people and can empathize with them. They understand another people almost as if they were inside the other person (Gardner, 1983). Nurses with strong interpersonal abilities might consider a leadership position or mental health nursing.

People with high *body-kinesthetic* abilities are able to use their bodies or parts of the body in a coordinated fashion. These individuals are athletes and are able to use their hands with dexterity (Gardner, 1983). Many areas of nursing require the skilled use of the hands. For example, an intravenous therapy nurse needs manual dexterity.

People with *musical* ability think in sounds and rhythms and are sensitive to pitch, rhythm, timbre and tone. They are often able to create, reproduce or recognize music (Gardner, 1983). There is no specific area of nursing that makes use of this ability. But music therapy can create relaxation that heals. Nurses can share their musical talents with patients.

Naturalistic ability often lends itself to nursing. Those with naturalistic talent are good with plants and/or animals and tend to feel comfortable in the outdoors (Gardner, 1999). Nurses who have a talent for the natural world of plants and animals might work as camp nurses in an area of the country with year-round camping weather. They also could use their talents to develop programs that use plants and/or animals for healing.

These eight abilities are not totally separate, but work together within individuals. For example, the ability to perceive space and depth is complementary with logical-mathematical ability in solving geometry problems and with body-kinesthetics in learning to drive an automobile. Linguistic and logical abilities are complementary when solving word problems. Logical, musical and spatial skills work well together in discerning certain patterns. The combination of abilities in each individual is as unique as a snow flake; there are no two alike.

Lynn reviewed her life from very early until the present to discern her talents. She found she always enjoyed reading, writing and working word puzzles. She remembered winning a PTA writing contest in fourth grade. This was one of the highlights of her school memories. Mathematics was a weaker area for Lynn, and although she was very good at problem-solving, she had no patience for complicated calculations. Lynn listed herself as a team player and able to get along with others. She enjoys and continues to enjoy working in groups but dislikes competitive games. During the review, Lynn found she is too busy to do much reflection and does not like all this self-examination that has become so popular today. She also remembers being a clumsy child and did not like physical education and handicrafts. She was the last kid on her block to learn to ride a bike, and learning to drive was a disaster. She had real trouble with depth perception and almost could not learn to parallel park. She enjoys listening to music but has never played an instrument and has no interest in doing so. She enjoys the outdoors but does not garden and has no pets. After reflection, Lynn agreed that her strongest abilities were linguistic and interpersonal.

Temperament/Type

Temperament describes personality, not behaviors or abilities. One of the most frequently used assessments of personality type or temperament is the Myers-Briggs Type Indicator (MBTI). The MBTI is based on Carl Jung's theory of personality and describes an individual's preferences for perceiving and processing information. The MBTI is administered to about two million people a year, making it the most widely used personality/temperament assessment test (Barbian, 2001). The four dichotomous scales of the MBTI are Extraversion and Introversion (E & I), Sensing and Intuition (S & N), Thinking and Feeling (T & F), and Judging and Perceiving (J & P). They are distinctly different and are defined below.

- Extraversion is when the person focuses on the outer world. Introversion is the opposite, the focus on the inner world.
- When in the sensing process, the person focuses on what is real, concrete and in the present; whereas, when in the intuitive process, the person tends to focus on possibilities and patterns.
- The thinker bases decisions on objectivity and logic and prefers to deal with data or things. In contrast, the feeler bases decisions on subjectivity and personal concerns and prefers to deal with people.
- Judging is associated with a preference for planning, organizing and seeking closure, while perceiving is associated with a flexible, spontaneous approach that seeks openness (Myers & McCaulley, 1985; Murray, 1990).

Type or temperament is very important in career decisions. An introvert prefers to be around one or two people, not a crowd. A feeler is at best when working around people, not with machines. A perceiving individual might prefer the spontaneity of the emergency department to the schedule of an operating room.

Lynn decided she was an extrovert. She focuses on the external world and enjoys being with others. She really does not like to spend much time reflecting inwardly. She believes she is an intuitive rather than a sensor. She is much more of an abstract thinker than a concrete thinker and searches for patterns and the big picture. Lynn is a feeler and thinks about things in a very subjective way. This subjectivity really allows her to be empathetic with others. Finally, Lynn is judging. She seeks order in her environment and seeks closure. She is really uncomfortable without a plan that is finally realized. So after thought and discussion, Lynn believes her MBTI to be ENFJ.

According to Bridges (1994), another part of temperament is an individual's activity pattern when faced with change. He describes the four patterns as inactivity, reactivity, proactivity and coactivity. Inactivity is an important pattern that allows for rest and recuperation. But if one is continuously inactive, then denial or powerlessness reigns. Chronic inactivity is not a way to maintain or recharge a career. Reactivity is when the person is always responding to an emergency. The reactor is not in control and frequently burns out. If an individual is reactive by nature and enjoys reacting, emergency and disaster nursing might be a great fit.

The proactive individual is the one who thinks of the solution ahead of time and thus is not forced to react. Innovators come up with great ideas. Coactivity is proactivity with a group of collaborators. The disadvantage of being coactive is the time it takes for a group to reach consensus and to act.

Lynn acknowledges she has spent too much of her adult life, both in her work as a staff nurse and in her role as a parent, moving between inactivity and reactivity. When confronted with change, she often freezes and then reacts out of desperation. This has sometimes caused her to be perceived as a shrew by co-workers and children.

Assets

Assets are advantages. Assets are finances, reputation, education, experience or anything that can be used as an advantage in starting a business or getting ahead in a job. Some assets, like education and experience, may need enhancement (Bridges, 1994). Individuals stalled in a career need to examine their assets by asking questions, such as "What are my assets and how would my education, experience, finances, etc. serve me?"

Lynn took stock of her assets and decided that her finances could not be considered an asset but were adequate. She had two years of general studies in a community college when she was thinking of majoring in English prior to meeting her husband and marrying. After her marriage, she entered the community college's associate degree in nursing program to become a nurse. So she has all her general studies completed, as well as a nursing degree. Early in her career, she received lots of praise for her patient teaching. Lynn organized outings and taught skills to the girl scouts.

So Lynn summarized her assets as experience as a teacher, completion of general studies, organizational skills and adequate finances.

Dutch (1997) reports each person possesses a unique combination of desires, abilities, temperament and assets. He points out that each individual is also greater than the sum of these talents. Thus, the review of one's D.A.T.A. must be written in a way that includes the times when work was enjoyed and they were successful. Then and only then will the stories provide themes that reveal a purpose and the D.A.T.A. that combined together to help the individual achieve that purpose.

Lynn's themes began to emerge early in her self-reflection. She was pleasantly surprised to remember winning the writing contest in fourth grade. She had also forgotten how much she loved to teach the scouts earlier in her life. The importance of being with others and affirming them almost shouted as a theme. As Lynn had gotten busy caring for her children and working, she had forgotten how much writing, teaching and being with others had meant to her. She had buried her personal dreams, abilities, temperament and assets in the day-to-day grind.

Opportunities

Opportunities in nursing careers are categorized by function, specialty and practice setting. Nurses can serve in a variety of functional roles, as direct bedside care providers, nurse educators, nurse managers, nurse executives, nurse researchers (nurse scientists), clinical nurse specialists, nurse consultants, nurse practitioners, case/care managers, nurse informaticists, nurse attorneys, etc. In addition to the clinical nurse specialist and nurse practitioner, there are other advanced practice roles, such as certified nurse anesthetists and certified nurse midwives, in which nurses have about 100 years of outstanding service. There are newer roles, such as legal consultants, forensic nurses, nurse entrepreneurs, quality managers, utilization managers, clinical research coordinators and more.

The clinical specialties include neurology, cardiovascular, oncology, urology, gastrointestinal, nephrology, orthopedic (known as medical-surgical specialties), critical care, perioperative, emergency, obstetric, neonatal, pediatric, gerontological, palliative and psychiatric. The practice settings include acute care; extended care (nursing homes, assisted living, adult day care); community (public health offices, schools, churches, homes and work places); ambulatory care (physician's office or ambulatory care center); health insurance companies; and universities. There is some kind of a career in nursing for almost any combination of dreams, abilities, temperament and assets.

As Lynn surveys the opportunities available, the role of nurse educator has an appeal. She realizes both her interest and abilities in writing and communicating, as well as her external focus, will serve her well as a teacher. Since early in her career, she has spent much time teaching patients. She thinks she might like to share her many years of clinical experience with other nurses as a staff developer. She also is interested in renewing her childhood ability and interest in writing.

Planning Outcome, Vision and Strategies

The career vision or outcome is grounded in the assessment of both self and the environmental opportunities. It must focus on what is possible and realistic for an individual for both short-term and long-term goals. The career vision or career outcome is the link between the person now and the person of the future (Donner & Wheeler, 2001). Lynn's short-term vision is to write an article for the hospital newsletter and volunteer to teach a patient education class or volunteer to teach nursing staff about a new therapeutic intervention. She would also like to continue writing and to eventually submit an article for publication. Seeing her name in print may recreate the same feelings of success she enjoyed as a fourth grade student winning a writing contest. One of her longer range outcomes is to return to school and hopefully use her past education as a foundation for earning a bachelor's degree in nursing and eventually a master's degree in nursing. This level of education should serve her well in realizing her five-year plan to work as a staff development specialist for her current employing agency. In 10 years, she would like to become a director of education for a healthcare agency.

Interventions/Strategies

The strategies implemented to make a vision a reality are blueprints for action. Barker (1992) states without action, a vision is only an unfulfilled dream and action without a vision just leads to the passage of time without any movement toward a goal. He concludes vision with action changes the world. For an individual with a stalled career, vision with action changes the future. However, the strategy selected must include specific activities, the time estimate for accomplishment and the needed resources (Donner & Wheeler, 2001).

Lynn has established her vision and now has to set up actions and a timeline for accomplishing them. Anderson (1992) suggests the best way to create a timeline is to work backwards from the part of the plan that will take the longest to accomplish. For Lynn, the outcome furthest away is obtaining the master's degree in nursing education and becoming a director of education. She needs to decide when she wants to graduate with the MSN and make that the furthest point on her timeline. She decides 10 years from January 2003 or January 2013 she would like to have an MSN and apply for a job as director of education. She knows she cannot do this without first earning a BSN, so she decides she would like to have her BSN by January 2008. In order to do that, she would like to start her BSN program no later than September 2004. Now she needs to find a school with a program that fits her needs, discuss the program with her manager and determine a workable schedule.

She establishes a time (June 2003) for talking to her manager about the possibility of employer support for her education. Working backwards again, she sets the date of May 2003 for finding a school program. Most importantly, she talks to her family immediately about their support in terms of assistance with household responsibilities and finances. She was pleasantly surprised to find her husband and children whole-heartedly supported her plan. Lynn set the timeline for volunteering to teach for staff development as February 2003, followed by volunteering the article in her agency's newsletter as March 2003. Lynn is excited with the possibilities for a "revved up" career.

IMPLEMENTATION

Once the strategies, timelines and resources have been decided, the implementation phase begins. There are several things to remember when implementing the plan for a "revved-up" career. One of the things to keep in mind is the need to market self. This means being able to find a mentor

(Donner & Wheeler, 2001) and project confidence, being self-reliant, showing initiative, being committed to professional development, demonstrating interpersonal competence, and being both flexible and savvy (Williams, 2000).

Marketing Self

Nurses are excellent at advocating for patients' achievement of health-care goals. This same kind of advocacy needs to be translated into self-advocacy so that career goals can be achieved. In order to market oneself, the person's unique set of desires, abilities, temperament and assets (D.A.T.A) must be described as the best fit for the job. In addition to developing a script that describes the match between the D.A.T.A. and the job, self-marketing includes establishing a network and acquiring a mentor. Self-marketing is about using resources to present the most positive image (Donner & Wheeler, 2001).

Finding a Mentor

Research findings demonstrate an active mentor assists in career goal achievement and increases job satisfaction for the protégé. Mentors are often confused with preceptors. Preceptors serve a narrow, prescribed function for a limited period of time as defined by the environment. The mentor's role has a broader scope that is not necessarily in the same work setting. It may include an orientation to certain work tasks, but it includes many other tasks, such as introduction to a career field, career guidance and inspiration. A mentor-protégé relationship is not for a prescribed period of time and usually lasts for years, even when one or both participants change jobs (Shaffer, 2001). See Chapter 24 for a discussion of mentorships and what they can offer the individual who is moving on from a stalled career.

Projecting Confidence

A nurse seeking new opportunities must exude confidence. Confidence, in this instance, is the belief in one's ability to succeed with additional career responsibilities. This self-belief must extend beyond the day-to-day work and into higher risk assignments and more visible positions (Williams, 2000).

Being Self-Reliant

There was a time not so long ago when administrators of organizations nearly instituted control mechanisms to ensure workers completed their tasks. Fortunately, there are no longer any controls, but managers do depend on the worker's trust in self and inner direction to complete the tasks of the job. Healthcare agencies, like many others, need nurses who are professionals and thus are self-reliant, because they cannot afford to assign enough supervisors to provide that kind of control (Williams, 2000).

Showing Initiative

Initiative is a move forward from self-reliance and requires that the worker understand what needs to be done and does it without needing to be told. It is getting to work on time and meeting deadlines. It is requesting feedback from colleagues and supervisors for constructive criticism (Chrisp, 1994).

Being Committed to Professional Development

Many nurses act as if the employer is responsible for their professional development. They only attend the programs provided by the employer. When a person wants to implement a career vision, there must be a commitment to personal professional development, which means keeping up by reading about what is happening in the field and keeping current by attending conferences and workshops (Chrisp, 1994).

Demonstrating Interpersonal Competence

Nurses must exhibit interpersonal competence or they will not be able to adequately care for patients. However, too frequently that same kind of interpersonal competence is not often extended to colleagues. "Horizontal violence" is a term that refers to interpersonal conflict among workers. Study findings continue to reveal there is blaming, back biting and other forms of aggression among nurses. This violence pits nurses against nurses (Jackson, Clare, & Mannix, 2002; Farrell, 2001). Interpersonal competence is not only between nurses and patients but must be expanded to include nurses' communication with other nurses. All nurses deserve the care and concern that patients receive. "Work goes better when we connect to our common humanity first" (Williamson, 2002, p. 105). Interpersonal competence requires respectful communication among colleagues in order to create a fully functioning team.

Being Flexible and Savvy

Flexibility is the ability to change with the situation. In a time when change is the only constant, flexibility is of the utmost importance. Thus, being able to let go and adapt is of the utmost importance in order to exist in the ever-changing environment.

Savvy is important. Savvy is being "in touch," and in this case, it means being able to see the big picture of an organization, as well as the job setting. It is almost impossible to move upward in an organization without having a sense of the organization and how to fit into it and be flexible.

Lynn realizes she lacks confidence, self-reliance and initiative. And because of these shortcomings, she has not been marketing herself. She also has no mentor. She has considered professional development the responsibility of her employer and has only participated in mandatory classes. Lynn is ashamed to say that she has participated in horizontal violence, not only against her colleagues, but against student nurses. She has made fun of the BSN students for their lack of practical knowledge and has berated her colleagues when they have made mistakes. Further, she has not always been flexible and has unsuccessfully tried to block changes in charting. In addition, Lynn has never seen the importance of organizational savvy until now.

Acknowledgement of these issues has been difficult because she is proud of her interpersonal skills with patients. However, she now realizes the reasons for her stalled career and the lack of job satisfaction. While she was providing competent patient care, she was not a steward of her work environment, nor was she growing professionally. Lynn is very excited about taking on a new work ethic with new behaviors as she implements her action plan.

EVALUATION OF OUTCOME ACHIEVEMENT

Evaluation is an ongoing process that begins with looking at short-term outcomes to see if they have been achieved. In Lynn's case, if she has written an article for the newsletter and taught a class for staff development, her short-term outcome has been met. If for some reason she does not accomplish these tasks, she needs to re-examine the self-assessment, the plan and the implementation strategies to determine what happened. Perhaps she really does not have the writing ability or interest. If that is the case, her self-assessment needs to be repeated. Maybe during planning she gave herself too short a timeline. If that is the case, she needs to change the plan. Or if she did not use initiative in implementing her plan, she needs to reexamine her strategies. She must do the same thing for her intermediate outcomes and for her long-term outcomes. Although evaluation is often seen as a process of judging outcome achievement, Lynn needs to evaluate the entire career development process. In order to do this, she will need the assistance of her mentor, colleagues, employer and family. Lynn will need to be gentle on herself initially.

Because change is not easy (Omaran, 1991), a journal might help Lynn monitor her progress toward outcome achievement (Chrisp, 1994). Her plan requires constant evaluation and adaptation, just as a patient care plan needs frequent evaluation. A nurse might plan to teach a patient and then find, on entrance to the room, that the patient is distraught and anxious. As a result of these findings, the nurse would postpone the teaching and offer the patient emotional support. A career plan must receive similar consideration. It requires constant re-evaluation and adjustment if the career goals and the actions are to be achieved (Donner & Wheeler, 2001).

CONCLUSION

Lynn is one of many nurses whose careers are stalled. In order to jump-start or "rev up" a stalled career, the nurse must perform a self-assessment, which includes an evaluation of dreams/desires, abilities, temperament and assets. After the self-assessment, the nurse needs to develop a career vision and a plan to achieve it. In order to implement the plan, the nurse must market self, which includes help from a mentor. The nurse also needs to project confidence, demonstrate self-reliance and initiative, exhibit interpersonal competence toward co-workers and supervisors, and be both flexible and organizationally savvy. Evaluation needs to be ongoing and include feedback from mentors, colleagues, employers and family. Jump-starting a stalled career is not easy but can lead to a career and personal renewal that once was just a dream.

REFERENCES

Anderson, L. (1992). Reviving your career dream. *Nursing*, 22(5), 121-122.

Barbian, J. (2001). Getting to know you. *Training*, 38(6), 60-64.

Barker, J. (1992) *Paradigms: The business of discovering the future*. New York, NY: Harper Collins.

Boyatzis, R., McKee, A., & Goleman, D. (2002). Re-awakening your passion for work. *Harvard Business Review, 80*(4), 86-94.

Bridges, W. (1994). *Job shift: How to prosper in a workplace without jobs*. Reading, MA: Addison-Wesley.

Bryan, M. (1997). *Career development manual* (2nd ed.). Waterloo, Ontario, Canada: Career Services, University of Waterloo.

Cannon, A. (2002, February 18). Left a good job for meaning: Some have responded to September 11 by trading stability for fulfilling careers. *U.S. News & World Report*, pp. 44-45.

Chrisp, D.R. (1994). Changing your specialty with confidence. *Nursing, 24*(12), 77-78.

Donner, G.J., & Wheeler, M.M. (2001). Career planning and development for nurses: The time has come. *International Nursing Review, 48*(2), 79-86.

Dutch, G. (1997). Helping people who hate their jobs. *National Consultation on Career Development.* Retrieved January 2, 2003, from http://icdl.uncg.edug/ft/0621000-06.html.

Farrell, G.A. (2001). From tall poppies to squashed weeds: Why don't nurses pull together more? *Journal of Advanced Nursing, 35*(1), 26-34.

Gardner, H. (1983). *Frames of mind: The theory of multiple intelligences*. New York, NY: Basic Books

Gardner, H. (1993a). *Multiple intelligences: The theory into practice*. New York, NY: Basic Books.

Gardner, H. (1993b). *Frames of mind: The theory of multiple intelligences* (10th anniversary ed.). New York, NY: Basic Books.

Gardner, H. (1999). Are there additional intelligences? The case for naturalist, spiritual, and existential intelligences. In J. Kane (Ed.), *Education, information and transformation* (pp. 111-131). Englewood Cliffs, NJ: Prentice Hall.

Greenblatt, A. & Greenblatt, P. (2001) *Integrating psychology and spirituality during career exploration. Staying innovative and change-focused in the new economy: A collection of special papers generated for the International Career Development Conference*. Retrieved January 2, 2003, from http://icdl.uncg.edu/pdf.102601-01.pdf.

Hilman, J. (1996). *The soul's code: In search of character and calling*. New York, NY: Random House.

Hudson, F.M. (1991). *The adult years: Mastering the art of self-renewal.* San Francisco, CA: Jossey-Bass.

Hudson, F.M. (1997). *Career plateau transitions in midlife, and how to manage them*. Greensboro, NC: ERIC Clearinghouse on Counseling and Student Services. Retrieved January 2, 2003, from http://icdl.uncg.edu/ft/051199-09.html.

Hughes, L. (2001). The poems: 1921-1940. In A. Rampersand (Ed.), *The collected works of Langston Hughes*. Columbia, MO: University of Missouri Press.

Imel, S. (2000*). Surviving career doldrums*. Eric Resource Information Center. Retrieved January 2, 2003, from http://ericacve.org/docgen.asp?tbl=pab&ID=98.

Jackson, D., Clare, J., & Mannix, J. (2002). Who would want to be a nurse? Violence in the workplace—a factor in recruitment and retention. *Journal of Nursing Management*, *10*(1), 13-21.

Kreuter, E.A. (1993). *Why career plateaus are healthy*. CPA in Industry. Retrieved January 2, 2002, from http://www.nysscpa.org/cpajounal/old/14522934.htm.

Lankard, B.A. (1993). *Career development through self-renewal*. ERIC Clearinghouse on Adult, Career, and Vocational Education (CE). Retreived January 2, 2002, from http://icdl.uncg.edu/ft/082099-14.html.

Murray, J.B. (1990). Review of research on the Myers-Briggs type indicator. *Perceptual and Motor Skills, 70*, 1187-1202.

Myers, I.B., & McCaulley, M.H. (1985). *Manual: A guide to the development and use of the Myers-Briggs Type Indicator*. Palo Alto, CA: Consulting Psychologists.

Omaran, S. (1991). Breathe new life into your career. *Nursing, 21*(12), 82-84.

Rampersad, A., & Roessal, D. (1995). *The collective poems of Langston Hughes* (Vintage Classics). New York, NY: Vintage Books.

Schlossberg, N.K. (1999). Lessons for life literacy: Examining non-event transitions. International Career Development Library. Retrieved January 2, 2003, from http://icdl.uncg.edu/ft/070600-01.html.

Shaffer, B. (2001). Win-win mentoring. *Dimensions of Critical Care Nursing, 20*(3) 36-39.

Williams, C. (2000). *Helping women shape a career path and life that works.* International Career Development Conference, November 2000. Retrieved January 2, 2003, from http://icdl.edu/ft/031401-15.html.

Williamson, M. (2002). *Everyday grace: Having hope, finding forgiveness, and making miracles.* New York: Riverhead.

Wong, T.P. (2003). *Promises of renewal.* Retrieved January 12, 2003, from http://www.meaning.ca/articles/presidents_column/print_copy/renewal_jan03.htm.

Chapter 18

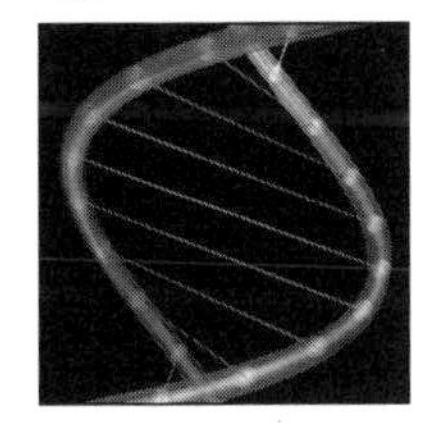

The Impaired Career

by Pam Reiter, Michaela Tolo & Cyndi McCullough

My road to recovery began the weekend before my 38th birthday. I told my husband about the drug abuse and decided to go through withdrawal over the weekend, so I would be ready for work again on Monday. I was shaking so hard, had severe pain from a fecal impaction, and could not get out of bed. I called in sick on Monday, and then on Tuesday, I tried to go to work. I thought I had licked the problem, but I had only been at work for one hour when I was shooting up again (P. Reiter, personal communication, June 2002).

A career can be significantly impaired due to mental and physical problems and/or chemical abuse. Chemical abuse (most often alcohol and drugs) among nurses has been a documented problem since the mid-19th century (West, 2002). The American Nurses Association (ANA) first addressed the issue in the 1980s. In 1984, the ANA defined the impaired nurse as "one who has impaired function which results from alcohol or drug misuse and which interferes with professional judgment and the delivery of safe, high-quality care" (p. 18). The ANA also helped state nurses associations (SNAs) establish assistance programs for impaired nurses. The disciplinary actions taken by state boards provide the most concrete evidence of impairment among nurses. In 1984, the ANA reported over half of all state board actions over a 12-month period were due to impaired functioning. Since that time, percentages have not been published. Fear of legal and occupational reprisal contributes to the difficulty in determining the national number of impaired nurses. Although exact numbers are not known, it is recognized that addiction to alcohol and drugs in nursing occurs as it does in other health professions.

On July 1, 2002, the ANA House of Delegates accepted a resolution reaffirming the nursing profession's response to the problems of addictions. The intent of the resolution is to bring about continuity of approaches and fairness so all nurses, regardless of geographic location, will be offered advocacy (ANA, 2002).

Factors Leading to Chemical Dependency

Many chemically dependent individuals have low self-esteem, and some have been abused as children. They often have difficulty making friends as children and thus feel lonely and alone as adults (West, 2002; Sullivan, Bissell, & Williams, 1988). Studies about the characteristics of substance-impaired nurses reveal the impaired nurse often has a family history of alcoholism and depression, has experienced sexual abuse, has been academically and professionally successful, and has an extensive medical history (Sullivan, 1987).

What happens when an individual is impaired? How does the nurse obtain another job? This chapter presents one nurse's story about her struggle with chemical (drug and alcohol) impairment, her voluntary surrender of licensure, and the steps she took to control her problem and have her license reinstated.

> *My name is Pam and this is my story. My mother was a public health nurse, and my father sold insurance. My parents grew up across the street from each other. My mother's father, my grandfather, was a country doctor, and my mother was reared by a governess. I am the middle child of three adopted children. Our family was one that didn't touch, hug or say "I love you." My older brother had medical problems, and my younger brother was always in trouble with the law, and they received much attention from my parents. There was much physical and emotional abuse in our home. For most of my childhood, I felt alone, lonely and left out. I was a shy and insecure teenager who was a little overweight. I started smoking in the 8th grade and drinking in the 10th grade to be accepted by my peers. I*

learned that when I was drunk, I could drown out some of the pain and endure it better.

These statements by Pam have been supported in the literature. For many abusers, there has not been positive support from anyone who cared. In addition, having access to drugs makes it easy to obtain them and when unhappy to use them (Finke, Hickman, & Miller, 1993).

While in nursing school, my aunt died and I went to help my parents settle her estate. My aunt had worked in a physician's office and left a bathroom cabinet full of drugs, mostly pain killers. My mother gave me the task of sorting through the drugs and disposing of them. I decided to keep some Darvocet, Tylenol with codeine and morphine just in case I needed it for back pain. That night, my parents, brother, niece and I went to dinner. My brother and father started yelling and fighting. My father was never happy unless everyone else was miserable. I couldn't take it anymore, so I swallowed some Darvocet and found it dulled both the back and emotional pain. I believe this is when I first got hooked on drugs. Later, I found the drugs worked even better with alcohol.

A sad and shocking fact is that many drug abusers learn how to obtain and use drugs from other professionals. Role modeling, availability of drugs and encouragement from others are leading causes of the expansion of drug abuse in nurses (Sullivan, Bissell, & Williams, 1988). Further, absence of drug inventory control often makes it easier for the abuser to obtain the drugs. Clearly, Pam experienced all of these situations.

After graduation, I worked five years as an RN and moved to another state to work in an ICU. While there, I married an RN and worked with him in the ICU. He was older than I, drank a lot and used drugs excessively. He often stole the drugs from the unit where we worked. He was also mentally abusive, and I developed migraine headaches. The marriage lasted two years.

After anesthetist school, I married again, had a miscarriage, tried again and was unable to get pregnant, and had fertility testing and drug therapy. Nothing worked and I was severely depressed. I started taking Tylox for the mental pain. On occasion, I observed other anesthesiologists falsifying narcotics records, and a resident once confided that she took and used some morphine. There were no checks and balances for the anesthesia drugs, so for the next five months I stole morphine. I was giving myself up to 12 mg IM per day. I was afraid to inject anything intravenously, so at first I only used oral and intramuscular injections. But after a while, I needed more, so I added drugs like Sufenta and Versed and started injecting them intravenously. Each time I stole drugs, I wished I would get caught. I wanted to quit, but I didn't know how. My codependent husband was not very supportive about the miscarriage and my depression, and if he knew I was using drugs, he ignored it. When I got drunk, he took care of me. I didn't know how to live without drugs and alcohol.

The Cry for Help

As if feeling alone is not bad enough, not having someone notice the escalating drug behavior, or notice and ignore it, is even worse. Yet over and over again, we hear about professionals who were using drugs and others who knew about the behavior but did nothing to help. This is known as enabling behavior.

Enabling is any behavior that serves to protect the abuser from the consequences of his or her use, thereby contributing to a worsening of the disease in the codependents, as well as the abuser. According to Tucker (2002), examples of enabling behaviors include:

- Denying the drinking or drug use is a problem
- Avoiding problems and conflicts that might cause the abuser to use alcohol and/or drugs
- Minimizing the problems associated with the use or amount used by the abuser
- Rationalizing the use
- Excusing the abuser's inappropriate behavior
- Protecting the abuser from the natural and logical consequences of chemical use
- Controlling people and situations in order to control chemical use
- Waiting and hoping things will get better

Confronting an individual about behavior specific to drug/alcohol abuse is difficult, and most professionals are not prepared to do this, thus they continue to enable. Pam's cry for help is an example of this phenomenon.

Even though I drank all the time, I did well in nursing school. I had no support system, no friends, my family didn't get along, and there was always a lot of yelling whenever we were together. Ultimately, I became bulimic. It was the only means of control I had. I really didn't want to drink all the time, but I didn't know how to stop. As a senior in college, I was required to complete a psychology project. I waited until the last minute, got drunk and tape recorded my story for the project. I received an "A" on the project, but my instructor never suggested counseling for me. My cry for help failed.

I hated work and the people I worked with, but I needed to be at work to get the drugs. The only time I didn't feel depressed was when I was high on alcohol or drugs. At first, I only used the drugs at home, but after a while, I started using them at work too. Deep down, I really wanted to stop stealing the drugs, and secretly I hoped I would get caught, but that never happened.

When the user has been caught or has been hospitalized, then the behavior is acknowledged. Frequently, professionals have difficulty believing their colleagues are doing wrong and often turn their backs on the situation. They may feel powerless to effectively confront the abuser and unfortunately avoid the confrontation that is needed (Tucker, 2002).

Substance-impaired nurses may share common risk factors, but the risk factors vary in the way they develop, progress and become severe (West, 2002). Being knowledgeable about risk factors that lead to substance-related disorders and discriminating between impairment and non-impairment based on risk factors will assure early intervention for the abuser and ultimately protect patients. In addition to the risk factors identified by Sullivan (1987), Haack (1988) lists burnout, depression and stress as risk factors for substance-related impairments.

When I reported I had a drug problem to my supervisor and needed to be hospitalized, he replied, "I thought you might," but he never confronted me about the problem. He said he had noticed my mood changes, absences from work and somewhat erratic behavior but never spoke directly to me about my drug problem. I felt betrayed.

Many healthcare professionals feel poorly prepared to address chemical dependency problems. Results of a survey of health professionals (including 100 nurses) conducted by Bissell and Jones (1981) indicated the professionals believed their education had not prepared them to recognize and deal with addiction problems. Tucker (2002) lists a number of characteristics of a chemically dependent nurse that help clarify why it is so difficult to spot the abuser. They are:

1. Chemical abuse usually occurs in adult life.
2. Initial use does not take place for recreation.
3. Use occurs in isolation rather than a social setting.
4. Abuser continues to meet work responsibilities.
5. Abuser has a traditional life attitude.
6. Abuser is demanding of self.
7. Abuser is often a male nurse; critical care and emergency room nurses are at high risk.
8. Abuser usually excels in school.
9. Abuser often has advanced degrees.
10. Abuser is often achievement oriented.
11. Abuser has demanding/responsible job.
12. Abuser is highly respected for excellent work.

Tucker (2002) also lists some problems affecting professionals who have contact with chemically dependent people. They include:

- Lack of knowledge about alcoholism/chemical dependency and the dynamics of recovery
- Mistaken belief the dependent could eliminate problems associated with use if s/he really wanted to
- Feeling powerless to effectively confront the substance abuser
- Possessing a live and let live mentality
- Resentment at being manipulated leads to emotional withdrawal from the substance abuser
- Fear of professional inadequacy leading to avoidance reaction
- Professional "no talk" rule associated with issues of confidentiality and politeness
- Discomfort with own chemical use or that of a family member

These issues need to be addressed and rectified so nursing can adequately support the impaired professional.

The Road to Recovery

The road to recovery often happens in one of two ways: the user initiates actions to change the behavior or the user is reported and required to seek therapy. Acknowledging there is a problem is the first step toward recovery. Denying the problem is common for those with a chemical dependency. Some people may even attribute their behavior to an underlying emotional problem. Sullivan, Bissell and Williams (1988) suggest there are three stages to the recovery process: intervention, treatment and re-entry to the profession.

Intervention

"Intervention" is the term used to describe a planned, structured method of helping the abuser get past the denial stage and to acknowledge there is a problem. The goal is to guide the abuser to agreeing to seek professional help. According to Sullivan, Bissell and Williams (1988), appropriate intervention begins with a willingness by those close to the troubled person to recognize the role they can play in confronting these difficult issues. It is not the role of friends and colleagues to diagnose chemical dependency; however, they must be aware of trouble signs and be prepared to offer assistance.

Intervention tactics range from informal conversations with friends to formal investigations and disciplinary actions. Intervention should not be a form of punishment. The goal is to guide the nurse safely into treatment. Employee assistance programs (EAPs) and state nurses associations' peer assistance committees are two resources that should be contacted to help plan interventions.

> *I found myself in the bathroom crying, so I told my co-workers I wasn't feeling well and needed to go home. I went home and tried to get drunk, but I didn't feel better. I was suicidal. I was planning on going to the hospital later that day to steal some drugs and overdose. The next day, a college classmate called and asked me what I had done the weekend before. I blurted out that I went through narcotic withdrawal. My classmate was shocked and told me I needed help. I told her I didn't know what to do. She called a treatment center in her city and inquired about how she could help me. Then she called my husband and told him what to do. He took me to the hospital where I was admitted to a lock-down unit with suicide precautions for two days. I was in detox for a week.*

The intervention for Pam went smoothly, but some do not. No matter how unpleasant or painful, intervention is preferable to job loss. According to Jefferson and Ensor (1982), a well-planned intervention should include the following:

- The intervention should be conducted when the event is fresh.
- There should be written documentation of each participant's concerns. Notes on specific times, dates and witnesses should be included.
- There should be a statement of desired outcomes and the consequences should they not be reached.
- The material should be presented in a kind and caring manner, but in a fair way.
- Follow-through after the intervention should be provided. This may mean accompanying the nurse to a treatment center if necessary.
- There should be a completed record once the intervention is over.

Treatment

Even with intervention, the road to recovery is not easy and doesn't always occur as planned. Family and co-worker support, an intent to change one's behavior, and an understanding of the fragility of the situation are necessary if recovery is to happen. There is often a denial of the condition and a persistent drive to minimize the situation.

The selection of treatment settings is often dictated by cost and insurance providers. When possible, consideration should be given to family situations, proximity of the treatment site to family and friends, and the level of staff expertise in treating the impaired professional. No matter what setting is chosen, the impaired professional is expected to abstain from all mood-altering drugs and participate in an appropriate 12-step recovery program. Some individuals can handle the recovery with ease as an outpatient, while others need a great deal of supervision and may require extended stay. Pam's situation illustrates this last point.

While in the lock-down unit, I met all kinds of resourceful people who knew how to get drugs. I made a deal with a guy to help me obtain drugs when I was released. He told the psychiatrist what I planned to do, and when the psychiatrist brought it up in a session with my husband, I denied it ever happened. They realized I was not going to make it in an outpatient treatment program, so arrangements were made for me to be dismissed and then readmitted the next day to an inpatient treatment facility. I failed to read my discharge instructions that specifically stated I needed to abstain from alcohol, and not realizing I had an alcohol problem, I went home and started drinking whiskey and Coke. I continued drinking until I went to the treatment center the next day. I even made my husband stop and buy a six-pack of beer that I also drank on the way to the treatment center.

The withdrawal period is often handled in an inpatient facility. The experience varies widely among chemically dependent people. Following withdrawal, a combination of therapy and education (primary treatment) begins. This may happen in an inpatient or an outpatient facility. Family and significant others are usually encouraged to attend these sessions. While some resist it, group therapy is important. It accomplishes the following:

- Allows the abusers to share commonalities and dissipates feelings of uniqueness
- Confronts the remaining denial and rationalizations
- Offers positive support for healthy coping behaviors
- Allows the abuser to help other group members

Group therapy proved to be an enlightening experience for Pam.

I didn't know I was an alcoholic until I attended group therapy. I thought I just had a drug problem. It was during group therapy sessions when others with drinking problems told their stories that I realized I was like them. I was an alcoholic and a drug abuser. It seemed like everyone had the same story, just a different version.

Recovery from drug abuse can be lengthy and difficult, but the real problem is regaining one's former work life, which means being reinstated as a licensed professional. The nurse can re-enter the workplace while receiving therapy, support and close monitoring. Groups such as Alcoholics Anonymous (AA) and Narcotics Anonymous (NA) provide a 12-step, structured recovery program. The only requirement for membership is the desire to stop drinking/using. Lifelong participation in mutual help groups is considered necessary for sustained recovery.

Re-entry Into the Profession

The goal of successful intervention and treatment of chemical abuse is re-entry to the workplace. Federal law specifies alcohol and drug abusers be protected as handicapped individuals and are thus protected from discriminatory employment practices. A prior history of chemical dependency, if there is a current sustained record of recovery, is not sufficient reason for discrimination. Federal law also assures confidentiality of any records of treatment received for alcohol or other drug abuse. However, licensing agencies may reveal a history of chemical dependency if sanctions have been placed on a nurse's license. Such action is a matter of public record (Sullivan, Bissell, & Williams, 1988).

There are a number of actions that must be taken and several processes that must be completed before any state will grant a license to a recovering drug abuser. The re-licensure of a nurse drug abuser is governed by the board of nursing in every state. "The state board seeks to identify and rehabilitate nurses whose competency may be impaired due to the abuse of drugs or alcohol so they may be treated and returned to or continue the practice of nursing in a manner that will benefit the public" (Sullivan, Bissell, & Williams, 1988, p. 158). The nurse practice act in every state specifies:

- Conditions under which the license is granted, revoked or withheld
- Options under which the board may issue suspensions, voluntary surrender of license and other forms of restriction

Boards of nursing are mostly reactive, limiting activities to cases that are reported to them. Most cases are reported to the board only when there is clear documented infringement of the law. Depending on the decision by the board, a nurse may need to consider a change in specialty or perhaps return to the former job with special provisions. Studies have shown that when recovering nurses return to jobs like anesthesia, emergency, intensive care, surgery and shock trauma, relapses often occur (Tucker, 2002).

If a nurse who uses drugs is permitted to return to the old job, there are usually special provisions, such as no access to narcotics. When the recovering nurse, supervisor and treatment counselor agree direct access to narcotics is no longer a threat to recovery, the nurse may be allowed to administer controlled substances. Most employers reassign a returning drug abuser to areas with little or no access to addictive drugs for a period of time while the nurse is being monitored. The monitoring process provides consistent documentation about continued abstinence while the nurse is in therapy. The purpose is twofold: (1) it protects patients from incompetent care and (2) it provides the recovering nurse with documentation of sustained recovery.

Returning to the former job with no access to narcotics requires cooperation from co-workers. This means the co-workers will be aware of the recovering nurse's problem. Being reassigned to a job that does not require narcotic distribution may be less stressful during the initial recovery period.

Eighteen months after I entered detox, I had my first job interview. I was so nervous and scared. What did they know about me? Did they know I had a drug problem? Should I tell the truth? The person interviewing me put me at ease, and I felt comfortable discussing my situation. I had learned in recovery that honesty is the best policy She told me she believed everyone deserves a second chance, and my background in surgery and anesthesia would be a positive addition to the team. I was hired because I had skills that would contribute to the team, not because they pitied me. I went from an environment where I worked independently with mostly men to a team environment with mostly women. For the first time in my career, I felt accepted, a part of the team and comfortable sharing my story. Since narcotics were not accessible in my department, there was no temptation at work. I just had to focus on learning my job and report to my supervisor when I was required to submit to random drug testing. For the first time in my life, I had a support system, and I even had fun at work!

The best-case scenario is one where the nurse returns to the former job after completing primary treatment, but this may not be possible. Attendance at support groups is essential during this time, and if the former job requires shift work, attending support groups regularly may be impossible. Exposure to drugs of addiction is considered unwise at this stage.

It is customary for the recovering nurse to sign a document specifying the expected behaviors while on the job such as:

- Consistent attendance at mutual help groups
- Documentation of continued treatment as recommended by a therapist
- Regular sessions with an employee assistance counselor

- Actions required of the nurse and employer if the nurse voluntarily resigns from the institution
- Submission to random urine screens and blood tests

Pam's Case Was Similar

My nursing and nurse anesthetist license were revoked by the state board of nursing and the medical board. I was assigned a probation monitor and an investigator. I never met the probation monitor (a nurse) in person, but we communicated by telephone. I met the investigator in person a couple times. Their responsibilities were to document continued abstinence and progress in therapy. When I was dismissed from formal treatment, I received a letter outlining the expected behaviors. They included:

- *Abstaining from alcohol use*
- *Participating in a voluntary drug testing program*
- *Attending support group meetings*
- *Finding a sponsor*
- *Assuring my supervisor submitted quarterly reports to the state board*
- *Finding a job that did not require contact with narcotics*

What I didn't receive was a specific timeline or specific instructions on getting my license reinstated. I was overcome with frustration and anger. I was dealing with problems I had never faced before while trying to remain sober. It was enough to cause a relapse, but I persevered.

There are many jobs in nursing that do not require a license. For instance, a nurse in recovery could function as a:

- Community nurse liaison
- Admission coordinator
- Case manager
- Research nurse
- Medical reviewer
- Utilization reviewer
- Nursing informatics specialist
- Discharge planner
- Employee health nurse
- Manager

One of the first things I had to do was find a job that did not require handling narcotics for 6 months. What I didn't know was that after the six months, I was supposed to have a plan for a gradual return to narcotic distribution with supervision. A friend helped me find a job. I selected to pursue the role of a pre-admission nurse in a hospital. I attended AA meetings once a week and submitted to random drug testing. My supervisor submitted reports about my performance to the state board of nursing.

Pam experienced a couple of setbacks during recovery, mainly due to miscommunication. Not finding a job with supervised narcotic distribution slowed the reinstatement of Pam's license. Another setback occurred when Pam needed knee surgery. During her brief pre-operative assessment with the surgeon, Pam mentioned her problems with alcohol and drug abuse, but she failed to mention the probation monitor would be contacting the physician. When the probation monitor called the physician and asked if Pam had discussed the fact she was in recovery, he didn't recall the situation and replied "no." The probation monitor informed the board of nursing and the state medical board that Pam was not following the rules. Pam was not notified of the situation.

Later, during Pam's appeal to the state medical board, she was permitted to defend herself. The physician sent a letter stating Pam's problems with alcohol and drug abuse were documented in the history and physical section of her medical record. After the appeal, Pam's license was reinstated. She resigned her admissions nurse position and actively pursued a nurse anesthetist job. If she did not find a job and was not actively working within a year, she would be required to retake her licensing board tests.

Pam's record indicates she abided by the rules of her probationary period. She did not require any further monitoring by the state board of nursing but is preparing for re-entry into a nurse anesthetist role. Pam has been placed on the drug Naltrexone for one year. Naltrexone is a drug that binds to narcotic receptor sites negating usual narcotic effects. It is used mainly to protect the patient in the event the recovering person relapses. The side effects include nausea, sleeplessness and headaches and have forced Pam to use other drugs to control the nausea and headaches. This minor inconvenience is worth it, because Pam has the opportunity to return to the career she loves.

I am currently celebrating three years of recovery and anxiously awaiting return to work. The past three years have been very difficult. My goal was to have my nursing license and my nurse anesthetist license reinstated and be working as a nurse anesthetist again. That process has taken longer than I expected. My privileges to practice have been reinstated. I applied for a nurse anesthetist position at a medical center, was offered and accepted the position, and am currently waiting for the credentialing department to complete its work. In retrospect, there are a few things I should have done that would have made the process easier, and there are a few things I believe the state board, probation monitor and investigator should have been more specific about. The following are lessons I learned from this experience:

- *Don't hold grudges. At times I was very angry at the state board of nursing, but one thing I learned in recovery was to accept responsibility for my actions. I am responsible for what happens to me. Holding grudges can cause a relapse and/or delay recovery.*
- *Support systems are essential. I never really had a support system until I entered recovery. I am required to attend a formal support group and I do it, but it is very difficult to find a group that I feel comfortable in. Often, my problems pale in comparison to others who are dealing with losing their families, source of income and friends. I continue to stay in contact with my former co-workers from my first job after recovery. I value their friendship and support. In addition, my dog and cat are very supportive and offer unconditional love.*
- *Follow rules to recovery. Rules of probation and steps to recovery need to be documented and available for constant review.*
- *Treatment does not end when you leave the hospital/treatment center. If you are assigned to an outpatient treatment center, required to attend AA or NA meetings, be randomly tested for drugs—do it! Find a job that allows you the flexibility to do this. It is your responsibility to invest the time and effort needed for recovery.*
- *Be persistent. Everything doesn't always go as planned. My license wasn't reinstated the first time. I didn't get along with my first sponsor, but I didn't give up. I found a sponsor I could relate to, and I fulfilled all obligations.*

CONCLUSION

Nurses are not immune to developing alcohol and drug problems. The existence of chemical abuse in the nursing profession is a significant problem; however, many of the important questions about chemical dependency in nursing remain unanswered. In addition to risking their own lives, nurses who abuse substances risk the lives of their patients and become financial liabilities for their employers. Unfortunately, the nurse who abuses chemicals is often not identified until the patient is at risk. Effective treatment programs are available. Having the courage to identify the nurse whose practice has become impaired because of the use of alcohol or other drugs is the responsibility of all professional people. Recovering from alcohol and drug abuse is a lifelong commitment and requires great inner strength. The words of Eleanor Roosevelt best describe this experience.

> *You gain strength, courage and confidence by every experience in which you really stop to look fear in the face. You are able to say to yourself, "I lived through this horror. I can take the next thing that comes along." . . . You must do the thing you think you cannot do.*

REFERENCES

American Nurses Association. (1984). *Addictions and psychological dysfunctions in nursing: The profession's response to the problem.* Kansas City, MO: Author.

Bissell, L., & Jones, R.W. (1981). The alcoholic nurse. *Nursing Outlook, 29*, 96-100.

Finke, L.M., Hickman, L.C., & Miller, E.L. (1993). Personal drug and alcohol use by staff nurses at work. *Addictions Nursing Network, 5*(1), 25-29.

Finke, L., Williams, J., & Stanley, R. (1996). Nurses referred to a peer assistance program for alcohol and drug problems. *Archives of Psychiatric Nursing, 10*(5), 319-324.

Haack, M.R. (1988). Stress and impairment among nursing students. *Research in Nursing and Health, 11*, 125-134.

Jefferson, L.V., & Ensor, B.E. (1982). Help for the helper: Confronting a chemically-impaired colleague. *American Journal of Nursing, 82*, 574-577.

Sullivan, E. (1987). A descriptive study of nurses recovering from chemical dependency. *Archives of Psychiatric Nursing, 1*, 194-200.

Sullivan, E., Bissell, L., & Williams, E. (1988). *Chemical dependency in nursing: The deadly diversion.* Menlo Park, CA: Addison-Wesley.

Tucker, K. (2002). *Professional enabling*. Retrieved August 21, 2002, from http://www.tktucker.net/nir/proena.txt.

West, M.M. (2002). Early risk indicators of substance abuse among nurses. *Journal of Nursing Scholarship, 34*(2), 187-193.

Chapter 19

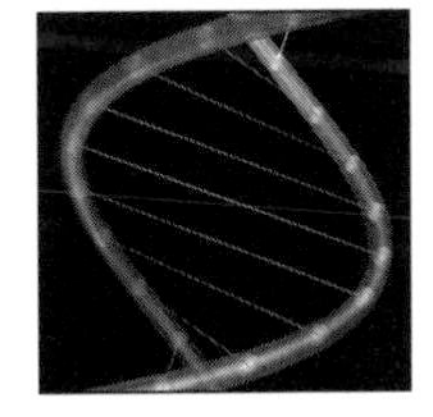

Overcoming Damage and Building New Credibility

by Edith Jenkins-Weinrub

INTRODUCTION

Understanding how a career path progresses and the many detours a career can take can be illustrated by comparing a person's human needs to the construct of a tree. This comparison between the two permits an explanation of why some people are able to overcome many career challenges and advance their careers and others cannot. Determining basic human needs and how that process is like the growth of a tree provides a framework for delineating career problems that need to be avoided. During the course of a person's career, mistakes are made and some of them are dreadful and have the potential for great damage to the person and the career. However, conversely, mistakes can be viewed as feedback and a lesson learned because of poor decisions and/or poor performance. Like a tree, the nurse's career can be rehabilitated and revitalized.

The purpose of this chapter is to demonstrate how a person, in this case a nurse, can overcome damage to self and build new credibility by comparing human needs with the growth and longevity of a tree. Using Maslow's Hierarchy of Needs and what we know about the growth and potential of trees, the case will be made that a damaged nurse can heal and regain credibility and a career be reinstated. To accomplish this task, a discussion is presented of Maslow's Hierarchy of Needs, followed by an analogous description of the life and potential of trees.

Nurses, like other human beings, are not perfect and may regret bad decisions and poor performance. However, making a mistake is not the end of a career. How the nurse moves on or recovers from the mistake is the important issue. Consequently, it is important to understand how career mistakes take place and how to avoid making them so there is no need to overcome career damage or rebuild credibility.

Nurses trying to overcome damaged credibility with other members of the health team can expect they will need to make some lifestyle changes, such as gain new skills, assume more or less responsibility, or re-examine their work life and their values. This re-examination will need to cover both internal and external factors that lead to career growth and satisfaction.

The damaged nurse needs to do a self-assessment by asking three questions:

- Which basic human needs were unmet?
- Which basic human needs were met?
- How will the unmet needs be addressed so damage to self is avoided?

HIERARCHY OF HUMAN NEEDS MODEL

The term "hierarchy of needs" was first introduced by Abraham Maslow, a psychologist, in his 1954 book *Motivation and Personality* (Witzel, 2002). According to Tomey (2000), individuals are different, thus needs vary in type and intensity for each individual. Individuals differ in the amount of satisfaction and fulfillment that is needed before the met goal becomes strong. For example, some people need six hours of sleep to function, and others need 10 hours of sleep. Pearson and Podeschi (1999) suggest the foundation of the Maslow model assumes that an individual's capacity for self-determination is significantly affected by the environment. They point out the model further suggests an individual needs both a good social environment and good emotional support to fulfill and satisfy the basic human need that leads to self-actualization.

Tomey (2000) and Huber (2000) are two authors who have conceptualized Maslow's model as a hierarchical pyramid of five categories of needs, which includes:

1. Biological/Physiological needs
2. Safety/Security needs
3. Belonging needs
4. Self-esteem
5. Self-actualization

Each level of the pyramid is dependent on the previous one. A person cannot move completely to a higher level without satisfying the previous level, and as a result, there may be "deficiency needs." These "deficiency needs" are viewed as disruptions or blockages that prevent individuals from progressing to the next level once a lower category of needs are met. Needs not met in an individual's life can cause disruptions.

Biological/Physiological Needs

Biological/physiological needs are those things that allow us to live, such as air, water, food, sleep and shelter. These needs are basic and allow for survival. They override all other needs, consequently individuals work hard to get these needs satisfied before they move on to other human needs. For example, not having a secure nursing job does not affect a nurse's ability to perform daily living activities. However, having basic biological/physiological needs threatened, such as not being able to sleep, could affect an individual's ability to sustain life.

Safety/Security Needs

Safety/security needs are threatened when we are faced with physical harm or a lack of emotional support or adequate finances. Everyone needs to feel safe and secure. For example, if a nurse is married to an abusive partner and fears physical harm, the need for safety/security is unmet.

Belonging Needs

Belonging needs are acceptance from others, having meaningful relationships and being part of a social group. Social support groups, such as family members, close friends and co-workers, reaffirm a person's competence and self-worth. This sense of belonging is evident when the members of these groups listen to each others' problems and give feedback. For some, belonging is missing. For example, there are few African-American, male nurses in a profession that is predominantly white and female. These male nurses have to search to find a professional group to which they can belong. The cultural and gender differences between nurses can be of some concern, for it means many nurses are forced to find support outside the profession.

Self-Esteem Needs

Self-esteem is the value people place on themselves. It is an assessment of self worth as a human being based on the approval or disapproval of others. Self-esteem needs are of two types: (1) confidence and mastery of task and (2) self-respect and desire for acceptance. Minchition (1993) claims high self-esteem individuals accept themselves unconditionally exactly as they are. They have control over their lives. Whereas individuals with low self-esteem often seem out of control and feel little intrinsic worth. Their value is in direct proportion to the value of their accomplishments. For example, C. J. acquired an associate degree in nursing by passing the RN-NCLEX examination and received a state nursing license that gave her a feeling of confidence and accomplishment. She enjoyed her work and had many ideas on how nursing could be improved and wanted to advance her career to management in order to implement these ideas. Two years later, Nurse C. J. decided to improve her knowledge and skill by seeking a bachelor's degree in nursing that later enabled her to get promoted to a charge nurse position of a nursing unit. Nurse C. J. felt even better about herself because she had her own ideas for nursing and was willing to follow the path to get them implemented. In addition, seeking formal education gave Nurse C. J. a feeling of increased self-esteem and respect from the members of the health team and her family.

Self-Actualization Needs

Self-actualization is the need to maximize potential. The term "self-actualization" is the highest level of fulfillment in meeting human needs. This means individuals have a feeling of accomplishment and responsibility, have a sense of importance, and seek opportunities for growth and self-fulfillment. For example, Nurse C. J., years later, received the outstanding nurse manager recognition from her peers and now is frequently asked to be a guest speaker at nursing conferences.

Goble (1972) asserts Maslow's self-actualization need is a process. According to Maslow (1956):

> *Self-actualization . . . tends to be seen as an ultimate or final state of affairs, a far goal, rather than a dynamic process, active throughout life. . . . If we define growth as the various processes which bring the person toward ultimate self-actualization, then this conforms better with the observed fact that it is going on all the time in the life history* (p. 25).

Goble stressed self-actualization is a process in development and a discovery of a person's true self and the development of existing and potential talents. One of the universal aspects of these self-actualized individuals is their ability to see life clearly, as it is rather than as they wish it to be. Goble further explains that individuals who self-actualize are more decisive and have a clear notion of what is right and what is wrong. They are able to make their own decisions even in the face of opposing popular opinion. Patterson (1985) agrees with Maslow's theory but argues that self-actualizing people are not afraid of the unknown and can tolerate doubt and uncertainty that accompany new and unfamiliar events.

In the *Gale Encyclopedia of Psychology* (Strickland, 2001), some of the behaviors that meet Maslow's self-actualization needs are listed. They are:

- Experiences life with the concentration of a child
- Tries something new
- Listens to one's own feelings rather than the voices of others
- Is honest
- Is willing to risk unpopularity by disagreeing with others
- Assumes responsibility
- Works hard at whatever is pursued
- Identifies and is willing to give up defenses

This discussion about Maslow's needs makes it clear if people's needs are not met, they get into trouble. The review of the hierarchy indicates if the individual is struggling to meet the basic needs of survival and security, there is little energy left to meet the higher-level needs. Nurses who get into trouble with drugs and alcohol, as the nurse in the previous chapter did, have either not had their higher-level needs met or are so busy trying to meet the lower-level ones, or both, that they are fragile victims of disaster.

CAREER TREE STRUCTURE

It has been said, "A palm tree can weather a storm by bending but never breaking." A palm tree has a sturdy root and trunk with a potential of growing as tall as 50 feet or more. It is also able to adapt, needs little maintenance, can avoid pests/distractions and has a long life. A nursing career is similar to the palm tree in many ways. Actually, five aspects of a palm tree and a nursing career are similar. They are adaptable, need safe and secure environments, have sturdy trunks and need continued maintenance, can avoid pests and distractions, and have long lives.

Adaptability

The first likeness between a palm tree and a nursing career is adaptability. Just as a tree adapts to changing times by bending to fit changing conditions so does a nursing career. However, the environment has the power to influence adaptability. For example, when a tree is planted, it is important to put it in an environment or climate that encourages growth and full potential. It is also important to determine if the tree's basic biological/physiological needs are being met. Therefore, it is not wise to plant a moisture-loving tree in a condition that lacks moisture. This will cause a deficit in the tree's ability to adapt to its environment and grow. Similarly, it is not wise to plan a nursing career in a work-setting environment that is not supportive and does not fit into the nurse's lifestyle.

Just as important as planting a tree is the right environment, the nursing career path selected must match the nurse's interests and enhance her or his ability to adapt and be successful. In a study by Nautam, Kahn, Angell and Cantarelli (2002), career was defined as "patterns of likes, dislikes, and indifferences regarding career-relevant occupations" (p. 290). Career interest was viewed in connection with a person's perceived ability to perform a given behavior or task. Schein (1993) asserts that all people develop some kind of picture of their work life and their role in it. For example, a nurse who can adapt to highly stressful emergencies may do well in an emergency department or intensive care unit; whereas, a nurse who needs less stress and more stability would not. Therefore, nurses need to include in their choice-making process a self-examination to determine adaptability.

Nurses need to explore their abilities, aspirations, interests and financial needs in order to save themselves disappointment and the expense of learning a skill that results in not being adequately prepared to adapt to demands of the profession. Poor adaptability leads to sloppy performance and can cast a cloud of doubt, distrust and credibility on the nurse.

Safe and Secure Environment

The second similarity between a palm tree and a nursing career is they both need a safe and secure environment. The root system of a tree provides two basic functions: (1) it absorbs key nutrients from the soil and (2) it anchors the tree firmly in the ground. To illustrate this point, if a tree is exposed to extreme direct sunlight, dry air, and very little or no water, the tree roots will die. In this case, the tree will not receive proper nourishment, which can negatively influence its growth.

Anchoring the roots in the ground provides safety and security. Similarly, the roots of a person are evident in the individual's values, beliefs, hopes and dreams, and the environment in which they live. An individual's family network and foundation are sources of nourishment and safety. Nurses often listen to valued family members and significant others because they provide guidance and guard the individual against unhealthy outside influences that can affect life and decision-making. For example, the nurse who gets into the drug scene listens to the wrong groups while ignoring the group (family) that cares the most. Another example is the troubled nurse who may not have a family that cares and can provide the feedback and support needed to make a change. In either instance, the nurse is void of safety and security. The following poem illustrates the importance and strength of the root system and its relationship to Maslow's Hierarchy of Needs.

THE OAK TREE

A mighty wind blew night and day.
It stole the oak tree's leaves away,
Then snapped its boughs and pulled its bark
Until the oak was tired and stark
But still the oak tree held its ground
While other trees fell all around.

The weary wind gave up and spoke,
"How can you still be standing, Oak?"
The oak tree said, "I know that you
Can break each branch of mine in two,
Carry every leaf away,
Shake my limbs, and make me sway.
But I have roots stretched in the earth,
Growing stronger, since my birth.
You'll never touch them, for you see,
They are the deepest part of me.
Until today, I wasn't sure
Of just how much I could endure.
But now I've found, with thanks to you,
I'm stronger than I ever knew."
(Hallmark, 2001)

Sturdy Trunk and Continued Maintenance

The third similarity between a palm tree and a nursing career is the need for a sturdy trunk and continued maintenance. The trunk of the tree must be sturdy or the branches will not be able to hold themselves up. A person's sturdiness, for overcoming the many challenges that must be faced, comes from the individual's personal attitude. According to Abramovitz (2002), attitude is an individual's personal strength. Attitude is how an individual responds to different situations. Attitudes can be positive or negative but more important is the way the individual controls them when certain events that happen cannot be controlled. If there is a tendency to not have a positive attitude when faced with difficult challenges and career setbacks, then working to gain positive thoughts is paramount. Abramovitz identified five steps for improving attitude when trying to build credibility, which include:

- Set reasonable goals
- Outline strategies for reaching those goals
- Hang out with positive people
- Focus on good rather than bad things
- Welcome changes as opportunities for growth rather than seeing them as threats

A beautiful tree has acceptance by others and is often a part of many gardens. However, to stay beautiful, the tree needs maintenance. For a nursing career to stay viable, it also needs maintenance. A tree's maintenance program consists of pruning and trimming branches. Pruning is a means of controlling the tree's growth and productivity. There are five reasons a nursing career also needs maintenance. The first is pruning. Pruning refers to doing what is necessary to keep a healthy career so that it can grow. Second is balance. To obtain balance means it is important to balance work with family and education. The third is training. Training refers to maintaining current nursing knowledge and skills that match the work setting. The fourth is restrict growth. Restricting growth means the nurse must restrict the use of time. We all live busy lives, and the demands of nursing can be overwhelming at times. There are only 24 hours in a day, and time must be used wisely otherwise there is a danger of getting involved in stress-reducing activities such as alcohol and drugs. Developing multiple nursing career paths can also lead to stress, which can then lead to unhealthy lifestyle activities. These activities can lead to unhealthy habits, such as being deceitful and not trustworthy, which can determine whether there is acceptance. The last reason for maintenance is to improve quality. Quality refers to the value of the nursing work performed. Is the work excellent or does it need to be improved?

A nurse's career maintenance program may consist of keeping nursing skills current and marketable. According to Martin (2001), effective career management is a combination of preparation undertaken by the individual and opportunities provided by the employer. However, due to changes in healthcare, the burden for career maintenance and management has shifted mainly to the individual. Martin describes these changes by stating, "Most organizations no longer offer the prospect of a lifetime career built on steady promotions in return for loyalty and commitment. But it is not only the attitudes of employers that have changed—so too have the expectations of those entering employment" (p. 32).

Pests/Distractions

The fourth similarity between the palm tree and a nursing career is the avoidance of pests and distractions. The American Heritage Dictionary (2002) defines "pest" as a thing or person that is persistently annoying and "distraction" as having attention diverted (p. 1040). Unwanted insects can plague a tree, and unwanted professional distractions can affect a nurse's employability. Maslow's needs for "belonging" and "self-esteem" must be examined to address the pests and distractions that can occur in a nurse's career.

Guilt, shame and worry are also examples of pests and distractions. Webster's New World Dictionary (Guralnick, 1982) defines guilt as "a painful feeling of self-reproach resulting from a belief that one has done something wrong" (p. 622). Shame is defined as "a painful feeling of having lost the respect of others because of improper behavior or incompetence" (p. 1308). Minchition (1993) proposes guilt and low self-esteem go hand in hand. Guilt is not just one emotion but is also a combination of feelings about experiences and actions. These feelings often result in anger, shame and embarrassment and the belief that there is a price to pay for the mistakes made.

Dyer (1996), a psychologist, agrees with Minchition's (1993) view on guilt. He also believes worry is the absence of positive thoughts coupled with mindless negative thinking that can paralyze mental processes and result in inappropriate choices and decisions. Minchition emphasizes how having low self-esteem and having unpleasant experiences contribute to guilt, shame and worry. Positive social support and feedback from family members, close friends and co-workers is needed to combat the guilt and worry. As discussed in the previous chapter, the pest or distraction for the nurse anesthetist, Pam, was alcohol and drugs. Pam felt alone, lonely and left out most of her earlier years. As a result, Pam did not have a strong sense of belonging or self-esteem; therefore, she used alcohol and drugs to escape not having her belonging needs satisfied by her parents. Further, the negative influence of Pam's first husband caused her to steal drugs from the workplace and not comply with drug treatment.

Examples of other pests and distractions are the negative activities a nurse might pursue. Such activities include nonprofessional conduct and activities that place a patient in a harmful situation. In both situations, the nurse may have to face legal issues. According to Monarch (2002) and Brent (2001), nurses are expected to use reasonable care and skill reflective of the standard of care to avoid legal action related to negligence or malpractice. Brent has listed seven grounds for nursing disciplinary actions:

- Violation of nursing practice act
- Abuse of alcohol or other habit-forming drugs

- Falsification and poor documentation of patient record
- Unprofessional conduct
- Conviction of a felony
- Negligence
- Unlawful acts

Three specific professional distractions occur frequently: (1) not having knowledge pertaining to professional practice standards, (2) disregard for policies and procedures, and (3) failure to meet obligations. Not knowing what is professionally expected is not acceptable. All nurses must adhere to the Nurse Practice Act, follow the institution's policies and procedures, and meet all assigned obligations. For example:

Early Friday morning, a young girl 14 years of age reports to a nurse case manager, S.R., in a community health center that her uncle had sexually abused her. The nurse case manager asks if the girl's parents are aware of the abuse. The young girl says yes, they have been aware for several months and have talked to the uncle. The parents have tried to reassure her that it would not happen again. The girl, however, says she is still afraid and has nightmares at times about the abuse. The nurse case manager talks to the girl and tells her she has not done anything wrong. She tells the girl that type of behavior is not acceptable and that it must stop, The nurse case manager says she will speak with the girl's parents. The nurse documents this information in the medical record along with her plan to speak with the parents. However, the nurse case manager goes on vacation the next day for two weeks, and when she returns back to work, she is informed that the young girl was raped by her uncle and is hospitalized. The young girl tells hospital officials that she reported her uncle's behavior to the nurse case manager in the community health center who said that the uncle's behavior would stop and would not happen again.

In this situation, the nurse case manager did not report the incident immediately to Child Protective Services before leaving duty. Further, the nurse did not inform the supervisor of the incident. Most importantly, the nurse did not follow the policies and procedures of the agency regarding the procedures for reporting sexual abuse. When hired, each employee is asked to read the Abuse Policies and Procedures. The employee signs a document that indicates they have read and understand the policy. In this case, there was a failure to follow the policy and procedures and a failure to meet expected obligations. The nurse allowed a distraction (her vacation) to deter her from doing what she is required by law to do and thus allowed a child to be harmed. The nurse's credibility is now is question, and her career is in deep trouble.

Longevity

The fifth likeness between a tree and a nurse career is longevity. Longevity and self-actualization are the highest level of human needs. Just as trees have different life spans, so do nurse careers. A nurse may spend many years as a staff nurse and then change career direction and become a nurse manager or administrator. Longevity in nursing begins with developing relationships, taking responsibility, making things happen, and not relying on others or placing blame.

One of the most influential relationships is the family. Family support is very important. The next set of important relationships are professional support groups, such as co-workers and other nurses, including the leadership team. Having people who support a nurse's efforts to help mentor and guide during difficult times can be the bridge that makes the difference. They can help the nurse see the situation from a different perspective, which will help the nurse develop resilience. Shrader (1999) suggests "resilience" gives one self-confidence to take risk and to withstand criticisms and setbacks. He further recommends when taking risks it is importance to put unpleasant situations in the past and move forward.

A PLAN FOR OVERCOMING DAMAGE AND BUILDING NEW CREDIBILITY

In the previous chapter, Nurse Pam's career was damaged because of chemical abuse (drug and alcohol). Understanding the misfortunes Pam experienced in her life and during her nursing career demonstrates the importance of actively maintaining a healthy career. Nurses need to take personal responsibility of their careers and not leave them to chance. There are five steps that can be used in designing and implementing a plan for overcoming career damage and building new credibility.

Many factors can damage a career, such as poor adaptability, not having an adequate root system or foundation, making poor choices related to career maintenance, not avoiding career distractions, and not satisfying the hierarchy of human needs. Once an unpleasant event has taken place and that event has damaged the nurse's reputation or nursing career, it is important to complete the following steps.

Get Ready

The first step is to get ready. To get ready involves awareness. Before getting ready to move forward, there must be awareness there was a mistake made or there was a potential for a mistake to be made. A self-examination must be accomplished to determine if the mistake was related to ability, performance or interest. After the assessment, accepting responsibility is next. Accepting responsibility requires personal strength. Honesty is necessary. Many people find it easier to blame someone or something than to accept their lack of knowledge, a mistake and/or a weakness.

Set Goals

The second step is to make some decisions and set some goals. Supportive individuals can help with the decision-making process. They can help clarify the lesson to be learned from this experience. These supportive individuals can also help clarify the goals and options. This pursuit of new directions is accomplished in several ways. One way is by providing examples of what the outcome likely will be in a similar situation with the same decision or goal. This process is very similar to an algorithm where there are multiple decisions and goals but each has a different specific outcome. For example, if the decision is to stay with the current position after an incident has occurred, is the work environment such that it will allow for rebuilding credibility? Is there emotional and professional support in the workplace? If not, what other options are available?

Draft a Plan of Action

The third step is to draft a course of action. It is important to allow enough time for thinking about the outcomes of the plan. It is also best to prepare a written plan with time limits set in weeks, months and years. Barriers must be identified that will get in the way of goal achievement. This will help keep the nurse focused on the target. Once whether to stay or move on is decided, it is important to have a positive attitude. Deciding what nursing skills will be necessary to transfer to a new job and what knowledge is essential in the new environment are also important. Anticipating success brings positive energy and effort to goal obtainment. Having a positive attitude builds credibility with others. Daily repeating of positive affirmation can hold off negative thinking and help keep the focus on the course of action.

Implement the Plan

The fourth step is to implement the plan. It takes determination and firmness of mind to implement a career plan when credibility is a major concern. There must be willingness to try something new, to risk being unpopular by disappointing or disagreeing with others, and to be willing to work hard. The individual must also have self-confidence to overcome distractions such as guilt, shame and worry that can act as barriers to the course of action. Positive social support and feedback from family members, close friends and co-workers is also a prerequisite for success.

Complete a Reflection and Evaluation

The fifth step is reflection and evaluation. Reflection involves taking time to put things in proper perspective; to replay incidents in the mind; and to reassess abilities, aspirations and financial needs. The evaluation process for overcoming damage and rebuilding credibility is a long process. Evaluation criteria need to be developed based on self-examination, career interest, established goals and timelines, and whether the outcomes were realized. The most important thing to remember is that a new day is just around the corner.

AFFIRMATION

I choose to see each incident in my life as beneficial to me in some way.
I choose to emphasize the positive aspects of every situation.
How I response is always my choice.
It is not what happens that causes me pain but my interpretation of it.
I take responsibility for making the world a happy place for myself.
I am willing to enjoy life.
I enjoy being alive.
Since I control my thoughts, I can decide to think positively about anything.
My happiness is not caused by people or events outside; I create it myself.
I refuse to become upset about matters outside my control.
My happiness depends on me (Minchition, 1993, pp. 219, 220.)

Table 19.1
Relationship Between Hierarchy of Needs and Career Tree Structure

HIERARCHY OF NEEDS	CAREER TREE STRUCTURE
Biological/Physiological	Adaptability Root System Growth Rate
Safety Belonging Self-Esteem	Maintenance Trunk/Stem Branches Pest/Distraction
Self-Actualization	Longevity and Leaves

REFERENCES

Abramovitz, M. (2002). The identity questions: What makes you? Here are some things to consider on your road to self-discovery. *Current Health 2, a Weekly Reader, 28*(8) 24-28.

American Heritage Dictionary (2002). *American heritage dictionary* (4th ed.). New York, NY: Houghton Mifflin.

Brent, N. (2001). *Nurses and the law: A guide to principles and applications*. Philadelphia, PA: W.B. Saunders.

Dyer, W. (1996) *Your sacred self. Making the decision to be free*. New York, NY: Harper.

Carlyle, R. (1989). Careers in crisis. *Datamation, 35*(16), 12-17.

Goble, F. (1972). *The third force: The psychology of Abraham Maslow a revolutionary new view of man.* New York, NY: Pocket Books.

Guralnick, D. (1982). *Webster's new world dictionary of the American language* (2nd ed.). New York, NY: Simon/Schuster.

Hallmark Cards (2001). *The oak tree*. Kansas City, MO: Author.

Huber, D. (2000). *Leadership and nursing care management*. Philadelphia, PA: W.B. Saunders.

Maddi, S.R., & Costa, P.T. (1972). *Humanism in personology: Allport, Maslow, and Murray*. Chicago, IL: Aldine & Atherton.

Martin, V. (2001). Open university: Developing as a manager part 1. *Nursing Management, 8*(7), 30-33.

Maslow, A.H. (1956). Defense and growth. *Merrill-Palmer Quarterly, 3*, 36-47.

Minchition, J. (1993). *Maximum self-esteem: The handbook for reclaiming your sense of self-worth.* Vanzant, MO: Arnford House.

Monarch, K. (2002*). Nursing and the law: Trends and issues.* Washington, DC: American Nurses Association.

Nautam M., Kahn, J., Angell, J., & Cantarelli, E. (2002). Identifying the antecedent in the relation between career interest and self-efficacy: Is it one, the other or both? *Journal of Counseling Psychology*, *49*(3), 290-301.

Patterson, C.H. (1985). *The therapeutic relationship.* Monterey, CA: Brooks/Cole.

Pearson, E.M., & Podeschi, R.L. (1999). Humanism and individualism: Maslow and his critics. *Adult Education Quarterly, 50*(1), 41-55.

Schein, E.H. (1993). *Career anchors: Discovering your real values.* Sydney, AU: Pfeiffer.

Shrader, R. (1999). Success is not an outcome, success is a way of living. *Vital Speeches, 65*(6), 504-508.

Strickland, B. (2001). *Gale encyclopedia of psychology* (2nd ed). Detroit, MI: Gale Group.

Tomey, A.M. (2000). *Guide to nursing management and leadership* (6th ed). St. Louis, MO: Mosby.

Witzel, M. (August, 2002). Motivations that push our buttons: A-A management of hierarchy of needs. *Financial Times*, p. 29.

Unit V

Useful Tools for Career Decision-Making

Chapter 20

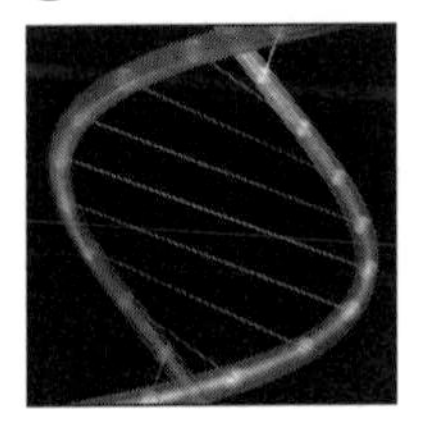

Searching

by Marcia Canton

INTRODUCTION

According to McKay (2002), the healthcare industry is huge. It encompasses a variety of occupations ranging from professionals who provide care, to ancillary workers who assist the professionals. Educational requirements for this wide range of career choices vary, as do credential and salary levels. Stable and secure positions have disappeared in the workplace. It is anticipated that many emerging careers will generate fewer new positions than in the past. Fields experiencing major growth will demand job applicants with specific academic majors and work experience.

According to the U.S. Bureau of Labor Statistics (2002), unemployment among government workers increased from 2.1 percent in September to 2.4 percent in October. Federal, state and local governments have perennial difficulty staffing 21 million positions across the United States. With the baby boomers reaching retirement age, the federal government faces critical shortages of talent in many specialties. Engineers, scientists, lawyers and professional managers are among those in high demand, according to Max Stier, president and CEO of the nonprofit Partnership for Public Service in Washington (2001).

As the nation shifts to a wartime economy, defense contractors large and small stand to reap hundreds of billions of dollars in new business. Hot specialties include systems engineers and integrators, software developers, information assurance professionals, and program and project managers. Security for the private sector and individual Americans is creating new job opportunities and adding distinction and monies to a once-sleepy profession.

The U.S. Bureau of Labor Statistics (2002) cites finance, insurance and real estate as positive aspects of the job market. However, the insurance and brokerage industries present a less optimistic picture. Whatever career is selected, careful planning and research are essential in order to make the right choice.

STEPS TO CAREER PLANNING SUCCESS

This chapter contains the steps that need to be taken to find a meaningful and ultimately rewarding career. These steps propose thoughtful criteria for seeking a career that is best suited to the needs of the job seeker and the employer, for a happy worker is an asset to the company just as an unhappy worker is a liability.

Conduct a Self-Assessment

The best way to begin the process of seeking a career is to complete a personal inventory. Abilities, interests and attitudes are revealed during a personal inventory. It is also important to review career development from time to time in order to determine if the career path is still relevant and satisfying. Career development is not a one-shot process. Just like the numerous choices made throughout life, career choices affect one's growth and development (Hunsaker & Cook, 2001); therefore, they need to be made in a thoughtful and systematic way.

The self-assessment also includes raising questions such as the following:

- How much thought has been given to what is wanted?
- What kind of salary is needed/desired?
- What kind of organization would be acceptable?
- Would a change in geographic location be considered?

These questions need to be answered before embarking on a search.

Search Out Career Options

Crucial to a successful job-search campaign is knowing how to research companies and organizations. Knowing as much as possible about the company or organization is important in order to tailor the resume and cover letter to a particular position. "Researching the company" is perceived as a critical factor in the evaluation of applicants, because employers believe the research effort reflects interest and enthusiasm. It demonstrates time has been taken to explore all aspects of the company. It also establishes a common base of knowledge for the job seeker and the employer from which questions can be asked (Crowther, 1993).

The research should begin by finding out about the knowledge and training needed for the position of interest. For example, what skills are needed to perform the job? What are the duties and responsibilities of the job? What are the working conditions? What is the salary range? It is also important to identify the opportunities for advancement and the future outlook of the job.

Knowing as much as possible about the company is essential and should include the following items of basic information about the company:

- Age of the company
- Services/products
- Competitors within the industry as a whole
- Growth patterns
- Reputation
- Divisions and subsidiaries and location/length of time established there
- Number of employees
- Record of sales
- Assets and earnings
- New products or projects
- Number of locations and foreign operations

A visit to a local career service center is a helpful way to locate the above information. Also, company profiles can be located in a volume of the *CPC Annual* or *Peterson's Annual Guide*. *Standard & Poor's Register* also has several volumes that include information on industry classifications, geographic locations, names and profiles of company executives, and company addresses.

Conducting an information interview with someone who holds the position of interest to obtain more detailed information about a particular career is also helpful. This strategy allows for a confirmation of the information gathered and often provides information not available in written form. Through this process, it is possible to gain an inside perspective of the job and the organization.

During the interview with the job holder, questions should be asked about the working environment, workplace changes and potential career paths available, if any. Personal opinions about the job should also be pursued.

When possible, the interview should cover a half day or an entire day so there is time to "shadow" the job holder at work. During this time, more in-depth questions can be asked. Usually being together provides firsthand information about the job, the work environment and the interactions with other workers.

If more information is needed in determining a fit with this position, it may be possible to work on a part-time basis or as a volunteer. Volunteering allows for a hands-on experience of the work environment and knowledge of the informal dynamics of the workplace.

Using the Internet in the Job Search

The amount of information processed over the Internet is doubling every 100 days, according to the U.S. Commerce Department (2002). In 1995, there were just 500 jobs sites online; in 1998, an estimated 100,000 sites had some job listings or job information on them. Undoubtedly, there are more today.

Instead of getting mired down in the overwhelming information on the Internet, it is more useful and expedient to focus on five essential tasks. The Internet should be used as a place to:

1. Search for vacancies listed by employers
2. Post a resume
3. Obtain some career counseling or job-hunting help
4. Research information about fields, occupations, companies, cities, geographical areas, etc.
5. Make contacts with people who can help locate information or help with an interview

Search for Vacancies on the Internet

An excellent resource for locating job opportunities is the Internet. Listed below are a few of the sites:

1. Dick Bolles, author of *What Color Is Your Parachute?* (2003), believes one of the best sites on the Net is America's Job Bank (AJB; http://www.careerbuilder.com). This site is maintained by the U.S. Public Employment Service and links 1,800 state employment service offices with job vacancies or postings. AJB lists between 250,000 and 750,000 vacancies daily, with 1,000 new listings added each day.
2. CareerPath.com (http://www.careerbuilder.com), says Bolles (2003), is one of the historic job sites on the Internet, which has merged with CareerBuilder. This is a useful site for classified ads.
3. CareerBuilder.com (http://www.careerbuilder.com) has become one of the largest job sites on the Web, rated #2 by the *Wall Street Journal* (1999), and "the most efficient online recruiting service among national recruiting brands" by Forrester Research (2000). This is a most important site because it has over 30 affiliates and powers 100 other career centers on the Web, including MSN.com and USATODAY.comJobBankUSA.
4. Jobs MetaSEARCH (http://www.jobbankusa.com/news1.html) is a meta-search site that contains a special section called Newspaper Search. Through this site, it is possible to link to the want ads of many of the U.S. newspapers that are not on CareerPath. Bolles (2003) believes this list is thorough and can be used to reach ads that are not readily visible.
5. Internet Press: Newspaper Mania Job Center (http://gallery.uunet.be/internetpress/link40.htm) is also referred to as a very complete site with links to over 11,000 Internet news sources. American Journalism Review Newslink (http://www.newslink.org/news.html) has been mentioned as an impressive, worldwide site with over 3,500 newspapers online. National Ad Search (http://www.nationaladsearch.com) has about 10,000 display ads culled from the Sunday newspapers in over 60 metropolitan areas in the U.S. This site is geared toward management, professional, technical and executive positions.
6. HandiLinks to Agencies (http://www.ahandyguide.com/cat1/employ.htm) links readers to employment agencies, temporary agencies, talent agencies and modeling agencies. A fee is often required.

Cover Letters on the Internet

Job hunting on the Internet is not some magic elixir that guarantees the location of a job (Bolles, 2003). Cover letters are also important and needed when searching for a position. Referred to as the best collection of resumes and letters on the Internet, William Frank's (1996) entire book *200 Letters for Job Hunters* is available free online. The site address for this resource is http://www.caareerlab.com/letters/.

Resume Services on the Internet

The same can be said about resume services. The Internet can provide the job searcher with help in the development of a resume. An excellent resource is http://www.yahoo.com/Business_and_Economy/Companies/Employment/Resume_Services/. This is a long list of agencies and individuals who are available to help with the writing of cover letters and resumes. There are also samples of resumes available for review that actually resulted in a job, if the job seeker is willing to pay a fee.

As soon as marketing preparation is under control, the next step is to write a cover letter. See Chapter 22 for a lengthy and helpful description of how to prepare a cover letter.

Posting the Resume

The resume is a critical part of the job search. It is the first impression given a future employer. If the resume is poorly organized or presented, there is little chance a job will be offered. The resume is a marketing tool that acts as a door opener and allows an employer to assess the job seeker's qualifications quickly in the prescreening process before an interview. Most resumes are initially read for 15 seconds or less if unsolicited. See Chapter 22 for a description of the types of resumes and how to prepare one.

Once the resume is complete, it is helpful to post it on the Internet. Weddle's Web guide (http://www.weddles.com) is a fascinating guide to some of the major resume-posting sites on the Web. It contains a great deal of information about each site. This would be a good place to begin.

America's Talent Bank (http://atb.mesc.state.mi.us/) is another site for posting a resume. It is maintained by the U.S. Department of Labor and is visited by employers looking for talent. (Note: registration is required.)

HeadHunter.NET (http://www.HeadHunter.NET/) is also a good site for posting a resume. Registration is also required at this site when a resume is posted.

For a fee, the job seeker can post a resume as a Web page using The World Wide Web Employment Office (http://www.employmentoffice.net). This site also has links to countries all around the world, with employment opportunities organized by occupation rather than by industry. The Riley Guide (http://www.rileyguide.com/resumes.html) is an updated public service and is noted as a first-class compilation of lists and charts of resume sites. JobBank USA's List of Resume Usenet Newsgroups (http://www.jobbankusa.com/useresum.html), as indicated by the title, limits its information to United States listings.

Prior to posting a resume, the job seeker must make sure it clearly identifies the person seeking a job; provides a means for the employer to contact the job seeker; identifies the job seeker's career skills, interests, strengths, focuses on key accomplishments; highlights educational successes; and uses action verbs.

SEEK CAREER COUNSELING AND JOB HUNTING ASSISTANCE

The essence of career planning is finding a match between one's qualifications and desires with what is available that fits those qualifications and desires. Career planning is a dynamic ongoing process of career development as a result of the ability to respond to change within self and the environment. Taking the time to build a foundation of knowledge about self and to explore other options that are appropriate can increase the chances of success enormously.

There are several career inventories for understanding personality type and career preferences. For example:

1. Strong Interest Inventory
2. Campbell Interest and Skill Survey
3. Myers-Briggs Type Indicator
4. SkillScan
5. Values Cards
6. Focus II

Focus II is an occupational computer program that offers self-assessment, as well as an opportunity to explore careers by related majors. It includes career overviews, salary, environment and training for over 1,000 occupations. These inventories can be found online at the Stanford University Career Development Center at www.stanford.edu/dept/CDC. Clicking on any one of the above inventories provides a complete description of each test.

Two of the most important factors to determine job satisfaction are to assess personality and attitudes. The two instruments preferred by most people are the Myers-Briggs Type Indicator and the Job Style Indicator. The Myers-Briggs Type Indicator (MBTI) is based on the work of Swiss psychologist Carl Jung and two American women, Katharine Briggs and Isabel Briggs Myers. A growing number of professionals recognize the strength and usefulness of the MBTI in their work with groups and with individuals in various organizations. Wherever the MBTI is used, it helps people become more self-aware, especially of their personality preferences for source of energy, information gathering and decision-making and how these preferences affect their approach to work and life in general.

The MBTI offers a straightforward and affirmative way to understand self. This model demonstrates how people's apparently random behavior is actually quite consistent, because it demonstrates how preference for receiving information is connected to decision-making and orientation to life.

The Job Style Indicator (JSI) was developed by Terry Anderson with Everett Robinson in 1988. It is a learning and communication tool for team development, performance improvement, job orientation and career planning. The authors of this instrument believe people who understand their work style behaviors that are appropriate for their jobs can be happier and productive at work. This instrument promotes a better understanding of work style behaviors required in a job and gives a clear view of the work style required. This instrument is accompanied by the Personal Style Indicator (PSI), a scientifically developed, self-administered, self-scoring learning and communication tool. It helps individuals identify their communication style when responding to people and tasks, to gain self-understanding and self-acceptance, and to identify the consequences of their interpersonal style when relating to others.

Some of these career inventories, like the Strong and the MBTI, require help from a career counselor. Others are self-tests, like the Holland Self-Directed Search and the Values Identification Inventory. If talking things out or individualized attention is preferred, a qualified career counselor should be contacted to help sort through the job seeker's interests and to make plans. A career counselor can help the job seeker focus on goals, prepare a resume and prepare for an interview.

RESEARCHING INFORMATION ABOUT FIELDS, CAREERS

Make Contacts

When it is clear who needs to be contacted, the Internet can be helpful. The following list of Internet sites can assist the job seeker in reaching the person(s) of choice.

1. http://www.555-1212.com/ is a site for finding the area code, telephone number, e-mail addresses and Web sites for many people, but often with less than 100% accuracy.
2. http://www.Four11.com is a database provided by Metromail.
3. http://www.switchboard.com is a database provider called Info-USA.
4. http://www.whowhere.com is a site with a variety of services, such as e-mail hookup, advanced community searches by location, school, personal interests, etc.
5. http://link-usa.com/zipcode is the site to find the zip codes for a particular city.

The use of one or more of these addresses should render pretty good results.

Marketing for the Position

When preparing for the job that best suits personal needs, the first step is to determine personal strengths and weaknesses. This should be followed by an evaluation of the current job and a projection of career interests in order to establish a career track or path. A careful analysis of the geographic areas of interest is important in order to decide on the ideal location for a new job.

Choosing where to work is one of the most important career decisions ever made (Hunsaker & Cook, 2001). Paramount is knowing whether the work environment offers personal satisfaction and career development. Careful selection of the organization is very important and can be accomplished by reading annual reports and relevant newspaper articles. Talking with others who are in a position to know about the policies and work environment of an organization is also a way to "scope out" the organization of interest.

Interviewing the Interviewer

While we all hear a lot about the interview of the applicant, interviewing the employer is less-frequently discussed. Being prepared for the questions to be asked is important, and preparation cannot be emphasized enough. However, being prepared about the organization of interest is equally important and desires equal if not more preparation. It is advisable to review the following list prepared by Chris Talarico and Associates (Seven things, n.d.) several days before an interview to get prepared for what needs to be asked of the employer.

1. Who are they (the prospective employers) and what do they do? Who owns the company? What are its products and services? How does the department of interest relate to the whole company? Facts should be gathered that are available to the public, such as the company's mission statement; its strategic objectives (stock write-ups, annual reports or internal documents); corporate values; and any current problems, challenges and changes the company is experiencing. This information can be obtained from any acquaintance of the company, from corporate public relations or personnel handouts, and from trade journals or company newsletters. Useful data can also be obtained from the business reference section of any major public or university library.
2. What has the company done? Has it recently merged or been deregulated? What have the last two or three years been like? What is known about the industry of which it's a part. What is the company's growth rate? Who are the competitors?
3. Where are they headed? What are the company's current predictions? What new products are on the horizon? How does the company stand in national and international competition? If they have new leadership, what goals have been announced?
4. Where is this company at an advantage or disadvantage? What are the trends in technology and profits?
5. What are the company's success factors? What influences the company's ability to achieve its targets? Do external factors, such

as the economy, competition and technology, affect the company's successes? Has the company had to cut costs, revitalize and penetrate new markets?

6. How does the job of interest contribute to the company's success? This may take more interpretation than research, but it is important to have a clear idea of how the department and job relate to the future success of the organization. Even if the job is at a lower level, it is important to understand how it relates to the company as a whole.

Chapter 22 contains a lengthy discussion of how to prepare for an interview and what to expect during the interview. The comments above are primarily about what the interviewee should know about the potential employer before the interview, so a match can occur between the interviewee's qualifications and desires and job/organization being considered.

Make a Decision and Set Up an Action Plan

Though it is not always obvious, people make a number of decisions during the course of a day that affect their lives. Yet, many people view decision-making as a grandiose task performed only by corporate executives and business leaders. Every time an action is taken toward a personal goal, freedom of choice is exercised, and the direction of life is altered.

Like major goals, major decisions are really the result of a series of smaller, more workable ones. Many of the decisions made daily were actually determined long ago and are now executed as a result of habit. At one time, we went through a process that led us to choose how we would handle each of these situations. Similarly, there is a process for making new decisions. The job seeker needs to learn more about this process as part of career growth. The more systematically decision-making is approached, the better the chance for making accurate and successful decisions.

Developing a career plan of action increases the chance for success and thus one's level of satisfaction. Once the decision to act has been clearly defined, it is time to gather data and analyze the information. The following questions need to be answered:

- How much information is necessary to reach a sound conclusion?
- How much time can be spent in determining and evaluating the facts surrounding this decision?
- What is already known about this situation?

The more information gathered about a particular problem, the more likely a satisfactory decision will be reached. By knowing what is wanted and when achievement is desired, it is fairly easy to make decisions. This planning must begin with a clear understanding of the job search process and the development of a job-search strategy.

After identifying and reviewing the alternatives, a decision can be made that offers the greatest probability of achieving the desired goal. Once the information and alternatives to the career decision have been examined, the choice is clear. Now, it is time to put these plans into action. The ability to act on the decisions is a direct reflection of progress made in the career development process.

CONCLUSION

Finding the right job can be both a rewarding and frustrating experience. Listed below are some tips that should make the job search easier.

- Involve friends and family. A support group, such as friends and family, offers encouragement and assistance during the job search.
- Allow a reasonable amount of time. Don't expect to find a job within a few days or weeks.
- Devote time to the job search. A thorough job search is hard work. Expect to spend several hours a day looking for a job.
- Be organized. Keep a record of all the places where an application has been submitted, of the people talked to and what responses were received.
- Meet with people who are interested in the field being pursued.
- Check job listings in the newspaper, classified advertising sections or with the state employment office. The state employment office also may be able to offer some job search assistance.

REFERENCES

Bolles, R.N. (2003). *What color is your parachute? A practical manual for job-hunters and career-changers* (2003 ed.). Berkeley, CA: Ten Speed Press.

Crowther, K.N.T. (1993). *Researching your way to a good job.* New York, NY: Wiley.

CPC Annual. (2002). *Employers and occupations.* Bethlehem, PA: College Placement Council.

Forrester Research. (2000). About Forrester research. Retrieved October 15, 2002, from www.forrester.com

Frank, W. (1996). *200 letters for job hunters.* Berkeley, CA: Ten Speed Press.

Hunsaker, P.L., & Cook, C.W. (2001). *Managing organizational behavior* (3rd ed.). New York, NY: McGraw-Hill.

McKay, D.R. (2002). Careers in allied health care. *Career planning.* Retrieved October 14, 2002, from http://careerplanning.about.com/library/weekly.

Partnership for Public Service. (2001). *NPR federal workers commentary.* Retrieved October 14, 2002, from http://www.ourpublicservice.org/pressrelease.3749/press-release.

Seven things to know in advance. (n.d.). Retrieved March 20, 2003, from http://christalarico.com/seven_things_to_know_in_advance.htm.

U.S. Bureau of Labor Statistics (2002, November). *Labor force statistics.* Washington, DC: Author.

U.S. Census Bureau. (2002). *Statistical abstract of the United States.* Retrieved October 15, 2002, from http://www.online.wsj.com/public/us.

U.S. Commerce Department. (2002). Statistical abstract of the United States, 1990-2000. Washington, DC: U.S. Government Printing Office.

Wall Street Journal. (1999, November). American business. Retrieved October 30, 2002, from http://www.online.wsj.com/public/us.

SUGGESTED READINGS

Allen, J.G. (1992). *The perfect follow-up method to get the job.* Toronto, ON: Wiley.

Burack, E.H., Albrecht, M., & Seitler, H. (1980). *Growing: A woman's guide to career exploration.* Belmont, CA: Lifetime Learning Publications.

Campbell, D. (1974). *If you don't know where you're going, you'll probably end up someplace else.* Niles, IL: Argus Communications.

Ceolin, D. (1995). *The idea guide: The step-by-step guide for planning and starting your own business.* Toronto, ON: Envision Communications.

Chin-Lee, C. (1993). *It's who you know.* Toronto, ON: Pfeiffer.

Cote, F. (1993). *The student guide to job hunting: Paths to success.* Peterborough, ON: Broadview Press.

Crystal, J.C. & Bolles, R.N. (1974). *Where do I go from here with my life?* New York, NY: Seabury Press.

Dillon, M. & Weissman, S. (1987). Relationship between personality types on the Strong-Campbell and Myers-Briggs instruments. *Measurement and Evaluation in Counseling and Development,* 20(2), 68-79.

Easto, L. (1993). *How to succeed in your own home business.* Willowdale, ON: HomeBusiness Press.

Easto, L. & Price, R. (1996). *From learning to earning: A student's guide to landing the right job.* Toronto, ON: Doubleday.

Figler, H. (1988). *The complete job-search handbook.* New York, NY: Henry Holt & Company.

Hachey, J. (1995). *The Canadian guide to working and living overseas.* Ottawa, ON: Intercultural Systems.

Hagberg, J. & Leider, R. (1983). *The inventurers: Excursions in life and career renewal.* Reading, MA: Addison-Wesley.

Haldane, B. (1974). *Career satisfaction and success: A guide to job freedom.* New York, NY: AMACOM.

Hall, D.T. (1976). *Careers in organizations.* Santa Monica, CA: Goodyear Publishing.

Hirsch, S.K. & Hemphill, K.J. (1984). *Personality, career and choice.* In Z. Leibowwitz & S. Hirsh. (Eds.), Career development: Current perspectives. Washington, DC: American Society for Training and Development Press.

Holland, J.L. (1973). *Making vocational choices: A theory of careers.* Engelwood Cliffs, NJ: Prentice-Hall.

Jacoby, P.F. (1981). Psychological types and career success in the accounting profession. *Research in Psychological Type, 4,* 24-37.

Kennedy, J. & Joyce L. (1995). *Hook up, get hired!* Toronto, ON: John Wiley & Sons.

Kennedy, J., & Morrow, T.J. (1994). *Electronic job search revolution.* Toronto, ON: Wiley.

Krannich, R.L., & Krannich C.R. (1989). *Network your way to job and career success.* Manassas, VA: Impact Publications.

Larson, J. & Comstock, C. (1994). *The new rules of the job search game: Who today's managers hire . . . and who they don't.* Holbrook, MA: Bob Adams.

Lathrop, R. (1977). *Who's hiring who?* Berkeley, CA: Ten Speed Press.

Lynch, R.G., Carpenter, M., & Schwartz, R.M. (1995). What makes the other guy tick? *Popular Government, 60*(4), 12-18.

MacDaid, G.P., McCaulley, M.H., & Kainz, R.I. (1986). *Atlas of type tables.* Gainesville, FL: Center for Application of Psychological Type.

Mathis, R.L. & Jackson, J.H. (2000). *Human resource management.* Mason, OH: South-Western College Publishing.

Myers, I.B. (1962). *Manual: The Myers-Briggs type indicator.* Palo Alto, CA: Consulting Psychologist Press.

Natter, F. (1981). The human factor: Psychological type in legal education. *Research in Psychological Type, 3,* 55-67.

Ohsawa, T. (1975, October). *MBTI experiences in Japan: Career choice, selection, placement and counseling for individual development.* Paper presented at the first national conference on the Myers-Briggs Type Indicator, Gainesville, FL.

Pinkley, J.W. (1983, November). The Myers-Briggs type indicator as an alternative in career counseling. *The Personnel and Guidance Journal, 62*(3), 173-177.

Royal Bank. (1990a). *Your business matters: Starting Out Right.* Ontario, Canada: Author.

Royal Bank. (1990b). *Your business matters: The Source Book.* Ontario, Canada: Author.

Schein, E.H. (1978). *Career dynamics: Matching individual and organizational titles.* Washington, DC: Addison-Wesley.

Senge, P.M. (1990). *The fifth discipline.* New York, NY: Doubleday.

Standard & Poor's Register—Biographical. (2002). *Bluesheet contents.* Retrieved October 28, 2002, from http://library.dialog.com/bluesheets.html/b10526.htm.

U.S. Department of Labor. (1977). *Dictionary of occupational titles.* Washington, DC: Author.

U.S. Department of Labor Statistics. (2002). *Occupational outlook handbook.* Washington, DC: Office of Occupational Statistics and Employment Projections.

Weaver, M. & de Presna O. (1994). *The online world: How to profit from the information superhighway.* Toronto, ON: Product Publications.

Woods, D. & Omerod, S.D. (1993). *Networking: How to enrich your life and get things done.* Toronto, ON: Pfeiffer.

The World Wide Web Employment Office. (2002). Retrieved October 15, 2002, from http://www.employmentoffice.net.

Chapter 21

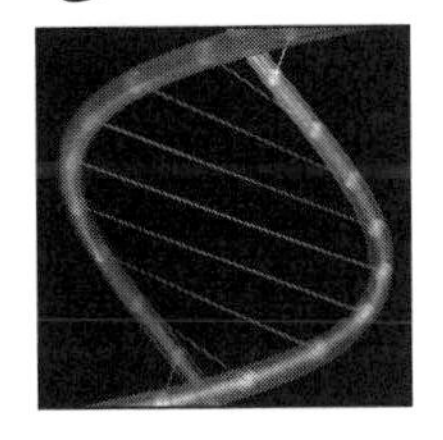

Matching

by Marcia Canton

INTRODUCTION

Here's the bad news. The U.S. Bureau of Labor Statistics (2002) reports that 67% of American workers don't like their jobs, and 41% of them are not employed in the fields that they studied in school. Gaps between an individual's skills and the job requirements are common factors that lead to job dissatisfaction. How well an employee is matched to a job affects the amount and quality of the employee's work. This matching also directly affects training and operating costs. Workers who are not able to produce the expected amount and quality of work can cost an organization a great deal of money and time. Estimates are that hiring an inappropriate employee can cost an employer three to five times that employee's salary before it is resolved. Yet, hiring mistakes are relatively common (Mathis & Jackson, 2000).

MEASURING THE MATCH BETWEEN DESIRE AND POSITION

Many people have been functioning in a position for a long period of time and yet do not have the same love for it or degree of accomplishment or hoped for income or career growth they had dreamed of. Pride in what is done is missing. However, they are clueless about what to do to bring that dream back on track. They vaguely think it is time for a new vision, a new sense of what to do with their work life.

The following questions should help the employee determine if the present job is the correct match:

- Do you know how you contribute to the overall success of the organization? What is your role in the big picture of the company? Has management acknowledged your contributions?
- Do you still expect great things from yourself and others? Are you part of a world-class work group? Are you receiving cross-training or rotational assignments to add to your personal and career development? Have you hit a ceiling in your growth and advancement?
- Are you seeing problems rather than challenges in your everyday work? Are you putting forth your share of solutions, creative answers?
- Are there too many times when it is difficult for you to do what you think is right or to maintain your integrity? Are there constant moral conflicts?
- Have you established a relationship with a mentor(s) inside or outside of the workplace? How has this association been helpful to you?
- Has your work positively or negatively affected your personal health and habits, as well as your relationships with family and friends?

These questions provide an opportunity to note if there is a pattern in the responses and if personal preferences match the job held. Unfortunately, many workers suffer from "career blues" where they lose their motivation for their chosen work and the pleasures they once derived from it (Ferris, Buckley, & Fedor, 2002).

Workers with career blues have become, to varying degrees, disengaged from their work, and although they may partially recognize that fact, they feel lost and uncertain about what to do about it. Most of us get the career blues from time to time; that's one reason why we take vacations, to refresh and renew our energies. But if the career blues linger, if the blues become a habit, the worker and the organization will suffer.

Languishing in career blues will get an individual along, but the worker will find no satisfaction or ways to excel while in that situation. Further, the organization takes risks with the mediocre performance and the continuation of old routines that come from tolerating more and more people doing only "good enough." These languishers have lost what are often called "E-factors"—energy, enthusiasm, excitement, effort and excellence. However, there is a way to move toward a personal state of career engagement wherein performance is not only at a higher level, but there is also more enjoyment in the level of performance.

Skills And Interests

Frequent job changes have become the norm rather than the exception. If a job change is in the near future, skill assessment is the best way to begin the process. Skills can be categorized into three groups: personal skills, information-based skills and transferable skills. Personal qualities are the traits acquired at birth that can be developed with practice, for example, patience, optimism and imagination.

Information-based skills are those skills learned on or off the job—a body of techniques, methods and knowledge gathered over the years. For example, a mastery of another language, software programming or karate skills.

Transferable skills are based on action—the ability to analyze, write, persuade or manage. It is these transferable skills that will facilitate a career change. Having a good sense of transferable skills makes the entire process of packaging and presenting these skills to a prospective employer much easier.

Pausing regularly to reflect on the level of engagement at work offers an opportunity to revisit a dream. There is a need to think about interests and the experiences that flow from those interests. There is also a need to identify what kind of school, religious, social or sports activities bring enjoyment and relief from the stresses of life. By making a list of 10 activities that have produced enjoyment over the past four years, it is possible to identify:

- What was important about those activities
- What challenges those activities offered
- What skills are needed to further develop satisfaction and enjoyment in those activities

Include in the list activities that bring enjoyment in school, volunteer work, leisure activities, and memberships in clubs or organization. The list should also include any social, civic or religious volunteering that has been conducted if it brought pleasure. After assessing this list for the activities that produce the most interest and satisfaction, it is possible to look for a career that offers the same kind of interest and satisfaction. Essentially, the task is to match personal interests and skills with career activities. Once a career that matches the identified interests and skills has been identified, it is time to revise the career goal.

GOAL SETTING

A career goal helps focus the individual on what she or he wants to do for a living. A career goal can be a specific job—such as doctor or teacher—or a career goal can be a particular field to work in, such as nursing, medicine or education.

Rather than limiting choices, a career goal should help one discover career possibilities that have not been thought of before. There are several job possibilities with any chosen career. For instance, if a medical career is selected, it could mean pursuing the role of scientist, researcher or clinician.

A career goal is also a guide for doing a job based on what is wanted rather than just drifting into a job. Generally, a career goal is based on the individual's skills and interests, career possibilities, and job trends.

Once a career has been selected, the next step is to think strategically about ways to accomplish the goal. Understanding and accomplishing the career goal will be a lot easier if there is a career plan. A career plan includes three important factors:

1. The individual's skills and interests
2. What career best suits those talents
3. What skills and training are needed for a match with the desired career

It is important at this point for the individual seeking a new career to not quit the current job without a game plan, no matter how awful it is. Identifying what is unbearable about the current job is important, as it is those activities that must be avoided in the next position. It is helpful to make a list of positive and negative factors of the present job in order to keep what is good and liked and eliminate what is disliked. If there is a feeling of uncertainty about what to do at this point, interests, skills and aptitudes can be measured by reliable evaluation instruments.

Before professionals can decide what they *want* to do, they should first identify what they *like* to do and what they're good at. It is useful to use a professional assessment tool (such as the Strong and Kuder Interest Inventory) or complete the following activities:

- Make a list of the activities you enjoy
- List what you like about those activities

Other tests can help the job seeker clarify interest, values and goals. Goal selection based on the individual's accumulated information should be consistent with his or her perceived capabilities and psychosocial characteristics and the requirements of the occupation. Argyris (1990) believes selected goals should be 1) challenging, 2) relevant to the individual's self-image, 3) set individually or collaboratively, and 4) implemented by independent effort.

In order to set career and personal goals, time should be devoted to looking at what is desired and what is known about self. For example:

- Where is the desired place to live?
- Who would be part of the desired life?
- What would relationships look like?
- What would happen during work? During leisure?
- What would the desired lifestyle look like?

The process of answering these questions can help an individual develop a personal vision. Once the worker has that vision, long-term and short-term goals can be developed. The worker's vision may be lofty or practical, such as raising a happy family in a wholesome environment, preparing for a carefree retirement, creating an estate, etc.

Knowing what is wanted from life will help a professional set career objectives, personal objectives and lifelong learning objectives. Life is comprised of several factors that work together to bring the balance needed for optimal wellness:

1. Physical (nutritious food, safe water, health, air, exercise)
2. Mental (intellectual challenges, knowledge, thoughts)
3. Emotional (feelings, belonging, security)
4. Philosophical (authenticity, spirituality, meaning, attitudes)
5. Social (relationships with others, friendships)
6. Career (finances, fulfillment)
7. Recreational (leisure, fun, sports)

A deficiency in any one of these areas will affect the other essential components, for example, overwork in a career can cause physical exhaustion leading to illness, disruption in social relationships and an inability to make sound decisions.

Thus sound, realistic goals are critical when developing a cognitive map for career advancement. Developing goals requires conscious projection into the future in order to bring clarity to the direction to be taken. A goal is the outcome and a plan is the strategy employed to get there. A plan details the activities necessary to accomplish the stated goal.

If the company of employment is liked but the job disliked, then it is best to pursue other opportunities inside before looking outside. Now is the time to make a commitment to stay on the job and do the best possible while investigating transfer opportunities. To the extent that it is possible, being honest with the boss is important. By emphasizing a willingness to continue with the company and do the best possible, the boss, as well as other company colleagues, may be able to help with a transfer.

An important strategy is to investigate the company's policies about transfers and management's tendency to follow them. Some companies encourage intra-company movement; others don't—even though they claim to do so. If there is evidence there will be no reprisals, talking to the human resources department is a good idea. Good selection and placement decisions are an important part of successful career planning.

Choosing the workplace is one of the most important career decisions made. The organization selected must provide the work environment necessary for career development and personal satisfaction. It can affect the future in numerous ways. It will determine opportunity for growth and advancement and financial status, and it may also determine the geographical location and the people with whom the job seeker identifies. It is, therefore, important to choose an organization carefully by reading annual reports and relevant newspaper articles. It is also advisable to talk with others who are in a position to know about the policies and work environment of a particular organization.

There are seven critical factors to consider prior to accepting a job:

1. The type of industry, its size growth rate and market potential
2. The facilities and working conditions and dress code
3. The level of stability of management and interest in employee well-being
4. The workers' duties and responsibilities and potential utilization of abilities
5. The potential for promotion and length of probation period
6. Compensation and other benefits
7. The organization's overall culture (e.g., How are decisions made? What are the core values of the organization?)

In terms of compensation and benefits, it is important to note that wage scales and employee benefits (vacations, pensions, etc.) generally have little impact on individual performance. People working only for money tend to become unhappy once the newness of the position is gone.

But these benefits do affect the employee's desire to remain with or leave the organization and the agency's ability to attract new employees. Salary is an important consideration, but being able to learn and get experience, liking the work and the people, and supporting the philosophy and goals of the organization are much more critical factors (Maslow, 1970).

It is also important to determine the organization's commitment to employee development. What type of training (inside or outside) does the company offer? Will this job assist the worker in learning new skills for future jobs? Most importantly, is this job compatible with the individual's goals? Organizations that use goal setting and performance appraisal systems seem to do so to strengthen performance outcomes (especially productivity).

Strive for personal mastery and continuous learning

Striving for personal mastery and continuous learning can be appraised by asking a few personal questions, such as:

- When have I felt energetic, harmonic, positive and unusually successful?
- When was I performing at my best?
- When did time seem to fly by?
- What was I doing when time was flying by?
- What parts of that activity were enjoyable?
- How did I feel at those times?

Those experiences may or may not have had anything to do with work. But thinking about them may surface a dream, a kind of feeling associated with the activity that defines how life should be experienced.

The identification of this set of feelings helps begin the thought process about how to recreate similar experiences at work. Research suggests that with intent and practice, one can recreate these internal flow experiences in other activities.

The search for an ideal career is a challenging process that requires personal mastery and continuous learning. Personal mastery is the phrase Senge (1990) uses for the discipline of personal growth and learning. People with high levels of personal mastery are continually expanding their abilities to create results in lives they truly seek.

Personal mastery goes beyond competence and skills, though it is grounded in competence and skills. It means approaching life as a creative work, living life from a creative, as opposed to reactive, viewpoint. The challenge for this new century is to make personal mastery a discipline—an activity that is integrated into our lives. This personal mastery means a special level of proficiency over people or things, not dominance.

People with high levels of personal mastery share several basic characteristics. They have a special sense of purpose that lies behind their visions and goals. To achieve this personal mastery:

- Learn how to perceive and work with forces of change rather than resist those forces.
- Become deeply inquisitive and committed to seeing reality more and more accurately.
- Feel connected to others and to life itself.
- Live in a continual learning mode.

Personal mastery is a lifelong discipline where we learn to remain open and continually strive for our stated goals. The more we practice achieving these higher virtues of life, the more we move toward personal and career success.

CONCLUSION

There are an abundance of opportunities for people interested in healthcare. Statistics indicate a growing need for home care aides, registered nurses, physician assistants, nurse practitioners, physical therapists, nontraditional health aides and physicians. Some of the biggest growth opportunities are expected to be for personal and home care aides, home health aides and nurses, and physical therapists and physical therapy assistants. The government even predicts continued growth opportunities for physicians, despite the current state of oversupply. To qualify for some positions (including physician, nurse, technicians and others), education is needed in addition to a strong network in a given area. Technical and administrative support are in high demand as the healthcare industry evolves in a competitive market.

A career path doesn't have to have a straightforward trajectory—it may be more like a maze than a path. People should periodically review their career development pathways and make mid-course corrections when necessary. Career development is not a one-shot process; professionals make numerous choices throughout life and these choices affect the way growth and development occur (Hunsaker & Cook, 1980).

Continual learning is a process everyone must adopt in order to move toward desired destinations. It helps to assess where we are now and what we want. "Learning" in this context does not mean acquiring more information, but expanding the ability to produce the results truly wanted in life.

Career development is not a one-shot attempt—it is an ongoing process where numerous choices must be made throughout life. Developing a systematic approach to search for the ideal career and striving continuously to grow and improve is a worthwhile and rewarding endeavor.

Re-Evaluation

Throughout a worker's career, re-evaluation is necessary. Professionals need to be intentional about their re-evaluation. Re-evaluation is about looking at life as an interconnected whole. Thus it is smart to revisit this process regularly, since priorities will most likely not remain the same.

Professionals need to determine whether the job is providing all the benefits hoped for (e.g., sense of accomplishment, income and career development). Is it time for a new vision, a new sense of what is important? Or are there changes that can be made within the present job? Or is a move warranted?

It is important to remember that the only predictable future is the one the individual creates. The best way to figure out specific life and career goals is to formalize the process. Taking time to answer the above questions that identify all of the specific goals and dreams for life and career is frequently necessary.

Successful professionals can sometimes feel trapped in career roles that no longer fit their personal goals, suit their skills or match their basic interests. It may take years before their discontent reaches a crescendo and they are ready to explore a change. Learning to listen to those warnings is the most difficult step in making a career change.

REFERENCES

Argyris, C. (1990). *Overcoming organizational defenses*. New York, NY: Prentice Hall.

Ferris, G.R., & Buckley, R., & Fedor, D.B. (2002). *Human resources management: Perspectives, context, functions, and outcomes*. Upper Saddle River, NJ: Prentice-Hall.

Hunsaker, P.L., & Cook, C.W. (2001). *Managing organizational behavior* (3rd ed.). New York, NY: McGraw-Hill.

Maslow, A.H. (1970). *Motivation and personality* (2nd ed.). New York, NY: Harper & Row.

Mathis, R.L. & Jackson, J.H. (2000). *Human resource management*. Mason, OH: South-Western College Publishing.

Senge, P.M. (1990). *The fifth discipline*. New York, NY: Doubleday.

U.S. Bureau of Labor Statistics (2002). *Occupational outlook handbook*. Washington, DC: Office of Occupational Statistics and Employment Projections.

SUGGESTED READINGS

DeGeus, A.P. (1988, March/April). Planning as learning. *Harvard Business Review*, pp. 70-74.

Drucker, P. (1992). The new society of organizations. *Harvard Business Review*, *5*, 95-105.

Handy, C. (1998). *The hungry spirit*. New York, NY: Broadway Books.

Kauffman, Jr., D. (1980). *Systems I: An introduction to systems thinking*. Minneapolis, MN: Future Systems, Inc.

Kets de Vries, M. (1994). CEOs also have the blues. *European Management Journal,12*(3), 275.

Merton, R.K. (1968). *Social theory and social structure*. New York, NY: Free Press.

McCleland, D.C. (1988). *Human motivation*. Cambridge, UK: Cambridge University Press.

Schein, E. (1978). *Career dynamics: Matching individual and organizational titles*. Reading, PA: Addison-Wesley.

Schor, J.B. (1993). *The overworked American*. New York, NY: Basic Books.

Schumacher, E.F. (1977). *A guide for the perplexed*. New York, NY: Harper and Row.

U.S. Department of Commerce (1988a). *Statistical abstract of the United States, 1982-1983*. Washington, DC: Bureau of Census.

United States Department of Commerce (1988b). *U.S. industrial outlook*. Washington, DC: Author.

Yankelovich, D. (1981). *New rules: Searching for self-fulfillment in a world turned upside down*. New York, NY: Random House.

Chapter 22

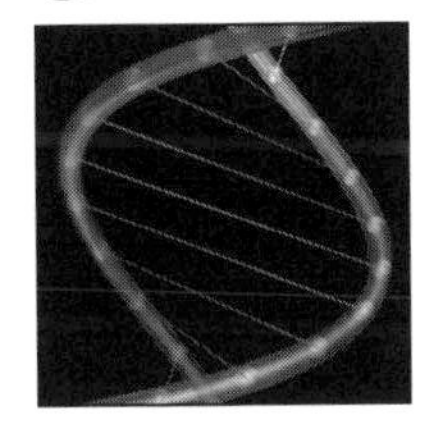

Choosing: Interviewing and Developing Resumes/CVs

by Mae Timmons

You have less than one minute to make a first impression on the individuals who are going to read your cover letter and resume/curriculum vitae (CV) and view you for the first time when you attend your first interview. The initial impression you make on an employer through applications, resumes, letters, telephone calls or informational interviews will determine whether the employer is interested in interviewing you and offering you a position (Krannich, 1997, p. 181).

INTRODUCTION

Major corporations spend millions of dollars to develop advertisements that will be seen for only a few seconds during the yearly Super Bowl extravaganza. Sometimes, the investment pays off and sometimes, it does not. If the advertisement was successful, it not only is discussed by millions of viewers on Monday morning but also may be seen as a rerun on many other programs during the following week. Career enthusiasts want to be as zealous as these advertisers when planning and preparing a resume/CV and cover letter and getting ready for an interview.

This chapter contains important information about actions that need to be taken so a good first impression is provided with the resume/CV and cover letter and during the interview. Following the actions presented in this chapter should motivate potential employers to invest more of their time considering the job seeker for a professional position in the healthcare arena.

Each of the tools discussed in this chapter has a specific purpose. The term *resume* comes from the French word résumé, which means "to summarize" (Oxford University Press, 1996). And that is just what a resume is—a summary of qualifications. The summary includes educational and professional accomplishments, skills, and related experiences. It is a marketing tool and a calling card to promote an individual to potential employers, primarily for the purpose of obtaining an interview. While many jobs require only a completed application form, the job seeker definitely should prepare a resume for influencing the person doing the hiring. Application forms do not substitute for resumes.

However, resumes are only as good as the cover letter that accompanies them. Several references support the fact that neglect of a well-executed cover letter may quickly kill the resume (Krannich & Krannich, 1994; Block & Betrus, 1999; Ireland, 2000; Ryan, 2003a). A cover letter is a well-organized, grammatically correct, typed document with content that serves as a complement, not a duplicate, of your resume. Its main purpose is to get the employer to take action on your resume. Consequently, the whole planning process in the construction of this letter should focus on persuading the employer to initiate an invitation for a job interview.

The interview is a meeting between the job seeker and one or more individuals who exchange information that serves to educate both about whether a mutually rewarding professional relationship can be formed. The information in this chapter provides the best methods for helping sell the job seeker during the interview and the typical questions that are asked by the interviewer and, more importantly, some pertinent questions the job seeker needs to ask prior to the end of the interview.

RESUME/CURRICULUM VITAE

Difference Between Resume and Curriculum Vitae (CV)

A resume is a detailed summary of an individual's professional experiences. These experiences usually include education, clinical experience or work history, projects, and awards. This document is designed to introduce the job seeker to potential employers and hopefully interest them in a follow-up interview. Often, the resume is the employer's first impression of the job seeker, so it is wise not to underestimate its importance. A resume is rarely more than one page.

A curriculum vitae (CV) contains the identical information as a resume; however, this document is usually designed for a job seeker who is interested in an academic or research position. The CV is usually more extensive in length, because the employer is probably seeking someone with extensive experience as a professional nurse, educator and/or researcher, as well as someone with a list of publications and/or research that have been completed or are in progress. Although there is no limitation on the length of a CV, it is important that it, like the resume, be written concisely. It is wise to check with the human resource or employment department of the potential employer if it is not clear whether a CV or a resume is expected.

Preparing a resume or a CV

It is very important to know how to construct an impressive resume. A better response can be expected if the resume or CV is well-organized and packed with relevant information to match and support the job seeker's professional or academic objective. Thus, it is important to allow sufficient time to plan and develop a resume/CV.

The first step in the preparation of a resume or CV is to review and document one's educational and professional history. Each of the areas that will be included in the resume or CV should be placed on a separate page. It is recommended a word processor be used, so after the lists are completed, the basic content of the resume or CV is completed. The items to include on these lists may include all schools attended, honors received, jobs held (paid and volunteer), duties performed, and any appropriate additional information.

Every single thing completed does not need to be included in these lists. Choices must be made about what to include or exclude. When preparing the list, think through the particular skills that would be important to the employer.

Content of the Resume or CV

Career counselors, human relations executives, employers and job experts disagree about what to include in the resume/CV. In fact, King and Sheldon (1996) state, "Ask a dozen different experts to tell you what to put in a resume and where to put it . . . and you'll get at least two dozen different answers, probably more" (p. 69). This dissention occurs because employers have different resume preferences and priorities. In addition, every job seeker has a different set of qualifications, skills and experience and thus different resume information.

The most important aspect when designing the resume is to match the resume to the employer's needs, state your accomplishments and qualifications in specific terms, and be clear and concise. Employers must be able to find the information they are seeking quickly and easily. Remember, you usually have just 30 seconds or less to get the attention of the person reading your resume.

Basic Information

The resume/CV should include the following information:

- Name
- Current and/or permanent address
- Telephone number
- E-mail address
- Education
- Employment history or skills and experience

Contact information is always placed at the beginning of any resume followed by education history and work history. Throughout the resume, all sections that contain information with dates should be presented in reverse chronological order, that is, from most recent backward (i.e., 2002-2000).

Name and Contact Information

Contact information is always presented first and in boldface type to make it more prominent. Full name (first and last names and middle initial), address, phone number and e-mail address are listed. It is important to present the actual name, not a nickname. Although a nickname may be preferred, for the purpose of the resume/CV, it is best to use the most professional version of the name. If the name is unusual or difficult to pronounce, a pronunciation guide may be helpful. For example, Dennia Kjar is pronounced "din-e-a car."

The name is probably the most important piece of information on the resume; it must be placed so it can be quickly and easily seen. Most people place the name at the top, middle or upper-right corner of the page. The reason for this placement is probably due to the fact that after the resume is read it will be filed with the left-hand side of the paper placed against the spine of a folder. Placing the name at the center on the far right of the page puts it where it will be noticed easily.

If the address is temporary (as in the case of a college student living away from home), both the temporary and permanent (or future) addresses and phone numbers should be included. It is better not to use a P.O. box number, because a home address conveys a more stable image. If, however, there is a specific reason not to distribute the street address, it is acceptable to use the post office address.

The phone number is the most crucial and most problematic element in the name header. The number should be listed where prospective employers can reach the job seeker during the day. This may create a problem if the job seeker's work hours are the same as the employer's. If including a work number may cause a problem, it is best not to include it but to leave a home number and a time to call.

Most individuals have answering machines, so it is appropriate to include a number that can receive a voice message. However, the outgoing message should sound professional and thus state the full or last name—not just a first name or nickname. People are usually very hesitant to leave a message when they do not know if they have reached the correct person. If there are other people living where the outgoing message is recorded, make sure the person answering the phone is able to answer the phone in a mature manner, accurately record the message and place the recorded message in a secure place. If a roommate, significant other or child does not have the capability to provide accurate information regarding calls, voice mail services may be a better way to record calls.

Listing an e-mail address can be a beneficial way to handle a job search. Providing an e-mail address will often expedite a potential employer's response, as well as demonstrate the job seeker is online savvy. A Web site that is devoted to a job search is also helpful and should be included in the heading along with your other contact information.

Personal information, such as social security number, birth date or marital status, should NOT be included in a resume or CV. These data are protected by current employment laws. Personal activities, such as sewing, hobbies, reading, skiing, etc. are not appropriate in a resume. These items may provide information about one's personality; however, most recruiters consider these items irrelevant.

Education

Education is always a point of interest to a prospective employer. This section is usually placed at or near the end of the resume unless education is highly relevant to the position sought, or the job seeker has no employment experience in the field being pursued but has a degree in that field.

If the job seeker has one or more college degrees, the date each degree was earned must be designated (last one first). The degree must be indicated (e.g., bachelor of arts or BA; bachelor of science, BS). Whichever form is used, they must be consistent throughout all listings. If honors were granted, they can be noted in an "Honors and Awards" section or with the educational listing.

If several schools were attended until the final degree was awarded, it is not necessary to list all the different schools that led to the achievement of the degree. List only those colleges where the degree was awarded. Listing more than that might cause the reader to think the job seeker tended to move around a lot without finishing things.

If the educational program has not been completed, list the name of the institution followed by the date of expected graduation and state "currently enrolled," or "in progress." If a minor or several courses in another field have been completed along with the professional degree, it would be wise to include this information. For example:

2003–University of California, San Francisco, San Francisco, CA–MSN

- 12 credits in Healthcare Business
- 9 credits in Computer Science

Unique educational experiences, such as spending a semester in course-related travel or related clinical experience in a foreign country, are also worth mentioning. These experiences may indicate you are a person who goes one step beyond the norm, who's open to new opportunities and challenges.

Another experience worth including in the resume is an internship. Along with the name and location of the institution and time spent in this experience, it is wise to include a brief summary of the experience.

Work Experience

A review of work experience with the latest one presented first is an essential aspect of the resume or CV. The work history section should contain a reverse chronological listing of each position and should contain the job title, name of the organization and location, and the starting and end dates of employment. Each experience should be listed with the dates of that experience and a very brief description of the job responsibilities. Every employer wants to know what the job entailed and the scope of the experience. It is important to be brief but to include the essence of the experience pointing out when there were delegations and when there were independent decisions required in the job.

If statements of accomplishments for each position are going to be included in the resume, it is important to use result-oriented verbs instead of functional verbs. An example of a statement that contains a functional verb is: "S*upervised* unlicensed personnel in the daily care of five to six acutely ill patients." To make this statement a result-oriented statement, the perspective employee may want to include the following statement instead: "Within one year of hire as a new graduate, established an effective working relationship when guiding unlicensed personnel in the daily care of five to six acutely ill patients. Several references (King & Sheldon, 1996; Bolles, 2003; Ireland, 2000; Ryan, 2003b; Yate, 2003) contain result-oriented verbs and further examples of result-oriented statements that can be reviewed for use in the resume.

Format of the Resume

The purpose of this section is to provide a model for the construction of a resume. Once it has been written, it can be converted into a format for e-mailing and posting on the Internet. There are three types of resumes to choose from: chronological, functional or a combination chronological/ functional one. The chronological resume is the standard resume used by most applicants.

Chronological Resume

The chronological format is the traditional and most commonly used resume format. It is so named because the core component of the resume is a chronological review of the employment history. This experience profile makes up about 70% of the resume and, in most cases, appears immediately after the job objective or skills summary. The following information is often included in this kind of resume:

- Dates of employment
- Employer's name and address
- Position held
- Responsibilities and accomplishments

Jennifer Jackson
34466 133rd St.
Omaha, NE 67812

Skills Experience	More than 10 years full-time experience as staff nurse in large, metropolitan acute care institution Extensive professional experience as direct care provider, supervisor of licensed and unlicensed personnel while directing care of 6 to 12 patients from acute to rehabilitative stages.
Employment History	
1997 – present	Great Plains Hospital, Omaha, NE Staff Nurse position in 35-bed Step-Down Unit Began as staff nurse caring for group of patients (6–8) during night shift. Progressed to weekend Charge Nurse for entire unit. Supervised average of 6 RNs, 3 LPNs and 5 Nursing Assistants.
1992 – 1997	Mid Plains Hospital, Summerset, IA Staff Nurse position in 25-bed Medical Surgical Unit Began as entry level RN caring for group of patients (4–5) during night shift. Worked with mentor for 6 months when first hired then progressed to care of patients assisted by LPNs and nursing assistants.
Volunteer Positions	
1997 to present	Health educator providing classess to clients at Planned Parenthood Women's Health Clinic
1994 to 1997	Mentor for nursing students at University of Iowa School of Nursing
Education	
1992	University of Iowa, School of Nursing, Athens, Iowa BSN
1990 – 1992	Mid Plains Community College General Education Courses
Professional Affiliations	
	Sigma Theta Tau International, Alpha Sigma Chapter since 1991 Nebraska Nurses Association, Secretary 1999 to present

---

Figure 22.1 *Sample of Chronological Resume*

Advantages and Disadvantages of the Chronological Resume

Employers can easily find what they are looking for in the chronological resume since it is an easy-to-follow snapshot of the employment history. It gives prominence to what many people consider the most important criteria for hiring: What the job seeker has done and is accomplishing right now. Describing the work history in reverse chronological fashion showcases the qualifications and strengths of the job seeker to good advantage.

According to Messmer (1995) and Ryan (2003b), chronological resumes can be troublesome if the individual is seeking a change in careers and the most recent position has no relationship to the job being sought. If the job seeker is looking for an entry-level position and has almost no work experience, this type of resume may be the best one. If the job seeker, however, has had several jobs over the past several years and less than one year in most of these or there are large gaps in the employment history, this type of resume may not be the best one to select.

Functional Resume

The functional resume summarizes accomplishments, qualifications and experience in areas of skill, rather than presenting a detailed description of specific jobs or volunteer positions. The groups that might be included are:

- Management experience
- Technical experience
- Customer service experience
- Leadership experience
- Computer experience
- Teaching experience

This alternative choice of resume formats is important if the job seeker does not have an extensive list of positions or if the pattern of employment has been sporadic. Less emphasis is placed on the when and where of work. Instead, the individual's accomplishments in the position(s) held are described. An example of a functional resume follows.

Jennifer Jackson

Campus Address	Permanent Address
3400 William St.	187777 Dodge St.
Omaha, NE 68106	Townsville, NE 65432
(402) 687-3442	(402) 888-2121

Professional Objective: To obtain a staff nurse position in a hospital that provides excellent care and incorporates cultural and socioeconomic issues as essential components of care delivery.

Education

University of Great Plains, School of Nursing, Omaha, NE
Bachelor of Science in Nursing, May 2003
Graduated Summa Cum Laude with a Business Health Minor
Activities:
Student Government, President
State Student Nurses Association, Vice-President
Great Plains Community College, Omaha, NE
Attended September 1999 to May 2001 to take General Education courses

Clinical Experience

Good Samaritan Assisted Living and Nursing Home Care of the Older Adult
Great Plains Hospital Adult Health & Leadership; Obstetrics; Specialized Environment
Children's Hospital Infant and Child Care
Open Door Mission & Mid Plains Psychiatric Institute Psychiatric Mental Health
Various community experiences in Nebraska and Iowa

Work Experience

Great Plains Hospital, Nursing Assistant, Sept 01 to May 03
Served as unlicensed personnel to nursing staff on step-down unit.

University of Great Plains, Office of Admissions Sept 01 to May 03
Work Study Student
Provided administrative support in busy office environment.
Answered phones and enthusiastically greeted potential students and their families. Assisted with Preview Days every semester.

Figure 22.2 *Sample of Functional Resume*

Advantages and Disadvantages of a Functional Resume

The chief advantage of a functional resume is that it enables the job seeker to focus on those aspects of his or her background most likely to be of special interest to a prospective employer. It calls particular emphasis to these accomplishments. On the other hand, since this type of resume may not be the typical format for some employers, they may view the resume with suspicion (Messmer, 1995, p. 72). Instead, these prospective employers may be more interested in learning where the job seeker received the accomplishments and skills.

Combination Resume

Some may find it easy to incorporate elements of both functional and chronological formats into the resume. This type of resume is sometimes referred to as the chrono-functional resume. For example, if the job seeker is applying for a nursing position that requires specific management skills, it may be appropriate to begin the resume with a functional-style listing of all the relevant management skills, followed by a traditional chronological listing of a work history.

Advantages and Disadvantages of a Combination Resume

The disadvantages identified for the chronological and functional resumes serve as an advantage for the chrono-functional resume. For example, if the job seeker is looking for a career change and wants to highlight general skills that would be beneficial to a new career, the chrono-functional resume may be helpful. The chrono-functional resume enables the job seeker to establish early on what has been accomplished and what skills and attributes can contribute to a new endeavor in addition to when and where these skills and accomplishments were obtained.

Format of the Curriculum Vitae (CV)

The job seeker should become familiar with the requirements of the academic field by asking colleagues or contacting professional associations for additional guidelines and examples. When applying to academic programs, it is wise to analyze the program's catalogs and brochures and look for key words and phrases to integrate into the CV.

The following list is provided as a guide for determining which categories of information to include in a CV:

- Education
- Master's thesis or project
- Dissertation title or topic
- Course highlights or areas of concentration in graduate study
- Teaching experience and interests

- Consulting experience
- Internships or graduate clinical experiences
- Publications
- Professional papers and presentations
- Grants received
- Professional association and committee leadership positions and activities
- Certificates and licensure
- Academic awards, scholarships and fellowships
- Technical and computer skills

Appearance of Resume/CV

Aside from the appropriate data, the resume/CV should also be clean, without typos or misspellings, and free of stains or creases. All word processing programs have spell-check capability, so the ease of editing the resume/CV on a computer has raised the stakes—typos are no longer acceptable or forgiven. It is also important to know the limitations of the spell-check program. For example, the program cannot distinguish between "to" and "too"; "was" and "were." Zurlinden (2002) offers several suggestions to ensure there are no mistakes on the document. These include:

- Prepare the resume and cover letter at least a day or two before they are to be submitted, so they can be proofread as if they were being read for the first time.
- Have knowledgeable colleagues read the resume/CV and cover letter to find mistakes.
- Read the resume/CV backwards from bottom to top and from right to left to find typos and misspellings. This process forces one to read the document letter by letter and word by word to find mistakes.
- Cut a small window approximately the size of a word in a piece of colored paper. Then use it to read the resume/CV and cover letter word by word while covering the rest of the document.
- Read the resume/CV aloud. Mistakes can often be heard that eyes ignore.
- Repeat the proofreading process after all corrections have been made. Corrections are as prone to mistakes as the original version.
- Accept that mistakes are hard to find but worth the effort to fix (p. 26).

Jennifer Jackson

Current Address	Permanent Address
5000 Greenwich Ave.	1200 F University St.
Blacktown, VA 24356	Warton, VA 21356
(540) 125-3445	(540) 345-7868

Education

2001	PhD, University of Storrs Department of Nursing, Storrs Connecticut Dissertation: Effects of Synchronous and Asynchronous Online Teaching Strategies to Develop Critical Thinking Skills of Nursing Students Registered in a Research Course
1995	MSN, Camden University School of Nursing Thesis: Comparison of Synchronous and Asynchronous Online Teaching Interventions Used to Teach Undergraduate Nursing Research Camden, AZ
1990	BSN, Sacred Heart College of Nursing Hartford, IL Graduated Magnum Cum Laude
Honors	Sigma Theta Tau International, Outstanding Doctoral Dissertation Award Phi Kappa Phi

Research Interests

Online Teaching Strategies for the Research Process
Alternative Teaching Strategies and Outcomes

Professional Experiences

1997 to present	Assistant Professor University of Storrs Department of Nursing, Storrs, CT
1995 – 1997	Research Assistant, Camden University School of Nursing
1992 – 1997	Instructor Camden University School of Nursing, Camden, AZ
1990 – 1997	Staff Nurse, Intensive Care Unit Camden University Hospital, Camden, AZ

Publications

Jackson, J. L. (2002). Effects of synchronous and asynchronous online teaching strategies to develop critical thinking skills of baccalaureate nursing students registered in a research course. *Journal of Computer Nursing, 12*(5), 125-132.

Jackson, J. L. (2000). Asynchronous and synchronous teaching strategies to promote critical thinking in baccalaureate nursing students. *Journal of Online Nursing Education, 3*(3), 46-52.

Jackson, J. L., & Bumgardner, S. (1998). Issues related to teaching theory courses to fast track BSN students using online strategies. *Journal of Online Nursing Education, 1*(4), 24-32.

Jackson, J. L., & Schother, D. (1996). Synthesis of research conducted on teaching strategies used for online education. *Online Journal of Knowledge Synthesis for Nursing, 10*(4).

Presentations

December 2002	Effects of synchronous and asynchronous online teaching strategies to develop critical thinking skills of nursing students registered in a research course. NLN Educational Summit, Bakersfield, IA
November 2000	Teaching strategies appropriate for promoting nursing students' critical thinking skills. Teaching Institute for Nurse Educators, Wellington, TX
June 1997	Summary of research conducted on differences of synchronous and asynchronous teaching strategies used for online education. National Online Teaching Conference, Stollard, CA

***Figure 22.3** Sample of Curriculum Vitae*

Final Production

Other points regarding the appearance of the resume/CV will assist in producing the final production of a well-designed document. For instance, use good quality paper—20-pound or heavier bond paper. The color of the paper should be conservative. Some authors recommend using only white paper with black ink. Others indicate that light tan (using brown ink), light gray (using black ink) and light blue are acceptable. All authors believe blue, yellow, green, pink, orange, red, or any other bright or pastel color should be avoided.

The document should be printed using a quality laser printer and be prepared using a 12-point type and fonts with serifs, e.g., Aa, Bb, Cc, Dd. Standard line spacing (single- or double-spacing) is appropriate rather than 1.5 or other spacing fractions. The same font and line spacing should be used throughout the document.

Cover Letters

The resume is only as good as the letter accompanying it (Krannich & Krannich, 1994). The purpose of the cover letter is to explain why the resume is being sent and helps to call attention to certain skills and qualifications of the job seeker. The most important part is that it should get the employer to take action on the resume. Thus, it is best to think of these letters as "interview generating" documents rather than a "cover letter."

Employers make quick judgments about the job seeker's professionalism, competence and personality based on limited information presented to them. Within a few seconds, the written message on a cover letter motivates them to select the job seeker or to take the job seeker out of consideration for a position. Employers do not want to be bothered with letters that make the job seeker appear disorganized, illiterate, likely to make errors or lacking the effort to ensure a top-rate letter.

The elements included in a cover letter shown in the sample are the same that are required for all business letters. The heading should include the job seeker's home address. Personal name stationary can be used and looks very professional; however, employers do not expect the job seeker to purchase pre-printed personal stationary for a cover letter.

Jennifer Jackson
515 Robin Lane Drive
Indianapolis, IN 47651

January 13, 2003

Mildred Bates, Director
Human Resources
Greater Mid Plains University Medical Center
4306 Conners Road
Indianapolis, IN 45676

Dear Mrs. Bates:

Please consider the accompanying resume as an application for the staff nurse position advertised today in the Indianapolis Star. As a recent graduate from a baccalaureate program, I believe I am well qualified for this entry-level position. Prior to completing my degree and becoming licensed, I worked as a nursing assistant and volunteer health worker. I have worked with many Registered Nurses on several units and have noted their professionalism and attention to cultural and socioeconomic aspects of patients. I have also experienced the effects of mentoring and concern professional nurses have for entry-level staff nurses.

I would appreciate an opportunity to interview for this position. The Greater Mid Plains University Medical Center has a well deserved reputation for excellent patient care. I learned about this reputation from patients I have cared for when they were hospitalized. I would be proud to contribute to the team effort at Greater Mid Plains.

I will call on Friday afternoon to see if you have any questions about my candidacy. I look forward to meeting with you and your staff.

Respectfully,

Jennifer L. Jackson

Figure 22.4 *Sample Cover Letter*

The date line comes immediately after the heading. The date can appear in month-day-year or day-month-year, e.g., November 12, 2002 or 12 November 2002. The date should be written in full rather than abbreviated.

The inside address consists of the recipient's title, name, position, and name and address of the institution. The letter should be addressed to a specific person instead of addressing the cover letter to "Dear Sir or Madam" or "To Whom it May Concern." The person's proper gender or professional title should also be included. It is important to find a specific contact or hiring manager at the institution in order to obtain the correct information. A receptionist or secretary will happily provide it. Remember to verify the spelling of the contact's name. These actions will ensure the cover letter and resume do not wind up in the wrong office.

The salutation or greeting should consist of the word "Dear" followed by the proper gender or professional title and surname of the individual. A colon should follow the individual's last name (e.g., Dear Mrs. Stevenson:).

A short and succinct one-page letter that highlights one or two points in your resume is sufficient. Three paragraphs will suffice. The first paragraph should state the job seeker's interest and purposes for writing. The second paragraph should highlight the job seeker's value to the employer. Finally, the third paragraph should state the time when the job seeker will call the individual to schedule an interview.

The intent is to avoid standard business language, but the letter must be interesting, honest and straightforward. It is important to demonstrate energy and enthusiasm through the use of words. For example, what type of impression does this letter leave on a reader?

> Dear Mr. Green:
>
> I'm writing in response to your recent ad for a staff nurse position at Great Plains Community Hospital. Please find enclosed a copy of my resume, which outlines my experiences in relationship to this position.
>
> Thank you for your consideration.

This letter is short and to the point; however, it does not grab the reader's attention, sustain interest, nor move anyone to action. It reads like hundreds of canned cover letters employers receive each day. Consider this alternative:

> Over the last three years, I managed a case load of six to 10 acutely ill patients on a step-down unit. Care of these patients was provided either by myself or with the help of unlicensed personnel, whom I

supervised. This position was a challenge since it was my first position as a staff nurse following graduation. I am now interested in assuming a similar challenge caring for patients in the intensive care unit at your institution. When I saw the posting of a full-time position on your Web site, I thought I would qualify for this position. If you are interested in learning more about my experience, let's talk soon about how I may become a contributing member of Grand Prairie Community Hospital Intensive Care Unit. In the meantime, please look over my enclosed resume. I will contact you on Monday, November 18, to see if you received these materials and to check your schedule for an interview.

I appreciate your time.

The six simple words written in the first example of a cover letter that may kill a job search effort are "Thank you for your consideration." This statement or "I look forward to hearing from you" are the most commonly used closings in job search letters and have been proven to be ineffective closings (Krannich & Krannich, 1994). Instead, it is wise to complete the letter with a follow-up statement that calls for the job seeker to initiate a specific action related to the contents of the letter. The statements may be worded as follows:

I will call your office Wednesday morning, November 14, to see if you received my resume and to schedule time for an interview.

Would next week be a good time to discuss my interests?

I will call your office at 3 pm on Monday, November 18, to check your schedule.

I appreciate your time.

Each of these statements (or something similar) specifies what the job seeker will do and when the expected actions will take place. The reader now knows what to expect next from the job seeker. Having the employer know what will occur next is the most important outcome the job seeker wants to achieve when developing a communication link with the reader.

Lastly, the closing statement can take various forms. The most standard and formal ones are:

Sincerely,
Sincerely yours,
Yours truly,
Respectfully,
Respectfully yours,

The signature information should be on two lines. The printed name should be typed four spaces below the closing with the actual signature between the closing and printed name.

Layout and Design

Block and Betrus (1999), Krannich and Krannich (1994), and Ryan (2003a) offer several suggestions on the layout and design of the cover letter. First, the letter should look clean, crisp, uncluttered and professional. It is important to pay attention to how the letter is laid out on the page. The cliché that "less is more" is a good rule to follow. White space should be generous. Margins should be at least 1 1/4 to 1 1/2 inches on the top, bottom and sides of the paper. A one-inch margin gives the letter a cluttered or unbalanced look.

Similar to any document that is sent to a prospective employer, grammatical, spelling and punctuation errors should be eliminated. These communicate a lack of competence and professionalism. Check and recheck the letter for errors by proofreading the cover letter at least twice. Have someone else read it also.

Avoid negative words and tones in the letter. Such words as "can't," "didn't" and "won't" can be eliminated for a more positive way of stating the negative. For example, instead of writing "I don't have any experience as a staff nurse since I just graduated," put the message in a more positive tone by using positive statements, such as:

> The mentoring experiences during my last semester in nursing school enabled me to learn how to organize and provide quality care for a group of four to five acutely ill patients in a step-down unit during a 12-hour shift. The goal of this experience was to provide safe, efficient and effective care to a group of patients with minimal supervision by the preceptor during the last month of the semester.

Effective Distribution

Distribution of the cover letter and resume plays an important role in demonstrating professional effort. The method of delivery can elicit an immediate response or no response at all. Some authors (Ireland, 2000; King & Sheldon, 1996; Krannich & Krannich, 1994; LeFevre, 1992) recommend the letter and resume should be sent in a 9″ x 12″ envelope instead of a #10 business envelope. This size envelope allows for the materials to arrive neat and flat. Thus, the receiver does not need to unfold the letter and resume and struggle to keep it flat should the paper tend to spring back to the folded position. The envelope paper stock should be the same color as the cover letter and resume.

In some cases, it may be beneficial to use a special delivery service for overnight delivery of the cover letter and resume. Such services may cost more than first-class delivery, but this method of delivery provides separate handling and quick delivery to the individual. The letter or resume should not be faxed unless requested by the appropriate person. Poor quality of fax paper and images does not enhance the professional image. If someone asks for the resume to be faxed, follow up by putting the original copies in the mail.

Follow-Up Phone Call

No matter which method of mailing is used, it is important to follow up with a telephone call after the letter and resume are sent. It is imperative to keep in mind that the individuals who receive the materials are very busy and receive many letters. Therefore, it is important to call the same day the individual is supposed to receive the materials. The phone call may include an introduction followed by inquiry if the materials had arrived. Since the job seeker included a day and time for contact in the cover letter, a desirable outcome should be expected. The employer may be available to talk to the job seeker at this time or a message can be left with the secretary for when the call can be completed. If the job seeker is unable to talk to the employer or his or her designate, useful information may still be obtained. The employer may have the secretary tell the job seeker there are no job openings at this time. If a rejection is obtained, the job seeker knows not to waste any more time with this institution. Other more promising job searches can then be pursued.

If the individual does respond positively and the job seeker talks to the employer/designate, it is important to remember that this is the first interview, even though the job seeker's primary purpose was to ask a few questions or schedule an appointment. The job seeker should be prepared to conduct an interview as soon as the follow-up call is made. Remember, it is important at this time to initiate proper telephone etiquette and assume a professional demeanor.

THE INTERVIEW

Preparation of the resume and cover letter is very important as part of the activities related to a job search. These documents and the application bring attention to the job seeker, but the interview is *the* most important step in the job search process (Krannich, 1997). The following discussion focuses on how to prepare for an interview and how to respond to the interview situation and the interviewer.

An interview is a two-way communication exchange between an interviewer and interviewee (Krannich, 1997). The general purpose of an interview is to determine whether the job seeker has the qualifications necessary to do the job and whether a mutually rewarding professional relationship can be formed. The interviewer seeks to explore the qualifications of the job seeker, but more importantly, the job seeker has an opportunity to use the interview period to ask pertinent questions in order to determine if it is possible to succeed in the position.

Purpose of the Interview

The job seeker should understand the purpose of the interview that has been scheduled. The first interview is usually a "screening" interview. The interviewer and job seeker use this time to determine the "fit" between the job seeker and the institution. The second interview, or follow-up interview, is designed for both the job seeker and interviewer to ask more probing questions that may confirm the "fit" between the parties. Frequently, the second interview may be the opportunity when the immediate supervisor meets the job seeker. This time together provides an opportunity for more probing questions by both the interviewer and job seeker.

The Interview Process

Interviews can take place in a variety of settings. They can occur in person or over the phone. The number of individuals who attend the interview may be only the interviewer and the job seeker or the interviewee and a panel of individuals who work at the institution. The number of times the interview may take place may be from one time to a series of interviews. All of these situations may occur in the same day or over a number of days or weeks. And each situation requires a different set of communication behaviors by the job seeker.

Overall Outline of the Interview

LeFevre (1992) offers a format for the four steps of the standard preliminary or screening interview. This interview usually takes 30 minutes with the following included in each step:

Step I:	The Warm-Up —greeting —establishing rapport —explaining structure of interview —verifying data on resume, etc.	4 minutes
Sept II:	Data Collection —asking open-ended questions —asking probing questions —asking closed questions —determining whether match exists —identifying strengths, liabilities	15 minutes
Step III:	Answer Questions/Offer Information —explaining training programs —describing position —answering candidate's questions	8 minutes
Step IV:	Closure of Interview —explaining what happens next —distributing brochures (pp. 65-66).	3 minutes

Preparation for the Job Interview

Preparation and practice are the keys to success for the job seeker for any interview. Several references (DeLuca, 1997; Restifo, 1997; Ryan, 2000) offer important steps that should be completed for adequate preparation for the interview. These steps include:

- Determine the purpose of the interview.
- Study the organization.
- Review questions that may be asked during the interview.
- Know questions that are inappropriate for both the interviewer and the job seeker.
- Plan to ask questions concerning the organization and the nature of the work.
- Develop polished interviewing skills.
- Plan for a positive image on the day of the interview.

"The more you practice, the better prepared [the job seeker] will be for the job interview" (Krannich, 1997, p. 240). Important facets the job seeker needs to practice before the interview include a "practice run" of possible responses to all questions that may be asked during the interview and a dress rehearsal where the job seeker dons the clothes that will be worn to the interview. The job seeker conducts a "practice run" with someone who evaluates how the job seeker answers questions, as well as evaluates the job seeker for evidence of positive and negative body language.

Becoming the Ultimate Candidate

There are many guidelines for increasing the job seeker's chances of getting a job offer. Some of these guidelines are summarized by Restifo (1997). He suggests (1) the job seeker schedule the appointment when it is best for the job seeker. The job seeker usually knows if morning or afternoon is best, so the interview should be scheduled accordingly. Detailed directions and parking information should be obtained ahead of time. A trial run of the facility at the time of day of the interview is helpful if the job seeker has never been there before. It is also a good idea to get a copy of the application form ahead of time so it can be completed. Also, the job seeker should bring extra copies of the resume to the interview. (2) A complete list of questions that can possibly be asked by the interviewer and questions that the job seeker should be ready to ask during the interview should be prepared. It is wise for the job seeker to practice answering these questions. A good test of the job seeker's readiness is to role-play the interview with a friend as the interviewer. (3) It is also wise to remember the interviewer is observing both the verbal and nonverbal communication skills of the job seeker. The interviewer will be observing speech, posture, eye contact, body language and enthusiasm. Practice enhances the likelihood of success, so it a good idea for the job seeker to rehearse until s/he is comfortable, confident and can spontaneously answer the practice questions. It is also wise to answer questions out loud in front of a mirror, relating everything the job seeker would like to tell the interviewer while watching facial expression and body language.

On the day of the interview, there are several items to take to the interview. A pen and paper can be used during the interview to take notes. The job seeker's planner or schedule should be taken to the interview to schedule a follow-up interview. It is also essential to be on time or, better yet, 10 to 15 minutes early. As a courtesy, the job seeker should sit when the interviewer does, not before, and should be sure to smile at everyone present, especially when offering a firm handshake.

The first 60 seconds are the most important part of the interview. This is when first impressions are made, so the job seeker needs to be alert and, from the start, put the best foot forward. The job seeker's communication style must meet that of the interviewer with responses kept brief—two minutes maximum—and to the point. Rushing to answer complex questions is discouraged. Asking for a few moments to organize a response before speaking is quite appropriate.

Researching the Organization

Any salesperson will verify the first step in making a sale is getting to know the customer. The same is true for the job seeker who wants to impress the interviewer. The job seeker needs to learn everything about the institution. Knowledge of various aspects of the institution should convince the interviewer that the job seeker is serious about the job and a career at the institution. So, before the interview, it is imperative the job seeker, who wants to work in a hospital setting, do some detective work and find the answers to the following questions:

- What is the registered bed capacity of the institution? What is the patient-to-staff ratio?
- What are the general characteristics of the patients who are admitted to the institution, e.g., age, gender, medical diagnosis, length of stay, method of payment?
- How do these general characteristics differ from patients who are admitted to competitive institutions in the immediate area?
- What is the average daily census? In the overall institution? In the unit that is of interest to the job seeker?
- Do community members (or former patients) view the institution's service as excellent or poor?
- What are the general opinions of the nurses who are currently employed about how staff members are treated at the institution?
- What skills are required to meet the requirements of the position?
- What is the typical salary range for the desired position in this hospital, and is it comparable to the salary of others in the same position in other hospitals?

- Are there career advancement possibilities, such as opportunities for continuing education and/or reimbursement for academic education?

The job seeker can find some of these answers from copies of the hospital's annual report, newsletters or any other materials available to the public that are easily accessible on the Web. The human relations department or personnel office may also provide brochures or other documents that can provide answers to these questions. The job seeker is also advised to contact an employee at the institution to learn about what really goes on. Further, the job seeker should be prepared to show how skills acquired in either the most current educational experience or previous jobs apply to the job at hand.

For the job seeker who is seeking a position in a school of nursing, there are specific questions that should be answered prior to the job interview. Examples of some of these questions follow:

- By whom and when were the institution and school of nursing accredited? When is the next accreditation period for the institution, as well as the nursing department?
- What are the general characteristics of the students who attend the school?
- What types of educational programs are offered in the entire institution?
- What are the various programs offered in the nursing department?
- Who are the educational competitors in the immediate community?
- What are the general components of the curriculum, i.e., mission statement, philosophy and conceptual framework of the nursing program, as well as the outcome competencies for the graduate of each nursing program?
- What courses are offered by each program of study in the school of nursing?
- What are the typical salary ranges for the desired position in other teaching institutions in the community?

Most of the answers to these questions for the job seeker who is interested in a position at an academic institution can be located in the college catalog. The catalog may be obtained by request from the Admissions

Office. Requests can also be made to obtain any brochures that describe the program to prospective students. It is also advised that the job seeker contact and interview faculty who are currently employed in the nursing school. A visit to the college's Web page is also an excellent place to obtain data about an academic institution.

Questions Frequently Asked During the Interview

It is important for the job seeker to prepare for the job interview by considering questions that may be asked, knowing how to respond to "illegal" questions that are not appropriate to ask, and preparing for questions that may be asked by the job seeker. Questions asked during an interview fall into one of three broad categories: closed, open and leading. The following questions for each of these categories are taken from various references, such as DeLuca (1997), King and Sheldon (1995), Krannich (1997), LeFevre (1992), and Messmer (1995). It is recommended the job seeker access these references to review suggested answers to the questions that follow.

Closed questions require a yes or no answer or one-word answer. Interviewers generally ask these questions to verify information on the resume or to set the stage for more probing questions. It is important to answer these questions directly and succinctly. Avoid lengthy answers. Wait until the interviewer makes further inquiry.

- Where did you go to school?
- How many years of experience do you have?
- How long did you work for . . .?
- How many patients/students/employees did you manage?
- Are you certified by any specialty? If so, who?

Open-ended questions require more than two or three words as a response. They give the job seeker an opportunity to elaborate on answers given to closed questions. It is important to frame answers to these questions that are relevant to the job that is sought. It is acceptable to ask the reviewer to narrow down the question somewhat if the question seems to be too broad to answer with a couple of words. For example, if an interviewer asks the job seeker to describe the last job, a counter response might be to say, "Is there a specific aspect of the job you would like to hear about?"

Examples of open questions related to educational background, work experience, career goals, personality and related concerns follow:

Education

- Describe your educational background.
- Why did you attend . . . college/university?
- Why did you major in . . .?
- What subjects did you enjoy the most? Least?
- If you could start over, what would you change about your education?

Work Experience

- Tell me about your last job.
- What was it like working for . . . hospital? School of nursing?
- Tell me about a time in which you had to handle an irate physician, co-worker, patient, student. How did you handle the situation and what were the results?
- What are your most important career accomplishments?
- Describe a typical day in your last job.
- Tell me about your previous bosses.
- Do you consider yourself a team player? How did the team function?
- What part of your last job did you enjoy the most? Least?
- What are your strengths? Weaknesses?
- How do you handle stress?
- Why did you leave your last job?

Career Goals

- Why did you become a nurse?
- What do you like best about being a nurse?
- What would you like to be doing in five years?
- How long would you stay if we were to offer you the position?
- Why should I hire you?
- Why do you want to make a career change?
- When would you be ready to begin work?
- What attracted you to our institution?
- What do you know about our hospital? School of nursing?
- What do you think you can bring to this institution?

Professional Activities and Other Concerns

- Tell me about yourself.
- What nursing organizations do you belong to?
- How do you remain current in your practice?
- What kind of recommendations will we receive from your references?
- What qualities do you admire in your co-workers? Supervisor?
- Describe a difficult decision you have made and the process you went through to reach that decision.
- How much initiative do you take?

Leading questions can be a minefield if the job seeker does not see them coming or is unable to recognize them. The interviewer who asks these types of questions may be trying to bait the job seeker a little—trying to get the job seeker to show something that the job seeker is trying to conceal. An example of this kind of question is: "I note you worked for hospital . . . That must have been a difficult place to work during the recent merger." If these kinds of questions are asked, the best thing to do is to refrain from being drawn into responses that will not help. Saying negative things about former employers could make the job seeker sound bitter—or worse, like someone who blames others for his or her own shortcomings. The best approach is to underplay the answer, as in, "It was difficult at times, but there were many positive aspects, also."

Illegal Questions

State and federal laws restrict employers from basing hiring decisions on age, gender, marital status, number of dependents, ancestry or race, as well as on many aspects of personal life, including religion and sexual orientation. Consider how the following questions could be answered:

- Are you married, divorced, separated or single?
- How old are you?
- Do you own a home or rent an apartment?
- Do you have any children?
- What does your spouse think about your career?
- Are you living with anyone?

It is wise not to become upset if one of these questions is asked by the interviewer. Some employers may ask questions just to see how the job seeker answers or reacts under stress. In some situations where there may be several individuals interviewing the job seeker, some of them may be ignorant of the law. It is best to briefly reply, remembering there is no obligation to answer questions protected by law.

The format of an interview may be an "encounter behavior" based interview. The statements included in this type of interview may be phrased as follows:

- Give me an example of a time when you . . .
- Give me an example of how . . .
- Tell me about how you . . .

Many references include these questions, as well as suggested answers for the job seeker to consider and practice prior to the actual interview. Bolles (2003) offers five basic questions that summarize the dozens and dozens of possible questions employers can ask the job seeker. These are:

- Why are you here?
- What can you do for us?
- What kind of person are you?
- What distinguishes you from 19 other people who have the same abilities as you do?
- Can I afford you?

Summary of the Interview

At the end of the interview, the interviewer usually offers general and specific information about the job and the institution. It is expected the job seeker will have some questions at this point. If the job seeker does not ask questions, the interviewer may get the impression the job seeker has received enough information about a most important career opportunity. Therefore, it is important for the job seeker to be prepared at each interview to have at least two or three questions during this part of the interview. Examples of the kind of questions to ask employers at some point are:

- What are the current major goals of the organization?
- What are the greatest strengths of this institution?
- What are the major duties and responsibilities of the job?
- What is the ideal type of person for this position?
- What would be my primary challenges if I were selected for this position?
- What type of people have been in this position previously?

- What is your timeline in filling this vacancy?
- Whom would I be working for in this position?
- How long is orientation, and what does it involve?
- How will I be evaluated?
- Are promotions and raises tied to performance criteria?
- How often are performance reviews conducted, and what is the process?
- What is the normal salary range for such a position?
- What is particularly unique about working for this organization?
- Could you describe the typical career path for this position?
- What does the future look like for this organization?

Just as Bolles (2003) recommended five questions the interviewer is interested in learning more about from the job seeker, there are five questions the job seeker could think about during the interview. These are:

- What does this job involve?
- Do my skills truly match this job?
- Are these the kind of people I would like to work with?
- If we like each other and both want to work together, can I persuade them there is something unique about me that makes me different from 19 other people who can do the same tasks?
- Can I persuade them to hire me at the salary I need or want?

Salary Negotiation

Salary should not be discussed until the end of the interviewing process when the offer of a position has been made. The job seeker wants the interviewer to be the first to mention a figure, if that is possible. If the interviewer asks the job seeker what they want for a salary, the job seeker needs to answer something similar to this: "Since the position was created by the institution, there must be a figure in mind, and I'd be interested in knowing what that is."

According to Cardillo (1997), the job seeker should be prepared ahead of time with a ballpark salary figure that is desired, based on knowledge of the institution's level of appointment and the accompanying salary scale. Benefits should be added to the salary, since they are a significant portion of the total compensation package. When offered an amount that is considerably less than the job seeker had hoped for, the job seeker might say after a slight pause, "I was hoping you would come in closer to (whatever amount the job seeker is hoping for or a littler higher), based on the level of responsibility and skill required to do the job." Remember, the job seeker can always come down with salary requests, but they cannot go up. With practice and development of assertive negotiating skills, the job seeker will become more comfortable with salary negotiation.

After the Interview—Thank You Letters

Every person the job seeker meets and talks to during a job interview should receive a note of thanks. This is best done immediately after the interview. It is advised the thank you note be written the same evening of the interview and mailed at the latest by the next morning.

The letter should contain information that lets the interviewer know the job seeker listened carefully, is aware of the institution's needs, and is prepared to offer a significant contribution to the organization. It is advised the letter include something specific about the way the job seeker was treated during the interview process or something said during the interview.

The letter should also mention anything the job seeker may have forgotten during the interview. It is important to emphasize points the job seeker wants the interviewer to remember and reiterate interest in speaking with him or her again.

Sharpening Job Interview Skills

Rather than make each interview a time to improve basic interviewing skills, it is important for the job seeker to practice the interview before the first interview opportunity. The first skill to acquire is the ability to listen. By the time nurses have graduated from nursing school and perhaps have held several positions, the skill of listening would seem second nature. Listening is not the primary skill . . . it is the ability to pay attention to, understand and thoroughly absorb what the other person is saying without misinterpreting, jumping to conclusions or allowing emotional responses to cloud the objectivity (Messmer, 1995). It is recommended the job seeker take many opportunities to practice listening skills prior to any interview session. Messmer (1995) recommends the job seeker videotape a show or newscast—anything with a good deal of dialogue. After taping the incident, the job seeker should then replay a section of the show without taking notes. After turning off the tape, the job seeker should write down (verbatim as much as possible) what one person said. A replay of the tape

January 16, 2003

Mrs. Janet Taylor
Manager, Telemetry Unit
MidWestern Medical Center
101 S. 42nd St.
Indianapolis, IN 43225

Dear Mrs. Taylor:

Thank you so much for taking the time to talk with me today about the staff nurse position on the Telemetry Unit at MidWestern Medical Center. I found our conversation to be very interesting and stimulating, especially the information you shared about the pilot program for mentoring new graduates that will be taking place on the Telemetry Unit. It was exciting to know there are institutions that are interested in assisting the new graduate make the transition from student to the first professional position. The experience of being a new graduate with an assigned mentor for the first six months of my "new" professional role should provide me with valuable experience that I can then share with new graduates in the future as their mentor.

It was a pleasure meeting with you today, and I look forward to hearing from you early next week to further discuss the staff nurse position.

Sincerely,

Jennifer L. Jackson
515 Robin Lane Drive
Indianapolis, IN 47651

Figure 22.5 *Sample Thank You Letter*

to verify how close the job seeker was able to recreate the conversation should be done next. This exercise should be repeated until the recall of conservations is close to the actual one.

The objective in this exercise is for the job seeker to listen carefully during an interview rather than primarily concentrating on getting information across to the interviewer. A pitfall to avoid in this situation is to only listen to the questions being asked. It is expected the job seeker will occasionally ask for clarification of any question in order to know exactly what the interviewer is trying to find out.

Most interviewers ask many of the same questions. So there is no excuse for not being prepared to answer the vast majority of questions the job seeker is likely to be asked. The job seeker should practice responses to these questions and still avoid sounding as though the answers have been memorized. The job seeker should have in mind the key points to get across when answering each question.

Ryan (2000) believes most questions only need a 60-second sell. During this 60-second time period, the job seeker should think of a 5-point agenda for each question. In order to accomplish this task, the job seeker needs to practice each of the "common questions" several times. It is advised the job seeker practice responses to these frequently asked questions with a peer who can provide honest feedback. These practice sessions should create confidence when the job seeker is actually being asked these questions during the interview session.

It is also recommended the job seeker tape these practice sessions, so when the sessions are played back, the peer and job seeker can evaluate them. The practice sessions should be as "real world" as possible, that is, the interviewer should sit across from the job seeker and have a list of questions. The job seeker should answer the questions as they would in the real interview. If the practice session is videotaped, both the peer and job seeker can assess the tape using a prepared evaluation form. It is recommended the form contain a Likert 5-point scale so both reviewers can critically assess the job seeker's posture, eye contact, pacing of the answers, emphasis and tone, distracting mannerisms, and quality of answers to the questions.

Dress for the Interview

Everything in this chapter has emphasized the importance of preparation, i.e., an impressive resume and cover letter and a successful interview. However, the appearance of the job seeker is also an important aspect of the interview process. In addition, the theme throughout this chapter, "first impressions matter," is equally important for the job seeker to remember when planning the wardrobe and hair style for the job interview. Before the job seeker has the chance to speak, the interviewer will notice how s/he is dressed. The interviewer may draw immediate conclusions about the individual's competence and personality based on appearance.

There are certain "rules of the game" when preparing to dress for an interview. This does not mean incompetent individuals get the job simply because they have dressed appropriately. Rather, it means qualified and competent job applicants can gain an extra edge over other qualified competent job applicants. The important part is to realize it is important to convey positive professional images.

A business suit is appropriate attire for both men and women job seekers. If a woman is not comfortable wearing a skirt that matches the jacket, it is appropriate to wear matching pants. It is important to choose a shade that enhances the job seeker's appearance. If the right color is not known, it is helpful to seek the advice of a colleague or a dress consultant. The style of the suit should be classic, well-tailored and well-styled. A conservative suit that has a timeless classic styling and also looks up-to-date will serve the job seeker not only for the interview, but it can be worn for years after the position is secured.

CONCLUSION

A significant amount of preparation is necessary to obtain a professional nursing position. The job seeker needs to begin this preparation well in advance of the actual job interview. The preparation begins with the development of a resume and cover letter that are organized and well-written. Once a job interview is scheduled, the job seeker needs to practice interviewing skills using a variety of methods.

After these preparations are completed, the job seeker needs to strategize ways to demonstrate evidence of seriousness of purpose and respect for the person who is doing the interviewing. After the interview has taken place, a meaningful thank you letter should be sent to everyone who was present at the interview. This chapter provides considerable information about how the job seeker can begin plans for these important functions. More specific details can be obtained from textbooks and the Internet. Job seekers should consult both and consider consulting colleagues, who are usually very helpful when a new job is being pursued.

REFERENCES

Block, J.A., & Betrus, M. (1999). *101 best cover letters*. New York, NY: McGraw-Hill.

Bolles, R.N. (2003). *What color is your parachute? A practical manual for job-hunters and career-changers* (2003 ed.). Berkeley, CA: Ten Speed Press.

Cardillo, D. (1997). *How to negotiate the salary you want! Nursing Spectrum student career fitness tool kit*. Hoffman Estates, IL: Nursing Spectrum.

DeLuca, M.J. (1997). *Best answers to the 201 most frequently asked interview questions*. New York: McGraw-Hill.

Ireland, S. (2000). *The complete idiot's guide to the perfect resume* (2nd ed.). Indianapolis, IN: Alpha Books.

Kennedy, J.L., & Morrow, T.J. (1995). *Electronic resume revolution: Creating a winning resume for the new world of job seeking* (2nd ed.). New York: John Wiley.

King, J.A., & Sheldon, B. (1996). *The smart woman's guide to resumes and job hunting*. Philadelphia, PA: Chelsea House.

Krannich, R.L. (1997). *Change your job, change your life: High impact strategies for finding great jobs into the 21st century* (6th ed.). Manassas Park, VA: Impact Publications.

Krannich, R.L., & Krannich, C.R. (1994*). Dynamite cover letters and other great job search letters! (*2nd ed.). Manassas Park, VA: Impact Publications.

LeFevre, J.L. (1992*). How you really get hired* (3rd ed.). New York, NY: Macmillian.

Messmer, M. (1995). *Job hunting for dummies*. Foster City, CA: IDG Books Worldwide.

Oxford University Press (1996). *The Oxford Dictionary and Thesaurus*. (p. 1287). New York: NY: Author.

Restifo, V. (1997). *Interviewing for career advancement. Nursing Spectrum student career fitness tool kit*. Hoffman Estates, IL: Nursing Spectrum.

Ryan, R. (2003a). *Winning cover letters* (2nd ed.). Hoboken, NJ: John Wiley.

Ryan, R. (2003b). *Winning resumes* (2nd ed.). Hoboken, NJ: John Wiley.

Ryan, R. (2000). *60 seconds & your're hired!* New York: Penguin Books.

Yate, M. (2003). *Resumes that knock 'em dead* (5th ed). Avon, MA: Adams Media Corporation.

Zurlinden, J. (2002). *Improving your resume's appearance. Nursing Spectrum student career fitness tool kit.* Hoffman Estates, IL: Nursing Spectrum.

Chapter 23

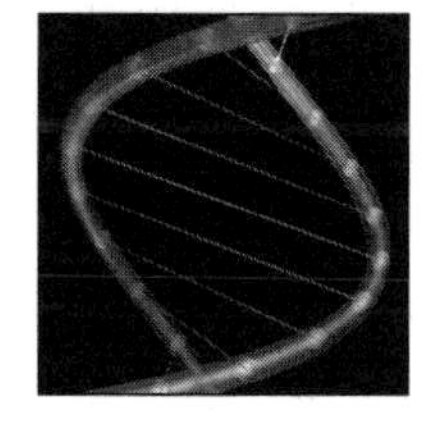

Building Support and Establishing Networks: Referrals and References

by Fay L. Bower

Few careers in life offer the rewards, stimulation and diverse opportunities of nursing. But sometimes we stumble over the pebbles in our path and momemtarily lose sight of these benefits (Klunder, 2002).

INTRODUCTION

Locating a position that is satisfying and leads to other opportunities can be a daunting task. Some people just don't know how to start. Others continue to locate and leave jobs because they did not do their homework about the positions before they accepted them or ask for help from a mentor or support person. And while there is no foolproof method for finding the perfect position, there are ways to pursue the search that result in satisfaction and future opportunities.

An important and useful way to pursue the search is to look to the people who have been helpful in the past when a daunting task was faced. This means there needs to be supportive people or linkages to those who can help when a need arises, such as trying to find the perfect position. According to Gruber-May (1997), networking is a critical component for any nurse's success in today's turbulent times. Once seen as a skill reserved for nurse executives, networking and support from people who care must now be developed by nurses at all levels. Ward, Embrey, Lowndes and Vernon (2002) have described how a group dedicated to meeting the networking needs of nurses evolved and how this group collaborated and developed an interactive network that significantly affected the clinical practice and work-related stress of its members. Thus, support groups alone or as a part of networks are an excellent way to seek help when one is searching for a new position or a change in work life.

Even though the value of networking is known, according to an April 2001 *Office Team Survey* (Cohen, 2000), 85% of workers polled said the emphasis on networking has increased in the last five years, and close to half said they felt only somewhat comfortable with the activity (http://www.jobspectrum.org/job workroom.html). Clearly, there is a need for more information about the value and use of support groups and networking and how they benefit the worker.

The remainder of this chapter is devoted to discussions about support groups and networks and how they are used to obtain referrals and references. Chapter 24, which follows, provides an in-depth discussion of the mentoring role, where other aspects of support and networking are developed.

SUPPORT GROUPS

The literature abounds with studies about and examples of how support groups have helped a variety of people. There are support groups for alcoholics, new mothers, people with mental illness, breast cancer victims, HIV/AIDS patients, parents with troubled children, etc.; there are also church support groups and professional organizations that act as a support when the need is consistent with the organization's goals. Support is not a new idea, and the process is not foreign to nurses; however, it may be a new idea when developing and managing a career. What makes it a new idea is not the process but the purpose of the support. In the instances cited above, the purpose of the support group is to help the individual adjust to a new role, a health problem or a new experience. In the context of this book, the support group, like those discussed, is a source for help, but it also provides access to those who can provide the information needed or to the people of influence who can open needed avenues or links to opportunities.

Support is also available from individuals and usually starts early in one's career. Many nurses establish support while in school. Others establish support in the first position from a more experienced nurse. Sometimes, this support lasts a lifetime, in other instances a different support person is selected as the career changes. Many times, the support person is one's mentor. However, support can be provided by anyone who knows and believes in the individual and is willing to provide help when asked.

A unique aspect of support is that some people ignore the need to enlist someone to be the support person. Like a mentor, support people are often very busy and don't have time to reach out. However, they are usually very ready to say "yes" when asked for help. The point is, if support is needed, asking for it may be necessary.

An important aspect of support is the ability to reciprocate. Those who want support must be willing to provide it when others are in need. While this may sound obvious, there are people who literally "drain" others; asking for help, needing validation and wanting others to assume their burdens. These kinds of individuals should seek professional support, for they are not going to find help for career development unless they are willing and able to be supportive to others.

Further, supportive people do not need to understand every aspect of the job search, but they should be able to provide advice about approach, dress, composure and how to reach those who can provide the professional linkages. The most important role of the supporter is to be a "sounding board" by listening and helping the job seeker think things through. For instance, the supporter could ask questions like these to help the job seeker think things through:

- Why are you seeking a new position?
- What do you know about the position you are pursuing?
- Who could help you learn more about the organization that you are interested in joining?
- Will the requirements of the position match your talents?
- What are the possibilities for advancement in the position you are considering?
- How will this position fit into your personal life?
- What does this position offer that your last one didn't offer?
- What are the advantages/disadvantages of this position?

The supporter can thus help the person consider all aspects before making a decision. Some supportive people might even go as far as making recommendations. That aspect of the relationship probably depends on the nature of the relationship, as some people would be uncomfortable providing a recommendation, while others would feel compelled to do so.

Networks

According to Girvin (1999), "Your career is in your hands—but others are often willing to lend a hand" (p. 14). She goes on to state, "Formal networking approaches should be prepared for meticulously. . . . If you waste your contact's time waffling around a subject, you may find that person is not willing to talk with you another time" (p. 15). This good advice by Girvin suggests the person seeking a career change must reach out to those who can help and be prepared to let them know specifically what is needed.

Networking is a process of creating a select group of individuals who can supply information and offer contacts or opportunities in order to reach the best outcomes for the person seeking help (Bower, 2000). The closest thing to knowing something is to know where to find it. Boer (n.d.) claims there are three kinds of networks: personal networks, social networks and professional networks.

Personal Networks

Personal networks are composed of like-minded friends whose eyes light up when they see you. They are the people who make you feel good or recharged. They love you and want to make you happy. Making time for your personal network is absolutely essential for motivation.

Social Networks

Social networks are networks of acquaintances you see less often. They are people you have fun with and see at parties or who enjoy similar hobbies, such as exercising, hiking, biking or going to the movies. Social networks play an important and unique role for the person seeking a career. They are the friends who are there to listen and provide feedback and support. They can also suggest and refer.

While a social network is not the usual source for linking to a job, it is often where the job seeker learns about opportunities. Many people develop social networks with those they work with. These people often know about what is available in the work world that might fit the career seeker's interests. In casual meetings and while having fun together, the career seeker may learn about an opportunity from those in the social network. Follow through via the professional network would be the next step, as those linkages are more likely to produce the kind of information needed when seeking a job change or new work experiences.

Professional Networks

Professional networks are groups of people you see more often than social acquaintances. You see them at alumni gatherings, professional meetings or in the workplace. Professional networks also include former co-workers, bosses, academic advisors, professors and memberships in business clubs, such as the Rotary Club, Kiwanis Club or any of the many nursing organizations (Boer, n.d.).

For career development, the professional network is probably the best resource. After learning about an opportunity from a friend or a work buddy, the best approach is to contact a member of the professional network who is the best source for accurate and up-to-date referral. For the development of a career, it is best to seek help from a professional network because it is these people who understand the rapidly changing healthcare scene.

Characteristics of Networks

Developing a network involves two people (and later more) in the establishment of a relationship because of mutual interest and trust. Networks can span a geographical or special interest area or be personally focused. They can also be age-related. Networks usually begin in school or the workplace as a helping relationship. However, networks have begun at workshops, conferences and other professional functions where individuals discovered they had something in common. Networks have even been established by people who have read about someone and called that person to talk. Over time, the relationship matures and, as trust develops, so does the network.

Clearly, those who have lived longer have a more complete picture of healthcare and its many changes. Conversely, those who are younger are free of the constraints older nurses may feel and can provide a vision free of "how it has always been done." Both perspectives are important because they provide a more complete view of any situation and should be included in the network composition.

Currency is another aspect of networking that is important. Knowing whether the informants are up-to-date on issues and thus are current could mean the difference between getting good information that broadens one's perspective and creates a proactive position or being stuck with data that are out-of-date and useless. This means the person seeking help from the network must be aware of the informant's activities, have a relationship that has been sustained over time, and have trust in the information received.

The people in the network must also be accessible. With e-mail, it is easy to locate people but "locating" is only half the task. How the question is posed and what the request is about are also important. Most networks function as a resource: The network provides people who can open doors, provide advice and locate others. Sometimes, the person you "network" with becomes a mentor, which is a relationship of far greater depth. In fact, many people find a mentor through the network; however, it is important not to mix the concepts, or one may become disappointed in the results.

Clearly, there is value to establishing a network, even though it is time-consuming and sometimes a complicated activity. According to Calano and Salzman (1988), the establishment of a network is worth the effort because it:

- Forces a broadening of perspectives
- Focuses on those who have the greatest potential for helping
- Highlights those in positions of authority who can offer assistance
- Fosters proactive behavior

Strategies for Developing Support Groups and Networks

Lesson 1. According to RoAne (1993), networking begins with capturing confidence. She points out that it is necessary to take the time to assess who we are, what we have done and what we know so we have an accurate picture of ourselves, because networking is a reciprocal process, an exchange of ideas, leads and suggestions. "Networking works for those who appreciate the path and process as well as the destination" (p. 11).

Lesson 2. The importance of a network and the ability to "schmooze" (Cohen, 2000) have led many to successful positions. Surveys have found the most successful way to find a new job or to make a business contact is in a casual setting—a cocktail party, dinner, post-conference mixer, etc. Being comfortable in those settings is important, or valuable career opportunities may be missed.

Lesson 3. Once in a setting that offers potential supporters, it is important to know how to introduce yourself. RoAne (1993) suggests a seven-to-nine-second introduction that pertains to the event is a good way to open the conversation.

Lesson 4. The next step is to scan the room and get a sense of who is there. Get familiar with the group before taking the next difficult step, breaking into the group. At this time, the usual convention of don't interrupt must be stretched. Try to pick up the thread of the conversation and add an inviting one or two comments. Follow up with an introduction of yourself and a compliment to one of the participants regarding his or her point of view, and before you know it, you are part of the conversation.

Lesson 5. While being a good conversationalist is important, being a good listener is equally important. Remembering something that was said can be used in a follow-up e-mail to keep the contact alive. For example, "Hi Dr. Smith, it was great talking with you last night at the conference. We should get together soon and continue that discussion. I find your perspective very interesting and would like to know more."

Lesson 6. According to Cohen (2000), Kate Koziel, president of K Squared Communications, a marketing and public relations firm based in Chicago, suggests wearing bright, attractive clothes is important because they are remembered, and thus you are remembered. Of course, the costume (dress and slacks) must be attractive and not bizarre, or else the memory of it may become a deterrent to a continuing relationship.

Lesson 7. Follow up, follow up, follow up. However, do not communicate with a fax message, for they are easy to discard, and a phone call usually ends up as voice mail, which is just as easy to discard. E-mails work the best. A short, concise e-mail is the best way to initially follow up. It is easy to respond to and helps give a sense of your interest. Of course, nothing replaces a lunch or dinner meeting to get better acquainted. Whatever method is used, be sure to remind the person of the original message so the importance of it is underscored.

Lesson 8. A network is not something you can establish overnight; it is the result of decades of work. Cohen (2000) claims if you haven't a network of supporters by the time you are 40, you are in trouble. Look around you, you no doubt have a cadre of supporters—school friends, work colleagues, teachers, clergy, etc. If they are not still an integral part of you life, call them and re-establish the relationship.

The lessons outlined above are just one way to begin a network. There are many others. An address book, collected business cards, the professional literature, a Christmas card list and a computer address book are excellent sources for the names of people who can become part of a support system and ultimately the network. Take the time to call, write or e-mail them. In no time at all, a network will be established. And it is always important to keep expanding the network with new people, especially as the job market changes and your interests and talents expand (Hansen, 2003).

Sustaining the Supporters and the Network

Establishing the network is only half of the process. Keeping it alive and useful is also important. Gruber-May (1997) offers 11 guidelines for keeping the supporters and networks functioning and available when needed.

1. Stay in touch. Do not overuse individuals in your network. Call if time lapses and there is no message from them.
2. Establish the relationship first; do business next. Members of your network are your allies. Do not misuse them.
3. Offer help to others. After you offer help, follow through. Give of yourself generously and often to the members of your network.
4. Follow up on all referrals. Report back and update the person who provided the referral.
5. Do not ask a favor that will make your network members uncomfortable. Do not put a person in the position of saying no.
6. Share information with your network, but use good judgment. Sharing critical business information is important, but be careful not to become labeled a "gossiper."
7. Technology has made the world a very small place. Do not burn bridges. Mean-spirited remarks and pettiness ruin one's reputation.
8. Avoid personal or private questions that make a person uncomfortable. Do not relate to someone in an interrogation manner. Ask open-ended questions and share in the conversation.
9. Return calls personally and in a *timely* manner. Do not ignore others, or they may not be there when needed.
10. Know when to use a personal touch. Send a handwritten thank you note, flowers or a small gift.
11. Give credit where credit is due. Put praise in writing. Make sure appreciation reaches not only the individual but also the supervisor/boss (p. 29).

One of the greatest values of a support person/group and a network is the way they can provide referrals and references once the individual has determined what direction to take. Frequently, as a career changes, so does the need for a referral and ultimately a reference.

REFERRALS AND REFERENCES

Referrals

There are two kinds of referrals: Those provided to the person seeking a new position and those provided to the employer looking for a new employee. Frequently, the person looking for a new position will want to know something about the position and the organization that is searching for someone new. Conversely, employers often get "good leads" regarding people they should consider for an open position. In the first instance, the person looking for a position may want more information than an ad can provide. This is when the network comes into play. There may be someone in the network who can provide information not usually available; someone who has inside experience who can determine if there would be a "good fit." When the employer seeks a referral, there may be someone in the network who knows about a position and refers a member of the network as a good candidate.

In addition, there are two kinds of referral formats. There are verbal and written referrals. Verbal referrals are informal and usually are provided "on the spot" without a lot of homework or investigation. The topic comes up between two people, and the conversation leads to a discussion that leads to a referral, i.e., "Joe is looking for a position. I think he would be an excellent choice for the position you are trying to fill." Or "Before you consider that job, I suggest you look into this one. It includes a better benefit package, and your chances for advancement are considerably better." Sometimes, the referral will be a phone call. Head hunters often use a phone call when trying to locate viable candidates.

Written referrals, on the other hand, are usually requested and are much more formal. People asking for written referrals want a great deal of information so they can determine if the person would fit into the organization and bring to it the talent needed. Sometimes, written referrals are addressed to an agency and request the CEO, COO or other managers to refer several people in the hopes that one of them will match the requirements for the position.

Whether the referral is for the individual seeking a position or for the employer searching for a new employee, there are certain criteria to consider. When asked to provide a referral, the following questions should be considered:

- What are the mission and goals of the organization?
- What is the nature of the position?
- What type of qualifications does the person need to be successful in the position?
- What does the benefit package include?
- What kind of work history should the applicant demonstrate?
- What are the opportunities for advancement?

Regardless of the kind of referral, once the position is pursued, a letter of reference will be needed. Unlike a referral, the letter of reference is a formal document that outlines many aspects of the candidate's work life and potential.

References

Most employers want reference letters to accompany the application for a position. In order to get the best reference letter, there are at least three things to consider: the qualifications of the writer, what the letter should say and how it should look. A good reference letter ought to be provided by a reputable individual who knows enough about the person to prepare a useful reference. It should also be on paper that includes the letterhead of the firm where the writer works and be copied to the person asking for the reference. Most organizations give the person applying for the position the option to see the letter or to not see it. However, unless the letter is not a good one, it is best to give a copy to the person who has asked for it. Better yet, it is not a good idea to write a reference letter for someone if positive things cannot be said. A good reference letter should contain something about the following:

1. The characteristics of the applicant. Is the person responsible, motivated, self-directed, etc.?
2. The ways the applicant works with other people. Is s/he a team player?
3. The person's communication style. Is the person able to clearly articulate a position? Write a coherent document?
4. The person's leadership style. Is the person able to "take the lead"? What is the person's leadership style? Authoritarian, participatory, laissez faire?
5. The person's strategies for handling conflict.
6. Special talents the person brings to the position.

Many organizations provide a reference form where the characteristics they are looking for are spelled out and a Likert scale provided for the referrer to complete. It is essential the person filling out the form be careful and note whether 1 is a high score or whether 5 is a high score. An error at this point could be fatal for the applicant.

Please complete this form by circling the appropriate number Please note the scale ranges from 5 – 0, with 5 being the highest mark. Please also provide comments in the space provided. The applicant whose name is on the accompanying release document has requested a reference from you. Please complete the form and sign it where indicated.

Thank You

IS DILIGENT	1	2	3	4	5
IS A CRITICAL THINKER	1	2	3	4	5
IS HONEST	1	2	3	4	5
SHOWS COMPASSION	1	2	3	4	5
IS COMMITTED TO THE JOB	1	2	3	4	5
COMMUNICATES EFFECTIVELY	1	2	3	4	5
IS EMOTIONALLY STABLE	1	2	3	4	5
HAS KNOWLEDGE OF THE FIELD	1	2	3	4	5
IS INNOVATIVE	1	2	3	4	5
DEMONSTRATES LEADERSHIP SKILLS	1	2	3	4	5
IS SELF-DIRECTED	1	2	3	4	5
COMPLIES WITH AGENCY RULES	1	2	3	4	5

In your own words, using the back of this form or an additional sheet, give a general assessment of the individual's strengths.

____

____

____________________ ____________________

Signature of the Respondent Date

Figure 23.1 *Sample Reference Form*

Many reference forms also provide an area for comments. It is best to put something in that comment space, because what is stated there could be what tips the decision in favor of the applicant. It is also very important the document be signed and a copy saved for the files.

Frequently, the employer asks for more than one reference. When this happens, it is important the individual seeking the position ask a variety of people for a reference. As a rule, it is NOT a good idea to ask a family member or a close colleague to write a reference letter. Their opinions are considered biased and thus less objective and not a valid view of the applicant's abilities. Letters from supervisors, managers, faculty, pastors/ priests, or anyone who knows about the job seeker's performance and can provide an authoritative comment are good sources for reference letters. They must also know something about the position being sought. Brochures and booklets about the agency, the job description and any information about the internal workings of the agency are good data for the writer to use when preparing the reference letter. It is the responsibility of the job seeker to provide these data to the person preparing the reference.

Reference Letter and the Recommendation Letter

Even though the reference letter is often used as a recommendation, they are not the same thing. The purpose of the reference letter is to provide the employer with information about the job seeker from someone the employer trusts; it is a written testimony supporting the applicant for employment. The writer often does make a recommendation; however, that is not the main reason for writing the letter. There are letters written that are purely letters of recommendation. Such letters suggest the applicant is "a fit" for a particular position and do not usually have the depth of information a reference letter would have, such as the applicant's ability to function in a particular role given the institution's particular needs.

SUMMARY

The quality of referrals and reference letters is all based on how well the support groups/individuals and networks are selected and sustained, since most letters are solicited from members of both. Thus, locating the

Mr. Bob Smith, Executive Director
Mt. Shasta Community Hospital
2340 Random Street, Suite #100
Redding, CA 95662

Dear Mr. Smith:

I have been asked by Lori Brown for a letter of recommendation, which I am pleased to provide because she is an outstanding nurse. I have known her for four years, and during that time I was her supervisor.

Lori is a conscientious self-directed person who always completes her assignments on time. She gets along well with her colleagues and is a team player. She can also assume a leadership position when it is needed. One of her most valuable traits is her ability to listen and reflect before making a move or saying anything. This thoughtful and careful approach has been beneficial for her and others on many occasions. She is very effective communicator.

A review of her work assignments also indicates she has been assigned some very difficult tasks and has completed them in a timely way and with few resources. Further, she is usually the first to offer to take a difficult assignment and can be counted on to do a stellar job.

Lori is particularly good at handling conflict in that she can stay calm, listens carefully and helps sort out the issues. She also is able to stay neutral while helping others hear the different positions. During labor negotiations, she was very helpful.

Knowing what I do about your organization, I believe Lori would bring to the operation some very valuable skills. Besides being a highly qualified nurse, she has other skills that would make her an important part of the management team. She can delegate appropriately, follows up on the delegation, and is always ready and able to support and provide help when necessary. I highly recommend Lori for the position of unit manager.

If you have any questions, please feel free to call me at 510-555-2000, Ext. #333.

Sincerely,

Nancy Torland, Assistant Chief Nurse Executive
Moorland Hospital
Turlock, CA 94566

Figure 23.2 *Sample Letter of Recommendation*

right people as supporters and members of the network is critical. Remember, "For what I lack in 'know how,' I more than make up for in who I know!" RoAne (1993, p. 25).

REFERENCES

Anders, R.I. (2000). Making the transition to the perioperative clinical educator role. *Perioperative Nursing, 9*(2), 53-56.

Boer, P. (n.d.). Advancing your career: Motivation, mentors, networks. Retrieved September 20, 2002, from http://content.monster.com/career/networking/advance_career/.

Bower, F.L. (2000). *Taking the lead: Personal qualities of effective leadership*. Philadelphia, PA: Saunders.

Calano, J., & Salzman, J. (1988). *Career tracking. The 26 success shortcuts to the top.* New York, NY: Simon & Shuster.

Cohen, S. (2000). *The rules of engagement: How to work a room*. Retrieved September 28, 2002, from http://www.jobspectrum.org/job_workroom.html.

Girvin, J. (1999). Networking for career planning. *NT Learn Curve, 2*(11), 14-15.

Gruber-May, J. (1997). Networking for nurses in today's turbulent times. *Orthopedic Nursing, 16*(2), 25-29.

Hansen, R.S. (2003). Networking your way to a new job. Retrieved March 7, 2003, from http://www.quintessentialcareers.com.

Klunder, V. (2002). Words of wisdom. *Opportunities to care: The Pfizer guide to careers in Nursing.* New York, NY: Pfizer.

RoAne, S. (1993). *The secrets of savvy networking: How to make the best connections for business and personal success*. New York, NY: Warner Books.

Ward, N., Embrey, N., Lowndes, C., & Vernon, K. (2002). Specialist nurse network improves MS practice. *Nursing Times, 98*(30), 34-36.

Chapter 24

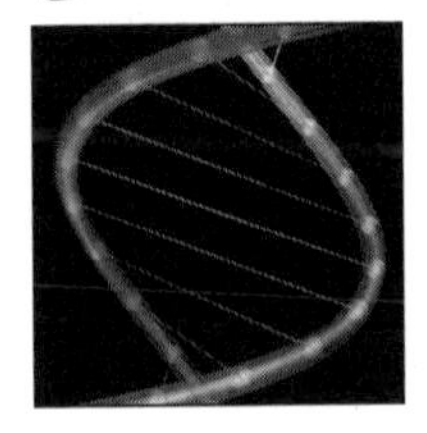

Mentoring

by Fay L. Bower

I'm in my fourth class, Advanced Nursing Roles and Concepts, and my class presentation is on the topic: power and leadership in nursing. I have been reading and researching like crazy and thought on a whim to drop you a line (found you on the Internet). While reading about a lot of great nurse educators, researchers, and theorists, I was overwhelmed with a sense of your mentorship/stewardship while I was a student. You were a huge part of the inspiration for me returning to school (Anonymous).

The above statement is what all mentors want to receive as validation that their efforts have made a difference in someone's life, especially when such a message comes "out of the blue" from someone you knew over 20 years ago. This statement also suggests that mentor relationships are more powerful than we understand and more lasting than we usually expect.

Definitions of Mentoring

Mentoring can be defined in many ways. The professional literature offers many similar but unique explanations of the purpose, composition and outcomes of mentoring.

Some authors view mentoring as a two-way exchange. According to Vance and Olson (1998), mentoring is a developmental, empowering and nurturing relationship that extends over time and in which mutual sharing, learning and growth occur in an atmosphere of respect, collegiality and affirmation. Gehrke (1988) believes the mentoring relationship can even be viewed as a gift-exchange. Whittaker and Cartwright (2000) suggest mentoring is a transforming experience. Barton (2001), former mentoring manager for Hewlett-Packard, reinforces the dictum that who you know is as important as what you know. She believes mentoring and networking go hand in hand for successful career advancement.

Other authors believe mentors have specific characteristics that allow them to facilitate the development of others. According to Taylor (1992), a mentor is someone who takes a personal interest in assisting another to develop the knowledge and skills needed to meet specific career goals. Williams and Blackburn (1988) believe the best way to mentor someone is to follow the tutorial model, whereby the selection of the protégé is specific, and the relationship is close and supervised. Bower (2000) suggests the mentor helps the novice become an expert by being a role model and facilitator of career development.

Hockenberry-Eaton and Kline (1995) believe an effective mentoring relationship must include a mentor who (1) is a leader, (2) has patience, (3) is caring and (4) is loyal. All authors who have written about mentoring agree there is a need for a trusting relationship in which there are positive outcomes for all involved. However, there are variations in the literature about the role of the mentor. Taylor (1992) believes the mentor is a teacher, coach, role model or confidant. Bower (2000) believes mentors are also consultants and referral agents who open doors of opportunity and help establish networks for the protégé. Kanter (1977), Levinson (1977) and Moore (1982) believe the major role of the mentor is to supervise the career development of the protégé. A close look at what occurs between mentors and their protégés suggests all of these roles are in operation at some time or other during the mentoring relationship. Valerie Restifo (2002) nicely sums up the characteristics of the mentor when she states "Mentors are smart people who choose to mentor other people who are hardworking, articulate, goal-driven, and professional" (p. 62). She outlines what to look for in a good mentor:

- Positive attitude and outlook
- Caring approach toward others
- Savvy insider, seasoned veteran and experienced practitioner (professional)

- Compatible, personal chemistry
- Model employee, exemplary professional
- Good communicator, especially listener
- Someone you trust, respect and admire
- Likes learning, loves people
- Experience as a protégé

Because mentoring occurs in many ways and with individuals of all ages, it is a very popular way for new professionals to learn their roles and to advance their careers. It is also an excellent way for seasoned professionals to make career changes. Whether the mentoring is beneficial for all involved or only for the protégé, most mentoring relationships develop and progress in a similar fashion. Presented below is a discussion of a model for a mentorship relationship regardless of purpose, composition or member characteristics.

Model for a Mentoring Relationship

Many models have been proposed for the mentoring relationship. Lee (1988) has proposed a four-phase process of initiation, cultivation, separation and transition. Zachary (2000) has proposed a four-phase cycle that includes preparing, negotiating, enabling and closing. Dortch and Joyner (2000) believe mentoring is a five-stage process and Parsloe and Wray (2000) offer "Seven Gold Rules of Simplicity" as a framework for mentoring. In this text, mentoring will follow the model offered by Bower (2000), which includes three phases:

- Introduction phase
- Goal-setting phase
- Working phase

Introduction Phase

During the introduction phase, two or more individuals come together to develop a relationship. Sometimes, this relationship is between a teacher and a student, or a worker and the supervisor, or an admirer and the one being admired. Note there is usually a difference between the person being mentored and the one doing the mentoring, which is often related to experience, position and capabilities. During this phase, each party is learning about the other. Even in those instances when the mentor is at a distance, there is a period of learning about the skills, linkages and capabilities of those involved. The stories presented here are examples of how the mentor relationship can occur even when the mentor is kept in the dark until the protégé is ready to present self.

Dr. Jane was a noted nurse researcher. Her research findings were published in many journals, and she served on many national committees. John wanted help with his research study and could not find anyone where he worked as a clinical nurse specialist who could help him. One day as he was reading the professional journals, looking for a conceptual model in which to frame his study, he ran across an article written by Dr. Jane. He also noted she lived in San Francisco and worked at a prominent medical center. The next day, he called the university and reached Dr. Jane. After telling her about his study and his need for help, she agreed to act as his consultant. This all occurred 10 years ago. Dr. Jane not only helped him with his study, she has been available to him as a role model, referral agent and teacher during those 10 years. Because of her connections, he has a new position in a different part of the country and has advanced to chief investigator on a huge government-funded research study.

This story illustrates the power of mentoring and how one nurse was able to initiate and create a mentoring relationship. Nurse Isabel had a different experience.

When Isabel was an RN/BSN student, she was approached one day by one of her instructors and asked if she needed help. Even though she was very motivated, she was having trouble in the community health experience making the adjustment from the hospital setting to entering the homes of her clients. She felt awkward, as an intruder, unable to speak and very frustrated. Her instructor offered to accompany her on a visit and acted as a role model. She reviewed their goals for the visit and helped Isabel plan the next visit. This relationship developed into a long and productive one where Isabel sought the advice of her former instructor even as she moved through the ranks of the health department to the position she holds today as the director of the public health department in a large metropolitan city.

Note, in the first case, the relationship was initiated by the protégé and in the second one by the mentor. Both methods work and are the ways that mentoring relationships begin. Someone has to initiate, and it takes both people to agree to work together. I doubt if the people in either of these relationships knew they would develop as they did. But it is not unusual for a brief encounter to develop into a long-time helping relationship.

There are times when one can be a mentor and not even know it. Comments like the following ones are examples of this unusual phenomenon: "I have followed your career for years and have patterned mine after yours." "Whenever I read about your activities, I feel as if I can do what I have wanted to do because you have set the stage." "You inspire me and thus free me from my fears of not succeeding." The importance of role modeling is clearly evident in these comments, and while the mentor may not have known about their impact, once these comments are made to the mentor, the relationship usually begins and can be implemented to a fuller extent. These statements also underscore the power of the role-modeling aspect of mentoring and the reason the protégé had the courage to initiate a more formal relationship.

Goal-Setting Phase

During the goal-setting phase, the direction of the relationship is set. To demonstrate the wide variety of ways this can happen, the following three stories are offered:

Irene is a nurse anesthesiologist. She liked what she was doing but thought having a medical degree would open other opportunities for her. She sought the advice of a nursing instructor at the local university about the best school to attend. They reviewed a long list of medical schools and where they were located. After an extensive review, she decided not to attend medical school but to pursue a PhD in nursing. She and the nurse instructor decided to establish a formal mentoring relationship so she could pursue other issues, such as professional memberships, career advancement, etc. They set an agenda of issues they would pursue and have been working together in a collegial relationship ever since.

This story is an example of a relationship that began with a focus on a single issue and then expanded to others. It is also a good example of how the mentor worked with Irene as they problem-solved together to build an agenda for future pursuit and how the mentor-protégé relationship shifted to a collegial one. The next story is quite different.

Nurse Bill had agreed to write a chapter in a book for a friend. He wrote and wrote and couldn't get anything in writing that he liked.

He realized he needed help, so he contacted a nurse author he had known when in school. He asked her to help him with his writing, and she agreed. Since that early encounter, he has written several chapters in books with her.

In this story, Bill and the author he contacted have remained as mentor and protégé because Bill realizes she has much more to offer him than he has for her. They focus only on writing and on ways he can improve his writing. Someday, he hopes to write a book of his own.

The next story is not uncommon and demonstrates another version of mentoring.

As a new graduate with a bachelor of science degree in nursing in a large medical center, Patty realized she needed a mentor. She wanted to make the transition from school to work smoother. Unlike her classmates who decided to "tough it out alone," she asked a staff nurse to be her mentor. The staff nurse refused stating she was too busy and referred Patty to the nurse supervisor. Afraid she would look incompetent, Patty did not contact the nurse supervisor. However, the nurse supervisor had talked with the staff nurse and decided to offer the new graduates preceptor experiences with experienced nurses who were willing to act as role models and teachers. The supervisor developed the preceptor program with advice from Patty. Today, the preceptor program is implemented in many units in the medical center and has made transition for new graduates much better.

These stories are offered as models of how mentoring can begin and how the agendas are set. They also illustrate the issues nurses face and why they need mentors.

Setting a goal for the mentoring experience doesn't always happen at the beginning of the relationship. Sometimes, the protégé is unclear about what is needed. And while the mentor is there just waiting for the time when it is right for goal-setting, nothing will happen until both parties are ready. Note, in the first scenario, the nurse and the mentor did not set the goal until they had reviewed schools for the protégé's original desire. It wasn't until they (together) determined what the nurse needed that a goal was determined. In the second scenario, the nurse knew from the beginning what he wanted from a mentor. And in the third story, the nurse knew from the beginning what she wanted but did not know how to implement her desire. In fact, it took someone else to set up a program that established mentorships in a formal way.

It is important to understand these variations in the search for a mentor because there are many, many ways mentoring can be pursued—just as there are many ways mentors can function. Most mentors are teachers and role models, but not all are consultants or referral agents. These variations are not because the mentor is not able to function in a variety of roles, but because it all depends on what the protégé wants and is able to accept.

Working Phase

The working phase begins at different times dependent on the individuals involved, the goal(s) of the relationship, and the time and effort expended by both parties. Ideally, the working phase begins when the goals are set and trust between both parties has been established; however, given the variability mentioned above, initiation into the working phase can happen quickly or be drawn out. Bower (2000) believes once the goals for the relationship are set, there are two stages to accomplish in the working phase:

- Exchange stage
- Transition stage

During the working phase, plans for personal development are established that are followed up with periodic suggestions, coaching with feedback and debriefings. It is through this process that close bonding and long-term attachments occur. Being available and showing interest in the protégé is invaluable and must continue throughout the relationship. For example:

John was a student in a BSN program when he started working with his mentor, the dean of the school of nursing. One of his comments many years later was: "I remember your open-door policy. The personal chats, discussions and invaluable professional discourses all created a foundation for me becoming a good and caring nurse.

Exchange Phase

A major part of the working phase is devoted to "exchange." As Bower (2000) points out in *Nurses Taking the Lead,* in the earlier part of the working phase of the mentor relationship, the mentor assumes much of the leadership. The mentor determines the activities and makes referrals for the protégé. But sometime into the relationship, the protégé begins to make suggestions and to pose ideas. When this happens, the relationship has advanced into the exchange phase. The mentor and the protégé begin to work as a team sharing responsibility for the direction and progression of the experience. Mentor relationships between individuals with equal status usually move quickly into this exchange phase.

One of the critical aspects of the exchange phase is the mentor's and protégé's abilities to communicate honestly. This means both parties must be able to offer and accept criticism and to truthfully dialogue. There are times when things do not go smoothly or advice did not pay off. The mentor and the protégé must be willing and able to deal with what occurs, good or bad, and to seek solutions that benefit both individuals.

Sometime during the exchange phase (the length varies), the protégé may begin to pull back, to need less supervision and attention. Some mentors may find this alarming and feel like a failure. To the contrary, it probably means the protégé is moving on and needs the help of the mentor less and less. It could also mean the protégé is moving into a different role as a colleague. Frequently, it means the relationship in entering the transition stage.

Transition Phase

The transition from being mentored to being a colleague is often very subtle and can happen at any time during the mentoring relationship. It is also possible to be mentored and be a colleague. However, most individuals move from a mentoring relationship into a colleague relationship, particularly if the protégé moves into a position of equal status with the mentor. According to Bower (2000), "One of the factors that initiates a transition, other than the fact that the career of the protégé is well on its way, is that the protégé starts to take on her or his own protégés. However, some would say the mentoring process is never really over …" (p. 263).

There are times when the mentor relationship goes dormant. The mentor and the protégé do not communicate or keep in contact. This lull does not mean the relationship is over. An important characteristic of mentoring relationships is that they can be operative or inoperative and then be reinstituted when the protégé needs help, support or advice. However, a sudden termination of dialog could mean there is trouble, so it is wise to determine what is happening. Silence could mean nothing is wrong, or it could mean the protégé is in need and cannot ask for help.

Restifo (2002) believes the mentor relationship lasts about five years. There are several reasons for this time frame: (1) the goals of the relationship have been met, (2) the relationship between the mentor and the protégé changes to a collegial one or (3) as the circumstances change, so does the relationship. However, "regardless of the duration of the experience, the resulting relationship is often long-term" (p. 61).

Characteristics of Good Mentors

Mentors must have certain qualifications to be effective in their roles. They must have experience and personal power; be interested in being a facilitator; understand different learning styles; have time to devote to the experience; have and use effective communication skills; be able to give feedback to the protégé; and, most of all, be able to provide leadership. According to Darby (2002), the mentor role is one of:

> *. . . listening, providing approval, and exploring various options when confronted with a problem. Many times, the mentor helps to reframe a given situation. Sometimes, the mentor engages in reframing when helping the [protégé] see a situation in a different way so that new possibilities become evident and frustrations are overcome. This requires engaging the imagination to help picture situations differently (p.32).*

Experience

Above all, good mentors must have had experience. The essential and most important value of experience is that it helps the protégé see what is possible and what they can learn from the experienced person. Sometimes, all it takes to become competent and to move forward is to have a little experience with an expert. But experience does not mean there is not room for more learning. Good mentors are always learning, and it is this very aspect the mentor wants the protégé to see and learn.

Mentors do not have to be in charge. In fact, the best mentor is often not the boss or someone in a high-level position. The mentor, though, does need to be competent and have an understanding of what the protégé wants to learn. Darrie's story is an example of the importance of experience.

> *Darrie wanted to become a home care nurse. She knew she had to learn more about nursing, so she sought the advice of her mentor from college about how she should proceed. While she knew the faculty person had been a home care nurse long ago, she also knew she would*

know the best way to get prepared. As she expected, the faculty person gave her a list of the programs she should consider and sent her to talk with a home care nurse who had been a student before Darrie. Darrie enrolled in school and completed her BSN degree and found a home care nurse position shortly after graduation.

Experience can be used in other ways, as is evident in Grace's story.

Grace had always admired her supervisor on the Pediatric Oncology Unit. When the supervisor left for a position in another hospital, Grace felt lost. She had been the protégé of the supervisor for several years and did not think she could manage without her. She even thought about leaving the hospital and obtaining a job where the supervisor now worked. However, the supervisor urged Grace to stay where she was and to use the skills and knowledge she had accrued over the years to help other nurses, particularly the new hires, gain competence and a sense of accomplishment just as she had done. It was this push by the supervisor that encouraged Grace to become a mentor. She became a good mentor and claimed her success as a mentor was due to the excellent mentoring she had received.

Interest in Being a Mentor

It is hard to imagine anyone wanting to be a mentor who did not have an interest in helping another learn and advance. However, it is not rare for a person to take on the responsibility of mentoring only to discover it is a task that demands personal interest in the learning process and how best to help the protégé. It takes a certain kind of person who is willing to devote time, effort and energy to helping another person enhance current knowledge and learn new skills. Frequently, the rewards are limited and the demands high, particularly when the demands of the mentor's position are also high and sometimes stressful. Being a mentor often means balancing responsibilities without much visible reward. Organization, time management and the allocation of personal time are essential for the mentor to learn.

Interest in being a mentor also includes understanding the needs and desires of the protégé. It means knowing the protégé's strengths and limitations, learning style, and the way s/he approaches and relates to others. Being aware of the protégé's goals and his or her expectations of the mentor also helps the mentor facilitate the relationship and ultimately the goals of the protégé. Showing interest by communicating and observing the protégé before the relationship is established is essential in order to avoid frustrating or negative outcomes.

Understanding Different Learning Styles

People don't learn in the same way. Some learners can "take off," that is, they need little assistance once they know what is expected. Others need a lot of direction and supervision. It is important to assess the protégé to determine exactly what style of learning is best for him or her. Mentors often become frustrated because the protégé seems uninterested in initiating anything, when in fact it is not a matter of interest but one of inability. Finding the right mix of initiation and facilitation is an important early assessment that is best accomplished during dialogue together.

Unlike a formal teaching experience, the teaching that occurs during a mentor relationship is usually spontaneous, individualized and time constrained. It often includes sharing, clarifying and explaining. There are usually no formal presentations, homework assignments or class notes. When the time is right, teaching occurs; therefore, the mentor must be alert; sensitive to the learner's needs; and willing to share, challenge and reinforce or correct the protégé's progress. The best mentors understand and appreciate learner differences and continue to use the adult learning principles listed below:

1. Demonstrate empathy, respect and consistency in your approaches.
2. View the experience as a partnership whereby the protégé and the mentor design, implement and evaluate the protégé's progress.
3. Create an environment that is conducive to learning, i.e., supportive, free from threat, encouraging of inquiry and trust.
4. Recognize the roles culture, maturation and leaning style play in the way the protégé learns and responds.
5. Suggest activities that are meaningful and consistent with the protégé's needs and goals (Bower & Lee, 2001, p. 15).

Have Time to Devote to the Experience

A frequent problem for mentors is having the time needed to give to the protégé. Many people agree to be a mentor only to discover it takes more time than they have to devote to the experience. The protégé needs the mentor to devote time to the facilitation of the goals for the experience. There is also a need for dialogue about the best activities for meeting those goals. To provide this kind of help, the mentor must know the protégé's capacity for learning and something about his or her coping skills. This means the mentor and the protégé must know each other on a personal level, sharing things about themselves that will help the relationship thrive and that will give the mentor the knowledge necessary for making decisions in the best interest of the protégé. It is also important for the protégé to know about the mentor so frustrations, misconceptions and anger do not enter the relationship. In order to know one another time must be devoted to the introduction phase and to the goal-setting phase of the relationship. Considerable time must also be devoted to the working phase when the mentor facilitates the protégé's activities to meet the goals. The next two stories are good examples of this need for "time" during the mentor relationship.

Harry was a new faculty member when he was assigned a faculty mentor. The college had a mentor program for all new faculty. Harry was excited about the program and liked his mentor immensely. However, it seemed every time he tried to contact her, she was too busy to see him. She didn't even answer his e-mails when he gave up trying to talk with her person-to-person. They talked at the beginning of the experience and he had sent her his goals. They had agreed to meet monthly, but he needed her more often and couldn't get her attention. What he did not know is she never used her e-mail and that she expected him to manage things until the monthly meeting and that she was very, very busy doing research so she could be promoted. Clearly, there were many problems with the arrangement that could have been dealt with if the two of them had talked more in the beginning and if the mentor had more interest and time for the experience. Jan, on the other hand, was overly conscientious with her protégé. She expected him to call her weekly and to submit a log of his activities. She was very busy and believed the experience could be managed by weekly phone calls, notes, logs and e-mail. Jan left many messages on his voice mail and dropped off his logs after they were reviewed. However, her protégé felt abandoned and wanted out but was afraid to offend Jan with a request for termination.

While both of these stories are negative examples of mentorships, they both highlight the importance of two facets of a mentoring relationship: interest in being a mentor and having time to devote to the relationship so both parties are satisfied.

Communicating Effectively

Being able to communicate effectively is also an important skill for the mentor. Being able to be an active listener and provide feedback (both reinforcing and corrective) are essential elements of a productive and satisfying mentor relationship. Darby (2002) believes mentors want and are capable of improvement, but without feedback, this goal cannot be met. Open communication, consistent verbal-nonverbal discussions, and being able to step back before responding are qualities of good communicators.

Because many mentor relationships may occur at a distance, the use of e-mail and the telephone as a means of communication are common. These media for communication must be handled carefully, for it is easy to send the wrong message by the tone of your voice or by the way the message is worded in an e-mail. One way to avoid miscommunication is to send the e-mail or make the telephone call when there are no other distractions. Being in a hurry, trying to multi-task and being tired are sure ways to foul up the communication. Another way to avoid miscommunication is to have scheduled times for meetings where the protégé and the mentor can devote time to discussing the protégé's progress. Scheduled meetings can be in-person, conducted as a telephone conference, or be messages sent by e-mail at designated times.

Providing Leadership

A major aspect of the mentoring relationship is the mentor's ability to provide leadership. Leadership, in this sense, is being able to be futuristic, proactive and yet grounded in reality. Bower (2000) states:

> *Leadership is defined differently today because what we face in this decade and what we will face in the next decade are different from what was previously experienced. In the 1950s, 1960s, 1970s, 1980s, [and 1990s], most nurses looked to others to provide "the way." Now it is the responsibility of every nurse to assume "the lead"* (p. 2).

What this statement suggests is that the mentor has a responsibility to provide leadership AND to help the protégé develop leadership skills. How is this accomplished? It is accomplished in a variety of ways. The mentor helps the protégé set goals, suggests actions when the protégé is without ideas and poses strategies for the protégé's consideration. Little by little the mentor backs away from being the initiator while helping the protégé accept responsibility for taking "the lead." It is a modeling experience as the mentor "opens doors" for the protégé and shows her or him how it is done.

"Taking the lead" means, according to Bower (2000), knowing self, looking forward, seeing the big picture, taking risks, recognizing the right time for action, being proactive, communicating effectively, mentoring others, letting go and taking on, and keeping informed. These strategies are important ways to "push the envelope" toward self-fulfillment and career development. They are also strategies the mentor uses as a role model in everything the mentor and protégé do together. They are strategies that allow the protégé to "make a difference" while learning. Bower sums up these characteristics by stating:

> *Taking the lead is being influential and thus means the [nurse] must not only be aware of opportunities and be skillful in the use of the principles but also see [self] as capable of initiating change* (p. 13).

Characteristics of Good Protégés

Just like mentors, protégés must exercise specific behaviors for success in the mentoring relationship. They must be motivated, be responsible, be ready and available for feedback, and understand their own strengths and limitations.

Being Motivated

Being motivated is an essential protégé characteristic. It is easy to seek new experiences, follow through on mentor suggestions, and reach new heights when you are ready, excited about the possibilities, and anxious to do a good job. Lethargy, laziness and disinterest dampen motivation and hamper opportunities. While working hard at the usual activities of work consumes much of ours lives, being able to try something new and having someone help you at the same time far outweighs the stress of any work life. Talking with the mentor or friends/family about negative feelings often keeps the protégé motivated.

Being motivated is not being ready to tackle anything. Again it is important to keep whatever is offered in perspective and weighed against whatever else is "on your plate." Frequent "check-ins" with the mentor are good ways to keep on track, be available for new experiences, and keep within your capabilities.

Being Responsible

It seems redundant to discuss responsibility, but it is easy to "duck" responsibility and find others at fault. For instance:

Betty and her mentor Laura had worked together for many months. Betty wanted to be a teacher just like Laura, so she accepted every opportunity to "sub" for her. One day, Betty arrived on campus to discover that she had missed an opportunity to teach the class. She immediately flew into a rage blaming Laura for not reminding her of the chance to teach. After cooling down, she realized she had not looked at her palm computer that morning where she had made a note of the subject being presented and her agreement to teach that day. She apologized to Laura and never again missed a responsibility to teach.

Taking responsibility for having the best possible learning experience is really the work of both the protégé and the mentor, but unless the protégé takes the lead, it may not happen.

The same is true of any problems that may arise during the mentor experience. Infrequently, the mentor and the protégé do not "click," that is, they do not relate well or communicate effectively. Rather than "make do" or struggle with it, the protégé should let the mentor know about the problem. Again, responsibility lies with the one most likely to benefit from the relationship, the protégé.

Being Ready and Available for Feedback

The best way to know how you are doing is to hear from those who can see you in action and know what you should be doing. That person could be the mentor or whoever the protégé is working with as part of the mentor experience. Being open and accepting of feedback, even when it is negative but constructive, is essential for growth and change.

If you view correction as an opportunity to do better and praise as validation of good performance, then growth and change are possible. Frequent one-to-one feedback is the best way to learn about your performance, but sometimes it is not possible, so feedback by other means is encouraged, such as e-mails, fax messages or telephone conversations. If there are time and space differences, it is wise to seek feedback. When nothing transpires between the mentor and the protégé, one never really knows if the performance is "on track," adequate or below par. This is one of the times the protégé must exercise responsibility to get the needed feedback.

An important way to get feedback is to have a conference with the mentor at regularly scheduled times. These conferences provide the protégé with progress checks so objectives/goals can be met, problems avoided and activities altered, if necessary. Frequent and open communication is absolutely essential, and while this kind of communication can occur at any time, it is best accomplished during a planned conference when there is no other intervening discussions or interruptions.

Understanding One's Strengths and Limitations

For the most productive and satisfying mentor experiences, it is best for the protégé to know about his or her strengths and limitations. For instance, if the protégé knows that certain activities frighten him or her, then it behooves the protégé to alert the mentor to those fears and to find ways to alleviate them. Ignoring fears will only make them worse.

The same is true about strengths. If the protégé knows s/he is very good at something, that strength should be acknowledged and capitalized on by asking for experiences that match that strength or build on it. It is also important to obtain rewards for what is completed well and to figure out how to remove the limitations. However, the key to doing well is to share this knowledge about self with the mentor so the most appropriate and growth-producing activities can be pursued (Bower & Lee, 2001).

Gwen was a very accomplished family nurse practitioner. However, every time she had to present at "rounds" she became speechless. She dreaded her turn at presenting. She knew the diagnosis and could recite the therapeutic protocol and follow-up procedures. She was an excellent one- on-one communicator, and her patients and their families admired and trusted her. To combat this fear of speaking before her colleagues, Gwen consulted her mentor, a physician she worked with, and he suggested she join a local Toast Master's Club. She followed his advice and soon learned to speak before crowds without fear. It wasn't long after that experience that she was able to present at rounds without clamming up and feeling like a failure.

This story presents two things to remember about mentoring. Mentors often have ideas that the protégé may not, and persistence pays off.

CONCLUSION

Other than marriage, mentor relationships are probably the closest, most intimate and most helpful relationships one can be part of. However, unlike marriage, the participants move on and away from each other as they were initially formed. But like a good marriage, the participants keep in touch and learn from one another over a long period of time and often grow professionally and personally. Even though every mentor relationship doesn't prosper and succeed, there is plenty of evidence those that do work have helped many people reach fulfillment.

REFERENCES

Barton, K. (2001). *Connecting with success: How to build a mentoring network to fast- forward your career.* New York, NY: Davies-Black.

Bower, F.L. (2000). *Nurses taking the lead.* Philadelphia, PA: Saunders.

Bower, F.L. (1993) *Women and mentoring.* In P.T. Mitchell (Ed.), Cracking the wall: *Women in higher education administration* (pp. 90-97). Washington, DC: College and University Personnel Association.

Bower, F.L., & Lee, C. (2001). *Preceptor manual for preceptors and family nurse practitioner students.* Oakland, CA: Holy Names College.

Darby, M. (2002). *Mentoring: Buzzword or breakthrough?* Retrieved August 28, 2002, from http://WWW.mdarby.com/files/beginning nursement.pdf.

Dortch, T.W., & Joyner, T. (2000). *The miracles of mentoring: The joy of investing in our future.* New York, NY: Doubleday.

Gehrke, N. (1988). *Toward a definition of mentoring. Theory into Practice,* 27(3), 190-194.

Hockenberry-Eaton, M., & Kline, N.E. (1995). Who is mentoring the nurse practitioner? *Journal of Pediatric Health Care, 9*(2), 94-95.

Kanter, R.M. (1977). *Men and women of the corporation.* New York, NY: Basic Books.

Lee, C. (1988). Need motivation and mentorship experiences of national and state leaders. *Dissertation Abstracts International, 49,* 4758.

Levinson, D. (1977). *The seasons of a man's life.* New York, NY: Alfred A. Knopf.

Moore, K.M. (1982). The role of mentors in developing leaders for academe. *Educational Record, 63,* 22-28.

Parsloe, E., & Wray, M. (2000). *Coaching and mentoring: Practical methods to improve learning.* London, England: Kogan Page.

Restifo, V. (2002). *Partnership: Making the most of mentoring. Nursing Spectrum student career fitness tool kit* (pp. 68-71). Newark, NJ: Nursing Spectrum.

Taylor, L.J. (1992). A survey of mentor-protégé relationships in academe. *Journal of Professional Nursing, 8,* 48-55.

Vance, C., & Olson, R. (1998). *The mentor connection in nursing.* New York, NY: Springer.

Whittaker, M., & Cartwright, A. (2000). *The mentoring manual.* Great Britain: Gower.

Williams, R., & Blackburn, R. (1988). Mentoring and junior faculty productivity. *Journal of Nursing Education, 27*(5), 204-209.

Zachary, L.J. (2000). *The mentor's guide: Facilitating effective leaning relationships.* San Francisco, CA: Jossey-Bass.

Index

C

D

E

I

M

N

O

S

T

Y

Z